Perspectives in
Behavioral Medicine

EATING, SLEEPING,
AND SEX

Perspectives in Behavioral Medicine

EATING, SLEEPING, AND SEX

Edited by

Albert J. Stunkard
University of Pennsylvania

Andrew Baum
USUHS School of Medicine

LEA LAWRENCE ERLBAUM ASSOCIATES, PUBLISHERS
1989 Hillsdale, New Jersey   Hove and London

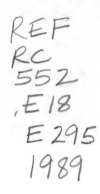

Lawrence Erlbaum Associates, Inc., Publishers
365 Broadway
Hillsdale, New Jersey 07642

Library of Congress Cataloging-in-Publication Data

Eating, sleeping, and sex / edited by Albert J. Stunkard and Andrew Baum.
    p.   cm.—(Perspectives in behavioral medicine)
  Includes bibliographies and index.
  ISBN 0-8058-0280-0
  1. Eating disorders. 2. Sleep disorders. 3. Psychosexual disorders. I. Stunkard,
Albert J., 1922– . II. Baum, Andrew. III. Series.
  [DNLM: 1. Appetite Disorders. 2. Behavior Therapy. 3. Obesity. 4. Sex
Disorders. 5. Sleep Disorders. WM 425 E14]
RC552.E18E295 1988
616.85′2—dc19
DNLM/DLC
for Library of Congress   88-24611
                                          CIP

Printed in the United States of America
10 9 8 7 6 5 4 3 2 1

CONTENTS

8

9

10

LIST OF CONTRIBUTORS

GENE G. ABEL, M.D.   Department of Psychiatry, School of Medicine, Emory University, P.O. Box AF, Atlanta, GA 30322

REUBIN ANDRES, Ph.D.   Clinical Director, Gerontology Research Center, National Institute on Aging, Frances Scott Key Hospital, Baltimore, MD 21224

JOHN McD. W. BRADFORD, M.B.   Director, Forensic Service, Royal Ottawa Hospital, University of Ottowa, Ottowa, Ontario, Canada K1Z7K4

KELLY D. BROWNELL, Ph.D.   Department of Psychiatry, University of Pennsylvania, 133 South 36th Street, Philadelphia, PA 19104

DAVID F. DINGES, Ph.D.   Unit for Experimental Psychology, The Institute of Pennsylvania Hospital, University of Pennsylvania, 111 North 49th Street, Philadelphia, PA 19139

M. R. C. GREENWOOD, Ph.D.   Chairperson, Department of Biology, Vassar College, Poughkeepsie, NY 12601

PETER J. HAURI, Ph.D.   Professor of Psychology, Co-Director, Behavioral Medicine Section, Dartmouth College, School of Medicine, Hanover, NH 03756

WILLIAM B. KANNEL, M.D.   Section of Preventative Medicine and Epidemiology, Boston University School of Medicine, 720 Harris Ave., Boston, MA 02118

DAVID J. KUPFER, M.D.   Chairman, Department of Psychiatry, University of Pittsburgh School of Medicine, 3811 O'Hara Street, Pittsburgh, PA 15213

JOHN E. MORLEY, M.D.   Director of Geriatric Research Education and Clinical Center, Veteran's Administration Medical Center (11E), 16111 Plummer Street, Sepulveda, CA 91343

PATRICIA SCHREINER-ENGEL, Ph.D.   Assistant Professor of Psychiatry, Mount Sinai School of Medicine, 5th Avenue & 100th Street, New York, NY 10029

ALBERT J. STUNKARD, M.D.   University of Pennsylvania, 133 South 36th Street, Suite 507, Philadelphia, PA 19104

G. TERRENCE WILSON, Ph.D.   Graduate School of Applied and Professional Psychology, Rutgers University, Box 819, Piscataway, NJ 08855-0819

INTRODUCTION

A thousand years ago in T'ang Dynasty China, some of the wisdom of the Buddhist tradition was distilled into cryptic sayings known as *"mondo,"* question-and-answer exchanges between Zen masters and their often hapless disciples. One question, now well-known in the West, epitomizes this puzzling form of discourse, "What is the sound of one hand clapping?" Not all Zen sayings are so opaque, however, and some are quite accessible:

> Disciple: "What is the Tao?"
> Master: "Everyday life is the Tao."
> Disciple: "What do you mean?"
> Master: "When you are hungry you eat, when you are thirsty you drink, when you meet a friend you greet him."
>
> Or, "How wonderful, how mysterious! I carry fuel, I draw water."

Although these sayings, no doubt, contain meanings within meanings, in one sense they are crystal clear, for they speak of the wonder of pure, natural acts, undefiled by our ruminations, free of neurotic elaborations. Eating, sleeping, sex—carrying fuel, drawing water—these are, indeed, the Tao.

This volume on our natural functions lets us see this wonder, heightened by its contrast with the sterile and joyless nature of these functions when they are in the service of neurotic processes. A salient characteristic of neurotic behavior is its tendency to go to extremes—too much or too little. This lack of balance, this failure of regulation, has traditionally been recognized in symbolic acts; in over-conscientiousness on the one hand and the criminal lack of conscience on the other. But the neurotic process also affects our biological functions. Thus, in the

1

chapters on eating, we consider the "too much" of obesity and the "too little" of that faulty method of controlling obesity known as "bulimia nervosa." The section on sleeping describes the age-old too little of insomnia and the too much of the disorders of excessive somnolence, such as sleepiness. In the chapters on sexuality, we encounter both the hypersexuality of criminal degree, including child molestation, as well as the hyposexuality of a newly recognized disorder—inhibited sexual desire.

EATING

Research on eating and its disorders has been unusually fruitful in the recent past, and these first chapters sparkle with intriguing new theories and fascinating new facts. The first five chapters on eating deal with excesses, four with the too much of obesity and one with the opposite pole of bulimia nervosa. Although this distribution of effort is the reverse of that in many psychiatric publications, it reflects the relative contributions of the two excesses to human suffering: Obesity is a far more prevalent disorder than bulimia or anorexia nervosa. The next two chapters deal with the old question, now being debated with increased intensity, "Is obesity bad for you?" Happily, these two chapters reach a high degree of consensus on this question that turns out to be far more complex than we had realized.

The chapter "Perspectives on Human Obesity" by Stunkard presents the first convincing evidence for the role of heredity in human obesity or fatness and thinness. We have long known from studies on animals that heredity *could* play a role in obesity. Fatness has been bred into pigs from the time that humans first began farming, and greyhounds are bred for thinness along with speed. Only recently, however, have twin and adoption studies shown that we humans are also creatures of our genetic endowment. Stunkard's chapter reviews the evidence for the genetic control of obesity in humans and then moves on to new studies of more and less successful methods of managing this disorder.

Greenwood's chapter, "Sexual Dimorphism and Obesity," presents an original synthesis of the extensive new data on the distribution of body fat and its significance. The differing fat distributions of men and women are the starting point for her essay on sexual dimorphism and on the differing functions that are served by body fat among women and men. Her animal experiments form the basis for her intriguing theory on the function of the inguinal fat depot in rats. According to Greenwood, the evolutionary function of this depot was as a site in which energy was stored during pregnancy, to be used later for lactation. The exquisite hormonal controls of this mechanism, the changes in food efficiency, and the concomitant changes in lipoprotein lipase activity at the different sites all speak to a major biological system subsuming mammalian reproduction. Rebuffe-Scrive has added important data on humans which strongly suggest that Greenwood's theory applies to humans as well as to rats.

Brownell and Stein's chapter, "Metabolic and Behavioral Effects of Weight Loss and Regain: A Review of the Animal and Human Literature," deals with some of the potential metabolic consequences of the current Western preoccupation with dieting. It would be difficult to overestimate the extent of this preoccupation. As Brownell and Stein point out, 90% of Americans feel that they are overweight, and 31% of women say that they diet at least once a month. It is well established that dieting promotes processes that impede its effectiveness, particularly a decrease in metabolic rate. That these processes may have long-term effects is demonstrated by reduced obese people whose caloric requirements are far lower than those estimated from their size. Brownell and Stein propose that such metabolic adaptation to dieting is increased by repeated cycles of dieting, and they present the intriguing theory that "dieting makes dieting harder." In support of this theory, they cite Brownell's already well-known experiment: When "dieted" for a second time, rats lost weight at half the rate of their first diet and regained the lost weight at three times the rate following their previous diet. The implications of this experiment for the vast numbers of American dieters are clear.

The always imaginative John Morley proposes another provocative challenge in his chapter, "Parallels in Neurotransmitter Control of Feeding and Memory," with its teleological speculations on the functions of opioid peptides and cholecystokinin (CCK). He begins with the observation (that will be news to many) that opioid peptides exist as far down the evolutionary scale as amoebae, whose feeding behavior they may modulate. The earliest evolutionary function of these peptides thus may have been to drive the search for food and to stimulate eating. The development of analgesia, according to this view, occurred later in evolution, to help organisms cope with the pain and danger of their foraging activities. Morley relates several of the other functions of the opioid peptides to such purposes (their enhancing effect on immune function and glucose metabolism and their inhibiting effect on gastric acid secretion, sexual performance, and reproductive hormones). When eating is terminated by satiety hormones, these hormones, such as CCK, act to enhance memory consolidation in order to help the animal remember the details of a successful foraging trip.

Wilson's scholarly chapter, "The Treatment of Bulimia Nervosa: A Cognitive-Social Learning Theory Analysis," is an insightful contribution to our understanding of bulimia. Particularly impressive is his analysis of the mechanism of "exposure and response prevention" in the treatment of bulimia. This measure, originally developed for compulsive behavior such as hand washing, consists of encouraging the patient to eat (exposure) and then preventing the subsequent vomiting (response prevention). It has been conceptualized as a means of eliciting and then extinguishing a classically conditioned reflex. Exposure and response prevention is now widely employed in treatment programs for bulimia, and it seems to be effective. Yet this effectiveness, Wilson argues, does not derive from its purported theoretical base—the extinction of conditioned responses. As he points out, experiments have clearly shown that eating does not arouse anxiety in bulimic patients, nor does vomiting reduce it.   /

Wilson proposes a new interpretation of exposure and response prevention, ascribing its effectiveness to the cognitions of mastery and self-efficacy that it elicits. And in true social learning theory style, he reinforces this interpretation by showing his new patients videotapes of his old patients learning to eat without vomiting.

The question of whether obesity is bad for you has become one of the most hotly debated issues in all of medicine. In recent years, the long-standing view that obesity is bad for you has been severely challenged by the iconoclastic analyses of Reubin Andres. The appearance of Dr. Andres on the same program with one of the most distinguished representatives of traditional views, Dr. William Kannel, former director of the landmark Framingham Study, seemed to promise a major confrontation. Instead, there emerged a surprising degree of consensus, which bodes well for our understanding of the risks of obesity.

Andres and Kannel agree that the question of the risks of obesity is far more complex than had been recognized in the earlier simplistic analyses and one which probably cannot be fully answered by the available data. For example, it has become clear that we need more information about such independent variables as the age of onset of the obesity, its duration, and, clearly of enormous importance, the distribution of body fat. More information about dependent variables is also needed, and we must specify far more clearly what risks are to be considered.

Traditional analyses have dealt primarily with total mortality. Finer-grained analyses have revealed that there are different risks for different diseases. As Kannel shows in his chapter, "Cardiovascular and Noncardiovascular Consequences of Obesity," obesity appears to *increase* the risk of cardiovascular disease but may *decrease* the risk of cancer and other noncardiovascular disease.

Just as Kannel has shown the need for disease-specific analyses of the effects of obesity, Andres has shown the need for age-specific analyses. Assessing the body weight associated with minimal mortality, Andres, in his chapter, "Does the 'Best' Body Weight Change with Age?" shows that this weight increases with increasing age. Optimal body weight may increase as much as 10 pounds for each decade of life. If so, the standard tables underestimate the risk of obesity below the age of 42 and overestimate it over the age of 42, and we need new, age-specific height-for-weight tables. Andres' chapter ends with such tables.

SLEEPING

The three chapters on sleep describe, in a moving fashion, the troubles that arise when sleep is not a simple consequence of going to bed at night and when it does not "knit up the ravelled sleeve of care." These chapters show gratifying progress in our understanding of sleep, its control mechanisms, and its conse-quences. This progress is particularly notable in the chapter by Kupfer and Reynolds, "Slow Wave Sleep as a 'Protective' Factor (Re-emergence of SWS)," and the authors show why we can expect continued progress: Comput-ers have markedly improved the capacity to analyze sleep records. Computer-generated analyses are already superseding the arcane up-and-down graphs that were the stock in trade of the sleep researcher of a few years ago.

In their chapter, Kupfer and Reynolds describe several consequences of the improved capability of analyzing sleep records and an intriguing two-process model of sleep. According to this theory, sleep is composed of two orthogonal processes. One process, reflected in slow-wave sleep, is sleep-dependent, builds up during the day, and is released at night. The other process, reflected in rapid eye movement (REM) sleep, is sleep-independent and circadian. The first pro-cess is closely linked to growth-hormone-releasing factor and to growth hor-mone, while the second process is linked to corticotropin-releasing factor and the hypothalamic-pituitary axis. The theory is particularly useful in interpreting the changes in both hormone levels and sleep during depressive illness: Depression is associated with decreased activity of the second process and increased activity of the first. Thus, depression is associated with a decrease in both the amount of slow wave sleep and growth hormone levels and an increase in both REM activity and hypersecretion of cortisol. This two-process model of sleep regula-tion not only integrates a wide variety of disparate findings, but permits predic-tions of potential therapeutic relevance.

The newly emerging field of disorders of excessive somnolence, particularly excessive daytime sleepiness, is described in detail in the chapter, "The Nature of Sleepiness: Causes, Contexts, and Consequences" by David Dinges, one of its leaders. As he points out, the study of sleepiness is fundamental to under-standing the function of sleep itself, and it is of great practical significance in understanding and preventing industrial accidents. The increase in shift work and the increasing demand for performance that requires continuous vigilance in monotonous environments greatly increases the probability of human error, as does night work, which occurs during the circadian nadir of alertness. The full extent of this problem is only now becoming widely recognized, although, as Dinges shows, experience from all parts of the world illustrates the dangers of shift- and night work. For example,

In Sweden in 1955, errors in 62,000 meter readings in a gas works peaked at 3:00 a.m.;

In Germany in 1974, 2,238 failures to respond to warning switches by train drivers peaked at 3:00 a.m.;

In Poland in 1974, 569 automobile drivers reported dozing with a peak at 4:00 a.m.; and

In the United States in 1978, 493 accidents by "dozing" truck drivers peaked at 5:00 a.m.

The nuclear-power industry is the most recent one to be affected by such human errors. The Chernobyl meltdown is reported to have involved human error at 1:23 a.m., while human error at three American nuclear power plants (including Three Mile Island) occurred at 1:35, 4:00, and 4:30 a.m., respectively.

Fortunately, recognition of this major occupational risk has been associated with the recent development of sensitive measures of sleepiness (and alertness). Two such measures are the one-minute reaction time and the measurement of sleep latency—the time from wakefulness to sleep onset when the subject is asked to try to go to sleep. These tests provide sensitive and reliable measures of sleepiness and hold the promise of preventing some of the problems, if used in both the clinic and the work place.

The chapter, "The Cognitive Behavioral Treatment of Insomnia," by Hauri has all the marks of a master clinician, and clinical skills are sorely needed for a condition that afflicts 15% of adult Americans. Hauri points out that effective treatment derives from accurate diagnosis. It is, therefore, worthy of note that careful diagnosis shows that at least half of all patients complaining of insomnia present with psychiatric or physical disorders. Treatment of these disorders is the first order of business, and the insomnia often responds promptly to such treatment.

For those who do not respond to treatment of an underlying disorder, a variety of approaches have been used, each with a measure of success. But, as Hauri notes, these various approaches tend to be technique-driven and often are insufficiently matched to the problems of the individual patient. The kind of individualization of treatment that Hauri describes should greatly increase the rate of success. What he does is clear and simple. I will not try to summarize an already admirably summarized approach, but instead invite the reader to enjoy this clearly written and carefully described program of treatment.

SEX

When we turn to the issue of sexual behavior, we again see its disorders in terms of excesses—of too much or too little. There is, however, a major difference between disorders of sexual function and those of eating and sleeping. Although disorders of eating and sleeping often involve others, particularly family members, they do not have the devastating effects of sexual assaults. Indeed, it is this effect of sexual dysfunction on others that renders it such a serious problem and it appears to be a problem that is far more extensive than we have realized.

Much of the research on sexual disorders derives from the pioneering work of

Masters and Johnson on inadequate sexual performance—impotence in men and anorgasmia in women. The recent research reported in this volume has revealed striking new dimensions of sexual disorders with at least as important contributions to human suffering.

Schreiner-Engel's chapter on "Low Sexual Desire: Biological Implications" describes a sexual disorder associated with little apparent distress on the part of the affected person. Curiously, the sexual function of persons with "inhibited sexual desire" may be quite adequate, and they may experience arousal and orgasm as readily as persons without the disorder. They simply show no sexual desire and they come to medical attention, if at all, only under pressure from their disappointed mates. Because the distress of these persons is so limited and they are so unlikely to complain, the extent of this disorder is still uncertain. The prognosis is believed to be poor. Schreiner-Engle's chapter describes one of the first controlled studies of inhibited sexual desire. It suggests that the disorder occurs primarily among persons with a lifetime diagnosis of affective disorder, that it usually begins during an episode of depression and continues long after recovery from other symptoms of the depression.

"The Organic Treatment of Violent Sexual Offenders," by John Bradford of Canada, describes a series of treatments with which we in the United States have had very little experience, although they have been used extensively in other parts of the world. They are based on the fact that reduction of the effects of androgenic hormones drastically reduces not only sexual drive but also the aggression of violent sex offenders. For many years, this effect could be achieved only by castration, and it has been extensively used in Europe for this purpose. I remember my mixed feelings several years ago as I watched Manfred Bleuler interview persons who had chosen castration over life imprisonment, a choice that Swiss law permitted to those convicted of violent sex crimes. At that time, castration seemed to be a horrendous penalty, and I was surprised at how well the subjects seemed to be functioning. Years later, with an appreciation of the havoc wrought by violent sexual offenders and of the results of castration cited by Bradford, this measure seems to be somewhat less horrendous. According to Bradford, the rates of recidivism reported from Europe following castration range between 2% and 7%; in the United States, recidivism is the rule.

The use of antiandrogens and hormonal agents makes this kind of treatment less of an all-or-none proposition, for it renders the antiandrogenic effects both reversible and titratable. Nevertheless, the use of these agents extends far beyond the purview of medicine into the realm of the criminal justice system; ultimately, decisions as to their use are political ones. In the absence of research in this country, which would provide the information necessary for such decisions, we must be indebted to Dr. Bradford and investigators in other countries for our growing knowledge of the use of chemical agents in the management of sexual offenders.

The reason why such unorthodox treatments may be considered more seriously in this country is made clear by the shocking figures reported by Abel in his chapter, "Behavioral Treatment of Child Molesters." According to Abel, the methods traditionally used for ascertainment of the frequency of child molestation have led to serious underestimates of the extent of the problem. He argues that the only way to obtain accurate information is through the offenders themselves, a process that requires elaborate legal safeguards to ensure confidentiality, followed by sensitive approaches to the offenders. Abel did just this, and his study of more than 400 child molesters has produced chilling results. Offenders against females had an average of 52 victims each, while those who offended against males had 150 victims each. Just the 400 offenders studied by Abel apparently committed a total of 76,000 molestations!

Abel points out that child molesters are rarely apprehended and that, when they are, rearrest records following incarceration and treatment are "of no value because recidivism post-treatment never led to arrest." Abel concludes that "20% of all females and 10% of all males have been or will be sexually assaulted in some way before reaching age 21." Clearly, child molestation is a public health problem of the greatest magnitude.

Abel's chapter is a fitting close to this volume, in alerting us to the dimensions of a disorder that far surpasses those of which we had been aware, and in setting the stage for programs of social action. Other chapters, as we have seen, also describe new dimensions of old problems, while some chapters describe new forms of disorder. Some chapters describe new treatment methods. All of them should be of value to those in the helping professions in their work and in calling attention to problems for which more help is needed. Finally, these examples of the distortions of our natural functions—our eating, sleeping, and sex—can also make us grateful for what we so often enjoy without a second thought: The undistorted exercise of these functions . . . "eating when hungry, drinking when thirsty, and greeting friends."

Albert J. Stunkard

1
PERSPECTIVES ON HUMAN OBESITY

Albert J. Stunkard
Department of Psychiatry,
University of Pennsylvania

This chapter describes some perspectives on human obesity that I have developed during three decades of work on this disorder. Even after these three decades, there is no general theory and that is a pity. A theory is the ideal way to advance research on a disease. Even when it is wrong (as it often is), or limited (as it always is), a theory is a powerful stimulus for research. Perspectives, by contrast, may be little more than glimpses of order in the chaos. If there is a choice, always choose a theory.

When I started research on obesity in 1953, it was in the framework of an ambitious theory—the glucostatic theory of the control of food intake. It was a heady time. Mayer had just proposed the theory (Mayer, 1953), and Van Itallie, Beaudoin, and he (1953) were busy testing it. Furthermore, it was holding up very well. All that remained was to apply it to obese persons, find out what had gone wrong with them, and put it right. I planned to allocate two years to the task.

Thirty-five years later, we still do not understand the control of food intake, and we are even further from a general theory of obesity. Understanding obesity has proved to be as difficult as treating it. Yet, in these years of research we have learned a great deal about obesity from a number of perspectives—from the genetic to the psychological to the sociological. And little by little we have come closer to our goal as physicians—the relief of suffering and the restoration of health.

What follows are some perspectives on human obesity; perspectives derived from two vantage points—the etiology of obesity and the treatment of obesity.

PERSPECTIVES ON THE ETIOLOGY OF HUMAN OBESITY

An attempt to understand the etiology of human obesity can start with one fact: Obesity is, to an extraordinary degree, a familial disorder. Figure 1.1 provides a clear illustration. Most of the children of lean parents are lean; half of the children of obese parents are obese (Garn, 1985).

What determines the familial nature of obesity? Is it due to genetic influences or to environmental influences or to an interaction between the two? Until recently, most of the evidence favored an environmental etiology. Much of this evidence was based on studies of the relationship between socioeconomic status and obesity. Figure 1.2 provides a striking illustration of this relationship: Obesity was six times more common among women of low socioeconomic status than among those of high socioeconomic status (Goldblatt, Moore, & Stunkard, 1965). Furthermore, this relationship was more than a correlational one. Figure 1.2 shows also that the socioeconomic status into which a women was born was almost as strong a predictor of obesity as was her own socioeconomic status. Being obese could, and did, result in a fall in socioeconomic status. The influence of socioeconomic status on obesity, however, was far stronger.

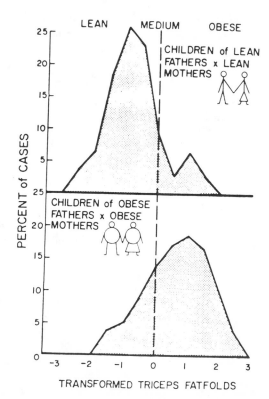

FIGURE 1.1. Relationship of parental fatness combination to the incidence of leanness and obesity in their children. Depending on the age of the children, two lean parents may yield close to 50% of lean progeny, and two obese parents will engender an equal proportion of obese children (Garn, 1985).

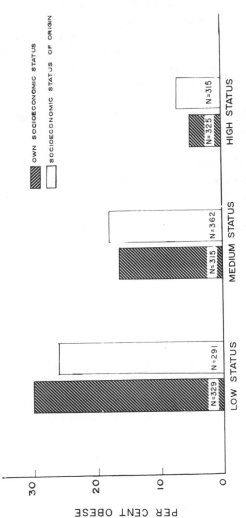

FIGURE 1.2. Decreasing prevalence of obesity with increase in own socioeco-nomic status (SES) and SES of origin (Goldblatt, Moore, & Stunkard, 1965).

Since this observation was first reported in 1965, no less than 32 studies have confirmed the inverse relationship between socioeconomic status and obesity among women, and it stands as one of the most robust findings in the obesity literature (Sobal & Stunkard, in press).

Further support for the influence of the environment on obesity is provided by a study of pet dogs: 44% of the dogs of overweight owners were overweight, as compared to 25% of the dogs of lean owners (Mason, 1972).

Evidence for a genetic influence in human obesity is of more recent origin. The first such evidence was obtained through twin studies. The basis for these studies is a comparison of the concordance rates for obesity of identical twins (who are genetically identical) with those of fraternal twins (who are no more similar, genetically, than siblings). The difference between the concordance rates of identical twins and those of fraternal twins provides a measure of the influence of genetics.

One large study examined the concordance rates for different degrees of overweight of more than 4,000 pairs of male twins, divided about equally between identical and fraternal twins (Stunkard, Foch, & Hrubec, 1986). The measure of fatness was the body-mass index (weight in kilograms divided by height in meters squared), which was estimated at age 20, when these men were inducted into the armed forces of the United States, and again 25 years later when they averaged 45 years of age. Table 1.1 shows that the concordance rates for lesser degrees of overweight were approximately twice as high among identical twins as among fraternal twins, suggesting a strong degree of genetic determination. Furthermore, differences in concordance rates between identical and

TABLE 1.1.   Probandwise concordance rates for various percentages of overweight Each twin whose weight exceeded a given criterion was included as a proband. At induction twins averaged 20 years of age; at follow-up they averaged 45 years of age (Stunkard et al, 1986a).

CONCORDANCE RATES

PERCENT OVERWEIGHT	AT INDUCTION		AT FOLLOW-UP	
	%MZ	%DZ	%MZ	%DZ
15	61	31	68	49
20	57	27	60	40
25	46	24	54	26
30	51	19	47	16
35	44	12	43	9
40	44	0	36	6

fraternal twins increased dramatically with the increase in the percentage of overweight.

Differences in concordance rates between identical and fraternal twin pairs indicates a genetic contribution to body-mass index, but it does not indicate the size of that contribution. For that purpose, a measure of heritability can be estimated to express the percentage of the variance that is accounted for by genetic factors. Heritability estimates obtained from twin studies of obesity and other disorders are listed in Table 1.2. These estimates show that genetic factors account for much of the variance in body-mass index in two previous studies of children and one previous study of adults. In the present study, the heritability of body-mass index was .77 at age 20 and .84 at age 45 (Stunkard et al., 1986a). In other words, approximately 80% of the variance in body mass may be due to genetic factors. Furthermore, a path analysis showed that genetic factors were largely responsible for the stability in body-mass index during the 25 years between the two measurements. These estimates of the contribution of genetics to body-mass index are larger than those of several other disorders, as shown in Table 1.2.

These figures on the heritability of human obesity are subject to three limitations. First, they are confined to men. Second, they are confined to men whose obesity began during adult life and, therefore, exclude men with juvenile-onset obesity. Third, heritability estimates based on twin data probably overestimate the contribution of genetic factors. Accordingly, it would be reassuring to sup-

HERITABILITY ESTIMATES
FROM TWIN STUDIES

Obesity (children)	.77
Obesity (children)	.88
Obesity (age 20)	.80
Obesity (age 20)	.77
Obesity (age 45)	.84
Schizophrenia	.68
Hypertension	.57
Alcoholism	.57
Cirrhosis	.53
Epilepsy	.50
Coronary	.49

TABLE 1.2.   Heritability estimates of twin studies of obesity and other medical conditions. The estimate of .80 at age 20 is from a Swedish study, those of .77 and .84 are from the study by Stunkard et al (1986a), the others are from various studies in the medical literature (Stunkard et al, 1986a).

plement twin studies with other methods of estimating the contribution of genetics to human obesity. One such method is adoption studies, and we have conducted two of them.

The rationale of adoption studies is simple: The adoptees are compared with both their biologic and their adoptive parents in regard to the trait under consideration. A relationship between adoptees and biologic parents indicates a genetic influence; a relationship between adoptees and adoptive parents indicates an environmental influence.

The first adoption study was carried out in Denmark, where we obtained full information about the height and weight of 3,580 adoptees who averaged 42 years of age (Stunkard, Sørensen, Hanis, Teasdale, Chakraborty, Schull, & Schulsinger, 1986b). The body-mass index of these adoptees was then calculated and arrayed across the spectrum from very thin to very fat. Out of this large population, we selected the study sample of 540 adoptees (half women and half men) which comprised the 4% thinnest, the 4% fattest, the 4% next to the fattest, and the 4% at the median of the distribution of their body-mass index. We then obtained information about the heights and weights of both biologic and adoptive parents, and calculated their body-mass index. Finally, we compared the weight class of the adoptees with the body-mass index of their biologic and adoptive parents. The results were unequivocal and dramatic.

There was a clear relationship between adoptee weight class and the body-mass index of the biologic parents; there was no relation between adoptee weight class and the body-mass index of the adoptive parents.

These relationships are shown in Figure 1.3, which depicts the mean body-mass index of parents of the four weight classes of adoptees. The body-mass index of the biologic parents increased with an increase in the weight class of adoptees. For biologic mothers, this relationship was highly significant ($p < 0.001$). The relationship between the mean body-mass index of biologic fathers and the weight class of the adoptees was also statistically significant ($p < 0.02$). A variety of other statistical tests confirmed this relationship between biologic parents and adoptees and the absence of a relationship between adoptive parents and adoptees.

This study confirmed the finding of the twin studies that heredity clearly plays a part in human obesity. It did not, however, indicate how large a part it plays. It is, therefore, gratifying that a very recent adoption study has provided such information (Price, Cadoret, Stunkard, & Troughton, 1987).

This study, carried out in Iowa, confirmed the findings from Denmark. As in the Danish study, it compared the body-mass index of a large number (357) of adult adoptees with the body-mass index of both their biologic and their adoptive parents. Once again, there was a strong relationship between the body-mass index of the adoptees and that of their biologic parents, and no relationship between the body-mass index of the adoptees and that of their adoptive parents.

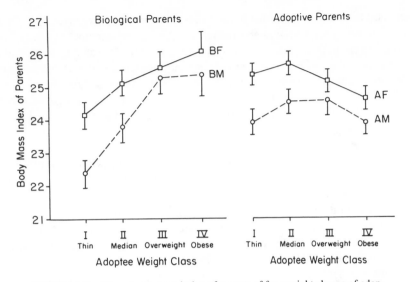

FIGURE 1.3.   Mean body-mass index of parents of four weight classes of adoptees. Note the increase in mean body-mass index of biologic parents with the increase in weight class of the adoptees. No such increase was found with adoptive parents. Bars represent 1 SEM. BF denotes biologic fathers, BM biologic mothers, AF adoptive fathers, and AM adoptive mothers (Stunkard et al. 1986b).

And, once again, the relationship between the biologic mothers and adoptees was stronger than that between the biologic fathers and adoptees.

Table 1.3 shows that the correlation between the body-mass index of the female adoptees and that of their biologic mothers was 0.40 ($p < 0.001$), while that of the female adoptees with that of their biologic fathers was 0.14 ($p <$

CORRELATION OF BODY MASS INDEX OF
FEMALE ADOPTEES WITH:

BIOLOGIC MOTHERS	0.40	$p < 0.001$
BIOLOGIC FATHERS	0.14	$p < 0.05$
ADOPTIVE MOTHERS	0.05	
ADOPTIVE FATHERS	-0.01	

TABLE 1.3.   The correlation coefficient of the body mass index of female adoptees with their biologic and adoptive parents (Price et al, 1987).

0.05). Table 1.3 also shows that there was no correlation between the body-mass index of the female adoptees and that of their adoptive parents.

The correlation between the body-mass index of the male adoptees and that of their biologic parents was not as strong as that between the female adoptees and their biologic parents and did not quite reach statistical significance.

These findings replicate the Danish results and confirm the strength of genetic influences on body-mass index. Furthermore, these influences show different patterns. In both Denmark and Iowa, the relationship between biologic mothers and their offspring was stronger than that between the biologic fathers and their offspring. This strong relationship between biologic mothers and their offspring, found in two very different populations, suggests that we are dealing with an important phenomenon. What is its cause?

One possibility is that the relationship is not due to genes at all, but is a gestational effect—the contribution of intrauterine life in the mother to the body-mass index of her offspring. We know that maternal starvation early in pregnancy during the Dutch Hunger Winter (Ravelli, Stein, & Susser, 1976) and the hyperglycemia of Pima Indian diabetics during pregnancy (Pettitt, Baird, Aleck, Bennett, & Knowles, 1983), favor the development of obesity. Although diabetes in the biologic mothers was not a cause in either the Danish or the Iowa studies, some other maternal influence may well have existed.

If the relationship is due to genes, one possibility is that it is due to mitochondrial genes, which are transmitted only by the mother. An intriguing aspect of this latter possibility is that decreased energy expenditure, presumably arising from altered mitochondrial function, has been implicated in a type of genetic obesity in the mouse (Coleman, 1985).

The extent of the relationship between biologic mothers and their daughters is also worthy of note. Since each parent contributes only half of the genes of each offspring, the correlation coefficient of 0.40, which we found, means that 64% of the variance on average is explained by the relationship between the biologic mother and her daughter. It is, of course, possible that nongenetic influences contributed to this high correlation and the purely genetic contribution may be closer to that reflected by the correlation between biologic mothers and their sons ($r = 0.15$).

These are new issues raised for the first time by the results of these studies. The attempts to understand them will help to define the agenda for future research in human obesity.

Where in the body are these genetic effects exerted? The answer is, "Almost anyplace." The central nervous system is an excellent candidate. Let us start with the cerebral cortex and perceptions of the palatability of foods; move to the limbic system, which may be involved in the emotions that facilitate or inhibit eating; go on to the hypothalamus, long recognized as a site for the control of ingestive behavior; and, in the brain stem, the area postrema, and the nucleus of the solitary tract, which may well contain a central mechanism for the regulation of body weight (Hyde & Miselis, 1983, Shapiro & Miselis, 1985). Leaving the brain stem, candidates for the site of a genetic influence may include the vagus nerve, including efferent impulses from the dorsal nucleus of vagus to the islet cells of the pancreas as well as to other endocrine systems.

The stomach has been implicated in the control of food intake (McHugh & Moran, 1985), and the sensitivity of the stomach and the afferent impulses leading from it via the vagus nerve could mediate genetic influences on the regulation of body weight. The anatomy of adipose tissue has long been recognized as a key factor in obesity, and there is compelling evidence of genetic influences on the development of adipose tissue in the Zucker obese rat (Johnson, Zucker, Cruce, & Hirsch, 1971). A single gene can prolong the period of adipose tissue proliferation among those Zucker rats destined to become obese, producing the greater adipose tissue of the fat rats as compared to their nonobese litter mates. Perhaps genes influence human obesity in a similar way. Finally, the "one gene—one enzyme" hypothesis (Beadle & Tatum, 1941) may well be exemplified by genetic determinants of lipoprotein lipase, an enzyme that has been called a "gatekeeper" for the entry of lipids into the adipose tissue cell (Brunzell & Greenwood, 1982).

In addition to the "where" of genetic influence on human obesity, there is the question of "how." The very different percentages of obese women in different socioeconomic strata tell us that genetic influences are modified by their interaction with the environment. One environmental influence is the character of the diet. Highly palatable and high-fat diets can produce dietary obesity in experimental animals. The degree of responsiveness to such diets may well be genetically determined, and some persons may be particularly vulnerable. The many different sites at which genes may exert their influence suggest that there are many different kinds of interactions between genes and environments.

For a long time it was not clear that genes influence human obesity. Now that we know that they do, we can begin to ask where and how they exert this influence. Research that investigates both the site of action and the method of action may be a fruitful starting point.

PERSPECTIVES DERIVED FROM
THE TREATMENT OF HUMAN OBESITY

Some of the perspectives on human obesity are derived from treatment. The treatment of obesity has recently been advanced by two new developments—a theory of obesity that has therapeutic relevance and a classification of obesity that has therapeutic consequences.

The theory states that obesity is a result of regulated processes that maintain body weight (and body fat) at a constant level, and that attempts to lower body weight (and body fat) are opposed by these processes. According to this theory, the origins of obesity reside in the forces that cause the regulated level of body weight—sometimes called a "set point"—to be elevated. This theory was first proposed to explain the remarkable stability of the body weight of most animals and the tendency of this weight to return to its baseline level after it had been either raised or lowered. The relevance of the theory to human obesity has become evident in recent years. Its usefulness in understanding different treatments of human obesity is illustrated in the sections that follow. But, first, let us consider the classification.

Classification of a disease ideally derives from an understanding of its etiology and pathogenesis, and we are far from such an understanding of obesity. But, for the clinician, the purpose of classification is to select the best treatment for a patient. For this purpose, our classification is useful. It is based on the severity of obesity—mild, moderate, and severe—characterized by body weights that are, respectively, 20 to 40% overweight, 41 to 100% overweight, and more than 100% overweight (Stunkard, 1984). Table 1.4 shows that the percentage of obese women falling into these categories is, respectively, 90.5, 9, and 0.5% (Vital and Health Statistics, 1983). The distribution of overweight among men is not currently available, but is believed to be similar to that for women. Note that these percentages are of the *obese* population, not of the total population, of which about 25% are considered to be obese.

The adipose tissue of mildly obese persons is usually hypertrophic, meaning that the adipose tissue cells are increased in size but not in number, while that of severely obese persons is both hypertrophic and hyperplastic, meaning that the adipose tissue cells are increased in both size and number. The adipose tissue of moderately obese persons lies between these extremes.

The complications of severe obesity are many and serious, including a 12-fold increase in mortality of men aged 25 to 34. The complications of mild and moderate obesity vary widely, depending on the existence of conditions such as

TABLE 1.4.   A classification of obesity together with prevalence, pathology, complications, and treatment of the three types (Stunkard, 1984).

Type	Classification of Obesity		
	Mild	Moderate	Severe
Percentage overweight	20–40%	41–100%	> 100%
Prevalence (among obese women)	90.5%	9.0%	0.5%
Pathology	Hypertrophic	Hypertrophic, hyperplastic	Hypertrophic, hyperplastic
Complications	Uncertain	Conditional	Severe
Treatment	Behavior therapy (lay)	Diet and behavior therapy (medical)	Surgical

hypertension and diabetes that are precipitated or exacerbated by obesity. These complications increase in frequency and severity with increasing body weight.

This classification has therapeutic implications. Severe obesity is best treated by surgical measures, and mild obesity by diet and behavior modification under lay auspices. The treatment of choice for moderate obesity is, as we shall see, uncertain.

TREATMENT OF SEVERE OBESITY

New surgical procedures have revolutionized the treatment of severe obesity, a condition associated with serious medical complications and one for which conservative treatment has been largely ineffective (Stunkard, Stinnett, & Smoller, 1986).

It is now generally agreed that the most effective surgical treatments for obesity are ones that restrict the volume of the stomach, and the vertical-banded gastroplasty has become the treatment of choice. This operation produces a stable pouch as small as 20 ml in volume, oriented along the lesser curvature of the stomach, with an outlet at the lower end of the pouch that measures no more than 5 cm in circumference. As a result, patients can consume only a very limited amount of food at any meal, and their food intake is drastically reduced. The resulting weight losses are impressive; very severely obese persons (200% or more overweight) lose about 50% of their excess weight or at least 50 kg, and lighter persons may lose an even greater percentage. Such weight loss produces a marked decrease in hypertension, diabetes, and other complications of obesity, and a marked improvement in psychosocial functioning. All reports agree on these facts, but even this rosy picture may underestimate the benefits of gastric-restriction surgery. The early reports used the time just before surgery as a control period. A more appropriate control period is previous occasions when the patient was losing weight without surgery. At such times, 50% of all persons experience untoward emotional responses, and the incidence and severity among severely obese persons are even greater (Stunkard & Rush, 1974).

In contrast to these rates of emotional disturbance following weight loss by medical treatment, weight loss following gastric-restriction surgery is associated with very little emotional disturbance. Figure 1.4 shows that, following such surgery, there was far less depression, anxiety, irritability, and preoccupation with food (Stunkard et al., 1986c). Furthermore, half of the patients reported an increase in positive emotions such as elation and self-confidence, in sharp contrast to the very limited number who reported such emotions during dieting. In addition, body-image disparagement decreased markedly following surgery. Before surgery in one series, 70% of the patients reported severe body-image disparagement, and only 11% reported no disparagement. By contrast, after surgery, only 4% reported severe body-image disparagement, and 45% reported

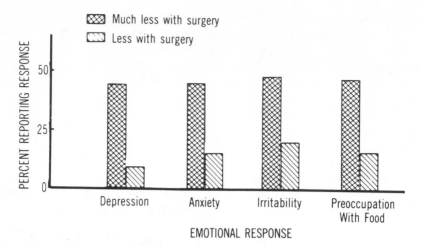

FIGURE 1.4. Comparison of emotional responses during weight loss by surgical and dietary treatments.

none. A notable aspect of these changes in body image is that they may occur within six months of surgery, when patients have lost only a fraction of their preoperative body weight and when they are still severely obese.

Another striking change that follows surgery is a change in food preferences. In one study, 50% of patients reported that high-density fat and high-density carbohydrates were no longer enjoyable, and smaller percentages reported a lack of enjoyment of high-fat meats and high-calorie beverages and an associated decrease in their consumption (Halmi, Mason, Falk, & Stunkard, 1981).

The final, striking effect of surgery for obesity is a paradox: During the period of rapid weight loss following surgery, patients who had formerly not begun to eat until later in the day reported a return of appetite for breakfast (Stunkard et al., 1986b).

The psychological changes following surgery for obesity are so profound as to suggest that the weight loss is due to major changes in the biology of the patients. Specifically, we have proposed that the operation leads to the lowering of a set point about which body weight is regulated (Stunkard et al., 1986c). If this idea is even approximately correct, it helps to explain how these patients can lose weight without any special effort for it suggests that a physiological regulation mediates the decrease in food intake rather than opposing it, as occurs during dieting. Persons who decrease their food intake in the service of a physiological regulation should experience far less difficulty than those who decrease their food intake in opposition to that regulation.

PHARMACOTHERAPY (AND BEHAVIOR THERAPY) OF OBESITY

Our understanding of the mechanism of action of appetite-suppressant medication began with a clinical trial. We compared behavior therapy with pharmacotherapy and a combination of the two (Craighead, Stunkard, & O'Brien, 1981). At the time of this trial, there had been thousands of studies of the pharmacotherapy of obesity and dozens of studies of behavior therapy of obesity, but few attempts to compare the two and none to combine them. In this study, 95 obese (60% overweight) women were treated for six months and reexamined one year later. In addition, 10 women were put on a waiting list to provide a (no-treatment) control group, and 10 others were treated in a doctor's office with the standard medical treatment of diet and drugs. Figure 1.5 shows the results of treatment and follow-up.

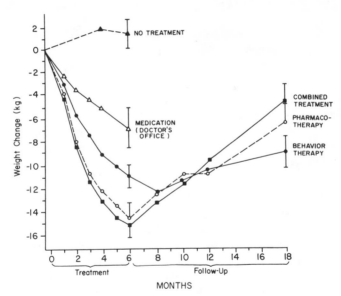

FIGURE 1.5.   Weight changes during 6-month treatment and 12-month follow-up. The three major treatment groups lost large amounts of weight during treatment: behavior therapy (closed circles), 10.9 kg; pharmacotherapy (open circles), 14.5 kg; and combined treatment (squares), 15.3 kg. The behavior-therapy group continued to lose weight for two months and then slowly regained it; pharmacotherapy and combined-treatment groups rapidly regained weight. Among control groups, the no-treatment (waiting-list) groups (closed triangles) gained weight; the physician's-office medication group (open triangles) lost 6 kg. Patients in control groups received additional treatment at 6 months, and so were not available for follow-up. Vertical lines represent 1 SEM (Craighead et al., 1981).

Patients in the behavior-modification condition lost 11.4 kg, while those in the medication condition lost significantly more—14.5 kg. Adding the two treatments had no effect on weight loss; patients in the combined treatment condition lost 15.0 kg. As expected, patients on the waiting list gained a small amount of weight, while those treated in the doctor's office condition lost 6.0 kg, less than those in the behavior-modification condition and far less than those in the pharmacotherapy condition (who had received comparable amounts of medication).

One year after the end of treatment, there was a striking reversal in the relative efficacy of the three major treatments. The behavior-therapy patients regained far less than did those who received pharmacotherapy or the combined treatment. During the year after treatment, behavior-therapy patients regained only 1.9 kg, compared to the pharmacotherapy patients whose net loss was only 6.3 kg. Combined-treatment patients regained even more weight than did the pharmacotherapy patients, for an even smaller net weight loss—no more than 4.6 kg. The long-term trend in weight loss thus strongly favored behavior therapy alone over the two treatments that employed pharmacotherapy.

A major lesson of this study was the surprising long-term effectiveness of behavior therapy, which is becoming the treatment of choice for mild obesity. An equally striking finding was the rapid regain of body weight by patients who had received pharmacotherapy, either alone or in combination with behavior therapy. In fact, adding pharmacotherapy to behavior therapy not only did not improve the long-term effects of the latter, it apparently compromised them. The long-term effects of behavior therapy were actually poorer if patients had also received pharmacotherapy than if they had not. This striking finding, which has since been replicated, cries out for an explanation.

Here it is. Medication lowers the body-weight set point of these patients, facilitating weight loss. When the medication is discontinued, however, the set point rises to its pretreatment level. The resulting biological pressures to gain weight to this higher level produce weight gains that are larger than those of patients who had lost weight without the help of medication (Stunkard, 1982). This rationale seems obvious. Why had it never been proposed before?

The most reasonable explanation is the long-standing belief in the development of tolerance to the effects of appetite-suppressant medication. Almost every textbook of medicine and pharmacology still cautions that the usefulness of appetite-suppressant medication is limited by the rapid development of tolerance. This belief is apparently based on the slowing of weight loss that occurs during treatment with such medication. Slowing weight loss, however, need not be due to tolerance. People clearly cannot keep losing weight indefinitely, and slowing of weight loss could be due to many reasons other than the development of tolerance. In fact, precisely such a slowing of weight loss is found in nondrug treatments for obesity, whether a little weight is lost, as with traditional diets, or much weight is lost, as with very-low-calorie diets, fasting, and surgical treatments. There is, thus, little evidence that tolerance develops during drug treatment. There is strong evidence that it does not:

This evidence is threefold. First, body weight rebounds when appetite medication is discontinued, as we have seen in Figure 1.5. If tolerance had developed, discontinuing medication should not have been followed by a rebound of body weight.

Second, weight losses in the medication conditions were more rapid than were those in the behavior-therapy condition for a full six months. If tolerance had developed, the weight losses in the pharmacotherapy conditions should have been slower than those in the behavior-therapy condition.

Third, hunger did not increase in the course of treatment. If tolerance had developed, hunger, which had been suppressed early in treatment, should have increased, and it did not.

The explanation that pharmacotherapy acts by lowering a body-weight set point was at first an ad hoc one, based, as was the explanation for the effects of gastric-restriction surgery, on clinical studies. Soon after the publication of our study, however, experiments with animals provided strong support for this explanation. Levitsky and his colleagues (Levitsky, Strupp, & Lupoli, 1982) showed that the effectiveness of an appetite-suppressant medication depends on the body weight of the animal to which it is administered. Thus, the administration of such an agent to a weight-deprived rat had no effect on its food intake; restoring its body weight to a normal level restored the ability of the agent to suppress food intake. Levitsky et al. (1982) concluded that their results "strongly support a weight-loss explanation of tolerance to the effects of anorexic drugs. What appears to be a pharmacological tolerance to the anorexic effects of chronic drug administration is merely a reflection of decreasing body weight."

These findings have important clinical and policy implications. The fact that tolerance does not develop to the effects of appetite-suppressant medication means that the old argument against its use—a loss of efficacy—is no longer valid. These agents retain their efficacy, and, paradoxically, this fact provides a new argument against their short-term use. For, if they retain their efficacy, discontinuing them permits the set point to rise to its previous level, subjecting patients to powerful pressures to regain the weight that they had lost.

Although short-term use of appetite-suppressant medication seems to be contraindicated, long-term use may not be. Indeed, the fact that such medication continues to be effective over long periods of time argues for long-term use. There is a large number of obese persons with hypertension, diabetes, and other disorders that are readily controlled by weight loss. Many of these people, however, cannot lose weight without medication. For them, the risks of long-term use of appetite-suppressant medication may well be outweighed by the benefits. These benefits may include not only control of these disorders, but also freedom from the risks of the chronic use of medications for their control.

INTENSIVE VERSUS EXTENSIVE APPLICATIONS OF BEHAVIOR THERAPY: WEIGHT-LOSS COMPETITIONS

The clinical trial described above provided convincing evidence of the usefulness of behavior therapy for the treatment of mild obesity. Subsequent efforts to increase the usefulness of behavior therapy have taken two quite different directions—increasing the *intensity* of treatment to produce larger weight losses and increasing the *extensiveness* of treatment to reach larger numbers of persons. The first attempt to increase the intensity of treatment was to combine behavior therapy with pharmacotherapy as described above. Clearly it was a failure.

The second attempt was to combine behavior therapy with very-low-calorie diets. We hoped that the large weight losses produced by these diets would not be followed by the kind of rebound in body weight that followed the discontinuation of pharmacotherapy. The results of these efforts were equivocal. Wadden and Stunkard (1986) showed that combining behavior therapy with very-low-calorie diets did, indeed, produce greater weight losses than did behavior therapy alone. Furthermore, following treatment, body weight was regained more slowly than following combined treatment with pharmacotherapy. Some weight was, however, regained, and we are left with an unanswered question. Is the weight loss worth the added effort and expense of the very-low-calorie diets? Perhaps only a cost-effectiveness analysis of these two treatments will answer this question, and we are proceeding with such an analysis.

In addition to efforts to increase the intensity of behavioral treatments, efforts have been made to increase the extensiveness of treatments and to apply them to large population groups. Behavior therapy is well suited to these efforts; it is easy to specify and, therefore, easy to teach and learn. Many of the key elements are available in easy-to-use treatment manuals (Brownell, 1985). As a result, behavior therapy for obesity has been administered by persons with less and less professional training to the point that lay persons now perform most of this therapy in the United States. Furthermore, the treatment is remarkably safe. We thus have a technology that can promise modest weight losses at low cost and minimal risk. Several vehicles can deliver this technology.

An obvious vehicle is the physician's office. Although few physicians themselves carry out behavioral weight-control programs, more and more of them are engaging nutritionists and nurses to conduct such programs within their practices. Hospitals are also establishing these programs in their outpatient departments, and behavioral psychologists have conducted weight-control programs for some years. By far the largest number of obese persons, however, is being treated under the auspices of lay-led groups.

Lay-led groups for obesity long antedate the development of behavioral weight control, and a large number of programs, both nonprofit and commercial, exist today. Unfortunately, these programs do not provide information about the results of their treatment, and information obtained by independent observers points to serious problems. For example, 50% of the members of one commercial weight-reduction group had dropped out of the program within 6 weeks and 70% in 12 weeks (Volkmar, Stunkard, Woolston, & Bailey, 1981). Similar dropout rates have been reported from four other studies conducted on three continents (Ashwell and Garrow, 1985).

A promising vehicle for the treatment of mild obesity is the work site. Most people spend more of their time at work than at any other activity, and the support of their fellow workers can encourage them to improve their health behaviors. Furthermore, weight-loss programs at the work site can be carried out by nonprofessionals just as effectively as by professionals and at a far lower cost. These favorable circumstances have attracted a large and growing number of industries to begin health promotions at the work site.

Despite the obvious potential of work-site weight control, the first results were disappointing. The problem was the same as that of the lay-led groups— very large dropout rates. The most intensive early treatment program was one adapted from a clinical format and applied at the work site of a large union in New York City (Brownell, Stunkard, & McKeon, 1985). During a period of three years, 172 women out of thousands in the union received a 16-week treatment program that was continually improved on the basis of prior results. Nevertheless, the dropout rate never fell below 34% and weight loss never exceeded 3.5 kg. These disappointing results provide the basis for appreciating a far more effective treatment measure—weight-loss competitions.

Weight-loss competitions at the work site are a major new development in the treatment of obesity (Brownell, Cohen, Stunkard, Felix, & Cooley, 1984). The first competition was initiated by a challenge from the management of a bank in a small town in north-central Pennsylvania to two competitor banks. The mechanics of the competition were simplicity itself. Bank members who wished to participate were weighed and given a modest weight-loss goal, which in no case exceeded 20 pounds. Crash dieting was, thereby, effectively discouraged. The winning team was the one that achieved the greatest percentage of its team goal, which was the sum of the weight-loss goals of each participant. Participants paid $5.00 to enter, and the pool of money was awarded to the winning team.

Participants were weighed weekly, at which time they received an installment of a treatment manual which described the standard measures for behavioral weight control. As soon as the weight losses had been determined each week, the progress of each team was calculated and relayed to the other banks. The results were promptly displayed in the lobby of each bank on large placards providing prompt feedback and incentives for further weight loss. The competition lasted for 12 weeks.

The first, striking effect of the competitions was the high level of participation. Almost every overweight person in each bank participated in the competition, and the attrition rate was no more than 0.5%. The contrast with traditional programs of weight loss at the work site could not have been stronger.

Substantial amounts of weight were lost. In the first competition, despite the shorter (12-week) duration of the program, the women lost 5.0 kg, significantly more than the 3.5 kg weight loss in the more traditional 16-week work-site program conducted by the union. Furthermore, there were substantial psychological benefits: A majority of employees reported increased morale and greater energy level, and 40% reported improved relations with coworkers and increased work performance.

Since this first effort, more than 30 weight-loss competitions have been held. They confirm the essential elements of the first program—very low attrition rates, weight losses of a pound per week, and marked improvement in morale and social functioning.

An important early discovery was that competitions are attractive to men, who do not usually take part in weight-loss programs. Even more striking, weight-loss competitions attract a larger number of blue-collar workers, a group that has traditionally been resistant to any form of health promotion.

In the course of these competitions, we have elucidated the effective elements of weight-loss competitions. They had initially been promoted as competitions, and we had, not unreasonably, assumed that competition was the effective element. As we assessed varying structures of competition, however, it became clear that this was not the case. Thus, the effectiveness of the programs decreased progressively as the intensity of individual competitiveness increased— from competitions between companies, to competitions between different divisions of a company, to competitions between individuals. Indeed, the competitions between individuals were so ineffective that very few women and only a minority of men lost any significant amount of weight.

These results led us to wonder whether cooperation might not be the critical element in the weight-loss competitions. We tested this hypothesis by conducting programs of pure cooperation, without any element of competition. Pure cooperation, however, proved as ineffective as pure competition: Very few men and only a minority of women lost any significant amount of weight.

It begins to appear that the effective element in weight-loss competitions is a combination of competition and cooperation. People do best when cooperating with each other in a competition against natural (business) competitors. This combination appeals to both men and women and arouses them to maximum effort.

An important aspect of weight-loss competitions is their very low cost. After the frustrating attempts to adapt clinical programs to the work site in the union program, the emergence of weight-loss competitions appears to realize the potential of work-site programs. It makes an effective treatment available to very large numbers of persons at very low cost.

The first estimates of the cost-effectiveness of weight-loss competitions were promising. Little professional time was required, workers could be weighed and receive instruction sheets in a few minutes during their lunch period, and demands on management were minimal. Since those first efforts, costs have been further reduced by the development of a manual for the conduct of weight-loss competitions. It is now possible to dispense with professional involvement, and programs can be administered by a small number of employees, largely in the course of their other duties.

The full merit of weight-loss competitions is revealed by cost-effectiveness analysis. In this analysis, we estimated the cost to lose 1% of body weight—the approximate amount of weight lost during one week of a standard weight-reduction program. This measure has proved to be a more useful measure than the apparently more common-sense one of pounds or kilograms. This usefulness is because weight loss is so dependent on body weight—heavier people lose weight more rapidly than do lighter people. The use of percentage rather than absolute weight loss controls for varying levels of body weight and makes it possible to compare programs which enroll persons with large differences in body weight.

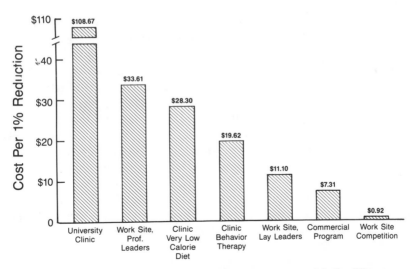

FIGURE 1.6.   The cost of 1% reduction in percentage overweight for different weight-loss programs. Estimates were obtained for a university clinic (Stanford Eating Disorders Program) and for a commercial group from Yates (1978), and for the work-site programs with professional and lay leaders from Brownell et al. (1984).

This measure was first used by Yates (1978) whose results, updated to reflect inflation, are shown in Figure 1.6, together with the results of the present and other comparable programs. Note the very large cost ($88.20) in a university-based program analyzed by Yates. Lesser, but still substantial, costs were incurred in the union program at the work site described by Brownell et al. (1985), in which the cost incurred by professionally led groups was significantly greater than that incurred by lay-led groups. The costs of treatment of individual patients in the doctor's office in the study of Craighead et al. (1981) were intermediate between those of the work site programs conducted by professional and by lay leaders. A very modest cost of $6.30 per 1% reduction in body weight was incurred during the commercial weight-loss program described by Yates, updated to reflect inflation. By contrast to the costs of these other methods, the cost of weight loss in the weight-loss competitions was less than $1.00 per 1% reduction in body weight!

SUMMARY AND CONCLUSIONS

Human obesity is a familial disorder. For some time it has been apparent that environmental influences can play an important part in human obesity. Recently, both adoption and twin studies have revealed an important genetic component. A major task for the future is understanding how specific genetic predispositions interact with specific environmental pressures to produce human obesity.

Treatment of obesity has become more effective in recent years. Gastric-restriction surgery has controlled the weight of a significant percentage of very severely obese persons, perhaps by a physiological mechanism such as lowering of a body-weight set point.

The regaining of weight that had been lost with the aid of appetite-suppressant medication has long been recognized. An explanation of this phenomenon is now at hand. Appetite-suppressant medication appears to act by lowering a body-weight set point. When the medication is discontinued, the resulting elevation of the set point subjects the patient to powerful pressures to regain the lost weight. By contrast, weight lost with the aid of behavior therapy is relatively well maintained.

A very recent development—weight-loss competitions at the work site—can reach large numbers of persons at very low cost to produce substantial weight losses. They show very promising cost-effectiveness ratios.

REFERENCES

Ashwell, M., & Garrow, J. S. (1975). A survey of three slimming and weight control organizations in the UK. *Nutrition, 29,* 346–356.

Beadle, G. W., & Tatum, E. L. (1941). Genetic control of biochemical reactions in *Neurospora*. *Proceedings of the National Academy of Sciences USA, 27*, 499–506.

Brownell, K. D. (1985). *The LEARN Program for weight control* (unpublished manual), University of Pennsylvania School of Medicine.

Brownell, K. D., Cohen, R. Y., Stunkard, A. J., Felix, M. R., & Cooley, N. B. (1984). Weight loss competitions at the work site: Impact on weight, morale and cost-effectiveness. *American Journal of Public Health, 74*, 1283–1285.

Brownell, K. D., Stunkard, A. J., & McKeon, P. E. (1985). Weight reduction at the work site: A promise partially fulfilled. *American Journal of Psychiatry, 142*, 47–51.

Brunzell, J. D., & Greenwood M. R. C. (1982). Lipoprotein lipase and the regulation of body weight. In P. B. Curtis-Prior, Ed., *Obesity* (pp. 175–199). New York: Elsevier.

Coleman, D. (1985). Increased metabolic efficiency in obese mutant mice. *International Journal of Obesity, 9*, Suppl. 2, 69–73.

Craighead, L. W., Stunkard, A. J., & O'Brien, R. (1981). Behavior therapy and pharmacotherapy of obesity. *Archives of General Psychiatry, 38*, 763–768.

Garn, S. M. (1985). Continuities and changes in fatness from infancy through adulthood. *Current Problems in Pediatrics, 15*, 1–47.

Goldblatt, P. B., Moore, M. E., & Stunkard, A. J. (1965). Social factors in obesity ■ *Journal of the American Medical Association, 192*, 1039–1044.

Halmi, D. A., Mason, E., Falk, J., & Stunkard, A. J. (1981). Appetitive behavior after gastric bypass for obesity. *International Journal of Obesity, 5*, 457–464.

Hyde, T. H., & Miselis, R. R. (1983). Effects of area postrema/caudal medial nucleus of solitary tract lesions on food intake and body weight. *American Journal of Physiology, 244*, R577–R587.

Johnson P. R., Zucker L. M., Cruce J. A. F., & Hirsch, J. (1971). Cellularity of adipose depots in the genetically obese Zucker rat. *Journal of Lipid Research, 12*, 706–713.

Levitsky, D. A., Strupp, B. J., & Lupoli, J. (1981). Tolerance to anorectic drugs: Pharmacological or artifactual. *Pharmacology and Biochemistry of Behavior, 14*, 661–667.

Mason, E. (1970). Obesity in pet dogs. Veterinary record, 1970; 86:612–616.

Mayer, J. (1953). Genetic, traumatic and environmental factors in the etiology of obesity. *Physiological Review, 33*, 472–485.

McHugh, P. R., & Moran, T. H. (1985). The stomach: A conception of its dynamic role in satiety. In J. P. Sprague & A. N. Epstein (Eds.), *Progress in psychobiology and physiological psychology* (Vol. 11, 199–232). New York: Academic Press.

Pettitt, D. J., Baird H. K., Aleck K. A., Bennett P. H., & Knowles W. C. (1983). Excessive obesity in offspring of Pima Indian women with diabetes during pregnancy. *New England Journal of Medicine, 308*, 242–245.

Price, R. A., Cadoret, R., Stunkard, A. J., & Troughton, E. (1987). Genetic contribution to human fatness: An adoption study. *American Journal of Psychiatry, 144*, 1003–1008.

Ravelli, G. P., Stein, Z., & Susser, M. (1976). Obesity in young men after famine exposure in utero and early pregnancy. *New England Journal of Medicine, 295*, 349–353.

Shapiro R. E., & Miselis, R. R. (1985). The central neural connections of the area postrema of the rat. *Journal of Comparative Neurology, 234*, 344–364.

Sobal, J., & Stunkard, A. J. (1986). *Socioeconomic status and obesity: A review of the literature*. Psychological Bulletin (in press).

Stunkard, A. J. (1982). Anorectic agents lower body weight set point. *Life Sciences, 30*, 2043–2055.

Stunkard, A. J. (1984). The current status of treatment for obesity in adults. In A. J. Stunkard & E. Stellar (Eds.), *Eating and its disorders* (pp. 157–174). New York: Raven Press.

Stunkard, A. J., Foch, T. T., & Hrubec, Z. (1986a). A twin study of human obesity. *Journal of the American Medical Association, 256*, 51–54.

Stunkard, A. J., Sørenson, T. A., Hanis, C., Teasdale, T.W., Chakraborty, R., Schull, W. J., &

Schulsinger (1986b). An adoption study of human obesity. *New England Journal of Medicine, 314*, 193–198.

Stunkard, A. J., & Rush, G. (1974). Dieting and depression reexamined: A critical review of reports of untoward responses during weight reduction for obesity. *Annals of Internal Medicine, 81*, 526–533.

Stunkard, A. J., Stinnett, J. L. & Smoller, J. W. (1986c). Psychological and social aspects of the surgical treatment of obesity. *American Journal of Psychiatry, 143*, 417–429.

Van Itallie, R. B., Beaudoin, R., & Mayer, J. (1953). Arteriovenous glucose differences, metabolic hypoglycemia and food intake in man. *American Journal of Clinical Nutrition, 1*, 208–213.

Vital and Health Statistics. (1983, February). Overweight and obese adults in the United States U.S. Dep. of Health Hum. Serv., Public Health Serv. National Center for Health Statistics, Series II, No. 230, Hyattsville, Maryland.

Volkmar, F. R., Stunkard, A. J., Woolston, J., & Bailey, B. A. (1981). High attrition rates in commercial weight reduction programs. *Archives of Internal Medicine, 141*, 426–428.

Wadden, T. A., & Stunkard, A. J. (1986). Controlled trial of very-low calorie diet, behavior therapy and their combination in the treatment of obesity. *Journal of Consulting and Clinical Psychology, 54*, 482–488.

Yates, B. T. (1978). Improving the cost-effectiveness of obesity programs: Three basic strategies for reducing the cost per pound. *International Journal of Obesity, 2*, 249–266.

2

SEXUAL DIMORPHISM AND OBESITY

M. R. C. Greenwood
Department of Biology,
Vassar College

Obesity is one of the nation's most prominent public health problems. Estimates of its prevalence include one third of the adult population (Van Itallie, 1985) and have suggested an increasing incidence among children. Over and over, the media and the public ask the question, If thin is in, why are there so many fat Americans? Are we a nation of gluttons, poorly disciplined and unable to restrain ourselves in the face of ever-increasingly available, tempting culinary delights, or are we the victims of metabolic alterations, not yet thoroughly understood, which make it difficult for many individuals to ever bring their own body somatotypes into congruence with that of the national ideal? Furthermore, although the psychosocial costs of obesity are increasingly recognized, the degree to which obesity poses a health-related risk is controversial.

Part of the confusion over what constitutes a health risk and what constitutes a social risk derives from the fact that much of our epidemiological data and intervention assessments come from data sets collected primarily on males. In contrast, much of the data base on treatment of obesity is derived from data sets comprised, in large part, of data collected on women. It appears that while there are more obese women than men and more women seek treatment, morbidity in women is less than that seen in men. This dimorphism in the prevalence and consequences of obesity may be related to biological differences between males and females which are at least partially related to the function of reproductive hormones on fat metabolism and fat deposition.

THE ROLE OF SEX HORMONES
IN THE REGULATION OF FATNESS

It is well known that sex hormones play significant roles in the distribution of fat in both males and females. These hormones are also important in the regulation of feeding behavior. For example, adult females of most mammalian species are fatter than males. This fatness is considered a secondary sexual characteristic and is under the influence of sex hormones (Gray & Greenwood, 1982; Krotkiewski, Sjostrom, Bjorntorp, & Smith, 1975; Wade & Gray, 1979). When male rats are castrated, they develop more fat. Also, body composition data for humans reveal that females are approximately 20–25% fat and males are 15–19% fat. Males given female sex steroids frequently develop fat deposits in areas that are normally lean in males.

A variety of animal studies have shown that the central or peripheral administration of estradiol suppresses feeding behavior and that progesterone can reverse this effect on feeding (Wade & Gray, 1979). Furthermore, it has been demonstrated that adipose tissue is a target tissue for steroid action and that the steroid receptor number is regionally specific (Gray & Wade, 1981). It is also known that female reproductive states such as pregnancy, lactation, and stage of reproductive cycle influence lipid metabolic pathways and the efficiency of nutrient utilization.

Less well appreciated, but of increasing prominence, is the importance of the regional localization of fat stores and the impact of this localization on risk factors in humans as well as in animals. Four decades ago, the distinguished French endocrinologist Jean Vague (1947) noted that the distribution of fat influenced risk for diabetic complications. In human males who become obese, the pattern of fat accumulation is generally in the abdominal region. This distribution has been called "abdominal," "central," and "android," respectively. Women, however, have two patterns of adiposity associated with the development of obesity. They, too, may have the abdominal accretion of fat, but a significant proportion of them, who may be equivalently obese, have a distribution of fat which is infrequently seen in males. This distribution is called "peripheral," "femoral," or "gynoid," respectively (see Figure 2.1). Among women who are equivalently obese, those with femoral or gynoid obesity show almost no increased risk for non-insulin-dependent diabetes or associated risk factors, such as increased plasma glucose and increased plasma immunoreactive insulin (Krotkiewski, Bjorntorp, Sjostrom, & Smith, 1983). Thus, on these measures, some very obese women have relatively "benign" fat. However, among both males and females with abdominal obesity, morbidity was highly correlated with increases in waist to hip (W/H) ratios. Increased W/H ratios have been indicated as risk factors for ischemic heart disease, stroke, and death, with larger increases when the ratio exceeded 1.0 (Krotkiewski et al., 1975). Thus, there is significant sexual dimorphism in the patterns of obesity which may

MALE

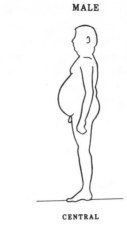

CENTRAL

FEMALE

FIGURE 2.1.   An illustration of the types of obesity that occur in males and females. Males develop predominantly centrally distributed fat. This pattern is called central, abdominal, or android obesity. Females develop two patterns of obesity, one of which is similar to that seen in males. The other form is typified by distribution of fat in the peripheral region, particularly in the hip region. This form is called peripheral, femoral, or gynoid obesity.

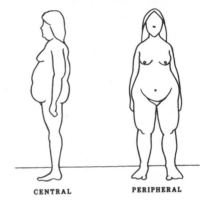

CENTRAL   PERIPHERAL

develop in males and females. This patterning influences health and demands further examination.

THE POSSIBLE ROLE OF FEMORAL FAT

We have recently hypothesized that in women, as well as in other mammals, metabolism of the femoral or peripheral fat may be specifically under female sex hormone control and represent a storage depot normally used during pregnancy and lactation (Greenwood, Savard, West, & Gray, 1985; Savard, Palmer, & Greenwood, 1986). In the course of a normal pregnancy in women and other mammals, fat is deposited in the body. In rats, this fat is deposited in most of the existing depots, but a preference for deposition in the subcutaneous inguinal depot is noted (Greenwood et al., 1985; Savard et al., 1986). The inguinal depot in rodents is thought by some to be similar to the femoral region in women. During lactation, fat is lost from all depots, but is preferentially lost from the inguinal depot (Steingrimsdottir, Brasel, & Greenwood, 1980).

Animal studies from this laboratory and others have shown that the regulation of this fat deposition and mobilization is primarily mediated through the action of the enzyme lipoprotein lipase (LPL). During pregnancy, LPL is elevated in adipose tissue, and this elevation is regionally specific (Savard et al., 1986; Steingrimsdottir et al., 1980). During lactation, the activity of LPL is nearly undectectable in adipose tissue, while rising manyfold in mammary tissue (Steingrimsdottir et al., 1980). Since LPL catalyzes the breakdown of circulating plasma triglycerides into free fatty acids (FFA) which are then available to the fat cell for reesterification, it has been named the "gatekeeper" enzyme (Greenwood et al., 1985). When LPL activity is high, the rate of entry of FFA into the fat depot is high; and when its activity is low, the entry of FFA to the fat depot is low. Thus, during the course of pregnancy and lactation, changes in LPL activity regulate the rate of storage of fat into individual depots during pregnancy but prevent the deposition of FFA into adipose tissue during lactation when it directs or "gates" substrate supply to mammary tissue milk synthesis. These effects of LPL activity in pregnancy and lactation are now known to be under the control of several steroid hormones and prolactin. In addition, other mechanisms, such as the regulation of thermogenesis (Moore, Gerada-Gettens, Horowitz, & Stern, 1986) and alterations in adipose tissue blood flow (Kava, West, Lukasik, Prinz, & Greenwood, 1986), all help to maintain the direction of nutrient flow and conserve energy substrate for needs associated with reproduction (see Table 2.1).

Table 2.1
Metabolic Alterations in Pregnancy and Lactation

	Pregnancy	Lactation
Food intake	+	+ + +
Food "efficiency"	+	−
Parametrial LPL	+	−
Inguinal LPL	+ +	− −
Mammary LPL	−	+ + +
Blood Flow, WAT	+	?
Blood Flow, IBAT	−	?

Net effect: Pregnancy: Increased nutrient flux to white adipose tissue WAT storage
Lactation: Decreased flux to WAT, increased to mammary tissue
NOTES: LPL—lipoprotein lipase
WAT—white adipose tissue
IBAT: Intrascapular brown adipose tissue

That such effects on fat metabolism in female rats occur should not be surprising, since overall food efficiency is markedly enhanced in female rats during pregnancy and lactation. Even before significant fetal demands on nutrient supply are evident, the female rat has adjusted her metabolism so that weight gain per gram of food eaten is increased (Savard et al., 1986). The evolution of such protective and adaptive metabolic responses may have served to ensure the livelihood of the fetuses and the mother during times of restricted feeding. In times of surfeit, these mechanisms may lead to increased adiposity, especially in genetically predisposed individuals. However, one can speculate that fat located in these femoral regions has future survival value and, thus, would be less associated with morbidity. Such an hypothesis is congruent with the current explanation for the mechanism by which abdominal fat is thought to affect cardiovascular and diabetic risk, for example, by perfusion of the mesentery and liver regions with locally high levels of circulating FFA, which then lead to insulin resistance and other metabolic complications associated with this effect.

Our laboratory asked the question of whether some fat depots might be "protected" in female rats, by examining competing demands of pregnancy and exercise on adipose tissue regional specificity (Savard et al., 1986). In this experiment, three groups of rats were studied. One group of rats was trained to swim. When they could swim continuously in agitated water for three hours a day, six days a week, they were mated and then allowed to continue on the swimming regimen for the remainder of pregnancy. A second group of rats was comprised of age-matched, pregnant but sedentary animals, and the third group was comprised of age-matched, nonpregnant controls. During the course of the pregnancy, the exercised group was able to maintain a growth curve comparable to the sedentary group but without increasing their food intake, a remarkable finding. Thus, the exercising pregnant female rat made significant adjustments in metabolism to preservation of body weight increments while expending significant amounts of energy on physical exercise. On the final day of pregnancy, both the sedentary and exercised groups had maintained a normal number of normal-weight pups (Savard et al., 1986).

However, the regional distribution of fat in the carcasses of the two pregnant groups was distinctly different. In the exercising female pregnant rat, the inguinal depot was preserved, while the parametrial depot was markedly reduced. Even in the face of endurance exercise, the female rat increased inguinal fat pad weight and fat cell size and showed an increase in inguinal adipose tissue LPL activity. The increased LPL activity was presumably the mechanism for increased fat deposition. Consequently, even when there are competing demands for lipid mobilization, such as those normally made by the physical demands of exercise, these are overriden in some fat depots by the primacy of the regulation of reproductive hormonal modulation. Thus, one can hypothesize that in some cases of human obesity, of the femoral or gynoid type, faulty performance of this set of control mechanisms may be the cause.

REGULATION OF REGIONAL FAT IN HUMANS

In humans, as well as in rodents, it has been noted that fat cell size and number vary from adipose tissue site to site. For example, it has been shown that normal weight young women have larger fat cells in the femoral-gluteal region than in the abdominal region, and the reverse is true for men (Sjostrom, Smith, Krotkiewski, & Bjorntorp, 1972). The importance of the femoral depot as a region in women specified for regulation by female sex steroids has been underscored recently by the investigations of Rebuffe-Scrive and co-investigators (Rebuffe-Scrive et al., 1985). In these studies, LPL activity was shown to be elevated in the femoral region as compared to the abdominal region. During pregnancy, a marked increase in LPL activity occurs in the femoral region, but not in the abdominal region. During lactation, LPL activity is preferentially reduced in this same region. Furthermore, after menopause, decreases in LPL activity occur in the femoral region. Such data argue strongly for a specific reproductive role for femoral fat in women. They also argue for a "gating" role for LPL in humans as well as in rats. More investigation is needed before we are able to define this role in humans.

The fact that LPL is playing a prominent role in the regional regulation of adipose tissue metabolism focuses attention on the genetic control of this enzyme. In fact, it has been shown in both humans and rodents that LPL is under significant genetic control. These observations, in combination with recent evidence that body fatness and fat distribution are also largely genetically controlled, may allow us to predict with much more validity those at risk for excess morbidity. Thus, future work may suggest that the genetic—environmental (G×E) interaction in the regulation of LPL's gating mechanism may, in fact, help to explain the particular regional accumulation of fat during the development of obesity and, thus, help to explain why some obese individuals seem to be at greater risk than others.

SUMMARY

There is sexual dimorphism in the regional distribution of adipose tissue. The regional distribution of adipose tissue is related to morbidity and suggests that at least some adipose tissue depots are under reproductive hormonal control. In females, the femoral region may have particular relevance to the reproductive status of the female and may be modulated by the regulation of lipoprotein lipase activity. Furthermore, while the accumulation of fat in the femoral or peripheral regions may have the same psychosocial impact, it appears to be less related to morbidity. In both males and females, the accumulation of fat in the abdominal region is associated with increased morbidity. Consequently, it is becoming increasingly clear that it is not the degree of obesity, per se, which is an indicator of associated risk factors, but rather the localization of the fat. Thus, regulatory errors in the regulation of specific adipose tissue depots may prove to be more significant in predicting the risk of obesity than putative overall regulatory signals.

ACKNOWLEDGMENTS

Some of the work reviewed in this manuscript was supported by NIH Grant HD12637, the NYSHRC, and the Canadian FRSQ. We thank James Brown for graphic services and Jerry Calvin for photographic assistance.

REFERENCES

Gray, J. M., & Greenwood, M. R. C. (1982). Time course of effects of ovarian hormones on food intake and metabolism. *American Journal of Physiology, 240,* E407–E412.

Gray, J. M., & Wade, G. N. (1981). Food intake, body weight and adiposity in female rats: Actions and interactions of progestins and antiestrogens. *American Journal of Physiology, 240,* E474–E481.

Greenwood, M. R. C., Savard, R., West, D. B., & Gray, J. M. (1985). The effects of sex hormones and pregnancy on the regulation of adipose tissue metabolism in rats. In J. Vague, Elsevier Science Publishers (Eds.), *Metabolic complications of human obesities* (pp. 131–139). New York: Elsevier.

Kava, R., West, D. B., Lukasik, V., Prinz, W. A., & Greenwood, M. R. C. (1986). Pregnancy alters blood flow to brown and white adipose tissue in the lean Zucker rat. *Federal Proceedings, 45*(3):601.

Krotkiewski, M., Bjorntorp, P., Sjostrom, S., & Smith, U. (1983). Impact of obesity on metabolism in men and women. Importance of regional adipose tissue distribution. *Journal of Clinical Investigation, 72,* 1150–1162.

Krotkiewski, M., Sjostrom, L., Bjorntorp, P., & Smith, U. (1975). Regional adipose tissue cellularity in relation to metabolism in young and middle aged women. *Metabolism, 24,* 703–710.

Moore, B. J., Gerada-Gettens, T., Horowitz, B. A., & Stern, J. S. (1986). Hyperprolactinemia stimulates food intake in the female rat. *Brain Research Bulletin, 17,* 563–569.

Rebuffe-Scrive, M., Enk, L., Crona, N., Lonroth, P., Abrahansson, L., Smith, U., & Bjorntorp, P. (1985). Fat cell metabolism in different regions in women: Effect of menstrual cycle, pregnancy and lactation. *Journal of Clinical Investigation, 75,* 1973–1976.

Savard, R., Palmer, J. E., & Greenwood, M. R. C. (1986). The effects of exercise training on adipose tissue metabolism in pregnant rats. *American Journal of Physiology, 250,* R837–R844.

Sjostrom, L., Smith, U., Krotkiewski, M., & Bjorntorp, P. (1972). Cellularity on different regions of adipose tissue in young men and women. *Metabolism, 21,* 1143–1153.

Steingrimsdottir, L., Brasel, J. A., & Greenwood, M. R. C. (1980). Lipoprotein lipase activity in mammary and several adipose tissue depots during pregnancy and lactation. *Metabolism, 29,* 837–841.

Vague, J. (1947). La differenciation sexuelle-facteur determinant des formes de l'obesité. *Presse Medicale, 30,* 339–340.

Van Itallie, T. B. (1985). Health implications of overweight and obesity in the United States. *Annals of Internal Medicine, 103,* 983–988.

Wade, G. N., & Gray, J. M. (1979). Gonadal effects on food intake and adiposity: A metabolic hypothesis. *Physiological Behavior, 22,* 583–593.

3

METABOLIC AND BEHAVIORAL EFFECTS OF WEIGHT LOSS AND REGAIN: A REVIEW OF THE ANIMAL AND HUMAN LITERATURE

Kelly D. Brownell
Leslie J. Stein
University of Pennsylvania School of Medicine
Department of Psychiatry

Dieting has become a preoccupation in many Western societies. Superimposed on a high prevalence of obesity is relentless pressure to be thin. The product is dieting. It is not confined to obese persons. Far more people feel that they are overweight than actually are by medical or reasonable social standards. A great deal has been written about the need for overweight people to lose weight and about the social disadvantages of being overweight. Relatively little attention has been paid to the possible hazards of dieting.

The purpose of this chapter is to examine the effects of weight loss and regain, particularly when such cycles occur repeatedly (the "yo-yo syndrome"). We will first review figures on the prevalence of dieting and will discuss the possible effects on both behavior and metabolism. We will cover data from human studies and then from the animal literature, and in concluding will propose specific mechanisms for how cycles of loss and regain may influence food efficiency, health, and the likelihood of eating disorders.

HOW COMMON IS DIETING?

A Gallup poll in November 1985 found that 90% of Americans feel that they are overweight. In this same poll, 31% of women said that they diet at least as often as once per month, and 16% said that they diet all of the time. In some of these chronic dieters, weight stays stable within the normal range because of the dieting. Others lose large amounts of weight and then regain, only to repeat the cycle when they are again seized by the need to be thin.

This pressure to be thin begins early and is especially pronounced in girls.

Before age 13, 80% of girls have been on a diet, compared to 10% of boys (Hawkins, Turell, & Jackson, 1983). In one survey of high school juniors and seniors, 125 of 195 girls (64%) said that they make a conscious effort to restrict food intake (Jakobovits, Halstead, Kelley, Roe, & Young, 1977).

It is apparent from these figures that there is an undercurrent of weight obsession in our society. Females are more subject to this phenomenon because of the emphasis on body shape in women and the physiological reality that women develop more body fat than men (Striegel-Moore, Silberstein, & Rodin, 1986). In a recent review and conceptual paper on risk factors for bulimia, Striegel-Moore et al. (1986) felt that the pressure to be thin is so pervasive among females that weight concerns could be considered normative. To understand the metabolic effects of all of this dieting, we must look first to the traditional concept of energy balance.

THE ENERGY-BALANCE CONCEPT: DO 3,500 CALORIES MAKE A POUND?

Basic laws of thermodynamics indicate that energy intake must equal energy expenditure or weight will change. Weight will increase if intake exceeds expenditure and will decrease if expenditure exceeds intake. That this occurs is beyond question. However, there are several common assumptions based on this law that are incorrect and imply more than can be delivered for many dieters.

There is the assumption, among many health professionals and the public in general, that individuals have specific metabolic requirements determined only by weight. For example, every person who weighs 180 pounds is thought to have a metabolic need for a certain number of calories. People at different weights would have different requirements, but the metabolic needs would be the same for people at a given weight. It comes a surprise to many clinicians, therefore, that one woman will lose weight on 1,200 calories per day, while another woman of the same weight will not. Some professionals would conclude that the second woman is not adhering to her diet and is underestimating what she eats.

The common practice is to attach specific numbers to these assumptions. This is where 3,500 calories are thought to equal one pound. The typical, but faulty arithmetic is as follows. An individual's daily calorie requirements are estimated by size, the most common factor being body weight multiplied by 15. As an example, a woman at 113 pounds (multiplied by 15 calories/pound) would have a daily need for 1,700 calories. If she consumes 1,200 calories/day, her daily deficit is 500 calories. Summed over one week, she would have a calorie deficit of 3,500 calories, or one pound's worth of calories. If this woman remained on 1,200 calories, she should lose one pound each week, except for a small decline because daily metabolic needs would be based on a declining body size. If only dieting were so simple!

There are large differences in metabolic needs across individuals. This is evident from research (Bray, 1976; Garrow, 1981, 1986; McArdle, Katch, & Katch, 1981) and from personal experience. Most of us know people who eat a great deal and maintain normal weight and others who eat little and struggle continuously to be thin. Part of this variation may be due to changes in energy balance produced by past or current dieting.

As we discuss below, metabolic requirements are lowered by dieting. Permanent effects may result when weight loss and regain occur repeatedly. If weight cycling lowers metabolic needs, dieting may make subsequent dieting more difficult. Weight loss would require greater and greater degrees of caloric restriction, perhaps producing the individuals who lose far less weight than predicted, even on strict diets.

HUMAN RESEARCH ON
WEIGHT LOSS AND REGAIN

Single Cycles of Loss and Regain

Weight loss and caloric restriction are greeted by a number of changes which impede further weight loss. In lean people exposed to starvation, these changes are adaptive and preserve critical body tissue in the face of energy depletion. The extent of adaptation to starvation has been documented in the classic work of Keys and colleagues at the University of Minnesota (Keys, Brozek, Henschel, Michelson, & Taylor, 1950). In the 1940s and early 1950s, this group completed careful studies on conscientious objectors who agreed to lose approximately 25% of their body weight in a trial of starvation. In addition to physical and psychological effects of starvation, these investigators found clear adaptive metabolic responses. It appeared, therefore, that the body can respond to weight loss by protecting itself. This may occur through more efficient use of ingested energy and/or lower energy expenditure for metabolic needs.

Similar adaptation may occur in obese persons who lose weight. One might question, however, whether the loss of weight in a lean person creates a similar physiological state as weight loss in an obese person who has many pounds to lose before vital functions are threatened. It is possible that the body responds to weight loss irrespective of absolute weight. Also, if some overweight persons are heavy due to an elevated body weight "set point," the body could seek to defend its elevated weight as vigorously as a thin person defends normal body stores (Keesey, 1986). The evidence which follows supports this view.

Lowered metabolic rate appears to be one mechanism for the energy conservation that accompanies dieting. This lowering has been documented in both lean and obese humans. An example is a study by Bray (1969), the results of which are displayed in Figure 3.1. Obese patients were maintained on 3,500 calories

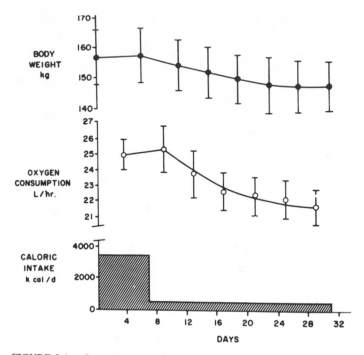

FIGURE 3.1.   Oxygen consumption in six obese patients during caloric restriction. After seven days on a 3,500-calorie diet, intake was restricted to 450 calories for 24 days. Body weight dropped less than 3%, while oxygen consumption declined by approximately 17%. (From Bray, 1969.)

per day and then were restricted to 450 calories per day for 24 days. These patients had a 3% drop in body weight, but a 17% decline in oxygen consumption. This indicates that physiological processes are activated by weight loss so that the body expends less energy for normal metabolic function.

Leibel and Hirsch (1984) reported remarkable findings from a group of reduced-obese humans (Figure 3.2). These individuals had lost a substantial amount of weight (52 kg) on a dietary program, but were still about 60% overweight. Their energy requirements were estimated from metabolic rates and were compared to their own figures before weight loss and to those of a control group of normal-weight persons.

When Leibel and Hirsch expressed calorie requirements as calories per square meter of body surface (to account for differences in body size), the reduced obese were 28% percent lower than their pre-weight loss level and were 25% lower than the level estimated from their body size. The daily calorie need for the reduced obese (2,171 kcal/d) was actually less than for the normal-weight controls (2,280 kcal/d), even though the reduced obese still weighed 60% (39 kg) more. Therefore, the reduced-obese persons had energy requirements far below

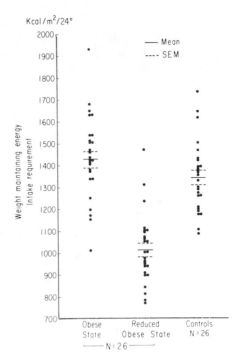

FIGURE 3.2. Seven-day, weight-maintaining energy-intake requirements (kcal/m²/d) in 26 patients studied when obese and after substantial weight loss (reduced-obese state) in comparison to requirements of 26 never-obese, normal-weight controls. In all instances except one in which there was no change, per-square-meter energy requirements declined with weight loss. (From Leibel & Hirsch, 1984.)

what would be predicted from their body size. They had not been able to reduce to ideal weight and were maintaining their elevated weights on fewer calories than normal-weight individuals who weighed far less.

There also appears to be an association between weight loss and changes in adipose tissue lipoprotein lipase (LPL) activity. LPL is considered the gatekeeper enzyme responsible for incorporation of lipid into fat cells, so when LPL activity is increased, more fat is stored given available circulating lipid. In two intriguing studies, Schwartz and Brunzell (1978, 1981) found that LPL activity was greatly increased in obese persons who had lost weight and was much higher than would be predicted by their weight per se. In the subset of subjects who later regained weight, LPL activity decreased.

> Because adipose tissue lipoprotein lipase activity does not "normalize" after weight loss, we hypothesize that this enzyme may play a counterregulatory role in resisting deviation from a "set point" for fat mass or fat cell size and thereby predispose to reattainment of the original obese state. (Schwartz & Brunzell, 1981, p. 1425)

These studies show clearly that the body makes adaptive changes in response to weight loss and calorie restriction. The effects are powerful and may help to explain why obese humans typically reach a plateau after the initial stages of weight loss and complain of failing to lose weight even when eating very little. A decline in metabolic rate and increased activity of adipose tissue LPL may be two of the mechanisms, but there may be others. Possibilities include changes in thyroid activity, fat cell morphology, and the thermic effect of food.

Multiple Cycles of Loss and Regain

The studies discussed above pertain to a single cycle of loss and regain. It is our contention that the metabolic adaptation to dieting is enhanced by repeated cycles of loss and regain. This issue has been studied more in animals (see below) than in humans, but what does exist is consistent with the view that repeated dieting may make dieting more difficult.

The clinical impression among professionals who work with dieters is that an extensive history of dieting is a negative prognostic sign. In our clinic at the University of Pennsylvania, it is our impression that women who have been on many diets are the ones who eat little and lose little, so their chance of long-term loss seems lower than that of the typical dieter. A study by Jeffery et al. (1984) confirms that an extensive dieting history is a poor prognostic sign. It is possible that some intrinsic metabolic factor has made these individuals more food efficient, so they are the ones who have had to diet many times and the ones who experience the most pressure to eat and gain weight. It is also possible, however, that their many bouts of dieting have induced this food efficiency and their resistance to weight loss.

One study attempted to examine this by evaluating weight loss in obese persons who had been on the same dietary program more than one time (Read, Blackburn, Wilson, & Brownell, 1986). A sample of 111 patients was identified from an outpatient clinic at Harvard University. These patients took part in an outpatient trial of the protein-sparing modified fast (Blackburn, Lynch, & Wong, 1986). After varying amounts of regain after the program ended, these patients re-enrolled and undertook the same diet a second time. The authors evaluated the rate of weight loss (pounds/week) in these individuals during their first and second time in the program (Figure 3.3).

The results showed substantially lower rates of weight loss the second time on the program as compared to the first. As Figure 3.3 shows, the rate of loss was almost a full pound/week less the second time on the diet. These authors noted that the results can be interpreted in many ways. One interpretation is that the adaptive metabolic processes we believe to result from dieting did occur, thereby slowing weight loss the second time. It is also possible, perhaps even likely based on clinical experience, that adherence to the diet was less rigorous the second time. The authors attempted to deal with this possibility by identifying a subsample of patients who had lost at least two pounds per week on both diets, their hypothesis being that deviation from this strict diet is unlikely to occur in

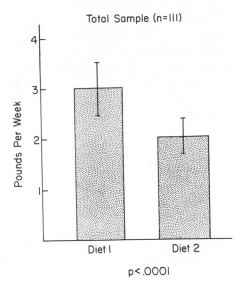

FIGURE 3.3. Mean weight loss per week on the first and second diets for subjects repeating an outpatient program of the protein-sparing modified fast. (From Read et al., 1986.)

patients losing at this rate. The data for these subjects are displayed in Figure 3.4. The same pattern emerges as for the total sample; that is, weight loss occurred more slowly in the second diet.

The data from the Read et al. (1986) study are certainly not conclusive. Only studies in metabolic units can help to isolate the effects of physiology from those of adherence. Such studies are needed to help define whether the putative effects of repeated dieting do occur and to identify the associated metabolic variables.

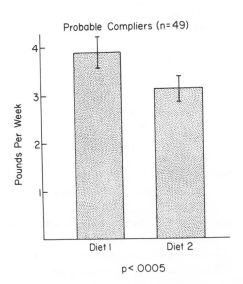

FIGURE 3.4. Weight loss per week for two trials of protein-sparing modified fast. Subjects are probable compliers, defined by weight loss of at least two pounds per week on both diets. (From Read et al., 1986.)

As we move from this section on human studies to our discussion of animal research, several conclusions are warranted. The first is that adaptive changes occur during weight loss that serve to actively resist further loss. Metabolic rate declines and similar changes may occur in other metabolic processes, including LPL activity. Few data exist on multiple cycles of loss and gain, but they do point to enhanced resistance to weight loss with successive cycles. As we discuss below, data from animal studies support the same conclusions.

ANIMAL RESEARCH ON WEIGHT LOSS AND REGAIN

Single Cycles of Weight Loss and Regain

Studies of normal-weight animals confirm that a single cycle of weight loss and regain is accompanied by physiological adaptations that favor increased energy deposition and rapid weight gain. Increased caloric intake is not necessary to compensate for weight lost during a diet or fast. Following a fast, rats recover to their original body weights even if food intake is restricted during the refeeding interval (Levitsky, Faust, & Glassman, 1976).

Several studies show how powerful these effects can be. Boyle, Storlien, and Keesey (1978) restricted the caloric intake of rats so that at the end of 6 weeks, the dieted rats weighed 81% less than did free-feeding controls. Over a 7-day refeeding period, the previously dieted rats ate less food but gained more weight than did non-dieted rats. Food efficiency (defined as weight gain per calorie ingested) was increased most in those rats which had ingested the fewest calories and had lost the most weight. A fivefold increase of food efficiency was reported by Bjorntorp and Yang (1982) over the 8 days following a 25% loss of body weight (induced by a 65-hour fast). The increase in food efficiency was so dramatic that no net increase of food intake was necessary to regain the lost body weight.

Several metabolic adaptations contribute to the enhanced food efficiency of weight-reduced animals. When Boyle, Storlien, Harper, and Keesey (1981) restricted food intake in rats over an 11-day period, resting metabolic rate fell 33% and remained decreased after 7 days of refeeding.

In an elegant series of experiments, Hill and colleagues first restricted food intake and then varied the amount that rats were allowed to eat during a 20-day refeeding period (Hill, Fried, & DiGirolamo, 1984; Hill, Latiff, & DiGirolamo, 1985). Rats lost significant amounts of both fat and protein during the fast. Animals allowed to refeed ad libitum did not increase food intake relative to controls, but instead gradually decreased energy expenditure during the refeeding period, which allowed them to regain all of the lost weight. Rats restricted during refeeding also decreased energy expenditure, but did so immediately upon the introduction of refeeding. The ultimate effect was to divert a greater proportion of ingested calories into restoration of depleted energy reserves. The degree of energy conservation was proportional to the degree of caloric restriction and was independent of whether fasting or gradual caloric restriction was used. When body weight was maintained at a reduced weight through caloric restriction, energy expenditure decreased further over time. A reduction of resting metabolic rate was the major means of energy conservation.

Further energy conservation during and after caloric restriction is achieved through reducing the thermic effect of food. Boyle et al. (1981) measured the increase in oxygen consumption following a standardized meal. Control rats showed an increase of 27%. Rats which had been calorically restricted for 10 days had a lower baseline oxygen consumption and showed no heat increment in response to the same meal. Intermediate responses were seen in rats which had been refed for 1 or 4 days. Again, the result is to enhance food efficiency by increasing the proportion of ingested calories, which are diverted to restoration of depleted energy reserves.

Multiple Cycles of Weight Loss and Regain in Animals

The responses to a single experience of weight loss represent adaptive responses to ensure survival. Metabolic adaptations act to minimize energy losses when calories are limited and to quickly replenish lost reserves when food is again freely available. If experience with food scarcity was repeated, it might be expected that further advantage would be conferred to organisms which adapt most quickly—that is, to those which lose more slowly and regain more quickly with repeated experience.

To test this hypothesis, Brownell, Greenwood, Stellar, and Shrager (1986) evaluated the effects of repeated cycles of weight loss and regain in obese rats (Figure 3.5). Male rats were fed a high-fat diet until they were 17% heavier than normal-weight controls. Half of these obese rats began two cycles of restriction and refeeding, while the other half remained statically obese on the high-fat diet. During the restrictions, the dieting rats were given 50% of the mean intake of normal-weight chow-fed controls (18 g chow/day). During the first cycle, the rats were restricted until they weighed the same as the normal-weight controls. They were then returned to ad libitum, high-fat diet and allowed to regain to the weight of non-dieted obese controls. Cycling rats then went through a second cycle, with weight loss equated to the loss of the first cycle (132 g). The animals were again allowed to regain to the weight of the non-dieted obese controls.

The results indicate that a single experience with caloric deprivation does enhance the response to subsequent restriction. The cycling rats lost 132 g in 21 days during the first restriction. The same weight loss required 46 days when the animals were restricted to 18 g/day a second time. The refeeding effect was even more pronounced. When restored to ad libitum food intake after the first diet, the cycling rats regained to the weights of the non-dieted obese rats in 46 days. The

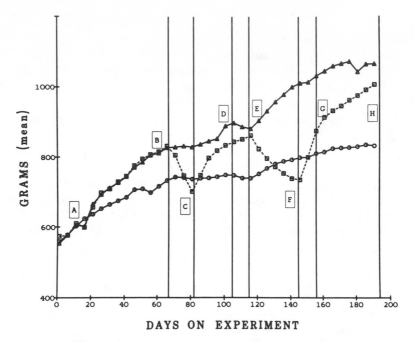

FIGURE 3.5.   Body weight changes in Chow Controls (Group 1), Obese Controls (Group 2), and Obese Cycling animals (Group 3), at the beginning of the experiment (A), beginning of the first restriction (B), end of the first weight loss period (C), point of weight regain to prediet weight (D), initiation of the second diet cycle (E), end of the second weight loss period (F), point of weight regain to predict weight (G), and end of experiment (H). (From Brownell et al., 1986.)

animals required only 14 days to regain the same amount of weight (157 g) during their second experience with refeeding. Thus, the cycling rats lost weight twice as quickly and gained weight three times more rapidly in the second cycle than in the first. Food efficiency of the cycling rats was significantly enhanced during the second period of refeeding (Figure 3.6). This effect was not attributable to age, as food efficiency of the non-dieted obese rats declined over the same interval.

Gray, Fisler, and Bray (1986) also reported that obese rats lose energy stores less quickly during a second experience with caloric restriction. In contrast, Cleary (1986) dieted and refed female, genetically obese Zucker rats four times. Each diet lasted for 3 weeks, during which the animals were given one-half of their ad libitum intake. The rats gained 4 g during the first 3-week diet, and then lost 10, 34, and 37 g during each of the subsequent diets. Although several factors, including age, degree of restriction, and composition of diet, might contribute to the differences among experiments, it is also possible that the response to weight cycling has a genetic component.

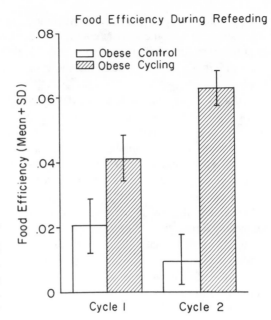

FIGURE 3.6. Food efficiency for Obese Cycling and Obese Control groups for the refeeding phases of Cycle 1 and Cycle 2. Food efficiency is calculated as the ratio of weight gain in grams to food intake in grams. (From Brownell et al., 1986.)

To summarize the animal literature, many questions remain to be answered regarding multiple cycles of weight loss and regain. The mechanism by which repeated experience with caloric deprivation enhances energy efficiency is not yet known. In the Brownell et al. (1986) study, cycled and noncycled obese rats did not differ in LPL activity, adipose tissue cellularity, body composition, or insulin concentrations at the end of the weight cycles, but measures need to be obtained during the dynamic stages of weight change. Metabolic rate and energy utilization need to be studied to determine whether the response to a single experience with caloric restriction can also explain the further increase in food efficiency observed during subsequent exposures. Then, factors responsible for the metabolic response to a single cycle of weight loss and regain, such as brown adipose tissue LPL activity (Fried, Hill, Nickel, & DiGirolamo, 1983), thyroid hormome levels, and sympathetic nervous system activity can be examined.

INTEGRATION AND IDENTIFICATION
OF RESEARCH NEEDS

Studies with both humans and animals show significant physiological changes in response to weight loss. Calorie restriction and the ensuing weight loss set into motion a series of adaptive or counterregulatory changes that serve to protect body weight, lean body mass, body fat, or some other related factor. Such a concept has intuitive appeal because it could help to explain the survival of some organisms and not others under conditions of energy deprivation. The organisms most likely to survive famine or restriction, and thereby to contribute to the gene pool, are those most efficient at conserving energy stores when food is not available.

We hypothesize that repeated cycles of weight loss and regain enhance food efficiency beyond the effects of a single bout of restriction and refeeding. An organism faced with repeated bouts of restriction would best adapt by increasing food efficiency more rapidly or to a greater extent with each successive restriction. This issue has been studied far too little to draw definite conclusions, but the evidence that does exist suggests that food efficiency increases as the number of restrictions increases.

What does this mean for human dieters? Dieting may be perceived by the body as a threat to some aspect of energy stores, even in the case of obese humans who presumably have much excess energy in storage. The body may respond to a diet by conserving energy stores and by increasing energy efficiency to minimize further weight loss. Stated another way, dieting may make dieting more difficult. If the body adapts to repeated cycles of loss and regain, food efficiency may increase to the point where people maintain high weights on surprisingly few calories and must follow remarkably austere diets to lose even a few pounds.

As is clear from the literature reviewed in this chapter, our ideas about responses to dieting must be considered speculative. There is much research to be done. Testing animals during many cycles of loss and regain will be important. Sex differences must be explored. The effects of weight cycling during critical stages of development have not been studied. Most of the possible mechanisms for the adaptive responses have not been identified.

Even less is known about weight cycling in humans. The effects on body composition, health risk, psychological status, and food efficiency need to be studied. Studies in metabolic settings will be the ultimate test of the questions posed here, but so little is known about weight cycling that there is a need for even descriptive information, prevalence studies on repeated dieting, and so forth. We hope that this chapter adds to the growing interest in the area.

ACKNOWLEDGMENT

This work was done as part of the Weight Cycling Project supported by the MacArthur Foundation.

REFERENCES

Bjorntorp, P., & Yang, M. U. (1982). Refeeding after fasting in the rat: Effects on body composition and food efficiency. *American Journal of Clinical Nutrition, 36*, 444–449.

Blackburn, G. L., Lynch, M. E., & Wong, S. L. (1986). The very-low-calorie diet: A weight reduction technique. In K. D. Brownell & J. P. Foreyt (Eds.), *Handbook of eating disorders: Physiology, psychology, and treatment of obesity, anorexia, and bulimia* (pp. 198–212). New York: Basic Books.

Boyle, P. C., Storlien, L. H., Harper, A. E., & Keesey, R. E. (1981). Oxygen consumption and locomotor activity during restricted feeding and realimentation. *American Journal of Physiology, 241,* R392–R387.

Boyle, P. C., Storlien, L. H., & Keesey, R. E. (1978). Increased efficiency of food utilization following weight loss. *Physiology and Behavior, 21,* 261–264.

Bray, G. A. (1969). Effect of caloric restriction on energy expenditure in obese patients. *Lancet, 2,* 397–398.

Bray, G. A. (1976). *The obese patient.* Philadelphia, W. B. Saunders.

Brownell, K. D., Greenwood, M. R. C., Stellar, E., & Shrager, E. E. (1986). The effects of repeated cycles of weight loss and regain in rats. *Physiology and Behavior, 38,* 459–464.

Cleary, M. P. (1986). Consequences of intermittent dieting/refeeding cycles in lean and obese female Zucker rats. *Journal of Nutrition, 116,* 290–303.

Fried, S. K., Hill, J. O., Nickel, M., & DiGirolamo, M. (1983). Novel regulation of lipoprotein lipase activity in rat brown adipose tissue: Effects of fasting and caloric restriction during refeeding. *Journal of Nutrition, 113,* 1870–1874.

Garrow, J. S. (1981). *Treat obesity seriously: A clinical manual.* Edinburgh: Churchill-Livingstone.

Garrow, J. S. (1986). Physiological aspects of obesity. In K. D. Brownell & J. P. Foreyt (Eds.), *Handbook of eating disorders: Physiology, psychology, and treatment of obesity, anorexia, and bulimia* (pp. 45–62). New York: Basic Books.

Gray, D. S., Fisler, J. S., & Bray, G. A. (1986). Effect of repeated weight loss and regain on percent body fat in obese rats. *Clinical Research, 34,* 512.

Hawkins, R. C., Turell, S., & Jackson L. J. (1983). Desirable and undesirable masculine and feminine traits in relation to students' dietary tendencies and body image dissatisfaction. *Sex Roles, 9,* 705–724.

Hill, J. O., Fried, S. K., & DiGirolamo, M. (1984). Effects of fasting and refeeding on utilization of ingested energy in rats. *American Journal of Physiology, 16,* R318–R327.

Hill, J. O., Latiff, A., & DiGirolamo, M. (1985). Effects of variable caloric restriction on utilization of ingested energy in rats. *American Journal of Physiology, 248,* R549–R559.

Jakobovits, C., Halstead, P., Kelley, L., Roe, D. A., & Young, C. M. (1977). Eating habits and nutrient intakes of college women over a thirty-year period. *Journal of the American Dietetic Association, 71,* 405–411.

Jeffery, R. W., Bjornson-Benson, W. M., Rosenthal, B. S., Lindquist, R. A., Kurth, C. L., & Johnson, S. L. (1984). Correlates of weight loss and its maintenance over two years of follow-up among middle-aged men. *Preventive Medicine, 13,* 155–168.

Keesey, R. E. (1986). A set-point theory of obesity. In K. D. Brownell & J. P. Foreyt (Eds.), *Handbook of eating disorders: Physiology, psychology, and treatment of obesity, anorexia, and bulimia* (pp. 63–87). New York: Basic Books.

Keys, A., Brozek, J., Henschel, A., Michelson, O., & Taylor, H. L. (1950. *The biology of human starvation, Volumes 1 and 2.* Minneapolis: University of Minnesota Press.

Leibel, R. L., & Hirsch, J. (1984). Diminished energy requirements in reduced-obese patients. *Metabolism, 33,* 164–170.

Levitsky, D. A., Faust, J., & Glassman, M. (1976). The ingestion of food and the recovery of body weight following fasting in the native rat. *Physiology and Behavior, 17,* 575–578.

McArdle, W. D., Katch, F. I., & Katch, V. L. (1981). *Exercise physiology: Energy, nutrition, and human performance.* Philadelphia: Lea & Febiger.

Read, J. L., Blackburn, G. L., Wilson, G. T., & Brownell, K. D. (1986). *Patterns of weight loss and regain in obese persons undergoing two successive trials of a protein-sparing modified fast.* Manuscript in preparation.

Schwartz, R. S., & Brunzell, J. D. (1978). Increased adipose tissue lipoprotein lipase activity in moderately obese men after weight reduction. *Lancet, 2,* 1230–1231.

Schwartz, R. S., & Brunzell, J. D. (1981). Increase of adipose tissue lipoprotein lipase activity with weight loss. *Journal of Clinical Investigation, 67,* 1425–1430.

Striegel-Moore, R. H., Silberstein, L. R., & Rodin, J. (1986). Toward an understanding of risk factors for bulimia. *American Psychologist, 42,* 246–263.

4

PARALLELS IN NEUROTRANSMITTER CONTROL OF FEEDING AND MEMORY

John E. Morley
Geriatric Research, Education and Clinical Center,
Sepulveda VA Medical Center

James F. Flood
Geriatric Research, Education and Clinical Center,
Sepulveda VA Medical Center
and
Department of Psychiatry & Biobehavioral Sciences,
UCLA School of Medicine

Arthur Cherkin
Geriatric Research, Education and Clinical Center,
Sepulveda VA Medical Center

James E. Mitchell
Department of Psychiatry,
University of Minnesota

In this chapter, we develop the hypothesis that the termination of a meal involves the interaction of cholecystokinin (CCK) and endogenous opioids. Further, the release of CCK during a meal leads to improved memory, while opioids impair memory. The modulation of feeding and of memory involve extremely complex processes (Morley & Levine, 1985; McGaugh, 1985). Within the central nervous system (CNS), both processes are regulated by a variety of neurotransmitters. We have suggested that, in the case of appetite regulation, these neurotransmitters interact in a cascade similar to the well-recognized cascade for complement fixation (Morley, 1980). Studies have suggested that it is the outcome of multiple neurotransmitter interactions that determines whether an organism is satiated or whether it is stimulated to forage for food and to eat. In addition to the *central* feeding system, it is now well established that a variety of peptide hormones are released peripherally during the passage of food through the gastrointestinal tract and that these peptides are responsible for sending satiety signals to the CNS. It is convenient to think of this system as the *"peripheral* satiety system."

As with feeding, multiple neurotransmitter interactions appear to be responsible for determining the ability of an organism to recall a learned task (Essman, 1983). During our studies on memory, we noticed that if mice were food deprived for 18 hours and then allowed to feed immediately after a brief training session, they had a better recall score than if feeding were delayed for 4 hours after training (Figure 4.1). We originally considered that this might be due to the food reward associated with training. However, during our studies of opioid modulation of memory, we were impressed by the memory-enhancing abilities of the opioid antagonists. These are both pharmacological satiety agents and anti-reward substances. This led us to ask whether the memory-enhancing properties of feeding following training were due to the release of gastrointestinal peptides. Our studies have demonstrated that nanogram doses of cholecystokinin-octapeptide (CCK-8) administered intraperitoneally enhanced recall. Is it possible that CCK-8 is the peripheral signal responsible for the memory-enhancing effect of feeding?

This review examines the effects of three peptide families, namely, CCK, opioids, and pancreatic polypeptide-neuropeptide Y, first on feeding and then on memory.

APPETITE REGULATION

Cholecystokinin and Food Intake

Since Sjodin (1972) originally noticed that an undesirable side effect of CCK in dogs was to decrease food intake, numerous studies have shown that CCK decreases food intake during a single meal (Morley, 1982; Smith, 1983). Al-

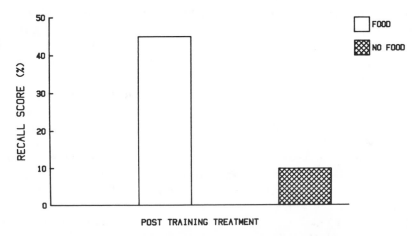

FIGURE 4.1.   Effect of eating on retention for T-maze footshock avoidance conditioning in 18-hour food-deprived mice.

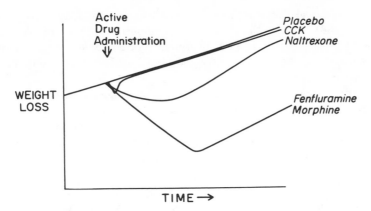

FIGURE 4.2.   Effects of long-term administration of pharmacological agents on weight loss.

though still controversial, it appears that at least at lower doses, CCK produces a true satiating effect, rather than decreasing food intake secondary to producing an aversive effect (Billington, Levine, & Morley, 1983). Whether or not peripheral CCK is a physiological satiety agent is uncertain. The CCK antagonist proglumide can enhance feeding under certain circumstances (Shillabeer & Davidson, 1984), and the lowest doses of exogenous CCK that decrease feeding produce the same magnitude of increase in circulating CCK as does feeding (Smith et al., 1985a). On the other hand, manipulations that cause CCK release can also enhance feeding (McLaughlin, Peikin, & Baile, 1983).

In the rat, CCK produces its effect on feeding by activating the ascending vagal fibers. Total (Morley et al., 1982a) and selective (Smith, Jerome, Cushin, Eterno, & Simansky, 1981) vagotomy, and lesioning the afferent vagal roots where they enter the spinal cord (Smith et al., 1985b), all block the effect of CCK on food intake. Within the CNS, lesions of the nucleus tractus solitarius (NTS) inhibit the effect of CCK on food intake (Crawley & Schwaber, 1984) and low-nanogram doses of CCK-8 inhibit feeding (Ritter & Landerheim, 1984). Fiber pathways run from the NTS to the paraventricular nucleus (PVN). Lesioning of these pathways (Crawley, Kiss, & Mezey, 1984) or of the PVN itself (Crawley & Kiss, 1985) inhibits the CCK effect on feeding. Low-nanogram doses of CCK injected directly into the PVN inhibit feeding, and CCK antibodies in the PVN enhance feeding (Faris, Scallet, Olney, Della-Fera, & Baile, 1984). Thus, CCK may support Dale's hypothesis, which states that one neurotransmitter repeatedly uses itself to transmit its message through the peripheral and central nervous system. It should, however, be pointed out that this elegantly dissected system may be unique to the rat, as vagotomy fails to inhibit the CCK effects on feeding in the dog (Levine, Sievert, Morley, Gosnell, & Silvis, 1984).

As is the case for opioid antagonists (see Figure 4.2), tolerance to the effects of CCK on food intake develops rapidly (Crawley & Beinfeld, 1983; West, Fey, & Woods, 1984). West et al. (1984) have demonstrated that this tolerance is behavioral tolerance, rather than true pharmacological tolerance. CCK continues to reduce the size of the meals ingested, but the animal adapts by increasing the number of meals eaten.

It has been suggested that CCK acts as a physiological antagonist of the endogenous opioid system (Faris, 1985). There is some evidence suggesting that CCK at high (possibly aversive) doses does decrease opioid-induced feeding (Morley, Levine, Kneip, Grace, & Billington, 1983a). However, in partial re-futation of this oversimplistic hypothesis, it should be pointed out that while opioids predominantly decrease the intake of high-energy (fatty) foods, this is not the case for CCK (Romsos, Gosnell, Morley, & Levine, 1987).

CCK and its analogues have been demonstrated to decrease feeding in humans (Kissileff, Pi-Sunyer, Thornton, & Smith, 1981; Pi-Sunyer, Kissileff, Thornton, & Smith, 1982; Shaw et al., 1985; Stacher, Steinringer, Schniever, Schneider, & Winklehner, 1982). The doses required are just below those that produce nausea and much higher than the doses required for gall-bladder contraction or pan-creatic enzyme secretion. CCK also delays gastric emptying, and this may play a role in its feeding-inhibitory doses in humans (Shaw et al., 1985).

Opioid Peptides and Feeding

Since the original description by Holtzman (1974) that naloxone decreases feed-ing in rats, multiple studies in a variety of species have shown that opioid antagonism will decrease food intake (Morley, Levine, Yim, & Lowy, 1983c). Similarly, it has been shown that a variety of opiate agonists will increase feeding. The studies using opiate agonists have shown that agonists that prefer-entially activate the kappa opioid receptor appear to be more effective at enhanc-ing food intake (Morley, Levine, Gosnell, & Billington, 1984; Reid, 1985). It should be noted that all the opiate agonists demonstrate inverted-U-shaped dose-response curves, with high doses inhibiting feeding. The effect is also state dependent, with food intake being suppressed by opiate agonists in food-de-prived animals.

Following the report by Grandison and Guidotti (1977) that beta endorphin injected into the ventromedial hypothalamus increases food intake, numerous studies have shown that central injection of opioid peptides or their analogues into the CNS enhances feeding (Morley et al., 1983c). The endogenous kappa agonists, dynorphin and alpha-neo-endorphin, appear to be particularly potent feeding enhancers (Morley et al., 1984). Further, Schulz, Wilhelm, and Dirlich (1984) have shown that antibodies to alpha-neo-endorphin, when injected into the area of the medial hypothalamus, inhibit feeding. A number of studies have demonstrated alterations in CNS dynorphin and beta-endorphin levels under conditions in which feeding behavior is altered (Levine et al., 1985b).

Microinjection studies have suggested three major sites of action for the opioids with the CNS. These are the paraventricular nucleus, the perifornical area of the lateral hypothalamus, and the amygdala (Gosnell, Morley, & Levine, 1986; Stanley, Lanthier, & Leibowitz, 1984). In the paraventricular nucleus, it appears that the endogenous kappa agonist, dynorphin, enhances food intake, whereas mu agonists are responsible for increasing drinking (Gosnell et al., 1986). Preliminary studies suggest that kappa agonists inhibit drinking while producing a diuresis; that is, their overall effect on water metabolism would be to dehydrate the organism. Lesion studies have suggested that opioid feeding pathways also involve the globus pallidus (Gosnell, Morley, & Levine, 1984) and the dorsal medial nucleus of the hypothalamus (Bellinger, Bernardis, & Williams, 1983).

The specific role of opioids in feeding is unclear. The opioid feeding system appears to control the ingestion of both foods with a high-fat content (Marks-Kaufmann, 1982) and foods that are perceived as highly palatable (LeMagnen, Marfaine-Gallut, Micelli, & Devos, 1980). In the studies by Kavaliers and Hirst (in press) in the slug (*Limax maximus*), it seems that mu opiates produce food-foraging behaviors, whereas kappa opiates are associated with ingestive behaviors. This is compatible with findings in deer, where it was shown that during the winter, when long distances need to be traversed to obtain food, naloxone suppresses both spontaneous locomotion and feeding, whereas in the summer, when food is abundant, naloxone only decreases feeding (Plotka, Morley, Levine, & Seal, 1985). A similar coupling between locomotor and feeding systems is seen in the wolf, an animal that travels an average of 37.5 kilometers between kills (Morley, Levine, Plotka, & Seal, 1983b). Our studies in the tiger suggested that naloxone enhances neophobia (Billington, Morley, Levine, Wright, & Seal, 1985a). This raises the possibility that increases in endogenous opioids play a role in recognition of good (nonpoisoned) foods. There are also data linking the opioid ingestive systems to the intake of salt-containing foods (Levine, Murray, Kneip, Grace, & Morley, 1982).

Opioid Peptides, Appetite, Food Intake, and Weight Loss in Humans

Opioid antagonists decrease food intake over a single meal in lean and obese subjects (Atkinson, 1982; Trenchard & Silverstone, 1983). Opioid antagonists have also been reported to decrease food intake in a patient with obesity secondary to ventromedial hypothalamic damage (Morley & Levine, 1982) and in genetic obesity of the Prader-Willi type (Kyriakides, Silverstone, Jeffcoate, & Laurance, 1980). In the patients with the Prader-Willi syndrome, cerebrospinal fluid levels of opioid peptides have been reported to be elevated (Krotkiewski, Fagerberg, Bjorntorp, & Terenius, 1983). Two patients with congenital indifference to pain and with massive obesity have also been found to have elevated opioid peptides in the CNS (Dunger, Leonard, Wolff, & Preece, 1980; Fraioli, Fabbri, & Moretti, 1981).

In humans, opioid antagonism preferentially decreases intake of high-fat-containing foods which, for the most part, are also the most palatable foods (Billington et al., 1985b; Cohen, Cohen, & Pickar, 1985). Naloxone has also been reported to decrease 2-deoxy-glucose-induced food intake in humans (Thompson, Welle, Lilivavat, Penicaud, & Campbell, 1983) and to limit the size of the binge in bulimic subjects (Jonas & Gold, 1986; Morley, Hernandez, & Flood, 1986).

The partial kappa agonist/mu antagonist, butorphanol tartrate, has been demonstrated to increase food intake in humans at low doses and to inhibit it at higher doses (Morley et al., 1984; Morley, Parker, & Levine, 1985c). Of particular interest in these studies is that, although opioid antagonists decrease food intake, they do this without altering the individual's perception of hunger or satiety. O'Brien, Stunkard, and Tesmes (1982) found no effect of naloxone on hunger or fullness. They did not, however, measure food intake. In the two studies where both satiety-analogue scales and food intake were measured (Thompson et al., 1983; Trenchard & Silverstone, 1983), there was no effect on satiety, despite the decrease in food intake. Similarly, butorphanol tartrate failed to alter the perception of hunger while increasing food intake (Morley et al., 1985c).

Because of the results in short-term animal and human studies and a number of uncontrolled studies with long-term administration of opioid antagonists in humans, it seemed that long-acting opioid antagonists which could be orally administered (e.g., naltrexone) might be useful anti-obesity agents. Five double-blind trials with naltrexone have been completed (Atkinson et al., 1985; Maggio et al., 1985; Malcom et al., 1985; Mitchell, Morley, Levine, Hatsukami, Gannon & Pfohl, 1987; Billington & Morley, 1987). Four out of the five studies failed to show an effect of naltrexone on weight loss. In the fifth study, Atkinson et al. (1985) showed a small effect in obese women, but no effect in obese men. The doses of naltrexone used in these studies were such that they produced an unacceptable rate of abnormal liver-function tests in the subjects receiving the active drug. Figure 4.2 shows idealized curves comparing the weight-suppressive effects of opiate antagonists to the classic anti-obesity drug, fenfluramine. Obviously, tolerance to the food-suppressive effects of opioid antagonists develops rapidly.

These studies in humans led to reevaluation of the animal data on opiate effects. Martin, Wikler, Eacles, and Prescor (1963) clearly showed that opiate agonists administered chronically cause weight loss and increased activity and metabolic rate. The weight loss seen following chronic opiate agonist administration cannot be explained by alterations in food intake (Levine et al., 1985a). Similarly, subjects on methadone maintenance are underweight while being hyperphagic (Tallman et al., 1984). Passive immunization with beta endorphin in rats leads to weight gain (McLaughlin et al., 1985). Recently, it has been shown that the weight loss that is associated with infections and cancer is secondary to interleukin stimulation of macrophages to produce a peptide hormone, cachectin (Beutler, Mahoney, LeTrang, Pekala, & Cerami, 1984). Cachectin is a potent inhibitor of lipogenic enzymes (Toste, Dieckmann, Beutler, Cerami, & Ringold, 1985). We have shown that opiates stimulate the interleukin receptor (Morley et al., 1985c; Morley et al., 1986). Thus, the weight loss secondary to chronic opiate administration may be due to cachectin release. Beta endorphin has also been shown to directly stimulate fat-cell lipolysis (Richter, Kerscher, & Schwandt, 1983).

A recent Hungarian study supports the concept that opiate agonists may be excellent anti-obesity agents (Balkanyi, Mohai, & Balkanyi, 1985). They used the mixed agonist/antagonist, nalorphine, which, in the absence of prior administration of a pure opiate agonist, displays mainly agonistic properties. Nalorphine produced marked weight loss in obese subjects. Should the effect of opiate agonists on weight loss be a peripheral one, as suggested above, it is possible that the development of quaternary opiate agonists or other forms of opiate agonists that cannot cross the blood-brain barrier may represent an ideal approach to obesity treatment.

Neuropeptide Y and Feeding

Neuropeptide Y (NPY), a member of the pancreatic polypeptide family, is a 36-amino-acid peptide (Tatemoto, 1982). It is widely distributed throughout the central and peripheral nervous system and has been demonstrated to have multiple effects after central administration (Gray & Morley, 1986). Clark, Kalra, Crowley, and Kalra (1984) first showed that NPY increased feeding in ovariectomized rats. Levine and Morley (1984) reported that NPY increased feeding in both food-deprived and non-food-deprived male rats after ventricular injection. Stanley and Leibowitz (1984) found that NPY increased feeding after direct injection into the PVN. NPY has also been shown to increase feeding in mice (Morley et al., 1986), in ground squirrels during the anorexic period just prior to hibernation (Nizielski, Gosnell, Morley, & Levine, in press), and in pigs (Parrott, Heavens, & Baldwin, 1986) after ventricular administration. In the chick, avian pancreatic popypeptide enhances feeding, while NPY fails to increase food intake (Steinman & Morley, 1986). NPY appears to be the single most potent orexigenic substance yet to be identified.

Tolerance to the orexigenic effects of NPY (Stanley, Kyrkouli, Lampert, & Leibowitz, 1985) or the structurally related peptide YY (PYY) (Morley, Levine, Grace, & Kneip, 1985b) does not appear to occur. Chronic administration of PYY leads to gross overdistention of the stomach, suggesting that central administration of the Y peptides can override the peripheral satiety system. NYP produces a highly specific increase in the intake of carbohydrate-rich foods (Levine et al., 1985c) in contradistinction to the increase in high-fat foods produced by the opioids (see above).

As NPY coexists with catecholamines in certain neurons and has been shown to be synergistic with norepinephrine in its effect on blood vessels, and norepinephrine is a potent enhancer of feeding, the relationship between norepinephrine and NPY has been studied in detail (Levine et al., 1985c). NPY increases both food and water intake, whereas norepinephrine decreases water intake. NPY is not additive or synergistic with norepinephrine, and its effects on food intake are not blocked by the alpha antagonist, phentolamine. Both vagotomy and adrenalectomy block the feeding effects of norepinephrine without altering the effects of NPY on ingestive behaviors. Thus, we have concluded that the effects of NPY and norepinephrine on feeding are not directly related.

Our pharmacological studies in genetic mice models of obesity suggested that the genetically obese diabetic mouse (cb/db) may have some excess production of NPY (Morley et al., 1986), as the dose-response curve for NPY-induced feeding is shifted to the right. No abnormalities in the response of genetically obese mice (ob/ob) to NPY could be demonstrated. Old mice have a normal response to NPY. This is in contrast to the findings suggesting that old rodents have a deficit in their opioid feeding system (Gosnell, Levine, & Morley, 1983; Kavaliers & Hirst, 1985).

Overall, NPY represents an extremely potent orexigenic agent. Because of the massive stomach overdistention produced by NPY and its selective increase in carbohydrate intake, it has been suggested that it may play a role in the pathophysiology of bulimia.

Feeding and Peptides: Summary

A number of peptides have been shown to modulate feeding after peripheral and central administration. CCK is a putative physiological satiety signal and appears to act as an indirect antagonist of opioid feeding systems. NPY is an extremely potent initiator of feeding that overcomes peripheral satiety signals. It appears to predominantly increase the intake of carbohydrate-rich foods.

MEMORY

As noted in the introduction, we observed that 18-hour food-deprived mice fed after a training session had better recall scores one week later than did unfed mice (Figure 1). Our subsequent exploration of the role of gastrointestinal peptides in memory modulation was of particular interest because of growing concern that the popular cholinergic hypothesis of geriatric dysfunction has been overemphasized at the expense of other memory-modulating systems (Flood & Cherkin, 1986). Indeed, an early proponent of the cholinergic hypothesis had clearly pointed out that cholinergic decline was likely to be only one component of memory impairment of the aged and the demented (Drachman, Glasser, Flemming, & Longnecker, 1982). Neuropeptides are among the other possible components now receiving attention (Fine, 1986).

Cholecystokinin and Memory

The memory-enhancing effects of feeding led us to postulate that these may be secondary to CCK release. When administered intraperitoneally, CCK-8 enhances memory in low-nanogram doses in mice when tested in an aversive T-maze paradigm (Figure 4.3). This effect of CCK-8 is time dependent, that is, it declines as the interval between training and injection is increased. The memory effect of CCK-8 produced an inverted-U-shaped dose-response curve. CCK-8 reverses amnesia induced by the cholinergic antagonist, scopolamine. The desulfated form of CCK-8 was 50-fold less potent than the sulfated form in enhancing memory.

Our data are similar to those previously reported by Fekete et al. (1984; Kadar, Fekete, & Telegdy, 1981) for the effects of CCK-8 on active and passive avoidance. However, they needed higher doses to produce the memory-enhancing effects. The higher doses that they needed for active avoidance could be due to the fact that CCK-8 is analgesic (Faris, 1985) and that they administered their CCK prior to training. The higher dose of CCK-8 in the passive-avoidance paradigm could be secondary to the inhibitory effects of CCK on locomotion and their use of an extinction paradigm, which makes interpretation of their results difficult. They also found that CCK-8 was active at very low doses when administered centrally. Administration of CCK-8 antibodies intracerebroventricularly produced the opposite effects to CCK-8 in their behavioral paradigm (Sziegel et al., 1985).

The mechanism by which CCK-8 produces its memory-enhancing effects after intraperitoneal administration at doses lower than those necessary for feeding inhibition has not been fully investigated. However, as the afferent vagal inputs to the nucleus tractus solitarius project to both the PVN and the amygdala,

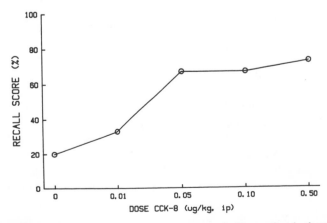

FIGURE 4.3 Effect of sulfated CCK-8 on memory for T-maze footshock avoidance conditioning.

it is tempting to speculate that CCK produces its memory-modulating effects by activating ascending vagal fibers which project from the nucleus tractus solitarius to the amygdala. Our preliminary data suggest that vagotomy blocks the memory-enhancing effect of intraperitoneal CCK-8 (0.5 ug/kg). As CCK-8 injected directly into the amygdala (Fekete et al., 1984) is active in memory tests, this suggests that, once again, CCK may confirn Dale's hypothesis.

Opioids and Memory

A number of studies in rodents have shown that opioid antagonists enhance memory (Gallagher, Rapp, & Fanelli, 1985; Izquierdo, 1979; Messing et al., 1979) and that beta endorphin produces a naloxone-reversible amnesia (Izquierdo & Dias, 1983). Preliminary studies have suggested that both aversive and non-aversive training is associated with the release of beta endorphin within the CNS (Izquierdo & Netto, 1985). Electroconvulsive shock is associated with retrograde amnesia. That this amnesia may be dependent on endogenous opioids is suggested by the fact that electroconvulsive shock is associated with the release of endogenous opioids (Dias, Perry, Carrasco, & Izquierdo, 1981) and that the amnesia it produces is reversed by naloxone (Carrasco, Dias, & Izquierdo, 1982). Studies by Reisberg et al. (1983) suggested that naloxone may improve memory in humans with Alzheimer's disease. Other studies, however, have shown that opioid antagonists have either no effect on memory (Cohen, Cohen, Weingartner, & Murphy, 1983; Hatsukami, Mitchell, Morley, Morgan, & Levine, 1986; Judd, Janowsky, Segul, & Huey, 1980; Steardo, Russo, Sorge, & Cardone, 1982; Volavka, Dornbuss, Mallya, & Cho, 1979) or even depress it (Cohen et al., 1983; Morley et al., 1980). Because of our heightened awareness of the occurrence of inverted-U-shaped dose-response curves produced by memory-modulating drugs (Cherkin & Flood, 1985; Flood, Smith, & Cherkin, 1983), we decided to examine in detail the characteristics of the opioid antagonist modulation of memory.

Our studies showed that the dose-response curve for the memory-enhancing effects of naloxone followed an inverted-U shape in two classes of animals (i.e., mice and chicks; Figure 4.4). The therapeutic window for the naloxone effect was estremely narrow. High doses of naloxone are amnestic. This suggests that the studies in which high doses of opioid antagonists were used in an attempt to replicate the memory-enhancing effects of naloxone in Alzheimer's disease adopted the wrong therapeutic tactics. Our preclinical data would suggest that before rejecting the role of opioid antagonism in memory in humans, individual dose-response curves need to be developed in each subject. These studies should emphasize intermediate rather than high doses of opioid antagonists.

Beta-funaltrexamine (B-FNA) is a long-acting antagonist of the mu opioid receptor (Ward, Portoghese, & Takemori, 1982). We have found that when B-FNA is administered 72 hours before training, it enhances subsequent retention

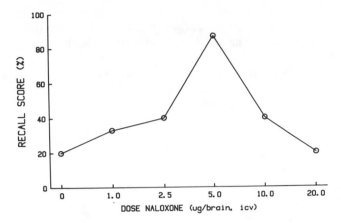

FIGURE 4.4a.   Effects of naloxone on memory in mice for T-maze footshock avoidance conditioning.

without altering acquisition of memory. When B-FNA is administered 24 hours before training, it completely blocks the memory-enhancing effects of naloxone, while failing to alter the memory-enhancing effects of other pharmacological agents, such as the cholinergic agonist, arecoline; the alpha-adrenergic agonist, clonidine; and the serotonin re-uptake blocker, fluoxetine.

Our finding is compatible with previous findings by Gallagher (1982) that the potency of opioid antagonists for inproving retrieval follows the order of affinity for the opioid mu receptors (i.e., diprenorphine > naltrexone > naloxone > levallorphan). Further, Izquierdo and Netto (1985) have shown that beta en-

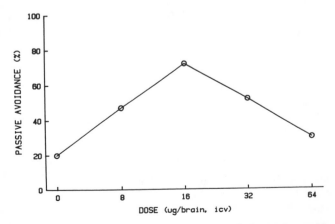

FIGURE 4.4b.   Effects of naloxone on memory in chicks for passive-avoidance conditioning.

dorphin, which has a high affinity for the mu receptor, is amnestic; whereas dynorphin (1-13) which is the endogenous ligand for the kappa receptor, fails to produce amnesia. These data are strongly suggestive that the memory-modulating effects of opioids involve the mu opioid receptor.

Whether opioids produce their depressant effect on memory through the cholinergic system is uncertain. Opioids inhibit acetylcholine turnover in both the septal-hippocampal and nucleus basalis-cortical cholinergic pathways (Pasternak & Wood, 1986). This inhibition of the cholinergic system appears to involve mu opioid agonists. On the other hand, naloxone still enhances memory in mice pretreated with an amnestic dose of the cholinergic antagonist, scopolamine (Flood, Cherkin, & Morley, 1985), suggesting that opioids can modulate memory independently of the cholinergic system. Combinations of naloxone and the cholinergic agonist, arecholine, partially antagonize the enhancing effects that each alone has on memory.

A Teleological Speculation on the Function of Opioids

Opioid peptides exist in unicellular organisms (LeRoith, Shiloach, & Roth, 1982), and opioids modulate feeding in amoeba (Josefsson & Johansson, 1979). There is no known analgesic system in these simple organisms. Thus, Morley and Levine (1982) have suggested that the primary function of opioids is to regulate the foraging for and ingestion of food. When food foraging causes the organism to run into danger, the utilization of opioidlike substances to produce analgesia makes eminent sense. Similarly, seen in this light, the enhancing effects of opioids on immune function (Morley, Kay, Alen, Moon, & Billington, 1985a) and glucose metabolism (Van Loon & Appel, 1981) and the inhibitory effects on gastric-acid secretion (Morley, 1982), sexual performance, and reproductive hormones (Morley, 1983) make teleological sense. When the animal is sated (post naloxone or low opioid state), memory consolidation would be enhanced, allowing the animal to remember the details of a successful foraging trip.

Neuropeptide Y and Memory

NPY occurs in high concentrations in the amygdala and the hippocampus (Gray & Morley, 1986). The highest concentration of NPY receptors is in the hippocampus (Chang, Lotte, & Chen, 1985). These anatomical findings suggested to us that NPY may play a role in memory processing. We found that, using the aversive T-maze model for memory in undertrained mice (Flood & Morley, 1986), NPY enhanced seven-day retention when administered immediately after training. This effect of NPY is time dependent. NPY reversed amnesia induced by the protein synthesis inhibitor, anisomycin, and the cholinergic antagonist, scopolamine. NPY does not alter acquisition, but does promote recall when administered prior to retention testing.

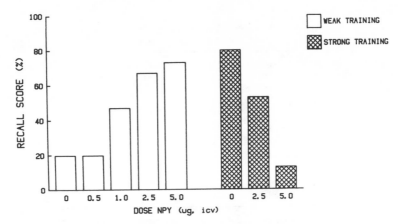

FIGURE 4.5   Effect of neuropeptide Y (NPY) on retention as a function of training strength during T-maze footshock avoidance conditioning.

As NPY enhances feeding, its effects on memory appear to be opposite on memory to those predicted for the opioids and CCK, where it is suggested that feeding enhancers should inhibit memory and feeding antagonists (satiety agents) should enhance memory. One possibility was that the memory-enhancing effect of NPY was nonspecific, secondary to the increased food intake releasing CCK. Preliminary data suggest that this is not the case, as NPY is equally effective in enhancing memory in the presence or absence of food.

However, NPY, when administered post-training to overtrained mice, is amnestic at the same doses that produce memory enhancement in undertrained mice (Figure 4.5). Should this amnestic effect of NPY be its predominant physiological role in memory modulation, its feeding and memory effects would be compatible with our hypothesis. Alternatively, NPY may be involved in different neuronal circuitry from that involved in the feeding-CCK-opioid pathway postulated here.

CONCLUSIONS

In this review, we have suggested that feeding leads to the peripheral release of the satiety peptide, CCK, which activates ascending vagal fibers. These fibers, through relays in the nucleus tractus solitarius, produce satiety secondary to messages transmitted to the paraventricular nucleus and enhance memory via circuitry projecting to the amygdala. CCK may produce both its inhibition of feeding and enhancement of memory by modulating central opioid systems. As can be seen in Table 4.1, not all neurotransmitters involved in the modulation of feeding and memory produce opposite effects in each system. This highlights the complexity of these two systems and suggests that, in the end, the decision of an

Table 4.1
Comparison between the Effects of Modulators
on Feeding and Memory

Modulator	Food Intake	Memory
Norepinephrine	↑	? ↑
Fluoxetine	↓	↑
Dopamine Agonists	↑ ↓	↑
Acetycholine Agonists	0	↑
Endogenous Opioids	↑	↓
Cholecystokinin	↓	↑
Neuropeptide Y	↑	↑ ↓
GABA Agonists	↑ ↓	↓
Dehydroepiandrosterone-sulfate	↓ *	↑

*Predominantly causes weight loss, rather than a reduction
in food intake.

organism to eat or to consolidate a memory involves multiple neurotransmitter interactions. As it was succinctly put by the British philosopher, Emerson Pugh, "If the human brain were so simple that we could understand it, we would be so simple that we couldn't."

REFERENCES

Atkinson, R. L. (1982). Naloxone decreases food intake in obese humans. *Journal Clinical Encocrinology Metabolism, 55,* 196–198.

Atkinson, R. L., Berke, L. K., Drake, C. R., Bibbs, M. L., Williams, F. L., & Kaiser, D. L. (1985). Effects of long-term with naltrexone on body weight in obesity. *Clinical Pharmacology Therapeutics, 38,* 419–422.

Balkanyi, I., Mohai, L., & Balkanyi, L. (1985). *A new approach to diminish the hunger of hyperphagic obese patients.* 4th Congress of the Hungarian Pharmacological Society, Budapest, Hungary.

Bartus, R. T., Dean, R. L., Beer, B., & Lippa, A. S. (1982). The cholinergic hypothesis of geriatric memory dysfunction. *Science, 217,* 408–417.

Bellinger, L. L., Bernardis, L. F., & Williams, F. E. (1983). Naloxone suppression of food and water intake and cholecystokinin reduction of feeding is attenuated in weanling rats with dorsomedial hypothalamic lesions. *Physiology Behavior, 31,* 839–846.

Beutler, B., Mahoney, J., LeTrang, N., Pekala, P., & Cerami, A. (1984). Purification of cachectin, a lipoprotein lipase suppressing hormone secreted by endotoxin induced RAW 26471 cells. *Journal Experimental Medicine, 161,* 984–995.

Billington, C. J., Levine, A. S., & Morley, J.E. (1983). Are peptides truly satiety agents? A method of testing for neurohumoral satiety effects. *American Journal Physiology, 245,* R920–R926.

Billington, C. J., & Morley, J. E. (1986). *Naltrexone administration to patients with Type II diabetes mellitus.* Manuscript in preparation.

Billington, C. J., Morley, J. E., Levine, A. S., Wright, F., & Seal, U.S. (1985a). Naloxone-induced suppression of feeding in tigers. *Physiology Behavior, 34,* 641–643.

Billington, C. J., Shafer, R. B., & Morley, J. E. (1985b). Effects of opioid blockade with nalmefene on older impotent men. *Endocrinology, 116*, 946A.

Carrasco, M. A., Dias, R. D., & Izquierdo, I. (1982). Naloxone reverses retrograde amnesia induced by electroconvulsive shock. *Behavior Neural Biology, 34*, 352–357.

Chang, R. S. L., Lotte, V. J., & Chen, T-B. (1985). Neuropeptide Y binding sites in rat brain labeled with 125I-Bolton-Hunter NPY. *Life Sciences, 37*, 2111–2122.

Cherkin, A., & Flood, J. F. (1985). Prospects for synergistic drug combinations for the treatment of senile amnesias, pp 169–183. In C. M. Gantz & T. Samorajski (Eds.), *Aging 2000: Our health care destiny. Volume 1: Biomedical issues* (pp. 169–183). New York: Springer-Verlag.

Clark, J. J., Kalra, P. S., Crowley, W. R., & Kalra, S. P. (1984). Neuropeptide Y and human pancreatic polypeptide stimulate feeding behavior in rats. *Endocrinology, 115*, 427–429.

Cohen, M. R., Cohen, R. M., & Pickar, D. (1985). Naloxone reduces food intake in humans. *Psychosomatic Medicine, 47*, 132–138.

Cohen, R. M., Cohen, M. R., Weingartner, H., & Murphy, D. (1983). High dose naloxone infusions affects task performance in normal subjects. *Archives General Psychiatry, 40*, 613–619.

Crawley, N. N., & Beinfeld, M. C. (1983). Rapid development of tolerance to the behavioral actions of cholecystokinin. *Nature, 302*, 703–706.

Crawley, J. N., & Kiss, J. Z. (1985). Paraventricular nucleus lesions abolish the inhibition of feeding induced by systemic cholecystokinin. *Peptides, 6*, 927–935.

Crawley, J. N., Kiss, J. Z., & Mezey, E. (1984). Bilateral midbrain transections block the behavioral effects of cholecystokinin on feeding and exploration in rats. *Brain Research, 322*, 312–321.

Crawley, J. N., & Schwaber, J. S. (1984). Abolition of the behavioral effects of cholecystokinin following bilateral radiofrequency lesions of the parvocellular subdivision of the nucleus tractus solitarius. *Brain Research, 295*, 289–299.

Dias, R. D., Perry, M. L., Carrasco, M. A., & Izquierdo, I. (1981). Effect of electroconvulsive shock on B-endorphin immunoreactivity of rat brain, pituitary gland and plasma. *Behavior Neural Biology, 32*, 265–268.

Drachman, D. A., Glasser, S., Flemming, P., & Longenecker, G. (1982). Memory decline in the aged: Treatment with lecithin and physostigmine. *Neurology, 32*, 944–950.

Dunger, D. G., Leonard, J. V., Wolff, O. M., & Preece, M. A. (1980). Effect of naloxone in a previously undescribed hypothalamic syndrome. *Lancet, 1*, 1277–1281.

Essman, W. B. (1983). *Clinical pharmacology of learning and memory.* New York: S.P. Medical and Scientific Books.

Faris, P. L. (1985). Role of cholecystokinin in the control of nociception and food intake. In H. Lal, F. LaBella, & J. Lane (Eds.), *Endocoids* (pp. 159–166). New York: Alan R. Liss, Inc.

Faris, P. L., Scallet, A. C., Olney, J. W., Della-Fera, M. A., & Baile, C. A. (1984). Behavioral and immunohistochemical analysis of cholecystokinin in the hypothalamic paraventricular nucleus. *Society Neuroscience Abstracts, 10*, 652.

Fekete, M., Lengyel, A., Hegedus, B., Penke, B., Zarandy, M., Toth, G. K., & Telegdy, G. (1984). Further analysis of the effects of cholecystokinin octapeptides on avoidance behavior in rats. *European Journal Pharmacology, 98*, 79–91.

Fine, A. (1986). Peptides and Alzheimer's disease. *Nature, 319*, 537–538.

Flood, J. F., & Cherkin, A. (1986). Scopolamine effects on memory retention in mice: A model of dementia? *Behavior Neural Biology, 45*, 169–184.

Flood, J. F., Cherkin, A., & Morley, J. E. (1985). Intracerebral naloxone enhances memory retention in chicks and mice. *Proceedings Society Neuroscience, 11*, 383.

Flood, J. F., & Morley, J. E. (1986). Neuropeptide Y modulates memory in mice. *Federation Proceedings, 45*, 917.

Flood, J. F., Smith, G. E., & Cherkin, A. (1983). Memory retention: Potentiation of cholinergic drug combinations in mice. *Neurobiology Aging, 4*, 37–43.

Fraioli, F., Fabbri, A., & Moretti, C. (1981). Endogenous opioid peptides and neuroendocrine correlations in a case of congenital indifference to pain. *Endocrinology, 108,* 238A.

Gallagher, M. (1982). Naloxone enhancement of memory processes: Effects of other opiate antagonists. *Behavior Neural Biology, 35,* 375–382.

Gallagher, M., Rapp, P. R., & Fanelli, R. J. (1985). Opiate antagonist facilitation of time-dependent memory processes: Dependence upon intact norepinephrine function. *Brain Research, 347,* 284–290.

Gosnell, B. A., Levine, A. S., & Morley, J. E. (1983). The effects of aging on opioid modulation of feeding in rats. *Life Sciences, 32,* 2793–2799.

Gosnell, B. A., Morley, J. E., & Levine, A. S. (1984). Lesions of the globus pallidus and striatum attenuate ketocyclazocine-induced feeding. *Physiology Behavior, 33,* 349–355.

Gosnell, B. A., Morley, J. E., & Levine, A. S. (1986). Opioid-induced feeding: Localization of sensitive brain sites. *Brain Research, 269,* 177–184.

Grandison, L., & Guidotti, A. (1977). Stimulation of food intake by muscimol and beta-endorphin. *Neuropharmacology, 16,* 533–536.

Gray, T. S., & Morley, J. E. (1986). Neuropeptide Y: Anatomical distribution and possible function in mammalian nervous system. *Life Sciences, 38,* 389–401.

Hatsukami, D. K., Mitchell, J. E., Morley, J. E., Morgan, S. F., & Levine, A. S. (1986). Effect of naltrexone on mood and cognitive functioning among overweight men. *Biological Psychiatry, 21,* 293–300.

Holtzman, S. G. (1974). Behavioral effects of separate and combined administration of naloxone and d-amphetamine. *Journal Pharmacology Experimental Therapeutics, 189,* 51–60.

Izquierdo, I. (1979). Effect of naloxone and morphine on various forms of memory in the rat: Possible role of endogenous opiate mechanisms in memory consolidation. *Psychopharmacology, 66,* 199–203.

Izquierdo, I., & Dias, R. D. (1983). Effect of ACTH, epinephrine, B-endorphin, naloxone and of the combination of naloxone and B-endorphin with ACTH or epinephrine on Memory consolidation. *Psychoneuroendocrinology, 8,* 81–87.

Izquierdo, I., & Netto, C. (1985). Role of B-endorphin in behavioral regulation. *Annual NY Academy Sciences, 444,* 162–177.

Jonas, J. M., & Gold, M. S. (1986). Naltrexone reverses bulimic symptoms. *Lancet, 1,* 807.

Josefsson, J.-O., & Johansson, P. (1979). Naloxone reversible effect of opioids on pinocytosis in amoeba protozoa. *Nature, 282,* 78–80.

Judd, J. L., Janowsky, D. S., Segul, D. S., & Huey, L. (1980). Naloxone-induced behavioral and physiological effects in normal and manic subjects. *Archives General Psychiatry, 37,* 583–586.

Kadar, T., Fekete, M., & Telegdy, G. (1981). Modulation of passive avoidance/behavior of rats by intracerebroventricular administration of cholecystokinin octopeptide sulfate ester and nonsulfated cholecystokinin octapeptide. *Acta Physiologia Academiae Scientarium Hungaricae, 58,* 269–274.

Kavaliers, M., & Hirst, M. (1985). The influence of opiate agonists on day-night feeding rhythms in young and old mice. *Brain Research, 326,* 160–167.

Kavaliers, M., & Hirst, M. (1987). Slugs and snails and opiate tales: Opioids and Feeding behavior in invertebrates. *Federation Proceedings, 46,* 168–173.

Kissileff, H. R., Pi-Sunyer, F. X., Thornton, J., & Smith, G. P. (1981). C-terminal octapeptide of cholecystokinin decreases food intake in man. *American Journal Clinical Nutrition, 34,* 154–166.

Krotkiewski, M., Fagerberg, B., Bjorntorp, P., & Terenius, L. (1983). Endorphins in genetic human obesity. *International Journal Obesity, 7,* 597–598.

Kyriakides, M., Silverstone, T., Jeffcoate, W., & Laurance, B. (1980). Effect of naloxone on hyperphagia in Prader-Willi syndrome. *Lancet, 1,* 876–877.

LeMagnen, J. P., Marfaing-Jallut, P., Micelli, D., & Devos, M. (1980). Pain modulating and reward systems: A single brain mechanism? *Pharmacology Biochemistry Behavior, 12,* 729–733.

LeRoith, D., Shiloach, J., & Roth, J. (1982). Is there an earlier phylogenetic precursor that is common to both the nervous and endocrine systems? *Peptides, 3,* 211–215.

Levine, A. S., Grace, M., Billington, C., Gosnell, B. A., Brown, D. M., & Morley, J. E. (1985a). Effect of chronic administration of morphine and nalmefene on food intake and body weight in diabetic and control rats. *Proceedings Society Neuroscience, 11,* 55.

Levine, A. S., & Morley, J. E. (1984). Neuropeptide Y: A potent inducer of consummatory behavior in rats. *Peptides, 5,* 1025–1029.

Levine, A. S., Morley, J. E., Gosnell, B. A., Billington, C. J., & Bartness, T. J. (1985b). Opioids and consummatory behavior. *Brain Research Bulletin, 14,* 663–672.

Levine, A. S., Morley, J. E., Grace, M., & Kneip, J. (1985c). A comparison between neuropeptide Y (NPY) and norepinephrine (NE) induced feeding. *Federation Proceedings, 44,* 546.

Levine, A. S., Murray, S. S., Kneip, J., Grace, M., & Morley, J. E. (1982). Flavor enhances the antidipsogenic effect of naloxone. *Physiology Behavior, 28,* 23–25.

Levine, A. S., Sievert, C. E., Morley, J. E., Gosnell, B. A., & Silvis, S. E. (1984). Peptidergic regulation of feeding in the dog (*Canis familiaris*). *Peptides, 5,* 675–678.

Maggio, C. A., Presta, E., Bracco, E. F., Vasselli, J. R., Kissileff, H. R., Pfohl, D. N., & Hashim, S. A. (1985). Naltrexone and human eating behavior: A dose-ranging inpatient trial in moderately obese men. *Brain Research Bulletin, 14,* 657–661.

Malcom, R., O'Neil, P. J., Sexauer, J. D., Riddle, F. E., Currey, H. S., & Counts, C. (1985). A controlled trial of naltrexone in obese humans. *International Journal Obesity, 9,* 347–353.

Marks-Kaufman, R. (1982). Increased fat consumption induced by morphine administration in rats. *Pharmacology Biochemistry Behavior, 16,* 949–955.

Martin, W. R., Wikler, A., Eacles, C. G., & Prescor, F. T. (1963). Tolerance to and physical dependence on morphine in rats. *Psychopharmacologia (Berlin), 4,* 247–260.

McGaugh, J. L. (1985). Peripheral and central adrenergic influences on brain peptides involved in the modulation of memory storage. *Annual NY Academy Sciences, 444,* 150–161.

McLaughlin, C. L., & Baile, C. A. (1985). Autoimmunization against beta-endorphin increased food intake and body weights of obese rats. *Physiology Behavior, 35,* 365–370.

McLaughlin, C. L., Peikin, S. R., & Baile, C. A. (1983). Trypsin inhibitor effects on food intake and weight gain in Zucker rats. *Physiology Behavior, 31,* 487–491.

Messing, R. B., Jensen, R. A., Martinez Jr., J. L., Speiherl, V. R., Vasques, B. J., Soumireu-Mourat, B., Liang, K. C., & McGaugh, J. L. (1979). Naloxone enhancement of memory. *Behavior Neural Biology, 27,* 266–275.

Mitchell, J. E., Morley, J. E. Levine, A. S., Hatsukami, D., Gannon, M., Pfohl, D. (1987). High dose naltrexone therapy and dietary counselling for obesity. *Biological Psychiatry 22,* 35–41. The Neural and Metabolic Bases of Feeding, Napa Valley, CA.

Morley, J. E. (1981). The neuroendocrine control of appetite. *Life Sciences, 27,* 355–368.

Morley, J. E. (1983). Neuroendocrine effects of endogenous opioid peptides in human subjects: A review Psychoneuroendocrinology 8:361–379.

Morley, J. E., Baranetsky, N. G., Wingert, T. D., Carlson, H. E., Hershman, J. M., Melmed, S., Levin, S. R., Jamison, K. R., Weitzmen, R., Chang, R. J., & Varner, A. A. (1980). Endocrine effects of naloxone-induced opiate receptor blockade. *Journal Clinical Endocrinology Metabolism, 50,* 251–257.

Morley, J. E., Hernandez, E. N., & Flood, J. F. (1986). Neuropeptide Y increases food intake in mice. *Federation Proceedings, 45,* 601.

Morley, J. E., Kay, N., Allen, J., Moon, T., & Billington, C. J. (1985a). Endorphins, immune function and cancer. *Psychopharmacology Bulletin, 21,* 3:485–488.

Morley, J. E., & Levine, A. S. (1982). The role of the endogenous opiates as regulators of appetite. *American Journal Clinical Nutrition, 35,* 757–761.

Morley, J. E., & Levine, A. S. (1985). Pharmacology of eating behavior. *Annual Review of Pharmacology and Toxicology, 25,* 127–146.

Morley, J. E., Levine, A. S., Gosnell, B. A., & Billington, C. J. (1984). Which opioid receptor mechanism modulates feeding? *Appetite, 5,* 61–68.

Morley, J. E., Levine, A. S., Grace, M., & Kneip, J. (1985b). Peptide YY (PYY)—a potent orexigenic agent. *Brain Research, 341,* 200–203.

Morley, J. E., Levine, A. S., Kneip, J., & Grace, M. (1982a). The effect of vagotomy on the satiety effects of neuropeptides and naloxone. *Life Sciences, 30,* 1943–1947.

Morley, J. E., Levine, A. S., Kneip, J., Grace, M., & Billington, J. S. (1983a). The effect of peripherally administered satiety substances on feeding induced by butorphanol tartrate. *Pharmacology Biochemistry Behavior, 19,* 577–582.

Morley, J. E., Levine, A. S., Plotka, E. D., & Seal, U. S. (1983b). The effect of naloxone on feeding and spontaneous locomotion in the wolf. *Physiology Behavior, 30,* 331–334.

Morley, J. E., Levine, A. S., & Silvis, S. E. (1982b). Central regulation of gastric acid secretion: The role of neuropeptides. *Life Sciences, 31,* 399–410.

Morley, J. E., Levine, A. S., Yim, G. K. W., & Lowy, M. T. (1983c). Opioid modulation of appetite. *Neuroscience Biobehavior Review, 7,* 281–305.

Morley, J. E., Mitchell, J. E., & Levine, A. S. (1985a). Neuropeptides as stimulators of feeding. *Psychopharmacology Bulletin.* 21:485–488.

Morley, J. E., Parker, S., & Levine, A. S. (1985c). Effect of butorphanol tartrate on food and water consumption in humans. *American Journal Clinical Nutrition, 42,* 1175–1178.

Nizielski, S. E., Gosnell, B. A., Morley, J. E., & Levine, A. S. (1985). Neuropeptide Y increases feeding in ground squirrel. *Federation Proceedings.* 44:545A.

O'Brien, C. P., Stunkard, A. J., & Tesmes, J. W. (1982). Absence of naloxone sensitivity in obese humans. *Psychosomatic Medicine, 44,* 215–218.

Parrott, R. F., Heavens, R. P., & Baldwin, B. A. (1986). Stimulation of feeding in the satiated pig by intracerebroventricular injection of neuropeptide Y. *Physiology Behavior, 36,* 523–525.

Pasternak, G. W., & Wood, P. J. (1986). Multiple mu opiate receptors. *Life Sciences, 38,* 1889–1898.

Pi-Sunyer, F. X., Kissileff, H. R., Thornton, J., & Smith, G. P. (1982). C-terminal octapeptide of CCK decreases food intake in obese men. *Physiology Behavior, 29,* 627–630.

Plotka, E. D., Morley, J. E., Levine, A. S., & Seal, U. S. (1985). Effects of opiate antagonists on feeding and spontaneous locomotion in deer. *Physiology Behavior, 35,* 965–969.

Reid, L. D. (1985). Endogenous opioid peptides and regulation of drinking and feeding. *American Journal Clinical Nutrition, 42,* 1099–1132.

Reisberg, B., Berris, S. H., Anand, R., Mir, P., Geibel, V., DeLeon, M. J., & Roberts, E. (1983). Effects of naloxone on senile dementia: A double-blind trial. *New England Journal Medicine, 108,* 721–722.

Richter, W. O., Kerscher P., & Schwandt, P. (1983). Beta-endorphin stimulates in vivo lipolysis in the rabbit. *Life Sciences, 33,* 743–746.

Ritter, R. C., & Landenheim, E. E. (1984). Fourth ventricle infusion of cholecystokinin suppresses feeding in rats. *Society Neuroscience Abstracts, 10,* 652.

Romsos, D. R., Gosnell, B. A., Morley, J. E., & Levine, A. S. (1987). Effects of kappa opiate agonists, cholecystokinin and bombesin on intake of diets varying in carbohydrate to fat ratio in rats. *Journal Nutrition, 117,* 976–985.

Schulz, R., Wilhelm, A., & Dirlich, G. (1984). Intracerebral injection of different antibodies against endogenous opioids suggested α-neo-endorphin participation in the control of feeding behavior. *Naumyn Schmiedebergs Archives Pharmacology, 326,* 222–226.

Shaw, M. J., Hughes, J. J., Morley, J. E., Levine, A. S., Silvis, S. E., & Shafer, R. B. (1985). Cholecystokinin octapeptide action on gastric emptying and food intake in normal and vagotomized man. *Annual New York Academy Sciences, 448,* 640–641.

Shillabeer, G., & Davidson, J. S. (1984). The cholecystokinin antagonist, proglumide, increases food intake in the rat. *Regulatory Peptides, 8,* 171–176.

Sjodin, L. (1972). Influence of secretin and cholecystokinin on canine gastric secretion elicited by food and exogenous gastrin. *Acta Physiology Scandinavia, 85,* 110–117.

Smith, G. P. (1983). The peripheral control of appetite. *Lancet, 2,* 88–90.

Smith, G. P., Greenberg, D., Falusco, J. D., Gibbs, J., Liddle, R. A., & Williams, J. A. (1985a). Plasma levels of cholecystokinin produced by satiating doses of exogenous CCK-8. *Society Neuroscience Abstracts, 11,* 557.

Smith, G. P., Jerome, C., Cushin, B. J., Eterno, R., & Simansky, K. J. (1981). Abdominal vagotomy blocks the satiety effect of cholecystokinin: A progress report. *Peptides, 2,* 57–59.

Smith, G. P., Jerome, C., & Norgren, R. (1985b). Afferent axons in abdominal vagus mediate satiety effect of cholecystokinin in rats. *American Journal Physiology, 249,* R638–R641.

Stacher, G., Steinringer, H., Schniever, G., Schneider, C., & Winklehner, S. (1982). Cholecystokinin octapeptide decreases intake of solid food in man. *Peptides, 3,* 133–136.

Stanley, B. G., Kyrkouli, S. E., Lampert, S., & Leibowitz, S. F. (1985). Hyperphagia and obesity induced by Neuropeptide Y injected chronically into the paraventricular hypothalamus of the rat. Proceedings Society Neuroscience 11:36, 1985.

Stanley, B. G., Lanthier, D., & Leibowitz, S. W. (1984). Feeding elicited by the opiate peptide D-ala-2-met enkephalinamide: Sites of action in the brain. *Society Neuroscience Abstracts, 10,* 1103.

Stanley, B. G., & Leibowitz, S. F. (1984). Neuropeptide Y: Stimulation of feeding and drinking by injection into the paraventricular nucleus. *Life Sciences, 33,* 2635–2642.

Steardo, L., Russo, G., Sorge, F., & Cardone, G. (1982). Effects of naloxone on memory in man. *Acta Neurology (Napoli), 37,* 117–126.

Steinman, J., & Morley, J. E. (1986). Effects of pancreatic polypeptides on food intake in chicks. *Federation Proceedings, 45,* 601.

Sziegel, Z. S., Fekete, M., Szipoes, I., Lengyel, A., Szender, I., Kardoos, A., & Telegdy, G. (1985). *Further analysis of the behavioral effects of cholecystokinin.* 4th Congress of Hungarian Pharmacological Society Abstracts, Budapest, Hungary.

Tallman, J. R., Willenbring, M. L., Carlson, G., Boosalis, M., Krahn, D. D., Levine, A. S., & Morley, J. E. (1984). Effect of chronic methadone use in humans on taste and dietary preference. *Federation Proceedings, 43,* 1058.

Tatemoto, K. (1982). Neuropeptide Y: Complete amino acid sequence of the brain peptide. *Proceedings National Academy Science USA, 79,* 5485–5489.

Thompson, D. A., Welle, S. L., Lilivavat, U., Penicaud, L., & Campbell, R. G. (1983). Opiate receptor blockade in man reduced 2-deoxy-d-glucose induced food intake but not hunger, thirst and hypothermia. *Life Sciences, 31,* 847–852.

Toste, F. M., Dieckmann, B., Beutler, B., Cerami, A., & Ringold, G. M. (1985). A macrophage factor inhibits adipocyte gene expression: An in vitro model of cachexia. *Science, 229,* 867–869.

Trenchard, E., & Silverstone, T. (1983). Naloxone reduces the food intake of normal human volunteers. *Appetite, 4,* 43–50.

Van Loon, G. R., & Appel, N. M. (1981). Endorphin-induced hyperglycemia is mediated by increased sympathetic outflow to adrenal medulla. *Brain Research, 204,* 236–241.

Volavka, J., Dornbuss, R., Mallya, A., & Cho, D. (1979). Naloxone fails to affect short-term memory in man. *Psychiatry Research, 1,* 89–92.

Ward, S. J., Portoghese, P. S., & Takemori, A. E. (1982). Pharmacological characterization in vivo of the novel opiate, B-funaltrexamine. *Journal Pharmacology Experimental Therapeutics, 220,* 494–498.

West, D. B., Fey, D., & Woods, S. C. (1984). Cholecystokinin persistently suppresses meal size but not food intake in free-feeding rats. *American Journal Physiology, 246,* R776–R787.

5

THE TREATMENT OF BULIMIA NERVOSA: A COGNITIVE-SOCIAL LEARNING ANALYSIS

G. Terence Wilson
Graduate School of Applied and Professional Psychology,
Rutgers University

Bulimia nervosa, as defined by Russell (1979) and Fairburn (1985), is a disorder characterized by binge eating which is accompanied by purging (typically self-induced vomiting) and an intense fear of weight gain. Body weight is normal (within 20%, plus or minus, of normative weight), although a history of weight disturbance is common. Although large quantities of food are often consumed rapidly, the distinguishing qualities of binge eating are basically subjective—the feeling of loss of control and the perception of excessive food intake (Fairburn, Cooper, & Cooper, 1986). As such, bulimia nervosa, as Fairburn notes, may be seen as a specific subtype of the less precise DSM-III definition of bulimia. In the latter, vomiting is not an essential feature of the diagnosis; nor is normal weight.

In the comments that follow, I examine the implications of existing evidence and conceptual models about the nature of bulimia nervosa for treatment, and, reciprocally, how the emerging findings of treatment outcome can guide our conceptualizations of bulimia nervosa.

The effective management of a clinical disorder, the etiology of which is not understood, is one of the realities of current clinical practice. Behavior therapists, particularly, have often concentrated on the modification of problems without necessarily linking them to etiology. Ultimately, however, the treatment of bulimia nervosa must derive logically from an adequate understanding of its etiology and maintenance. Whether bulimia nervosa is viewed as a symptom of affective illness (Hudson, Pope, & Jonas, 1984), a product of a pathological family system (Schwartz, Barrett, & Saba, 1984), a conditioned response maintained by negative reinforcement (Leitenberg, Gross, Peterson, & Rosen, 1984), or a consequence of dysfunctional cognitions (Fairburn, 1985) would seem to have decisive implications for the choice of treatment methods and the specific target of intervention. In reciprocal fashion, the results of different treatments can bear importantly on the analysis of the nature of the disorder. Although it would be an error to infer etiology from the modification of a problem, the outcome of treatment may provide a powerful test of some of the predictions of different conceptualizations of bulimia nervosa.

CONCEPTUAL MODELS OF BULIMIA NERVOSA

We do not, as yet, have an adequate knowledge of the etiology and maintenance of bulimia nervosa. Not surprisingly, different theories abound.

Bulimia as a Form of Affective Disorder

The notion that bulimia is a form of affective disorder has attracted much attention (Hudson et al., 1984). One source of evidence for this view is that depression is often a prominent part of the clinical picture of patients with bulimia nervosa. The available evidence, however, suggests that in the majority of patients, this depression is the consequence rather than the cause of bulimia (Wilson, 1986a). Cognitive-behavioral treatment that successfully eliminates binge eating and vomiting reliably results in highly significant reductions in depression and other forms of psychopathology as well (Fairburn, Kirk, O'Connor, & Cooper, 1986; Kirkley, Schneider, Agras, & Bachman, 1985; Wilson, Rossiter, Kleifield, & Lindholm, 1986a).

Another argument for conceptualizing bulimia as a form of affective disorder is the effect of antidepressant drugs (Hudson et al., 1984). Two observations are pertinent here. First, the outcome evidence on the effects of antidepressant medication on binge eating and vomiting is conflicting (Sabine, Yonace, Farrington, Barratt, & Wakeling, 1983; Wilson, 1986a). Moreover, pretreatment levels of depression are unrelated to positive response to medication (Agras, Dorlan, Kirkley, Arnow, & Bachman, 1987; Brotman, Herzog, & Woods, 1984; Walsh, Stuart, Roose, Gladis, & Glassman, 1984). Second, even if it is granted that the drugs work, alternative interpretations of their efficacy can be readily generated, as noted below.

A third line of reasoning for this view derives from studies showing a higher prevalence of affective illness among family members of bulimics as opposed to controls (Hudson, Pope, Jonas, & Yurgelin-Todd, 1983: Kog & Vandereycken, 1985; Lee, Rush, & Mitchell, 1985). A well-controlled study by Stern et al. (1984) failed to replicate these results, however. Moreover, it may be that the high incidence of family members with depression occurs primarily in those bulimic patients who themselves are depressed (Wilson & Lindholm, 1987). This suggests that the family connection lies in the concomitant depressive disorder rather than bulimia nervosa per se. Finally, family history of depression seems unrelated to treatment outcome using cognitive-behavioral methods (Wilson et al., 1986a). The number of patients in this study was small, however ($n = 17$). Better-controlled studies of this possible relationship, using more rigorous assessment of family history, seem to be indicated.

A fourth argument in favor of viewing bulimia nervosa as a form of affective illness stresses the similarity in response to the Dexamethasome Suppression Test in bulimic and depressed patients, respectively. However, alternative explanations of these results (e.g., the neuroendocrine effects of dieting and purging) are possible (Lee et al., 1985).

The Family-Systems Model

The family-systems view of bulimia nervosa is shared by many clinical practitioners. This focus seems to come partly from well-known analyses of the families of anorexics (Minuchin, Rosman, & Baker, 1978) and as a corollary of family therapy in general enjoying the popularity that it does in clinical practice.

Available data indicate that families of bulimics show significant levels of disturbance. Garner, Garfinkel, and O'Shaughnessy (1985), for example, found that the families of normal-weight bulimics were akin to those of bulimic anorexics and that both showed greater disturbance than the families of anorexics of the restricting type. Similarly, both Kog, Vertommen, and Degroote (1985) and Strober (1981) found more family conflict in families of normal-weight bulimics and bulimic anorectics than in those of restricting anorectics. Johnson, Lewis, and Hagman (1984) cite data showing that, compared to normal controls, the families of bulimics were more disorganized, more conflicted, but had a greater achievement orientation. Johnson et al. suggest that these findings indicate that an unstructured family environment may be a critical factor in the development of bulimia. Although data of the latter kind do implicate the role of family factors in bulimia nervosa, only longitudinal research will be able to untangle cause, correlation, and consequence in this association.

Preliminary findings from a prospective study of 15-year-old English school girls, by Johnson-Sabine, Wood, Mann, and Wakeling (1985), suggest that there is no specific association between abnormal eating attitudes and self-reported social stress, the latter including home life. In this study, "abnormal attitudes toward eating" are defined in terms of scores on the Eating Attitudes Test (EAT). There is no direct evidence that this test predicts subsequent development of anorexia or bulimia nervosa, however.

With respect to treatment, there is no direct evidence, of which I am aware, in favor of family therapy. Rather, there is evidence against such a view. Cognitive-behavioral treatment of individual bulimic patients, without any involvement of family members and without a specific focus on family affairs, has produced consistently positive—and lasting—findings (Fairburn et al., 1986;

Lacey, 1983; Wilson et al., 1986a). In the absence of the latter ingredients, the family-therapy model must predict therapeutic failure. My own clinical impressions are that direct reduction or elimination of binge eating and vomiting (bulimic "symptoms," according to some) may, in some cases, result in more satisfying interpersonal relationships and improved family harmony. The significance of these findings for the role of a disordered family environment in the development of bulimia nervosa is, at present, unclear. The systematic assessment of family interaction and other intimate interpersonal relationships throughout the course of therapy and during follow-up has been relatively ignored in the treatment of bulimia nervosa. We need to know more about this relationship.

I have already referred to the data indicating greater prevalence of affective disorders among family members of bulimics than controls. Family histories of both substance abuse and eating disorders have also been linked to binge eating and bulimia. Leon, Carroll, Chernyk, and Finn (1985) found that a family history of substance abuse was associated with binge eating among female college students, but not among males. Leon et al. also reported that 51% of a sample of diagnosed bulimic patients had "one or more first-degree relatives specifically diagnosed by a health professional as chemically dependent" (p. 53). Yet, the presence of a positive family history of substance abuse was not significantly associated with chemical dependency in the bulimics or frequency of binge eating or purging.

In a well-controlled investigation, Strober, Morrell, Burroughs, Salkin, and Jacobs (1985) found a higher rate of eating disorders (anorexia nervosa, bulimia nervosa, and subclinical anorexia nervosa) in first-degree relatives of anorexic patients than in those of non-anorexic psychiatric control probands. I am unaware of a comparable study of the families of normal-weight patients with bulimia nervosa, but this seems to be a potentially productive line of research, given the view that bulimia is a consistent and distinctive disorder that varies across the full spectrum of body weight (Garner et al., 1985; Leon et al., 1985).

The Anxiety Model

The anxiety model of bulimia nervosa (Rosen & Leitenberg, 1982) draws an explicit analogy between the behavioral conceptualization of obsessive-compulsive disorders and bulimia. As Rosen and Leitenberg put it,

> . . . binge eating and vomiting seem linked in a vicious circle by anxiety. . . . Eating elicits this anxiety (binging dramatically so); vomiting reduces it. Once an individual has learned that vomiting following food intake leads to anxiety reduction, rational fears no longer inhibit overeating. Thus the driving force of this disorder may be vomiting, not binging. . . . (p. 118)

This model has proved heuristic and, as detailed below, has led to the use of exposure and response prevention (well-established methods in the treatment of anxiety disorders) in the treatment of bulimia nervosa (Johnson, Schlundt, & Jarrell, 1986; Leitenberg et al.. 1984). Briefly, patients are systematically instructed to binge to the point where they would typically vomit, but are encouraged to resist vomiting (prevent the escape/avoidance response).

There are a number of difficulties with the anxiety model, however. These may be summarized as follows: (1) The model addresses the maintenance of the binge-vomit cycle, but is silent on the reasons for the initial development of disordered or binge eating, which then triggers the vomiting. Furthermore, it does not take into account the cognitive and psychosocial factors which are plausibly linked to the development and determinants of bulimia (see below). (2) The model is an extension of Mowrer's (1960) two-factor theory, in which escape/avoidance behavior is directly motivated by anxiety conceptualized as conditioned autonomic arousal. The reduction of this physiological arousal maintains the escape/avoidance behavior through the process of negative reinforcement. Yet, this two-factor theory has been shown to be untenable. Conditioned anxiety is not causally related to avoidance behavior (e.g., vomiting): both anxiety arousal and avoidance appear to be correlated coeffects of some central mediating process (Bandura, 1978). It has been largely abandoned, or at least seriously modified, as an explanatory model of the development and maintenance of phobic disorders (Bandura, 1978, 1982), sexual disorders (Beck & Barlow, 1984), and another form of substance abuse—alcoholism (Wilson, 1987).

In each of these other clinical disorders to which I refer, the noncognitive two-factor theory has yielded to a distinctly more cognitive account that comprises attentional and attributional processes, and efficacy and outcome expectations (O'Leary & Wilson, 1987). There is no reason to expect any difference with bulimia nervosa. Furthermore, this cognitive emphasis lends itself well to accommodating both the psychosocial factors that seem to be related to the onset of bulimia (Striegel-Moore, Silberstein, & Rodin, 1986) and a broader array of potentially more useful treatment strategies than exposure and response prevention.

Williamson, Kelley, Davis. Ruggiero, and Veitia (1985) have expanded Rosen and Leitenberg's (1982) anxiety model. In their version, other psychopathological states (e.g., depression), distorted body image, stress, and interpersonal issues function as background factors that exacerbate the binge-purge cycle that is the crux of the Rosen and Leitenberg model. Even this expanded model deemphasizes cognitive processes. Binge eating is attributed to a biological demand (food deprivation), and anxiety is still defined as physiological arousal. Important psychosocial processes behind binge eating still receive little emphasis. (3) Some of the predictions of the anxiety model have not received empirical support in behavioral treatment studies. I discuss these inconsistencies below. (4) The analogy to obsessive-compulsive disorders, while clearly heuristic, is imperfect, as I will also discuss later. The issues in using exposure and response prevention with bulimics are more complex. There seems to be a discrepancy between the effects of treating obsessive-compulsives with exposure and response prevention and those obtained in the treatment of bulimics.

The Role of Cognitions

Dysfunctional cognitions and values about their body weight and shape are a particularly prominent feature of patients with bulimia nervosa. Fremouw and Heyneman (1983) showed that overweight bulimics, relative to nonbulimic controls, displayed a distinguishable cognitive style. They evaluated themselves more negatively following a failure experience. and they were more dichotomous or extreme in their evaluative style. Ruderman (1985) found that, among female college students, those who scored high on a test of bulimia (the BULIT: Smith & Thelen, 1984) were also significantly more prone to distorted cognitions of a rigid, perfectionistic, and demanding nature. The prominence of these dysfunctional cognitions has led to cognitive conceptualizations of the disorder. Fairburn (1985), for example, has stated that

> the extreme dieting, vomiting, and laxative abuse, the preoccupation with food and eating, the sensitivity to changes in shape and weight, and the frequent weighing or total avoidance of weighing are all comprehensible, once it has been appreciated that these patients believe that their shape and weight are of fundamental importance and that both must be kept under strict control. Even the apparently paradoxical binge eating can be understood in cognitive terms, since it seems that it may represent a secondary response to extreme dietary restraint. . . . Thus, rather than being simply symptomatic of bulimia, these beliefs and values appear to be of primary importance in the maintenance of the condition (pp. 160–191)

Fairburn's (1985) framework fits both experimental findings and clinical observations. One advantage is that it dovetails with Polivy and Herman's (1985) theory of dietary restraint. According to this theory, restrained eaters actively diet to achieve a desired, but less than biologically optimal weight, and become preoccupied with control over food intake. The Restraint Scale, a questionnaire measure of this construct, has consistently predicted certain types of eating behavior. One phenomenon has been referred to as "counterregulatory eating." Specifically, following an initial food "preload," restrained eaters consume more on a standardized eating task (counterregulate) than do unrestrained eaters who reduce (regulate) their intake. Moreover, Polivy and Herman assume that counterregulation is cognitively mediated.

Clinical experience indicates that bulimics binge when they transgress their characteristically rigid and unrealistic dietary standards. If it is assumed that binge eating is a form of counterregulation, it then follows that dieting should be a precursor. Consistently, the data show that bulimics start binge eating following a severe diet (Johnson-Sabine et al., 1985). Laboratory studies have also shown that individuals high in dietary restraint, in contrast to their unrestrained peers, tend to counterregulate when stressed or depressed (Polivy, Herman, Olmsted, & Jazwinski, 1984: Ruderman, 1985). Negative emotional states frequently trigger binge eating in bulimics (Johnson, Stuckey, Lewis, & Schwartz, 1982; Wilson et al., 1986a).

A Cognitive-Social Learning Model of Bulimia Nervosa

Figure 5.1 provides a brief model of bulimia nervosa that summarizes some of these points.

WOMEN AND WEIGHT: THE PSYCHOSOCIAL CONTEXT.   One of the overriding characteristics of bulimia nervosa is that it is almost exclusively confined to women. Any theory of bulimia must account for this striking imbalance in prevalance between the sexes.

Recent reviews by Rodin, Silberstein, and Striegel-Moore (1985) and Striegel-Moore et al. (1986) have synthesized the observations of several investigators in indicating why women are singularly at risk for eating disorders in general and bulimia in particular. Column 1 of the model shown here, the primary cognitive dysfunction, emphasizes the drive for a slim and svelte body. This concern is often dysfunctional to women, but hardly irrational. As Rodin and her colleagues note, women's fear of overweight is well-grounded in society's negative view of obesity, particularly in women. The evidence seems to be quite consistent that females, far more than males, incur negative psychosocial consequences for being overweight. Being physically attractive is clearly rewarded in our society. Again, this is more significant for women than men, apparently throughout the life cycle. For women, body weight and shape are the central determinants of their perception as being physically attractive. For men, these attributes are important, but not as central in perceived attractiveness.

PSYCHOSOCIAL VERSUS BIOLOGICAL DEMANDS.   These psychosocial pressures on women frequently conflict with biological reality. Contrary to old beliefs that weight could be controlled given sufficient care and effort, we now know that body weight is regulated significantly by genetic and biological factors, factors which are more of a problem for women than for men. In general, these biological influences predestine women to be fatter than men, and certainly fatter than the current psychosocial thin ideal. There is evidence that the pressures on women to be thin have increased over recent years; for example, the study showing that *Playboy* centerfolds have become progressively thinner over the years (Garner, Garfinkel, Schwartz, & Thompson, 1980). During the same time period, however, women under the age of 30 years have increased in body weight, according to the Metropolitan life-insurance norms.

Confronted with this discrepancy, and motivated by a not entirely unreasonable fear of overweight (see Column 2, Figure 5.1), women go on diets. In the

Cognitions	Fear	Dietary Practices	Binge Eating	Purging	Post-Purge Psychological Effects
Dysfunctional attitude/Cognitions about body weight and shape; emphasis on thinness	→ Fear of weight gain	→ Restrained eating pattern a. stringent diet b. diet pills c. physical exercise	→ Binges (counter-regulation) following violation of excessively rigid dietary standards (AVE) Negative affect (stress, depression, anger) will facilitate counter-regulation, particularly in individuals with low self-efficacy. Undetermined genetic, familial, personality, or learning factors place a subset of restrained eaters at risk for developing the clinical disorder	→ a. self-induced vomiting b. laxative, stricter diet/periods of starvation	→ First, anxiety reduction and physical relief; second, guilt and depression; low self-esteem, fear about psychological/physical consequences; purification promise—"I'll never do it again," increased dietary restraint

FIGURE 5.1.   A model of the binge-purge sequence.

felicitous phrasing of columnist Russell Baker, "Whom nature has fashioned to go through life bearing flesh can achieve tautly boned angularity only by submitting to the most unnatural sufferings". Diets, or restrained eating practices (see Column 3, Figure 5.1), are often unrealistic (given biological boundaries) and unhealthy. The result is a pattern of repeated "on a diet/off a diet" cycles that have a variety of negative biological and psychological effects. The biological effects, which include decreased metabolic rate and lower thermogenic response to food intake, will only make it increasingly more difficult for the woman to attain her ideal weight. Psychologically, the sense of deprivation or unrealistically rigid standards of dietary restraint leave the woman vulnerable to counterregulation, or what Marlatt (1985), in the related context of other substance-abuse disorders, has termed the "abstinence violation effect" (AVE; see Column 4, Figure 1).[1] According to Polivy and Herman (1985), it is this cognitively mediated disinhibition of restrained eating (counterregulation) that initiates overeating or binge eating. The extent of the binge eating, once initiated, may be influenced by physiological factors, such as hypothesized impaired hunger or satiety signals as a result of dieting and irregular eating patterns. Binge eating leads to purging (Column 5), the consequences of which ultimately feed back to initiate the same cycle once again (Column 6).

LIMITATIONS OF THE MODEL.   The obvious limitation of the model is that only a relatively small subset of the normal-weight restrained eaters described here develop the clinical disorder of bulimia nervosa. Similarly, Fairburn et al. (1986) ponder why "some patients with overvalued ideas concerning their shape and weight successfully maintain control over eating (i.e., restricting anorexics), whereas others experience episodes of bulimia (i.e., bulimic anorexics and patients with bulimia nervosa)." (p. 402) Both of these groups are subjected to the psychosocial influences described above. Both respond with dietary restraint and weight loss, but a different pattern emerges. The critical factors that result in bulimia nervosa are unknown. Possibilities, which are not necessarily mutually exclusive, include genetic, familial, personality, and specific social-learning factors. Family history seems to be a likely influence. For example, Strober et al. (1985) not only showed the familial transmission of anorexia nervosa, but also found that restricter and bulimic forms of anorexia tended to segregate within families, suggesting specificity of transmission of bulimia. The mechanisms responsible for this familial transmission are unknown.

A second limitation of this cognitive-social learning model concerns the questions that have been raised about the concept and measurement of dietary restraint as developed by Polivy and Herman (1985). Dietary restraint is not a unitary concept (Ruderman, 1985; Stunkard & Messick, 1985), and the strictly cognitive interpretation of restraint-related phenomena, such as counterregulatory binge eating, has been challenged (Lowe, in press). Nonetheless, irrespective of these concerns, Polivy and Herman's restraint theory continues to show both heuristic and clinical utility.

IMPLICATIONS FOR RESEARCH AND THERAPY.   My foregoing comments, illustrating what, as Striegel-Moore et al. (1986) point out, are normative concerns about body weight and shape among women in our society, have implications both for therapy and research on the determinants and consequences of bulimia. With respect to therapy, these psychosocial factors have to be addressed in treatment. It will be inadequate to treat bulimia nervosa as a clinical disorder that is separate from these normative concerns (e.g., simply as a symptom of an underlying affective illness).

For research purposes, the line of reasoning pursued here suggests a control group that might usefully be included in future studies of individuals with bulimia nervosa. I am referring to a comparison group of nonbulimic subjects who, nevertheless, are restrained eaters. Existing data point to considerable overlap between women with and without eating disorders in terms of attitudes about weight and food (Garner, Olmsted, & Polivy, 1983).

A study by Garner, Olmsted, Polivy, and Garfinkel (1984) showed that weight-preoccupied women [selected on the basis of extreme scores on the Drive for Thinness subscale of the Eating Disorders Inventory (EDI)] resembled matched anorexic patients in many ways. A subset of these weight-preoccupied women "scored as high or higher than the anorexia nervosa group on all EDI subscales" (p. 263). Rossiter (1986) found no differences between patients with bulimia nervosa and nonbulimic, but highly restrained controls on most of the subscales of the EDI. The exceptions were the Bulimia, Interoceptive Awareness, and Ineffectiveness subscales. Nor did patients with bulimia nervosa report greater fear of weight gain or frequency with which they thought about food than highly restrained, nonbulimic controls, although both groups differed from unrestrained controls. Excluding highly restrained, but nonbulimic women from studies of bulimia (Huon & Brown, 1986; Willmuth, Leitenberg, Rosen, Fondacaro, & Gross, 1985) tends to downplay the normative considerations described above. Comparisons with nonbulimic, restrained eaters will reveal the distinctive psychological and pathophysiological processes of individuals with bulimia nervosa and facilitate the search for causal mechanisms.

Cognitive Processing in Patients with Bulimia Nervosa

Given the assumption of the primacy of attitudes and dysfunctional cognitions in bulimia nervosa, it would seem to be important to study these putative cognitive processes directly. My students and I have completed two studies in this area.

One study explored the question of whether bulimic patients selectively process information related to typical bulimic concerns—body weight and parts, bingeing, and purging. Following Mathews and MacLeod's (1985) study of danger schemata in patients with anxiety states, we used the Stroop Color Naming Task, in which subjects are asked to name the ink color in which words are printed and to ignore the word content. Interference effects occur, as indexed by longer latencies in naming the colors, when cognitive representations of the irrelevant word content are concurrently activated and thus compete for processing resources. The cognitive model predicts that bulimics should be selectively slowed in naming color words related to their concerns because of the activation of what may loosely be called a "bulimic schema."

The color-naming performance of patients with bulimia nervosa and two control groups—subjects high in eating restraint, but nonbulimic; and matched counterparts who were unrestrained eaters—was measured. The bulimics were significantly slower in naming the color of the target words than were the unrestrained eaters, but they did not differ from the restrained eaters, who also took longer on the task than the unrestrained eaters. This lack of difference between the patients with bulimia nervosa and normal subjects high in eating restraint underscores the similarity between bulimic patients and weight-conscious women.

A second study examined body-image estimation and evaluation in patients with bulimia nervosa and matched nonbulimic restrained and unrestrained eaters (Lindholm & Wilson, 1988). Contrary to some reports (Thompson, Berland, Linton, & Weinsier, 1986), but consistent with others (e.g., Birtchnell, Lacey, & Harte, 1985; Huon & Brown, 1986), outpatients did not overestimate their body size. Moreover, in line with so many other measures, patients with bulimia nervosa did not differ significantly from nonbulimic, highly restrained controls. The patients did, however, show a more negative evaluation of their bodies than did unrestrained controls.

TREATMENT OF BULIMIC NERVOSA: OUTCOME AND IMPLICATIONS

Assuming that dysfunctional cognitions concerning body weight and shape are seminal to the understanding and treatment of bulimia nervosa, the next questions are What specifically needs to be changed and how is this best accomplished? Polivy et al. (1984) have proposed that their cognitive theory of eating restraint applies to patients with bulimia nervosa. Extrapolating from their model, they have argued that

> If the cognitive (diet quota) boundary could be made more flexible, so that it bends rather than breaks under caloric pressure, it could prevent further consumption following lapses. One way to do this might be to encourage dieters to eat small amounts of "forbidden" foods and to accept occasional "splurges" as treats instead of unforgivable (no turning back now) disasters. . . . This restructuring of both cognitive and eating patterns would allow the cognitive diet boundary to remain more often unbreached and also would serve to reduce the dichotomy inherent in "diet" thinking. (p. 120)

This suggested treatment strategy essentially formed the basis of Fairburn's (1984) treatment program, which, showing very successful results in an uncontrolled clinical series, has influenced subsequent cognitive-behavioral treatment programs (Wilson, 1986a).

Cognitive-Restructuring Strategies

Several different psychological treatments for bulimia have incorporated cognitive-restructuring procedures, in one form or another, even when therapy is not necessarily labeled as "cognitive behavioral." Some therapeutic systems, such as multimodal therapy (Lazarus, 1981) and the three-systems model of emotion (Hugdahl, 1981), hold that cognitive-restructuring procedures, drawn mainly from the cognitive therapies of Beck (1976) and Ellis (1970), are required to modify dysfunctional cognitive processes. I have detailed the conceptual and empirical limitations of this reasoning elsewhere (Wilson, 1982). Suffice it to point out here that in terms of social-learning theory, behavioral procedures are the most effective means of producing changes in cognitive processes (Bandura, 1982). The latter point has been amply documented in the treatment of phobic disorders. Several studies have shown that primarily verbal or symbolic methods have proved ineffective, whereas performance-based procedures have produced significant changes in behavior and cognitive processes (Rachman & Wilson, 1980). There would seem to be no reason to expect other than the same pattern in the treatment of bulimia nervosa.

The major problems in using verbal cognitive-restructuring procedures with bulimics are that some patients find that using the typical cognitive methods do not prevent the binge/purge, or that they simply fail to implement cognitive self-regulatory strategies that, at other times, have proved effective (Rossiter & Wilson, 1985; Wilson et al., 1986a). In the latter cases, it seems as though patients have made up their minds to binge or purge before they have a chance to challenge dysfunctional thoughts. One of my patients described this phenomenon as "the hand being quicker than the mind." Of course, this does not always occur, and rational challenging of dysfunctional thoughts may often prove to be effective. When there is an anticipatory awareness of the binge, cognitive self-control strategies are most likely to be effective. A lack of awareness of "automatic" binge eating seems to require alternative treatment interventions.

Controlled studies have yielded results ranging from modest to highly positive. Kirkley et al. (1985) compared a cognitive-behavioral treatment modeled after Fairburn's (1984) program to a nondirective control treatment. The cognitive-behavioral treatment consisted primarily of dietary management, cognitive restructuring, "interpersonal problem solving related to deficient assertive skills," and relaxation training. The nondirective control group discussed their food choices, eating frequency, eating rate, binge patterns, vomiting rituals, the role of stress in their bulimia, and ideas about forbidden foods, but were not instructed as to how to alter these behaviors. The cognitive-behavioral treatment produced significantly greater reductions in binge eating and vomiting. Both treatments showed significant reductions in depression, anxiety, and cognitions associated with eating disorders. However, the superiority of the cognitive-behavioral treatment at posttreatment had disappeared at a three-month follow-up. Although five patients had ceased binge eating and vomiting compared to only one in the control treatment, 23% of the cognitive-behavioral group and only 11% of the control group had relapsed. At follow-up, 77% and 78% of each group showed decreased vomiting frequencies of at least 60%.

Lee and Rush (1986) compared a cognitive-behavioral group treatment to a waiting-list control condition. The treatment initially emphasized relaxation training as a substitute for binge eating and as a means of coping with the negative affect that triggered binges. Thereafter, group discussion was aimed at identifying and altering dysfunctional thoughts about eating and weight. Ten of 14 patients were arbitrarily classified as "treatment responders" because they had decreased their binge eating by at least 50%. Three of 14 patients in the wait-list group could be so classified. Only 4 treated patients and 1 control subject were abstinent at posttreatment. Pretreatment binge frequency was unrelated to treatment response. Following treatment, vomiting declined from 13 to 4.2 times a week, with the wait-list group unchanged. Seven of the treated and one of the control patients were "treatment responders" (using a 50% cutoff), but only two of the treated patients had ceased vomiting. A 3–4-month follow-up showed that the treated patients maintained their improvement. Treated patients had significant reductions in depression at posttreatment and follow-up. The lack of control for attention-placebo factors makes it impossible to attribute changes to the treatment itself.

Ordman and Kirschenbaum (1985) also compared a treatment consisting of cognitive restructuring, behavioral techniques, and "process-oriented psycho-therapy" to a waiting-list control group. Treatment, averaging 15 weekly sessions in duration, produced greater reductions in binge-purge frequencies than the control group. Nevertheless, at posttreatment, 3 patients were still bingeing-vomiting more than once a week, and only 2 were abstinent. No follow-up was reported. Reductions in depression and general psychological adjustment assessed by the SCL-90 (Derogatis, 1977) were obtained following treatment, but patients did not score in the normative range of these measures.

The most encouraging findings have been reported by Fairburn et al. (1986). They showed that both Fairburn's (1984) cognitive-behavioral treatment (CBT) and a short-term form of focal psychotherapy largely eliminated binge eating and vomiting in patients with relatively severe bulimia nervosa, improvements that were maintained over a one-year follow-up. The CBT treatment was superior to psychotherapy in terms of its effects on patients' general clinical status, psycho-pathology, social adjustment, and self-assessment of outcome. Lacey (1983), using a more eclectic treatment, but with an emphasis on cognitive restructuring, also reported substantial improvement in his bulimic patients at posttreatment and over a two-year follow-up.

Exposure and Response Prevention

It is important to point out that in Fairburn's (1984) program, explicit behavioral procedures are used to achieve the cognitive changes deemed critical to eliminating bulimia. Examples include the instructions to patients to eat three meals a day, regularly; to gradually introduce "forbidden" foods into their diet; and to weigh themselves only once a week. These instructions are designed to disconfirm rigid and dysfunctional cognitions about obsessive concern with dieting and the putative effects of eating in a more normal fashion. Fairburn notes that as patients follow these behavioral instructions, their dysfunctional cognitions decline and no "formal cognitive restructuring" is required. We have found, however, that at least for some patients, encouraging them to comply with behavioral interventions such as these is a difficult matter (Wilson, Rossiter, Lindholm, & Tebbutt, 1986b). Here cognitive restructuring may be invaluable not so much as a means of stopping binges or purges directly, but in preparing patients for the use of behavioral procedures and facilitating compliance with specific behavioral procedures, such as exposure and response prevention.

Exposure and response prevention is a behavioral technique that warrants particular attention, both because of its theoretical appeal and its empirical track record with clinical disorders, including bulimia nervosa. The use of exposure and response prevention [which we refer to as "exposure and vomit prevention" (EVP) in this context; Wilson et al., 1986a] in the treatment of bulimia nervosa derived, as I noted before, from Rosen and Leitenberg's (1982) analysis of the disorder in terms of the two-factor, anxiety-reduction model. Treatment is directed at preventing vomiting and ensuring exposure to the cues that elicit this behavior. Uncontrolled clinical series (Giles, Young, & Young, 1985; Wilson et al., 1986b) and studies using single-case experimental designs have shown that EVP appears to be an effective technique (Leitenberg et al., 1984: Rossiter & Wilson, 1985). The point here is that it need not, however, be predicated on the adoption of the now questionable two-factor formulation of the extinction of avoidance/compulsive behavior. Cognitive-learning theory holds that behavioral procedures such as EVP work not because they produce extinction of classically conditioned anxiety responses, but because they alter mediating cognitive processes encapsulated in the concept of self-efficacy (Bandura, 1982; Wilson et al., 1986b). Behavioral procedures are reliably more effective than cognitive (verbal) methods in changing both avoidance behavior and related cognitive processes (Rachman & Wilson, 1980). EVP, then, would be preferred to verbal cognitive-restructuring methods in changing the dysfunctional attitudes and cognitions that characterize bulimia nervosa.

EMPIRICAL FINDINGS.   Consistent with the foregoing predictions, EVP appears to be more effective than verbal cognitive restructuring (Rossiter & Wilson, 1985; Wilson et al., 1986a). In the latter study, EVP produced significantly greater change than cognitive restructuring alone—a verbal/symbolic technique—in both binge/vomiting frequency and self-efficacy. A post-hoc classification of patients from both treatments into responders and nonresponders shows no difference in self-efficacy prior to therapy, but significantly greater self-efficacy among responders at posttreatment. Similarly, Schneider and O'Leary (1986) found that increases in self-efficacy following cognitive-behavioral treatment were associated with reductions in vomiting frequency in high-risk situations, such as negative moods.

Another major prediction of self-efficacy theory is that clients' efficacy expectations at posttreatment significantly influence the probability of relapse. The higher the strength of self-efficacy, the more persistent clients will be in coping constructively with high-risk situations without resort to substance abuse. To test this prediction of self-efficacy theory, we compared clients who were either abstinent or improved at posttreatment and who maintained their therapeutically induced success at follow-up with abstinent or improved clients at posttreatment but who subsequently relapsed. The former group showed significantly greater increases in efficacy expectations following treatment than the latter (Wilson et al., 1986b). Consistent with this general finding, Schneider and O'Leary (1986) have reported that efficacy ratings of ability to resist binge eating in negative mood states may predict which mood states are probable antecedents of binge eating in individual clients.

Other findings are inconsistent with the anxiety model of EVP but not the cognitive-social learning conceptualization. The anxiety model states that binge eating initially reduces the negative emotional state that triggers the binge. Binge eating leads to a fear of gaining weight, however, which is then reduced by self-induced vomiting (Leitenberg et al., 1984). Imaginal representation of the stimuli proximally antecedent to the binge, on the one hand, and vomiting on the other should elicit the autonomic arousal which has been used to define the anxiety state (Borkovec, 1978). Yet, consistently our research shows that specific binge-related images do not elicit significantly greater heart rate than does a neutral image (Rossiter & Wilson, 1985; Wilson et al., 1986a). Leitenberg et al. (1984) also failed to obtain increases in heart rate (HR) while their bulimic patients were actually eating. In the latter study, HR was desynchronous with both eating and self-report of anxiety. Patients in my research similarly showed desynchrony between changes in HR to imaginal representations of bingeing and binge/vomit scenes. Williamson et al. (1985) also failed to show that bulimics responded with greater psychophysiological arousal than did normal controls while eating a standard meal. A subsequent analysis showed that the most severe bulimics reacted more autonomically than did nonbulimic controls.

In an additional departure from the findings with the treatment of phobic disorders, HR in the bulimic patients in the Wilson et al. (1986b) study did not show a significant reduction from pre- to posttreatment in their EVP treatment. Rather, HR remained stable across different stimuli and assessment phases of the study. These data are consistent with other reports that patients with bulimia nervosa show less autonomic reactivity than do either normals or anorexics who do not vomit (Calloway, Fonagy, & Wakeling, 1983; Rossiter, 1986; Salkind, Fincham, & Silverstone, 1980). These data are inconsistent with the two-factor anxiety-reduction explanation of bulimia nervosa and the mechanisms responsible for EVP's success.

We have evidence of another discrepancy between the treatment of bulimics and obsessive-compulsives with exposure and response prevention. Rossiter and Wilson (1985) found that their three patients treated successfully with EVP showed habituation of anxiety (Subjective Units of Disturbance) within each treatment session. However, only one patient showed habituation across sessions. A second showed no between-session habituation, and the third showed a slight increase. This pattern is inconsistent with the findings from the treatment of obsessive-compulsives, where lack of habituation across sessions has predicted treatment failure (Foa & Emmelkamp, 1983). We have since replicated this inconsistency (Wilson et al., 1986a). Some of our most successful patients have shown an increase in SUDS across EVP sessions (i.e., a failure of habituation as it is defined in the anxiety-disorders literature), whereas treatment failures have shown habituation. These data dovetail with Leitenberg et al.'s (1984) findings. In that study, one subject reported increased anxiety ratings across sessions despite showing the greatest reduction in daily vomiting frequency. Another subject, who showed habituation across sessions, failed to show any reduction in daily vomiting. The reasons for these discrepancies and their implications require further analysis.

Body-image disturbance (BID) has been proposed as a cognitive/perceptual mechanism responsible for anorexia nervosa (Bruch, 1973) and bulimia nervosa (Freeman, Beach, Davis, & Solyom, 1985: Touyz, Beumont, Collins, McCabe, & Jupp, 1984). In this connection, Freeman et al. (1985) have reported that of bulimic patients who no longer binged and vomited at posttreatment, only those who showed positive changes in BID maintained their therapeutic improvement. Failure to produce changes in BID, regardless of changes in binge eating and vomiting frequencies, predicted relapse. This pattern of findings is consistent with what we know about social cognition and the importance of effecting changes in relevant cognitive schemata if durable improvement is to be achieved (Goldfried & Robins, 1983; Wilson, 1986b). Experimental analyses of the relative predictive power of BID and the more focused measures of self-efficacy in coping with high-risk situations in relation to maintenance of therapeutic improvement are warranted.

Freeman et al.'s (1985) finding complements one of Fairburn and Cooper's

(1984a) findings from their community study of binge eating and self-induced vomiting. They classified subjects according to frequencies of vomiting: those who vomited once a week or less; those who vomited between 2 and 6 times a week; and those who vomited at least once a day. These groups were, to use Fairburn and Cooper's words, "remarkably similar" on other measures, including psychiatric symptomatology. These researchers concluded that

> behavioural indices of bulimia nervosa, such as the frequency of binge eating or self-induced vomiting, may be poor measures of clinical severity, since people with markedly different eating habits may nevertheless have all the other characteristic features of the condition to an equivalent degree. (p. 409)

Garner et al. (1984) issued a similar caveat, as noted above. These findings fit well with the cognitive-social learning analysis of bulimia nervosa and indicate that a straightforward behavioristic approach is necessarily limited.

CLINICAL CONSIDERATIONS.   One of the problems with the anxiety model of bulimia nervosa was that likening the use of EVP with bulimia nervosa to that of obsessive-compulsive disorders has its limitations. For example, the compulsive handwasher can be assured that if he refrains from washing his hands after touching a "contaminated" object, no adverse consequence will follow. Disconfirmation of the patient's fear is unequivocal. The same cannot be said of the person with bulimia nervosa. In her case, engaging in a binge and then refraining from vomiting *may* result in what for the patient is a particularly dreaded outcome—weight gain. Accordingly, this possibility, and the fear, conflict, and resistance it breeds, must be addressed in treatment. In the process, the psychosocial context described by Striegel-Moore et al. (1986) and others necessarily features prominently in therapy.

The forms of resistance to a procedure such as EVP, ranging from dropping out of therapy to participating in but undermining the technique, are described by Wilson et al. (1986b). Overcoming this resistance requires a good therapeutic relationship in which the therapist is seen as both credible and trustworthy, a careful explanation of the rationale behind the technique, and intensive cognitive restructuring devoted to attitudes and fears about weight control. An important aspect of the latter is helping the patient to define her self-worth in terms other than physical appearance and moving her toward an acceptance of her body shape and weight. Inevitably, in this part of therapy, patients have to be helped to cope better with societal pressures to look slim and svelte, regardless of biological boundaries on eating and weight management. Influenced by Beck's (1976) cognitive therapy, we frame the exposure and response prevention sessions as a behavioral experiment, the outcome of which the patient must discover for herself. We emphasize to each patient that whereas most of our patients who have participated in this procedure have not gained weight, there is no guarantee that *she* will not. However, in the event that she does gain weight, we can teach her healthier, more sensible, yet effective methods for weight control. It is my impression that this directness and candor is most helpful in overcoming reluctance to participate in the technique. It is also useful to inform patients that self-induced vomiting does not ensure that they eliminate all of the calories they had ingested. This is one reason that most patients do not always gain weight when they cease the binge/purge cycle (Fairburn et al., 1986). And as several investigators have pointed out, bulimics may believe that they would gain weight by eating normally if they did not purge.

We are also testing the following strategy for overcoming resistance. We videotaped successfully treated patients discussing their initial emotional response when the therapist introduced the procedure—how they felt threatened, anxious, or angry. They relate how they were helped, however, as they persevered with the procedure. This strategy—which we call "vicarious pre-therapy exposure"—has its origins in social-learning theory on the one hand and client-centered therapy on the other. In terms of the former, the guiding principle is vicarious learning (specifically, the use of a coping as opposed to a mastery model—one who admits freely to strong initial resistance but who gradually learns to value the technique). The latter involves what Truax (1963) called "vicarious therapy pretraining"—a means of providing both cognitive and experiential structuring of "how to be a good client." Our initial clinical impressions are encouraging.

In sum, our use of EVP is guided by social-learning theory. The method is aimed at altering patients' perceptions and beliefs about themselves and their eating, and at developing a sense of efficacy. In this connection, it is noteworthy that Garner et al. (1984) found that the ineffectiveness subscale of the EDI was one of only two that differentiated anorexic patients from their weight-occupied controls. These same authors recall that Bruch (1973) emphasized ineffectiveness as the primary "ego deficit" from which other cognitive/perceptual problems derive. Self-efficacy provides a more sharply defined analysis of "ineffectiveness," and social-learning theory offers demonstrably more powerful treatment methods for increasing a sense of efficacy.

Parenthetically, although Rosen and Leitenberg (1982) derived their exposure and response prevention treatment from animal-conditioning research and tend to discuss it as a conditioning treatment, they also observe that a goal of their therapy is the modification of irrational beliefs.

Can the Cognitive-Social Learning Model Account for the Results of Pharmacotherapy?

Different studies of the effects of treating bulimics with antidepressant drugs have yielded conflicting findings (Wilson, 1986a). Moreover, even the studies showing positive results can be criticized on methodological grounds (Yager,

1985). Nevertheless, it seems reasonable to assume that antidepressant drugs (typically imipramine and MAOIs) are effective, at least in the short-term, with some patients (Agras et al. 1987). Any comprehensive cognitive-social learning account of bulimic nervosa must account for these results.

Pope et al.'s (1983) original notion that antidepressant medication is effective because bulimia nervosa is really a form of affective illness now seems untenable for the majority of bulimics. Walsh et al. (1984) have proposed an alternative mechanism for the effects of antidepressant drugs. They suggest that these drugs reduce the anxiety or tension that often precedes binge eating. Studies have shown that coping with negative emotional states is the main proximal precipitant of binge eating (Johnson et al., 1982: Wilson et al., 1986a). Furthermore, it appears that self-induced vomiting, which initially serves to reduce the fear of weight gain, secondarily, for some bulimics, comes to function as a generalized reinforcer by virtue of reduction of dysphoric feelings. As Johnson and Larson (1982) put it, many bulimics who originally purged so that they could binge subsequently binge so that they can purge.

Both the tricyclics and MAOIs, as investigators in the area of anxiety disorders have stressed (Marks et al., 1983; Zitrin, Klein, Woerner, & Ross, 1983), have general antidysphoria and anti-anxiety as well as antidepressant effects.[2]

Walsh et al.'s (1984) proposal is plausible, and it lends itself to an explanation of how a cognitive-behavioral analysis can subsume the successful results of antidepressant drug treatment. In this context, both cognitive-behavioral strategies and drug treatment are designed to counteract the negative psychosocial factors (anxiety, stress, and the like) that are the antecedents to bingeing or vomiting. The critical question then is whether antidepressant drugs, seen in this light, offer any distinctive benefits above those conferred by cognitive-behavioral treatments aimed at the same target variables. There is evidence that drug treatment is marked by high rates of relapse when the drug is withdrawn. Although cognitive-behavioral treatments are hardly free from problems of relapse, the long-term effects seem to be superior to those achieved with drug treatment. This finding, together with other factors such as the need to be selective with patients for whom antidepressant drugs are appropriate (Walsh et al., 1984), suggest that cognitive-behavioral treatments are generally to be preferred as an initial treatment for most patients.

Prognostic Factors

Treatment effects bear on the nature of bulimia nervosa in still other ways. Fairburn and Cooper (1984b) found that in their study of the clinical characteristics of patients with bulimia nervosa, roughly 25% had had anorexia nervosa in the past. Yet, patients in this subgroup did not differ in terms of current clinical features from those without such a history. Leon et al. (1985) reported the same finding. However, the presence of a history of anorexia nervosa or a history of low body weight may well prove to be an important predictor of treatment outcome. Wilson et al. (1986a) found that their patients with the lowest past weights fared poorly on outcome. In particular, these subjects accounted for all of the dropouts. Agras et al. (1987) have reported a strong association between previous lowest weight and response to imipramine treatment, suggesting that this is an important prognostic factor. These findings are consistent with Hawkins' (1984) and Lacey's (1983) reports that patients with anorectic tendencies have a poor prognosis.

Garner et al. (1985) found that on both clinical and psychometric measures, normal-weight bulimics resembled bulimic anorexics and that both groups differed from anorexics of the restricting type. They accordingly emphasized that their results "failed to support the diagnostic distinction between bulimia in anorexic women and bulimia of equal severity in normal weight women" (p. 581).[3]

It can be argued, however, that the results of treatment outcome do support an important diagnostic distinction. All in all, the results on the treatment of bulimics give cause for cautious optimism. Consider the positive findings of studies by Connors, Johnson, and Stuckey (1984), Fairburn et al. (1986), Kirkley et al. (1985), Lacey (1983), Leitenberg et al. (1984), Wilson et al. (1986b)—not to mention some of the positive findings with pharmacological treatment (Agras et al., 1987; Walsh et al., 1984)—among others. Much of this treatment, it should also be emphasized, consisted of relatively brief, outpatient therapy. Compare these findings to the less positive outcomes obtained with anorexia nervosa (Agras & Kraemer, 1984), even after much lengthier and usually inpatient treatment. This differential response rate to treatment must reflect on differences in the two sets of patients in question.

CONCLUDING COMMENTS

A cognitive-behavioral analysis accommodates much of the available evidence on the nature of bulimia nervosa. It seems best suited to conceptualizing the maintenance and modification of bulimia. It does not offer a complete or adequate explanation of etiology and encounters difficulties in accommodating some of the existing knowledge about the development of eating disorders. We do not know why only a subset of weight-troubled, restrained eaters become bulimic, while others do not. As yet undetermined biological, personal, and familial factors are, singly and in combination, all plausible possibilities.

A cognitive-behavioral perspective does lead directly to specific treatment strategies that have thus far yielded encouraging success. Several findings from the treatment literature are consistent with this approach. For example, there is the superiority of behaviorally based methods (e.g., EVP) over verbal procedures (e.g., cognitive restructuring). It appears that specific behavioral methods must be implemented within a treatment that addresses the psychosocial determinants of bulimia nervosa. This fits well with the cognitive-social learning model and less well with a more traditional conditioning framework. Most importantly, this approach is heuristic—it points to several lines of experimental inquiry that are likely to advance our knowledge in this area.

We do not yet have reliably effective treatment methods for the full spectrum of patients with bulimia nervosa, nor do we have established prognostic indicators. We are far from answering the ultimate treatment outcome question: What treatment, applied by whom, is most effective for what problem in which person? (Paul, 1967). The literature unmistakably informs us that there is considerable heterogeneity among patients with bulimia nervosa. It would be a mistake to search for the bulimic personality, just as the quest for a uniform personality has proved futile in other areas. Future treatment studies, in particular, need to assess, more objectively and systematically than heretofore, the varying forms of psychopathology that may accompany bulimia nervosa and relate them to short- and long-term outcomes.

REFERENCES

Agras, W. S., Dorlan, B., Kirkley, B., Arnow, B., & Bachman, J. (1987). Imipramine in the treatment of bulimia: A double-blind controlled study. *International Journal of Eating Disorders, 6*, 29–38.

Agras, W. S., & Kraemer, H. (1984). The treatment of anorexia nervosa: Do different treatments have different outcomes? In A. J. Stunkard & E. Stellar (Eds.), *Eating and its disorders* (pp. 193–208). New York: Raven Press.

Bandura, A. (1978). Reflections on self-efficacy. *Advances in Behaviour Research and Therapy, 1*, 237–269.

Bandura, A. (1982). Self-efficacy mechanisms in human agency. *American Psychologist, 37*, 122–147.

Beck, A. T. (1976). *Cognitive therapy and the emotional disorders.* New York: International Universities Press.

Beck, G., & Barlow, D. (1984). Current conceptualizations of sexual dysfunction: A review and an alternative perspective. *Clinical Psychology Review, 4*, 363–378.

Birtchnell, S., Lacey, J. H., & Harte, A. (1985). Body image distortion in bulimia nervosa. *British Journal of Psychiatry, 147*, 408–412.

Borkovec, T. D. (1978). Self-efficacy: Cause or reflection of behavioral change? *Advances in Behaviour Research and Therapy, 1*, 163–170.

Brotman, A. W., Herzog, D. B., & Woods, S. W. (1984). Antidepressant treatment of bulimia: The relationship between bingeing and depressive symptomatology. *Journal of Clinical Psychology, 45*, 7–9.

Bruch, H. (1973). *Eating disorders: Obesity, anorexia nervosa and the person within.* New York: Basic Books.

Calloway, P., Fonagy, P., & Wakeling, A. (1983). Autonomic arousal in eating disorders: Further evidence for the clinical subdivision of anorexia nervosa. *British Journal of Psychiatry, 142*, 38–42.

Connors, M., Johnson, C., & Stuckey, M. K. (1984). Treatment of bulimia with brief psycho-educational group therapy. *American Journal of Psychiatry, 141*, 1512–1516.

Cooper, P. J., & Fairburn, C. G. (in press). The depressive symptoms of bulimia nervosa. *British Journal of Psychiatry*.

Derogatis, L. R. (1977). *SCL-90: Administration, scoring and procedures manual for the R(evised) version*. Baltimore: Johns Hopkins University, School of Medicine.

Ellis, A. (1970). *The essence of rational psychotherapy: A comprehensive approach to treatment*. New York: Institute for Rational Living.

Fairburn, C. G. (1984). Bulimia: Its epidemiology and management. In A. J. Stunkard & E. Stellar (Eds.), *Eating and its disorders*. New York: Raven Press.

Fairburn, C. G. (1985). A cognitive-behavioural treatment of bulimia. In D. M. Garner & P. E. Garfinkel (Eds.), *Handbook on psychotherapy for anorexia nervosa and bulimia* (pp. 160–192). New York: Guilford.

Fairburn, C. G., Cooper, Z., & Cooper, P. (1986). The clinical features and maintenance of bulimia nervosa. In K. D. Brownell & J. Foreyt (Eds.), *Physiology, psychology and treatment of eating disorders* (pp. 389–404). New York: Basic Books.

Fairburn, C. G., & Cooper, P. J. (1984a). Binge eating, self-induced vomiting and laxative abuse: A community study. *Psychological Medicine, 14*, 401–410.

Fairburn, C. G., & Cooper, P. J. (1984b). The clinical features of bulimia nervosa. *British Journal of Psychiatry, 144*, 238–246.

Fairburn, C. G., Kirk, J., O'Connor, M., & Cooper, P. (1986). A comparison of two psychological treatments for bulimia nervosa. *Behaviour Research and Therapy, 24*, 629–644.

Foa, E., & Emmelkamp, P. M. (Eds.). (1983). *Failures in behavior therapy*. New York: Wiley.

Freeman, R. J., Beach, B., Davis, R., & Solyom, L. (1985). The prediction of relapse in bulimia nervosa. *Journal of Psychiatric Research, 19*, 349–353.

Freemouw, W. J., & Heyneman, N. E. (1983). Cognitive styles and bulimia. *The Behavior Therapist, 6*, 143–144.

Garner, D., Garfinkel, P., & O'Shaughnessy, M. (1985). The validity of the distinction between bulimia with and without anorexia nervosa. *American Journal of Psychiatry, 142*, 581–587.

Garner, D. M., Garinkel, P., Schwartz, D., & Thompson, M. (1980). Cultural expectations of thinness in women. *Psychological Reports, 47*, 483–491.

Garner, D. M., Olmsted, M., & Polivy, J. (1983). Development and validation of a multidimensional eating disorder inventory for anorexia nervosa and bulimia. *International Journal of Eating Disorders, 2*, 15–34.

Garner, D. M., Olmsted, M., Polivy, J., & Garfinkel, P. E. (1984). Comparison between weight-preoccupied women and anorexia nervosa. *Psychosomatic Medicine, 46*, 255–266.

Giles, T. R., Young, R. R., & Young, D. E. (1985). Behavioral treatment of severe bulimia. *Behavior Therapy, 16*, 393–405.

Glynn, S., & Ruderman, A. (1985). *The development and validation of an eating self-efficacy scale*. Unpublished manuscript, University of Illinois at Chicago.

Goldfried, M., & Robins, C. (1983). Self-schemas, cognitive bias, and the processing of therapeutic experiences. In P. C. Kendall (Ed.), *Advances in cognitive-behavioral research and therapy* (Vol. 2). New York: Academic Press.

Gormally, J. (1984). The obese binge eater: Diagnosis, etiology, and clinical issues. In R. C. Hawkins, W. Fremouw, & P. Clement (Eds.), *The binge-purge syndrome* (pp. 47–73). New York: Springer.

Hawkins, R. C. (1984, November). *Cognitive-behavioral treatment of bulimia: Overview and clinical data*. Paper presented at Association for Advancement of Behavior Therapy, Philadelphia.

Herzog, D. B. (1984). Are anorexic and bulimic patients depressed? *American Journal of Psychiatry, 141*, 1594–1597.

Hudson, J. I., Pope, H. G., & Jonas, J. M. (1984). Treatment of bulimia with antidepressants: Theoretical considerations and clinical findings. In A. J. Stunkard & E. Stellar (Eds.), *Eating and its disorders*. New York: Raven Press.

Hudson, J. I., Pope, H. G., Jonas, J. M., & Yurgelin-Todd, D. (1983). Family history study of anorexia nervosa and bulimia. *British Journal of Psychiatry, 142,* 133–138.

Hugdahl, K. (1981). The three-systems model of fear and emotion—a critical examination. *Behaviour Research and Therapy, 19,* 75–86.

Huon, G. F., & Brown, L. B. (1986). Body images in anorexia nervosa and bulimia nervosa. *The International Journal of Eating Disorders, 5,* 421–440.

Johnson, C., & Larson, R. (1982). Bulimia: An analysis of moods and behavior. *Psychosomatic Medicine, 44,* 333–345.

Johnson, C., Lewis, C., & Hagman, J. (1984). The syndrome of bulimia. *Psychiatric Clinics of North America, 7,* 247–273.

Johnson, C. L., Stuckey, M. K., Lewis, L. D., & Schwartz, D. M. (1982). Bulimia: A descriptive survey of 316 cases. *International Journal of Eating Disorders, 2,* 1–15.

Johnson, W., Schlundt, D., & Jarrell, M. (1986). Exposure and response prevention, training in energy balance, and problem solving therapy for bulimia nervosa. *International Journal of Eating Disorders, 5,* 35–46.

Johnson-Sabine, E., Wood, K., Mann, A., & Wakeling, A. (1985). A study of the association of current social pressures with abnormal eating attitudes. *International Journal of Eating Disorders, 4,* 101–106.

Kirkley, B. G., Schneider, J. A., Agras, W. S., & Bachman, J. A. (1985). A comparison of two group treatments for bulimia. *Journal of Consulting and Clinical Psychology, 53,* 43–48.

Kog, E., & Vandereycken, W. (1985). Family characteristics of anorexia nervosa and bulimia: A review of the research literature. *Clinical Psychology Review, 5,* 159–180.

Kog, E., Vertommen, H., & Degroote, T. (1985). Family interaction research in anorexia nervosa: The use and measure of a self-report questionnaire. *International Journal of Family Psychiatry, 6,* 227–244.

Lacey, J. H. (1983). Bulimia nervosa, binge eating, and psychogenic vomiting: A controlled treatment study and long term outcome. *British Medical Journal, 286,* 1609–1613.

Lazarus, A. A. (1981). *The practice of multimodal therapy.* New York: Springer.

Lee, N. F., & Rush, A. J. (1986). Cognitive-behavioral group therapy for bulimia. *The International Journal of Eating Disorders, 5,* 599–616.

Lee, M., Rush, A. J., & Mitchell, J. E. (1985). Bulimia and depression. *Journal of Affective Disorders, 9,* 231–238.

Leitenberg, H., Gross, J., Peterson, J., & Rosen, J. C. (1984). Analysis of an anxiety model and the process of change during exposure plus response prevention treatment of bulimia nervosa. *Behavior Therapy, 15,* 3–20.

Leon, G., Carroll, K., Chernyk, B., & Finn, B. (1985). Binge eating and associated habit patterns within college student and identified bulimic populations. *The International Journal of Eating Disorders, 4,* 43–58.

Lindholm, L., & Wilson, G. T. (1988). Body imge assessment in patients with bulimia nervosa and normal controls. *International Journal of Eating Disorders, 7,* 527–540.

Lowe, M. R. (inpress). Set point, restraint, and the limits of weight loss: A critical analysis. In W. G. Johnson (Ed.), *Advances in eating disorders* (Vol. 1). Greenwich, CT: JAI Press.

Marks, M., Gray, S., Cohen, D., Hill, R., Mawson, D., Ramm, E., & Stern, R. S. (1983). Imipramine and brief therapist-aided exposure in agoraphobics having self-exposure homework. *Archives of General Psychiatry, 40,* 153–162.

Marlatt, G. A. (1985). Relapse prevention: Theoretical rationale and overview of the model. In G. A. Marlatt & J. Gordon (Eds.), *Relapse prevention.* New York: Guilford. pp. 3–70.

Mathews, A., & MacLeod, C. (1985). Selective processing of threat cues in anxiety states. *Behaviour Research and Therapy, 23,* 563–569.

Minuchin, S., Rosman, B., & Baker, L. (1978). *Psychosomatic families: Anorexia nervosa in context.* Cambridge, MA: Harvard University Press.

Mowrer, O. H. (1960). *Learning theory and behavior.* New York: Wiley.

O'Leary, K. D., & Wilson, G. T. (1987). *Behavior therapy: Application and outcome.* Englewood Cliffs, NJ: Prentice-Hall.

Ordman, A. M., & Kirschenbaum, D. S. (1985). Cognitive-behavioral therapy for bulimia: An initial outcome study. *Journal of Consulting and Clinical Psychology, 53,* 305–313.

Paul, G. L. (1967). Outcome research in psychotherapy. *Journal of Consulting Psychology, 31,* 109–118.

Polivy, J., & Herman. P. (1985). Dieting and binging: A causal analysis. *American Psychologist, 40,* 193–201.

Polivy, J., Herman, C. P., Olmsted, M., & Jazwinski, C. (1984). Restraint and binge eating. In R. C. Hawkins, W. J. Fremouw, & P. Clement (Eds). *The binge-purge syndrome* (pp. 104–122). New York: Springer.

Pope, H. G., Hudson, H. I., Jonas, J. M., & Yurgelun-Todd, D. (1983). Antidepressant treatment of bulimia: Preliminary experience and practical recommendations. *Journal of Clinical Psychopharmacology, 3,* 274–281.

Rachman, S. & Wilson, G. T. (1980). *Effects of the psychological therapies.* Oxford: Pergamon Press.

Rodin, J., Silberstein, L., & Striegel-Moore, R. (1985). Women and weight: A normative discontent. In T. Sonderegger (Ed.), *Psychology and gender: Nebraska symposium on motivation* (pp. 267–307). Lincoln, NE: University of Nebraska Press.

Rosen, J. C., & Leitenberg, E. (1982). Bulimia nervosa: Treatment with exposure and response prevention. *Behavior Therapy, 13,* 117–124.

Rossiter, E. M. (1986). *Psychological and psychophysiological characteristics of patients with bulimia nervosa, and nonbulimic restrained or unrestrained eaters.* Unpublished doctoral dissertation, Rutgers University, New Brunswick, NJ.

Rossiter, E. M., & Wilson, G. T. (1985). Cognitive restructuring and response prevention in the treatment of bulimia nervosa. *Behaviour Research and Therapy, 23,* 349–360.

Ruderman, A. (1985). Dysphoric mood and overeating: A test of restraint theory's disinhibition hypothesis. *Journal of Abnormal Psychology, 94,* 78–85.

Russell, G. (1979). Bulimia nervosa: An ominous variant of anorexia nervosa. *Psychological Medicine, 9,* 429–448.

Sabine, E. J., Yonace, A., Farrington, A. J., Barratt, K. H., & Wakeling, A. (1983). Bulimia nervosa: A placebo controlled double-blind therapeutic trial of mianserin. *British Journal of Clinical Pharmacology, 15,* 195S–202S.

Salkind, M. R., Fincham, J., & Silverstone, T. (1980). Is anorexia nervosa a phobic disorder? A psychophysiological inquiry. *Biological Psychiatry, 15,* 803–808.

Schneider, J., & O'Leary, A. (1986). *The role of perceived self-efficacy in recovery from bulimia: A preliminary examination.* Unpublished manuscript, Stanford University.

Schwartz, R. C., Barrett, M., & Saba, G. (1984). Family therapy for bulimia. In D. M. Garner & P. Garfinkel (Eds.), *Handbook of psychotherapy for anorexia nervosa and bulimia* (pp. 280–310). New York: Guilford.

Smith, M. C., & Thelen, M. H. (1984). Development and validation of a test for bulimia. *Journal of Consulting and Clinical Psychology, 52,* 863–872.

Stern, S. L., Dixon, K., Nemzer, E., Lake, M., Sansone, R., Smeltzer, M., Lantz, S., & Schrier, S. (1984). Affective disorder in the families of women with normal weight bulimia. *American Journal of Psychiatry, 141,* 1224–1227.

Striegel-Moore, R., Silberstein, L., & Rodin, J. (1986). Toward an understanding of risk ractors for bulimia. *American Psychologist, 41,* 246–263.

Strober, M. (1981). The significance of bulimia in juvenile anorexia nervosa: An exploration of possible etiologic factors. *International Journal of Eating Disorders, 1,* 28–43.

Strober, M., Morrell, W., Burroughs, J., Salkin, B., & Jacobs, C. (1985). A controlled family study of anorexia nervosa. *Journal of Psychiatric Research, 19,* 239–246.

Stunkard, A. J., & Messick, S. (1985). The three-factor eating questionnaire to measure dietary restraint, disinhibition, and hunger. *Journal of Psychosomatic Research, 29,* 71–83.

Thompson, J. K., Berland, N., Linton, P., & Weinsier, R. (1986). Utilization of a self-adjusting light beam in the objective assessment of body distortion in seven eating disorder groups. *International Journal of Eating Disorders, 5,* 113–120.

Touyz, S., Beumont, P., Collins, J., McCabe, M., & Jupp, J. (1984). Body shape perception and its disturbance in anorexia nervosa. *British Journal of Psychiatry, 144,* 167–171.

Truax, C. (1963). Discussed in A. Goldstein, K. Heller, & L. Sechrest (Eds.). (1966). *Psychotherapy and the psychology of behavior change.* New York: Wiley.

Walsh, T. B., Stuart, J. W., Roose, S. P., Gladis, M., & Glassman, A. H. (1984). Treatment of bulimia with phenelzine: A double-blind placebo-controlled study. *Archives of General Psychiatry, 41,* 1105–1109.

Williamson, D., Kelley, M. L., Davis, C. J., Ruggiero, L., & Veitia, M. C. (1985). The psychophysiology of bulimia. *Advances in Behaviour Research and Therapy, 7,* 163–172.

Willmuth, M. E., Leitenberg, H., Rosen, J., Fondacaro, K., & Gross, J. (1985). Body size distortion in bulimia nervosa. *International Journal of Eating Disorders, 4,* 71–78.

Wilson, G. T. (1982). Clinical issues and strategies in behavior therapy. In C. M. Franks, G. T. Wilson, P. Kendall, & K. Brownell (Eds.), *Annual review of behavior therapy: Theory and practice* (Vol. 8, pp. 305–345). New York: Guilford.

Wilson, G. T. (1985). Fear reduction methods and the treatment of anxiety disorders. In C. M. Franks, G. T. Wilson, P. Kendall, & K. Brownell (Eds.), *Annual review of behavior therapy* (Vol. 10, pp. 87–122). New York: Guilford.

Wilson, G. T. (1986a). Cognitive-behavioral and pharmacological therapies for bulimia. In K. D. Brownell & J. Foreyt (Eds.), *Physiology, psychology, and treatment of eating disorders* (pp. 450–475). New York: Basic Books.

Wilson, G. T. (1986b). Social psychological concepts in the theory and practice of behavior therapy. In P. Eelen & O. Fontaine (Eds.), *Behavior therapy: Beyond the conditioning framework.* Hillsdale, NJ: Lawrence Erlbaum. Pp. 150–179.

Wilson, G. T. (1987). Cognitive studies in alcoholism. *Journal of Consulting and Clinical Psychology, 55,* 310–324.

Wilson, G. T., & Lindholm. L. (1987). Bulimia nervoda and depression. *International Journal of Eating Disorders, 6,* 725–732.

Wilson, G. T., Rossiter, E., Kleifield, E., & Lindholm, L. (1986a). Cognitive-behavioral treatment of bulimia nervosa: A controlled evaluation. *Behaviour Research and Therapy, 24,* 277–288.

Wilson, G. T., Rossiter, E., Lindholm, L., & Tebbut, J. (1986b). *Cognitive-behavioral treatment of bulimia nervosa: Clinical issues and findings.* Unpublished manuscript, Rutgers University, New Brunswick, NJ.

Yager, J. (1985). The treatment of bulimia: An overview. In P. S. Powers & R. C. Fernandez (Eds.), *Current treatment of anorexia nervosa and bulimia.* New York: Karger.

Yates, A. J., & Sambrailo. F. (1984). Bulimia nervosa: A descriptive and therapeutic study. *Behaviour Research and Therapy, 22,* 503–518.

Zitrin, C. M., Klein, D. E., Woerner, M. G., & Ross, D. C. (1983). Treatment of phobias. *Archives of General Psychiatry, 40,* 125–138.

AUTHOR NOTES

*Preparation of this paper was made possible by grant MH40237 from NIMH. The contributions of Elise Rossiter and Linnea Lindholm are gratefully acknowledged.

[1]Gormally (1984) has reported that binge eating is most probable when individuals' perceived self-efficacy in this respect is low. This view fits with the data, discussed below, on the possible predictive value of self-efficacy in the treatment of patients with bulimia nervosa. Furthermore, Glynn and Ruderman (1985) have shown that women generally report lower self-efficacy in controlling overeating than men, a finding that meshes with the higher incidence of the disorder in women.

[2]I have elsewhere commented on the parallel that might be drawn between the behavioral and pharmacological treatment of anxiety disorders (e.g., agoraphobia) on the one hand and bulimia nervosa on the other (Wilson, 1986b). Exposure and response prevention squares off against imipramine as possibly the most effective treatment methods in both disorders. And there is continuing debate about conflicting drug findings and the putative mechanisms by which the drugs might exert their effect (Wilson, 1985).

[3]Contrary to Garner et al.'s (1984) findings, Herzog (1984) found a significantly higher rate of major depression in patients with anorexia nervosa than in those with bulimia.

6

DOES THE "BEST" BODY WEIGHT CHANGE WITH AGE?

Reubin Andres
National Institute on Aging

For every complex question there is always a
simple answer and it is always wrong.
—H. L. Mencken

The purpose of this chapter is limited to an analysis of the "weights for heights" associated with lowest total mortality—the basis for the weight goals in use in the United States for the past 45 years. As an essential aspect of this analysis, the issue of age effects on the weight-for-height association with mortality will be examined.

Several facts need to be listed, if only to emphasize the complexity of these analyses:

1. The weight-for-height tables that have been the standard for the U.S. for over 40 years have been constructed by actuaries of the Metropolitan Life Insurance Company. Three sets have been issued, all with the same familiar structure of separate tables for men and women and a range of weights for each of three body frame sizes for individual, one-inch increments in height. The 1942–1943 tables were called "Ideal," (*Statistical Bulletin*, 1942, 1943), the 1959 tables "Desirable" (*Statistical Bulletin*, 1959), and the most recent set simply "1983" (*Statistical Bulletin*, 1983). The 1942–1943 tables have passed into history, except for the fact that the phrase "ideal body weight" still appears in scientific publications, even though the authors used the 1959 or 1983 tables as their reference base for computing the degree of overweight in their subjects. The 1959 tables still find favor despite the fact that subjects were enrolled in the insurance study (Society of Actuaries, 1959) that provided the data for those tables some 35 to 50 years ago! The 1983 tables have been widely criticized, perhaps more so than the 1959 tables, undoubtedly because weights were modes-

tly liberalized. Thus, the Consensus Conference Statement on Health Implications of Obesity (1985), while noting that confusion exists over which table to use, states that "It is recognized that such increased body weight [which the 1983 tables allow] may contribute to high blood pressure, hypercholesterolemia, and glucose tolerance or similar risk factors, apart from the impact of weight on mortality." Further on: "Although not a specific recommendation of the panel, use of the lower weights [i.e., the 1959 tables] as goals would be advisable in the presence of any of the complications or risk factors . . . " such as those noted above.

It should be noted that even the 1983 tables are based on data from subjects enrolled some 15 to 35 years ago (Society of Actuaries, 1980). It is, of course, an integral feature of the design of prospective studies which provide mortality data that enrollment of subjects must occur years before data can be analyzed and reported. Still, other features being equal (or even favoring the 1983 tables, such as a distinctly higher percentage of subjects whose weights and heights were actually measured), it is difficult to defend a decision to favor a table that is based on the mortality experience of a population studied mainly in the 1930s and 1940s over one based on a similar population studied mainly in the 1950s and 1960s. I venture the suggestion that had the 1983 tables *lowered* the estimates of "best" weights as compared to the 1959 tables, they would have been hailed rather than criticized. We will never know. The Metropolitan Life Insurance Company actuaries simply went where the data took them—and the data took them to higher weights.

2. From all of this, a second fact emerges. The Metropolitan tables are based, as they emphasize, on total mortality as the dependent or outcome variable. Tables can, indeed, be constructed based on disease-specific mortality (coronary artery disease, cancers, diabetes, pneumonia and influenza, etc.) or on weight-for-height association with other risk factors (serum lipids, glucose tolerance, blood pressure, etc.). The uncomfortable fact is that separate tables would be needed for each dependent variable examined. The provision of a relatively simple table of weights which could be recommended to the public as a goal would be impossible. Theoretically, it would be possible to "weight" the various deleterious (and advantageous?) aspects of body weight to come up with a table based on "global health" or "quality of life," but that is far beyond what anyone has attempted, to date. It is total mortality which, in a sense, provides its own weighting for all of the specific causes of death. Furthermore, it is total mortality that has been the golden standard—or the golden outcome—for weight tables since the 1942–1943 Ideal Weight Tables.

3. The very fact that the traditional tables provide lower as well as upper limits indicates that the relationship of weight for height to mortality is not a simple linear one but, rather, better described as quadratic or U-shaped (or J-

shaped). There is, thus, a range of weights about the nadir of such a curve at which mortality is at its lowest, and it is this nadir which must be computed.

4. There are technical complexities involved in the use of weight for height as a surrogate for true fatness. The provision of weight ranges for three separate body frames is a gesture made at "correcting" for bony size; the elbow breadth is used to categorize body frame. The division of an overall weight range into three separate ranges must have been based on sweet reasonableness, since elbow breadths were not measured as a component of the insurance examination. But bony size is only part of this complexity. Muscle mass varies greatly among individuals. No prospective population studies to date have estimated muscle mass, skeletal mass, and fat mass of the subjects. And if such data were available, it would not provide practical guidelines to individuals who would need to have their body compositions determined in order to have an appropriate weight goal. So, for the time being, it is body weight that will occupy our attention. It is what we can analyze. Data from many populations have been published.

5. The population of "insured lives" studied by the insurance industry (Society of Actuaries, 1959, 1980) has been criticized on many counts. A sample of these criticisms includes: (1) cigarette smoking (an obesity confound) was not taken into account; (2) the subjects were largely Caucasian and middle class; (3) some subjects obtained more than one policy, each of which was separately counted; (4) a small fraction of the 1979 study and a larger fraction of the 1959 study did not have weights and heights measures—the subject's own statements were accepted; and (5) the mortality rate of the insured population is considerably lower than that of the overall U.S. population (the insured group had to have passed a medical examination in order to be included). A large number of studies have now been reported from the U.S., Europe, Japan, Israel, Australia, and several South Pacific islands.

There are still no reports from the major developing regions of the world. Such studies would not be immediately contributory to decision making for recommendations to the U.S. population; but, on the other hand, the standard tables in use here are probably irrelevant for a large percentage of the world's population. There are, sadly, almost no studies on the two major U.S. minority populations, Blacks and Latinos. And this leads us to the next point.

6. There is increasing evidence that not only is the amount of body fat important, but its pattern of distribution is important also (Vague & Bjorntorp, 1985). Only a population of middle-aged men in Gothenburg, Sweden has had mortality correlated with both obesity and fat distribution (Andres, 1985). The results are surprising. The Swedish men were divided for analysis into 9 groups—tertiles of body-mass index and tertiles of waist : hip circumferential ratios (WHR). Mortality was highest in the group with highest WHR and lowest body-mass index (sic). Studies in other populations are clearly needed. Strong

associations of WHR with such risk factors as glucose intolerance, hyper-lipidemia, and hypertension have also been reported (Vague et al., 1985). Since the fat-distribution pattern is genetically determined and since large racial differences exist in these patterns, weight recommendations in future tables will almost certainly have to take this variable into consideration.

With all of these problems in mind but, for the moment, in the background, we can consider whether the current standard, the 1983 Metropolitan tables, adequately describe the experience of the insured population as reported (Society of Actuaries, 1980). As clinical gerontologists, we have become sensitive to the fact that normative standards for clinical tests must frequently be age specific if gross overdiagnosis of abnormality (disease) is to be avoided. Thus, when we noted that the 1959 tables were said to be for persons ''aged 25 and over'' and the 1983 tables for persons 25 to 59 years of age (still a large age spread), we deemed it necessary to examine the possible impact of age on recommended weights. The rule that we had been taught to follow concerning body weight was that the best weight was that of the average, quite lean young adult, perhaps 20–25 years of age, and that that weight should be maintained throughout the life span. This rule then represented an example of a normative standard which did not change with age. Fortunately, the experience of the insurance industry is reported in tabular form in great detail (Society of Actuaries, 1980) so that independent analyses can be made. Mortality ratios are presented for men and for women for each decade of life from 20–29 to 60–69 years for each of five height ranges (from very short to very tall) and for 10-pound increments in body weight. We converted each height-weight group into a body-mass index (BMI; wt/ht^2, kg/m^2). For each age-sex group we then computed the quadratic relationship between BMI and mortality ratio. The number of deaths in each of the BMI groups was taken into account; that is, the data were appropriately ''weighted.'' Then, for the five age groups of men and of women, the nadir of the curve was computed (the BMI associated with lowest mortality). The two points of intersection of the curve with the 1.00 mortality ratio line (the mean mortality for that age-sex group) provided the range of BMIs associated with less-than-average mortality. The magnitude of the ranges that we computed is similar to those in the 1983 Metropolitan tables (the range from the lower weight for the small frame to the upper weight for the large frame). The Metropolitan actuaries have not reported how they computed the ranges in their tables, but the comparability between our ranges and theirs suggests that they also chose to select that range of weights associated with less-than-average mortality.

Our analyses demonstrated, however, that the BMI at the nadirs of the quadratic curves for both men and women increased with increased age (Andres, 1985). Furthermore, there was no consistent difference between the values of the BMI at nadir for men and women. The magnitude of the increase in BMI with age amounted to a weight increase of about 10 pounds per decade of life. We have, therefore, constructed an age-specific table (Table 6.1) of weights for heights which is no more complex than the 1983 Metropolitan table. Our table, the Gerontology Research Center (GRC) table, has a range of weights for each inch of height for each of five ages, but without separate tables for men and women and without division into frame sizes. The BMIs of the midpoints of the range of weights in the GRC table range linearly from 20.4 at age 25 to 26.8 at age 65. These can be compared with the midpoints of the total range of weights reported by Metropolitan (*Statistical Bulletin,* 1984). The mean BMI for the average American woman (64 inches tall) is 23.0, and for the average American man (69 inches tall) is 23.5. These BMIs are equivalent to what the GRC table recommends (by interpolation) for 41- and 44-year-old individuals. Since the Metropolitan tables are for individuals aged 25–59 years (average, 42 years), it can be seen that the GRC and Metropolitan 1983 tables actually are, on the

Table 6.1

Comparison of the Weight-for-height Tables from Actuarial Data:
Non-age-corrected Metropolitan Life Insurance Company
and Age-specific Gerontology Research Center Recommendations

Height		Metropolitan 1983 Weights*		Gerontology Research Center*				
		Men	Women	Age-specific Weight Range for Men and Women				
Feet	Inches	25–59 Yrs.		25 Yrs.	35 Yrs.	45 Yrs.	55 Yrs.	65 Yrs.
4	10		100–131	84–111	92–119	99–127	107–135	115–142
4	11		101–134	87–115	95–123	103–131	111–139	119–147
5	0		103–137	90–119	98–127	106–135	114–143	123–152
5	1	123–145	105–140	93–123	101–131	110–140	118–148	127–157
5	2	125–148	108–144	96–127	105–136	113–144	122–153	131–163
5	3	127–151	111–148	99–131	108–140	117–149	126–158	135–168
5	4	129–155	114–152	102–135	112–145	121–154	130–163	140–173
5	5	131–159	117–156	106–140	115–149	125–159	134–168	144–179
5	6	133–163	120–160	109–144	119–154	129–164	138–174	148–184
5	7	135–167	123–164	112–148	122–159	133–169	143–179	153–190
5	8	137–171	126–167	116–153	126–163	137–174	147–184	158–196
5	9	139–175	129–170	119–157	130–168	141–179	151–190	162–201
5	10	141–179	132–173	122–162	134–173	145–184	156–195	167–207
5	11	144–183	135–176	126–167	137–178	149–190	160–201	172–213
6	0	147–187		129–171	141–183	153–195	165–207	177–219
6	1	150–192		133–176	145–188	157–200	169–213	182–225
6	2	153–197		137–181	149–194	162–206	174–219	187–232
6	3	157–202		141–186	153–199	166–212	179–225	192–238
6	4			144–191	157–205	171–218	184–231	197–244

*Values in this table are for height without shoes and weight without clothes.
From Society of Actuaries (1980).

average, in remarkably close agreement. The differences in the tables are largely a consequence of the fact that Metropolitan lumped data for the broad age range of 25–59 years, while we constructed an age-specific table.

It is not entirely clear why Metropolitan chose to exclude data from the men and women in the 60–69 year decade of life. It could not be due to an inadequate number of deaths at that age. The mortality experience for the 60–69-year-old men was more extensive than for that of any of the age decades for women; furthermore, the number of deaths among the 60–69-year-old women was about equal to that of the 30–39-year-old women, and much greater than that for the 20–29-year-old women. Perhaps the very high BMIs at the nadir of the curves for the 60–69-year-old men and women (close to 27 kg/m^2) would have raised the mean values of BMI in a table that was not age specific to a level that was uncomfortably high. A significant increase would have been necessary had the age range in the Metropolitan tables been extended to 25–69 years. As we noted previously, the 1983 revisions received serious criticism, even for the small increase in weights (or BMIs) over those in the 1959 tables. A still higher increase may have been considered imprudent, and age-specific tables were evidently not considered acceptable.

Still, 60–69-year-old men and women have a right to expect advice on what they should weigh. The Metropolitan tables provide no guidance, although data for basing such recommendations are available in the insurance data set (Society of Actuaries, 1980). The solution to this problem, we believe, is the one that we have offered: Provide age-specific tables.

The progressive increase in "best" weight with age in the GRC table is based on cross-sectional weight-height measurements with follow-up of mortality. Thus, the GRC table should be interpreted as indicating that the best weight for survival for 65-year-old men and women is higher than the best weight for 25-year-olds. The logical implication is that actual weight gain (longitudinally) is associated with lower mortality. Reports of true longitudinal data are rare, however. Such studies would have repeatedly measured weights and heights over the adult life span, or at least over a significant portion of it. Mortality could then be related to levels of weight and to changes in weight with time. Two studies not only report BMIs at two stages of life, but also the effect of changes in BMI (Paffenbarger, Hyde, Wing, & Hsieh, 1986, study of Harvard students; Avons, Ducimetiere, & Rakotovao, 1983, study of Paris civil servants). Both studies report mortality experience related to weight in early adult life and in middle age or older and also present the effect of weight change between those ages on mortality. Initial weight and change in weight are, however, not considered together in a common analysis. A very obese 20-year-old would be expected to benefit from weight loss, while an excessively lean 20-year-old might be expected to benefit from weight gain. This kind of analysis, the examination of the effect on mortality of change in body weight related to initial body weight, has not been reported.

Still, there is considerable "tracking" in body weight over time. Obese young adults are more likely to be obese older adults than their leaner colleagues. Even though we do not have reports including weight and weight change in a single analysis, it might still be instructive to examine simply the effect of weight change on mortality after middle age.

The Paffenbarger study (Paffenbarger et al., 1986) involved measured weight and height on entry to Harvard College and values reported on questionnaires when the alumni were aged 35 to 74 years. The Avons study (Avons et al., 1983) involved measured weight and height at age 43–53 years and weight at age 20 by recall. Mortality rates were computed for each of five weight-change categories in each study. The Harvard study reports BMI in U.S. customary units, pounds and inches; the BMIs reported below have converted their values to metric units. Highest mortality for the Harvard alumni occurred in the group that, on average, gained the least weight, a BMI increase of less than 2.1 kg/m^2, followed by the group whose increase was 2.1 to 2.8. Lowest mortality occurred in those whose BMI increased from 2.8 to 3.5, but the two groups who gained from 3.5 to 4.2 and more than 4.2 kg/m^2 also had low mortality. In the Paris civil servants, highest mortality occurred in those whose weight gain was less than about 0.5 kg/m^2 or whose BMI fell (i.e., who lost weight). Next highest mortality occurred in the group whose gain in BMI exceeded about 6.5 kg/m^2, and lowest mortality occurred in the middle 3 of 5 groups, those whose BMI gain ranged from about 0.5 to 6.5. It can be computed from these reported BMI changes that unless the Harvard men gained about 23 pounds, mortality was high. In the Paris study, a gain of about 3 to 37 pounds was associated with the lowest mortality.

Longitudinal change in body weight is clearly a parameter which should be considered, but analysis of these results raises another question. Could the high mortality in those who lost weight or whose weight gain was relatively small be a consequence of illness which caused weight loss and which increased mortality? This remains a possibility. Still, increase in mortality at the other end of the weight-change spectrum either did not occur at all (Paffenbarger et al., 1986) or occurred only at very high levels of weight increase (Avons et al., 1983). These two longitudinal studies are at least consistent with the conclusion derived from cross-sectional insurance data that best weight increases with age.

We have, elsewhere, summarized our analysis of reports on 31 populations that examined the weight-mortality association (Andres, Elahi, Tobin, & Muller, 1985). We can ask whether these studies also support our conclusion that the Metropolitan 1983 tables provide weight goals that are inappropriately low for older individuals. The studies provide data on 57 different groups of individuals, mainly in Europe and the U.S., who are 50 or more years of age. In general, the lowest mortality in those studies occurs at BMIs far above the BMI at the midpoint of the medium frame of the Metropolitan 1983 tables, a commonly used reference value. Only in 1 of 35 male groups and in 3 of 23 female groups were BMIs below 22.5 for women and 22.4 for men, the cut points selected. If this analysis is limited to studies on U.S. populations, then only 1 of the 11 groups of older women and none of the 18 groups of older men had nadirs below those cut points. In fact, no male group had a nadir as low as 23.5, nor did any other female group. We conclude from this survey that not only are the Metropolitan weight standards too low for the insured population of older individuals, but that the overwhelming consensus of other studies worldwide demonstrate the incorrectness of applying Metropolitan 1983 standards to older individuals. The 1959 Metropolitan tables are even more inappropriate since the BMIs of the midpoint of the medium frame in those tables are about 21.6 for men and 21.2 for women, very much lower than the best BMIs computed in other studies.

The 1959 tables were certainly deemed acceptable by obesity authorities: They were the basis of the construction of the so-called "Fogarty tables" in the report of an NIH conference in 1973 (Bray, 1975). The 1983 tables (as well as the 1959 tables) have recently received a similar vote of confidence by an NIH panel (Consensus Conference Statement, 1985). In essence, then, the mortality experience of this insured population has been accepted as the basis of weight goals for the American public, despite the recognized limitations, some of which were noted above and which were also pointed out in the Consensus Conference Statement (1985).

Our analyses of these insurance data (Society of Actuaries, 1980) clearly demonstrate a powerful effect of age on the obesity-mortality curves in men and women. It is, then, no great leap of logic to accept the necessity of age-specific goals. If one accepts the validity of the insurance data set as a source for the construction of weight goals, there is no escaping the equal validity of providing age-specific goals.

To get to know a truth properly, one must polemicize it.—Novalis [Friedrich von Hardenberg]

REFERENCES

Andres, R. (1985). Mortality and obesity: The rationale for age-specific height-weight tables. In R. Andres, E. L. Bierman, & W. R. Hazzard (Eds.), *Principles of geriatric medicine* (pp. 311–318). New York: McGraw-Hill.

Andres, R., Elahi, D., Tobin, J. D., & Muller, D. (1985). Impact of age on weight goals. *Annals of Internal Medicine, 103,* 1030–1033.

Avons, P., Ducimetiere, P., & Rakotovao, R. (1983). Weight and mortality. *Lancet, 1,* 1104.

Bray, G. A. (Ed.). (1975). *Obesity in perspective: A conference sponsored by the John A. Fogarty International Center for Advanced Study in the Health Sciences* (Vol. 2, Part 1). Washington, D.C.: U.S. Government Printing Office, DHEW Publication No. (NIH) 75-708.

Ideal weights for women. (1942). *Statistical Bulletin, 23* (October), 6–8.

Ideal weights for women. (1943). *Statistical Bulletin, 24* (June), 6–8.

Measurement of overweight. (1984). *Statistical Bulletin, 65*(1), 20–23.

National Institutes of Health Consensus Development Panel on the Health Implications of Obesity. (1985). Health implications of obesity: National Institutes of Health Consensus Development Conference Statement. *Annals of Internal Medicine, 103,* 1073–1077.

New weight standards for men and women. (1959). *Statistical Bulletin, 40* (November–December), 1–3.

1983 Metropolitan height and weight tables. (1983). *Statistical Bulletin, 64* (January–June), 2.

Paffenbarger, R. S., Jr., Hyde, R. T., Wing, A. L., & Hsieh, C.-C. (1986). Physical activity, all-cause mortality, and longevity of college alumni. *New England Journal of Medicine, 314,* 605–613.

Society of Actuaries and Association of Life Insurance Medical Directors of America. (1959). *Build and blood pressure study.* Chicago, IL: Author.

Society of Actuaries and Association of Life Insurance Medical Directors of America. (1980). *Build study 1979.* Chicago, IL: Author.

Vague, J., & Bjorntorp, P., (Eds.). (1985). *Metabolic complications of human obesities.* Amsterdam: Excerpta Medica.

7

CARDIOVASCULAR AND NONCARDIOVASCULAR CONSEQUENCES OF OBESITY

William B. Kannel
Section of Preventive Medicine and Epidemiology,
Boston University School of Medicine

L. Adrienne Cupples
School of Public Health,
Boston University School of Medicine

There is long-standing interest in obesity as a predisposing factor for cardiovascular disease in particular and as a force of mortality in general (Bray, 1979; The Health Implications of Obesity, 1985). Insurance industry data has, for some time, recognized that obesity is linked to premature mortality (Lew, 1985). However, controversy has evolved concerning optimal weights and the independent contribution of obesity to cardiovascular disease (Mann, 1985; Keys, 1980; Anares, 1985). It now appears that not only is the general level of adiposity important, but that there is variable metabolic effect depending on how the fat is distributed (Bjorntorp, 1985).

This report examines the relation of various measures of adiposity to development of cardiovascular and noncardiovascular morbidity and mortality. It is based on 30 years of follow-up of the Framingham Study cohort, classified by their risk factor make-up, including weight. Findings are compared to other investigations.

THE FRAMINGHAM STUDY

A cohort made up of a two-thirds representative sample of 9,831 Framingham residents was recruited, who were between ages 30 and 62 years between 1948 and 1953 (Dawber, 1951). These subjects were then re-examined biennially for development of cardiovascular disease. Height and weight has been recorded on each biennial examination, along with other suspected risk factors, including blood pressure, serum cholesterol, blood sugar, cigarette habit, and uric acid (Shurtleff, 1974).

At the time of the fourth biennial examination, 2,420 women and 1,934 men aged 34–68 had some additional measurements of body configuration and fat distribution. Measurements obtained included height, weight, waist circumference, upper arm, lower arm, and wrist circumference; and subscapular, triceps, abdominal, and quadriceps skinfolds.

Evidence of development of cardiovascular disease was documented from biennial clinic examinations, hospital protocols, medical examiner's reports, and information from attending physicians. Minimal criteria for clinical events were applied by a panel of physicians to validate all newly acquired cardiovascular occurrences. Cardiovascular outcomes included: coronary heart disease, stroke, cardiac failure, or occlusive peripheral arterial disease (Shurtleff, 1974).

The statistical method used to explore the relation of risk factors in general and adiposity in particular to occurrence of cardiovascular and noncardiovascular morbidity and mortality was logistic regression analysis. This allows an assessment of the relationship of obesity to morbidity and mortality, adjusting for age and other risk factors associated both with adiposity and cardiovascular disease (Shurtleff, 1974).

PREVALENCE OF OBESITY

Obesity is defined as an excessive storage of energy in the form of fat. It has been variously defined and measured. A common and utilitarian way to characterize obesity is to take weight and height into account. Accepting 20% above desirable weight as obesity [a body-mass index (BMI) of 27.8 for men and 27.3 for women], there are 34 million adult Americans who are obese. However, depending on definitions, obesity (excess body fat) affects from one-tenth to one-third of the adult population in the U.S. (Abraham, 1980; United States DHEW 1971–1974). Paradoxically, obesity appears to be more prevalent in low- rather than high-income subgroups of the population and afflicts black more than white women. There is a virtual epidemic of obesity in middle-aged black women. Compared to a 30% prevalence in white women 45–55 years of age, 60% of black women are obese (Van Italli, 1985).

Although obesity is more prevalent in women than in men, secular trends indicate that men are fattening. The secular trends in weight, geographic variation, and social-class differences attest to powerful environmental influences on the prevalence of obesity.

Whatever the definition of obesity, it is highly prevalent in the U.S. Weight tends to increase with age through early adult life, and the prevalence of obesity mounts until late in life (Van Italli, 1985). Overweight increases with age until age 55 and then falls off. In women, the prevalence of obesity increases until age 65.

GENETIC AND ENVIRONMENTAL DETERMINANTS

Strategies for disease control are dependent on the extent to which obesity is predominantly genetic or acquired. Clinical and public health efforts at controlling obesity have focused on overall obesity, and thus far little attention has been given to patterns of obesity. More research is needed on the genetic and environmental influences on fat patterns.

Overall obesity has a genetic component, but this may only be permissive, requiring excess calories and a sedentary life-style for it to become manifest. Central obesity is more commonly associated with adult onset than lifelong obesity. This is inferred from the fact that lifelong obesity is associated with hyperplastic, rather than hypertrophic obesity. However, direct data do not seem to confirm any relation between fat patterning and age of onset of obesity or weight gain (Joos, 1984; Ashwell, 1978). Because the fat pattern is preserved on undergoing weight loss, there may well be a genetic component to central obesity (Ashwell, 1978).

The correlations of height and weight (Quetelet Index) were studied in adult relatives participating in the Farmingham Study, comparing body size in two generations. Height correlations suggested a large genetic component. For weight, the pattern was difficult to interpret, and data did not support a sizable genetic contribution. However, there was marked resemblance for obesity among first-degree relatives, but even spouses tended to share obesity, particularly older spouses. However, twin studies show a genetic influence.

MORTALITY

The association between body weight and overall mortality has been examined extensively with variable results: a quadratic relationship with excessive mortality at both extremes of weight; a progressive increase with weight; a monotonic decrease with increasing weight; and no association whatsoever (Stallones, 1985). For mortality from CHD, studies have also been divided between those positive and those showing no associatons (Stallones, 1985).

There is no question about a low body weight or weight loss being an ominous finding regarding overall mortality, particularly in the elderly. In the elderly of both sexes, the pattern of mortality in relation to relative weight (or BMI) is quadratic with excess mortality at both extremes of the weight distribution (Figure 7.1). Taking this at face value, relative weights a bit on the plump side would appear to be optimal. In the Framingham data in men, there is no indication that this ''optimal'' point increases with age; in women, there is a suggestion that it may.

The question arises as to why there is an excess mortality at low weights. Is

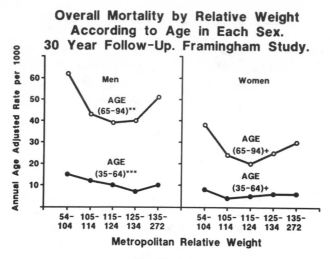

FIGURE 7.1.

this a real biological phenomenon? Does moderate adiposity have survival value? It certainly could in a hostile climate with an intermittent food supply. Data from the Framingham Study suggest that this excess mortality may derive from three factors: subclinical disease leading to weight loss and eventual death; a mixture of noncardiovascular and cardiovascular causes of death; and confounding with cigarette smoking.

If one examines risk of mortality in terms of cardiovascular and noncardiovascular mortality, then it appears that for noncardiovascular and cancer mortality there is a negative trend, whereas for cardiovascular events weight carries a more quadratic risk (Figure 7.2). If one examines the relationship of adiposity to cardiovascular disease adding those events which are nonfatal with those that are, then the trends are more positive with increasing weight. This suggests that illnesses leading to death may be responsible for both weight loss and death (Figure 7.3).

An examination of long-term versus short-term impacts of obesity indicate a more direct relationship for long-term mortality with little excess mortality at low weights (Figure 7.4). For cardiovascular events, Cox proportional-hazards analysis indicates an increasing impact of obesity with the passage of time (Hubert, 1983).

It is conceivable that adiposity has some survival value going into an acute cardiovascular event. To examine this possibility, case-fatality rates were evaluated to determine whether the age-adjusted ratio of fatal to total cardiovascular event rates were related to degree of overweight (Table 7.1). This analysis shows no clear survival advantage in those who are overweight. Nor does it protect against sudden death (Table 7.2).

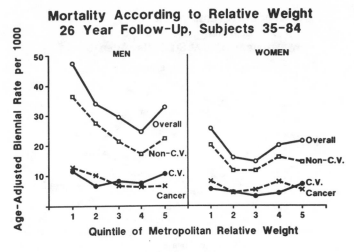

FIGURE 7.2.

There is a tendency for those who are underweight to smoke more than those who are overweight (Jarret, 1982). Cigarette smoking is a powerful contributor to mortality. An examination of the relationship of relative weight to mortality in cigarette smokers shows the usual excess mortality at low weights, whereas in nonsmokers, this increased mortality is not apparent (Garrison, 1985). The quadratic relationship of overall mortality is in part a function of the inverse relation

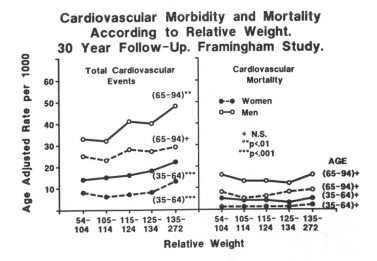

FIGURE 7.3.

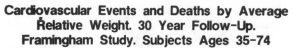

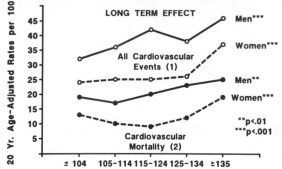

Cardiovascular Events and Deaths by Average Relative Weight. 30 Year Follow-Up. Framingham Study. Subjects Ages 35-74

Average Metropolitan Weight Over Six Biennial Examinations
(1) Persons free of C-V Dis. at Exam 6.   (2) Persons alive at Exam 6

FIGURE 7.4.

of noncardiovascular and the positive relation of cardiovascular mortality to overweight.

DURATION OF FOLLOW-UP

The duration of follow-up influences the relationship between mortality and relative weight. Based on 30 years of follow-up of men in the Framingham Study, the pattern of mortality was observed to change from an inverse relation

Table 7.1
Proportion of Cardiovascular Events Fatal by Relative
Weight, 30-year Follow-up of Framingham Study

	Persons Free of Interim CV Disease			
	Age-adjusted, Percent Fatal			
Metropolitan relative weight	*Men*		*Women*	
	35–64	*65–94*	*35–64*	*65–94*
54–104	29	45	13	36
105–114	20	25	17	26
115–124	13	34	14	22
125–134	11	23	13	22
135–272	18	31	15	37
Total	18	32	11	31

Table 7.2

Proportion of CHD Deaths and Coronary Attacks
as Sudden deaths by Weight in Men, 30-Year Follow-up
of Framingham Study

Metropolitan relative weight	Percent of CHD Deaths[1]		Percent of CHD Attacks[1]	
	35–64	65–94	35–64	65–94
54–104	40	50	29	25
105–114	50	31	12.5	12
115–124	50	38	12.5	20
125–134	67	33	11	20
135–272	60	44	17	21
Total	50	43	11	20

Persons free of interim CHD. [1]Age-adjusted

the first six years to a U-shaped one with minimum mortality at relative weights between 100 and 109 in nonsmoking men (Stallones, 1985). Long-term follow-up for cardiovascular morbidity and mortality in relation to relative weight at initial examination shows a significant relationship, even taking associated risk factors into account (Table 7.3).

Framingham data indicate that the prognostic importance of obesity varies by age, smoking status, duration of follow-up, and whether the mortality is from cardiovascular or noncardiovascular causes.

Evaluation of the true relation between body weight and mortality requires

Table 7.3

Multivariate Logistic Regression Coefficients for MRW Exam 1
26-year follow-up

Event	Men (N = 2,197)	Women (N = 2,714)
Coronary disease	0.012***	0.008**
Angina (AP)	0.014***	0.007*
CHD other than AP	0.009**	0.010***
Congestive heart failure	0.014**	0.015***
Atherothrombotic brain infarction	0.004	0.012**
Death from CHD	0.009*	0.010**
Death from CVD	0.006	0.008**
Total CVD	0.009**	0.009***

Regressions include adjustments for age, systolic BP, serum cholesterol, cigarettes/day, glucose intolerance (no/yes), and ECG-LVH (no, possible, definite) at exam 1.

$*p < 0.05$, $**p < 0.01$, $***p < 0.001$

that the effect be studied apart from low socioeconomic status, cigarette smoking, and poor health. Aside from the cited data of the Framingham Study, the extensive data from the American Cancer Society and insurance companies allow such an evaluation. These investigations, involving 4 million insured persons and over 1 million studied by the American Cancer Society, have provided information on the impact of over- and underweight on mortality in healthy, middle-class Americans free of physical impairments and low socioeconomic status often associated with weight (Lew, 1985a). The Cancer Society Study also eliminated confounding by smoking. These investigations showed that mortality rises steadily with increasing weight (Lew, 1979b). The insurance data indicated that among overweight persons, mortality is initially low but increases to excessive levels after about 15 years (Lew, 1985a).

CARDIOVASCULAR MORBIDITY

In contrast to mortality, nonfatal cardiovascular events are positively related to relative weight, with little evidence for an excess mortality at low relative weights. This is the case for cardiovascular events in general and for CHD in particular (Table 7.4). This is, again, even more apparent when long-term morbidity is examined (Table 7.3; Hubert et al., 1983).

However, there are some curious anomalies which are observed. Angina and intermittent claudication are both transient ischemic phenomena on an occlusive atherosclerotic basis. Yet, angina is clearly related to relative weight at all ages, whereas intermittent claudication is not (Figure 7.5).

Table 7.4
Risk of Coronary Events by Relative Weight
30-Year Follow-up, Framingham Study, Men, Aged 35–94

Metropolitan relative weight	Age-adjusted Annual Rate Per 1,000			
	Myocardial Infarction		Coronary Disease[1]	
	35–64	65–94	35–64	65–94
54–104	5	10	10	19
105–114	6	13	11	21
115–124	6	14	12	25
125–134	7	15	14	27
135–272	7	18	17	33

[1] Any clinical manifestation of coronary heart disease.

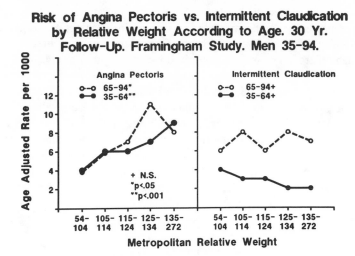

FIGURE 7.5.

NONCARDIOVASCULAR MORBIDITY AND MORTALITY

Clinical observations have connected obesity with a wide variety of noncar-diovascular illness, as well as diseases of the heart and blood vessels. It imposes substantial psychosocial penalties. The NHANES I and II, in the period 1971 to 1980, indicated a threefold excess of hypertension; a twofold excess of hyper-cholesterolemia (>250 mg/dl); and a threefold increase of prevalence of diabetes associated with obesity (Van Italli 1985).

Epidemiological studies have indicated that obese women, regardless of smoking habits, have an excessive mortality from cancers of the biliary tract, breast, uterus, and ovaries; obese men, from cancers of the colon, rectum, and prostate (Garfinkle, 1985). An association of obesity with gout and hyper-uricemia has long been recognized (Bray, 1979a). Osteoarthritis has been incon-sistently linked to obesity (Bray, 1985b). Epidemiologic, insurance, and clinical data firmly link obesity and gallstone disease (Bray, 1979a; Friedman, 1966). Increased mortality from digestive disease (chiefly gall-bladder disease) has been documented by the American Cancer Society Study (Lew, 1979). Weight is clearly the most important contributor to gallstone disease, considering age and parity. In the Framingham Study, 20% overweight doubled the risk of gall-bladder disease (Friedman, 1966). This may be due to secretion of a more concentrated bile, more saturated with cholesterol (Bray, 1979a).

Pulmonary functional abnormalities have been found in the obese. These include decreased expiratory reserve volume, decreased maximum voluntary ventilation, and reduced lung volume. Significant alterations in pulmonary function occur primarily in the massively obese or in conjunction with attendant cardiovascular or respiratory problems. Compliance of the chest wall is decreased, and there is greater work required for breathing. The obesity-hyperventilation syndrome, which may be related to sleep apnea, is relatively rare.

Obese men tend to have decreased serum testosterone and increased estradiol and estrone. In obese women, there is increased ovarian hyalinization and atersia of follices (Bray, 1985b). Menstrual irregularities are more common in obese women. Hormonal abnormalities in obese women are reversible with weight loss. Acanthosis nigrans has been found to occur in association with obesity.

In the Framingham Study, relative weight has been found to be related to fibrinogen values which may have implications for thrombotic occlusive occurrences.

PSYCHOSOCIAL ASPECTS

There is prejudice and discrimination against obesity. One might also expect psychological disturbance, but studies fail to show any more disturbance of mental health in the obese than among lean persons (Wadden, 1985). Parental disapproval of obesity may result in disparagement of body image in juveniles. Dieting to reduce weight may result in emotional reactions including depression, irritability, weakness, and nervousness, but these are not confined to the obese.

BODY-FAT DISTRIBUTION

There is a fairly strong intercorrelation among the various measures of adiposity, which makes it difficult to disassociate the effects of each. Body fat, as such, is not directly measured in epidemiologic studies, which rely on weight-for-height indices or skinfold measurements. Body-fat distribution has been incriminated as a determinant of various metabolic disorders (Vague, 1956; Albrink, 1964; Feldman, 1969; Sims, 1979; Blair, 1984). Epidemiologic studies have not adequately assessed adiposity consistently or well.

Many studies have shown that diabetics tend to have a central or upper body-fat distribution, particularly in women (Joos, 1984; Feldman, 1969: Sims, 1979: Mueller, 1984; Hartz, 1983a; Hartz, 1984b: Kissebah, 1982). Central obesity has also been found in hypertensives (Blair, 1984). Within a defined weight stratum, an increased waist/hip ratio has been found to predispose to gall-bladder disease and menstrual disorders, as well as to diabetes and hypertension (Hartz, 1983a; Hartz, 1984b).

There is evidence that persons whose obesity is predominantly of the upper-body distribution are more insulin resistant than are comparably obese persons

Table 7.5

Independent Contribution of Various Indices
of Obesity to Incidence of CHD, 22-year Follow-up,
Framingham Study, Subjects Aged 36–68

Standard Multivariate Logistic Regression Coefficients

Obesity Index	Men	Women
Subscapular Skinfold	.306**	.183*
Abdominal Skinfold	.265**	—
Waist Circumference	.162*	—
Body-mass Index	.185**	.136*

Covariables: Systolic BP, cholesterol, glucose, cigarettes, ECG-LVH, and age.

(Kissebah, 1982; Kratkiewski, 1983; Evans, 1984; Ward, 1985). Upper-body obesity appears to be primarily hypertrophic, and lower-body obesity hyperplastic (Kissebah, 1982; Krotkiewski, 1983), and it is enlarged fat cells which are insulin resistant (Salans, 1968; Olefsky, 1976). However, this insulin-receptor defect is not confined to fat cells and is also demonstrated in muscle and monocytes. Hypertriglyceridemia is also more strongly associated with central- or upper-body obesity (Krotkiewski, 1983; Evans, 1984). Lower HDL has also been found.

Three studies have examined the effects of fat patterning on the occurrence of cardiovascular end points, prospectively (Lapidus, 1984; Larsson, 1984; Stokes, 1985). Two Swedish studies found that waist/hip ratios were predictive of coronary disease, stroke, and overall mortality independent of conventional cardiovascular risk factors in women, but not in men (Lapidus, 1984; Larsson, 1984). In the Framingham Study, subscapular skinfold in both sexes was strongly and independently predictive of CHD, taking other risk factors into account (Table 7.5). Abdominal skinfold and waist circumference were less powerfully but also independently predictive of CHD in men. This suggests a unique contribution of central obesity.

WEIGHT TRENDS

An examination of weight trends was carried out in the Framingham Study including level, variation, trend, and recent loss. Subjects were placed at risk according to these parameters, measured over a 14-year baseline period, and survival was determined over the next 18 years using a Cox proportional-hazards model. This analysis showed that the maximum BMI over time or earliest BMI values most distant from death were more strongly related than current BMI measures to future mortality.

In nonsmokers in both sexes, higher levels of adiposity were associated with excess mortality, particularly mortality due to cardiovascular disease. Maximum or long-past adiposity had a stronger relation to mortality than did the more current BMI. In smokers, a negative weight trend over 14 years was associated with excess mortality in both sexes.

Recent weight loss in men was also found to be associated with increased mortality. This was true for both cardiovascular mortality and cancer deaths. The negative trend for smokers and the increased mortality with recent weight loss at least partially explains why many studies find a quadratic (U-shaped) mortality trend for weight.

Although recent weight loss appears to be associated with excessive cardiovascular mortality, long-term trends have a different connotation. In the Framingham cohort, those who gained weight after completion of musculoskeletal growth at age 25 (and, hence, put on fat) had a distinctly increased tendency to develop cardiovascular disease, the risk increasing with the amount of weight gained (Table 7.6). Those who lost weight were at decreased risk in the long term. These long-term weight trends were directly related to cardiovascular disease, taking the weight level and coexistent risk factors into account.

It is possible that repeated unsuccessful attempts to lose excess weight might be more metabolically detrimental than a stable same average weight. Analysis at Framingham suggests that variation in weight is not associated with excess mortality. However, because variation is highly correlated with other patterns of weight change, this is difficult to interpret (Table 7.7).

Cancer death, on the other hand, was related to variability in weight in both sexes, and also to recent weight loss in smokers and to a negative trend in weight in women.

Table 7.6

Relative Odds of Cardiovascular Disease
According to Change in Relative Weight
Between Age 25 and Initial Exam, Framingham
Study, Subjects Aged 32–64

Unit Weight Change	Relative Odds	
	Men	Women
−10	.88	.93
None	1.00	1.00
+10	1.13	1.08
+20	1.29	1.17
+30	1.46	1.26

Adjusted for age, relative weight at age 25, and coexistent CV risk-factor level.

Table 7.7

Risk of Cardiovascular Events and Deaths by Variation in
Relative Weight, 30-year Follow-up, Framingham Study

Coefficient of Variation of MRW[3]	20-year Age-adjusted Rate Per 100			
	Cardiovascular Events[2]		Cardiovascular Deaths[1]	
	Men	Women	Men	Women
<2	39	23	21	10
2–3	37	27	19	11
3–4	41	27	20	13
4–5	42	28	20	12
>5	37	30	23	15

[1] Variation in weight over first 6 biennial exams.
[2] Persons free of CV disease
[3] persons alive at Exam 6.
No significant trends.

ATHEROGENIC ACCOMPANIMENTS

Weight gain tends to promote atherogenic risk factors, and weight loss is associated with improvement in these traits. Because of the powerful influence of adiposity on atherogenic factors, control and correction of obesity holds great promise as a hygienic approach to avoidance of atherosclerotic disease.

Epidemiologic evidence indicates that the risk of cardiovascular events is two to six times greater for the diabetic at any age than for the nondiabetic. There is a close connection between obesity, overnutrition, and Type II diabetes. Weight control can definitely modify the severity of diabetes and may retard the time of onset of this form of diabetes. Obesity is closely related to diabetes because it induces resistance to endogenous insulin. Although the pathogenesis of diabetes in the obese remains uncertain, data suggest that enlargement of adipocytes, rather than total body fat, is more closely correlated with insulin resistance. This may be related to the finding that central obesity characterized by a large waist-to-hip ratio is more strongly related to diabetes (Hartz, 1983a). Thus, adult-onset, hyperinsulinemic, keto-resistant diabetes is definitely related to weight gain, and the diabetes induced accelerates and aggravates atherogenesis, leading to an excess development of cardiovascular disease. The effect is more pronounced in women and eliminates their advantage over men against atherosclerotic cardiovascular disease.

There is a marked rise in serum cholesterol in American men from levels of 150 mg/dl during adolescence, to over 200 mg/dl by age 40, which corresponds to weight trends (Kannel, 1979c). It has been repeatedly shown that as adults alter their weight, cholesterol values change correspondingly (Kannel, 1979c; Ashley, 1974). The relation between obesity and LDL cholesterol, HDL cholesterol, and VLDL cholesterol has been investigated in 4,260 young adults participating in the Framingham offspring study. An inverse relation between obesity and HDL cholesterol was found in all age-sex groups between 29 and 49 years of age. LDL cholesterol was positively related to degree of adiposity. As a result, there are substantial differences in the ratio of LDL/HDL or total cholesterol/HDL cholesterol in lean compared to obese persons. This is important because this ratio has proved to be the best indicator of CHD risk (Kannel, 1983). Triglyceride is also increased with adiposity, but the atherogenic potential of this feature of weight gain is uncertain. The association between HDL cholesterol and obesity is strongest, varying little by age and sex. Triglyceride is a close second, but, unlike HDL cholesterol, it and other lipids were more closely associated with obesity in men than women and in younger than older persons.

There is a large, convincing body of evidence linking obesity and hypertension, including population-based studies and controlled intervention trials (Non-Pharmacologic approaches to the Control of High Blood Pressure, 1986; Chiana, 1969; Kannel, 1967b; Frohlich, 1983; Voors, 1977). This has been observed in all cultures, including primitive societies, and has been shown in relation to both systolic and diastolic blood pressure. In populations which do not tend to fatten with age, there is no age-related rise in blood pressure (Chiang, 1969). The relationship has been demonstrated at all ages, including children and adolescents (Voors, 1977).

The Framingham Study has shown that relative body weight, change in weight, and skinfold thickness are related to blood pressure and development of hypertension (Kannel, 1967b). It is estimated that as much as 70% of newly developed hypertension in the Framingham offspring study was directly attributable to weight. These findings are not unique to Framingham. Other longitudinal studies have documented the importance of obesity and weight gain in the evolution of hypertension (Paffenbarger, 1968; Oberman, 1975; Johnson, 1975; Heyden, 1969).

The Framingham Study also showed that lean hypertensives are more likely to gain weight than lean normotensive persons (Kannel, 1967). Those familially predisposed to hypertension developed hypertension in excess independent of weight, but if overweight was also present, risk was further escalated three- to fourfold (Stamler, 1979).

Central, hypertrophic obesity is alleged to predispose more particularly than more generalized hyperplastic obesity (Blair, 1984). A variety of mechanisms have been proposed as to the pathophysiology of hypertension in obesity, including expanded blood volume and increased cardiac output, increased dietary sodium and vascular responses to it, and increased adrenergic participation (Dustan, 1985).

There is clear evidence that weight reduction is associated with a fall in pressure in both normotensive and hypertensive persons. This is usually associated with a contraction of plasma volume; a decline in cardiac output; a slowing of heart rate; and a decrease in cholesterol, uric acid, and glucose (Reisen, 1983).

OPTIMAL WEIGHT

The optimal weight for survival and avoidance of obesity-related cardiovascular and noncardiovascular illness is difficult to specify. Data from the huge American Cancer Society and insurance studies provide the most convincing data because they are confined to the middle class, without health impairments and confounding low socioeconomic status, and can examine the effect in non-smokers. These investigations indicate that the lowest mortality occurs among persons who are somewhat underweight (Lew, 1985a; Lew, 1979b). The study of insured persons indicated some excess mortality in those who were underweight, but this declined with time, whereas the mortality among the overweight persons increased with time (Lew, 1985a).

Whether optimal weights vary by age is a matter of dispute (Andres, 1985). This determination is confounded by long- and short-term effects, by cigarette smoking (Garrison, 1985), and by an influence of subclinical illness on weight. Also, it is not clear whether total mortality should be the criterion. The quality of life must be considered, as well as the length of it.

Deficiencies and inconsistencies in the epidemiologic information on relative underweight makes it difficult to establish the lower limit of optimal weight. It is more realistic to define relative weights associated with increased risk of specific morbid events and mortality among those who are overweight. It is also possible to specify the metabolic penalties of obesity in the promotion of hypercholesterolemia, diabetes, and hyperuricemia. Because obesity promotes atherosclerotic cardiovascular disease by aggravating these atherogenic traits, optimal weight would be that which optimizes the cardiovascular-risk profile.

There are a number of well-documented adverse metabolic consequences of obesity which can account for the excessive morbidity and mortality which has been noted in overweight persons. For excess mortality at lean body weights, no reasonable hypotheses are available for a causal relationship, as there have been no metabolic derangements noted. Implicit in recommending an optimal weight is the assumption that the extent of adiposity directly contributes to excess morbidity and mortality through some plausible mechanism. Since this is lacking for leanness, it is more likely that some underlying pathology is responsible for both the leanness (or weight loss) and the excessive mortality. It is likely that there is pathology at both extremes of the distribution of any biological variable, including weight. For overweight, a direct causal link is plausible; whereas for leanness, there is only guilt by association.

PENALTIES OF UNDERWEIGHT

There is considerable epidemiologic data which suggest that underweight may entail some health risks. This was not supported by the Build and Blood Pressure Study (1959), which found that minimum mortality occurred well below average weight. Subsequent insurance studies and a number of other epidemiologic studies have found a U-shaped relationship between weight and mortality (Keys, 1980; Dyer, 1975). The Whitehall Study found that mortality patterns varied by age, with a monotonic positive relationship in the 40s; a quadratic relationship in the 50s; and an inverse relationship in the 60s.

In the American Cancer Society Studies, underweight men (20% or more below average weight) had mortality rates 25% higher than those of average weight (Lew, 1979b). Studies in northern and central Italy indicate that in rural communities, leaner persons have a shorter life expectancy.

This evaluation is complex, and it is necessary to address specific causes of mortality. In a Scottish study, cardiovascular mortality rates increased with fatness; whereas in lung-cancer mortality, the obese had the lowest rate, even in nonsmokers (Garn, 1983).

INDEPENDENT CONTRIBUTION

There has been dissent concerning the role of obesity as a cardiovascular risk factor (Mann, 1985; Keys, 1980). This stems from a consideration of obesity as an independent statistical predictor of cardiovascular disease. However, it is important to recognize that a variable such as obesity can be an important intermediary in the pathogenesis of disease, even though it is not a significant predictor in multivariate analysis when other covariates are taken into account (Keys, 1980). Since obesity predisposes to hypertension, low-HDL cholesterol, and glucose intolerance, the public-health significance of obesity is not refuted by its poor performance in a multivariate statistical model. It is likely that obesity predisposes to cardiovascular disease precisely by promoting these atherogenic traits.

Adiposity, whether measured by relative weight or subscapular skinfold, is an independent contributor to CHD incidence in particular (Table 7.3, 7.5). This is true, even taking into account serum total cholesterol, systolic blood pressure, blood glucose, ECG-LVH, and cigarette smoking. The independent contribution is more apparent for long-standing obesity either because of a time-dose product of metabolic influences or less confounding by recent weight change. Also, there is some indication that obesity originating early in adult life may be more detrimental than that acquired later in life.

THE DESIRABILITY OF REDUCING OVERWEIGHT

There is no acceptable evidence that weight reduction improves the prognosis of the obese over those who remain corpulent. However, there is good evidence that persons who become overweight incur a number of metabolic disadvantages which are reversible with weight loss (Abraham & Johnson, 1980). Largely as a result of these metabolic aberrations, but also independently, the obese are subject to excessive cardiovascular morbidity and mortality (NIH Consensus Development Statement, 1985; Larsson, 1984; Hubert, 1983).

Nevertheless, there are no good data on the efficacy of weight loss in long-standing and substantial obesity. There is also little information on the prognostic outlook in those obese who repeatedly fail in their attempts to lose weight (the common experience), compared to those who remain steadfastly obese. It is possible that weight fluctuations may be harmful.

However, it is clear that substantial overweight shortens life and predisposes to cardiovascular disease, gall-bladder disease, arthritis, cancer, diabetes, gout, and hypertension. It also imposes psychosocial penalties. Obesity would appear to be a much underrated risk factor for cardiovascular disease. Avoidance and correction of obesity would appear to be one of the chief hygienic measures available for the improvement of *all* of the major cardiovascular risk factors. It appears to be one of the chief determinants of the high level of cardiovascular risk factors. Because of this and its great prevalence in the U.S., a large percentage of the cardiovascular disease in the country can be attributed to unrestrained weight gain.

We urgently need better measures for achieving sustained weight reduction in the obese, but, even more, we need a greater sense of urgency about moderate obesity so that we can keep it from progressing inexorably to long-standing and massive intractable adiposity.

Weight reduction can be lifesaving for persons with extreme, massive obesity (100 pounds over desirable weight). Weight reduction can be justifiably recommended for persons more than 20% above desirable weights (BMIs of 27.2 and 26.9 for men and women, respectively). For less obese persons with cardiovascular risk factors, lesser degrees of obesity merit treatment, in order to improve glucose intolerance, hypertension, hypercholesterolemia, hypertriglyceridemia, reduced HDL cholesterol, and hyperuricemia.

Excessive weight imposes direct functional penalties on the heart, lungs, and skeleton. Exercise tolerance can be improved in coronary patients; breathing improved in chronic obstructive lung disease; and pain-free ambulation improved in patients with osteoarthritis of the spine, knees, and hips.

Concern about the large and growing numbers of overweight Americans is widespread. A good case can be made for consideration of obesity as a leading health hazard because of its great prevalence, association with major cardiovascular risk factors, and independent contribution to cardiovascular disease. However, we are still uncertain about its causes and biological consequences, despite many studies over the past several decades. It is often difficult to decide whether metabolic aberrations in the obese are the cause of obesity, a result of it, or a consequence of other factors leading to obesity.

Many unresolved issues remain to be unraveled. Are the consequences of early-onset generalized obesity the same as late onset of central obesity? Exactly how does putting on weight raise the blood pressure, impair glucose tolerance, increase uric acid, lower HDL cholesterol, and raise triglyceride? What is the optimal weight for longevity and avoidance of cardiovascular disease? Why is adiposity inversely or quadratically related to overall mortality and cardiovascular mortality, and directly related to nonfatal cardiovascular morbidity? Is it harmful to repeatedly attempt to lose weight, only to regain it? What factors regulate the regional distribution of fat, and how is this best assessed? Why should central obesity affect blood pressure and glucose tolerance more than generalized obesity? Do people differ in their thermogenic response to overfeeding?

Although there are many unresolved issues, obesity control nevertheless has great promise for avoiding illness. No other hygienic measure can correct the full array of atherogenic traits predisposing a person to accelerated atherogenesis. Avoidance of weight gain prior to middle age is a rational means for reducing the annual toll of cardiovascular mortality. Weight control is a logical first approach to correction of mild to moderate hypertension, dyslipidemia, impaired glucose tolerance, and hyperuricemia. Weight control can also minimize drug dosage needed to treat hypertension, diabetes, and dyslipidemia. Correction of overweight should improve exercise tolerance in persons with established coronary heart disease and cardiac failure.

It is not likely that a convincing demonstration of the efficacy of correcting obesity will become available, because of our inability to achieve sustained weight loss. However, there is a sound rationale and great potential benefit which should assign a high priority for weight control as a means for disease prevention. The continued high prevalence of obesity and the ineffective state of treatment indicate a need to find better ways to avoid unrestrained weight gain. Barriers to achieving this goal are ignorance about the pathogenesis of the condition, vested interests which promote obesity, and life-styles which maintain sloth and gluttony. Because long-standing obesity is often intractable, a greater sense of urgency about emerging obesity is needed.

ACKNOWLEDGMENT

Supported by contract numbers NIH-NO1-HV-92922 and NIH-NO1-HV-52971.

REFERENCES

Abraham, S., & Johnson, C. L. (1980). Prevalence of obesity in adults in the United States. *American Journal of Clinical Nutrition, 33*, 364–369.

Albrink, M. J., & Meigs, J. W. (1964). Interrelationships between skinfold thickness, serum lipids and blood sugar in normal men. *American Journal of Clinical Nutrition, 15*, 255–261.

Andres, R., Elahi, D., Tobin, J. D., Muller, D. C., & Brant, L. (1985). Impact of age on weight goals. *Annals of Internal Medicine, 103*, 1030–1033.

Ashley, F. W., & Kannel, W. B. (1974). Relation of weight change to changes in atherogenic traits: The Framingham study. *Journal of Chronic Disease, 27*, 103–114.

Ashwell, M., Chinn, S., Stulley, S., & Garrow, J. S. (1978). Female fat distribution. A photographic and cellularity study. *International Journal of Obesity, 2*, 289–302.

Bjorntorp, P. (1985). Regional patterns of fat distribution. *Annals of Internal Medicine, 103*, 994–995.

Blair, D., Habicht, J. P., Sims, E. A. H., Sylvester, D., & Abraham, S. (1984). Evidence for an increased risk of hypertension with centrally located body fat and the effect of race and sex on this risk. *American Journal of Epidemiology, 119*, 526–540.

Bray, G. A. (Ed.). (1979). *Obesity in America.* Bethesda, MD: National Institutes of Health, NIH Publication No. 4:79–359.

Bray, G. A. (1985). Complications of obesity. *Annals of Internal Medicine, 103*, 1052–1062.

Chiang, B. N., Perlman, L. V., & Epstein, F. H. (1969). Overweight and hypertension. *Circulation, 39*, 403–421.

Dawber, T. R., Meadors, G. F., & Moore, F. E. (1951). Epidemiological approaches to heart disease. The Framingham study. *American Journal of Public Health, 41*, 279.

Dustan, H. P. (1985). Obesity and hypertension. *Annals of Internal Medicine, 103*, 1047–1049.

Dyer, A. G., Stamler, J., Berkson, D. M., & Lindberg, H. A. (1975). Relationship of relative weight and BMI to 14-year mortality in the Chicago Peoples Gas Co. Study, *Journal of Chronic Disease, 28*, 109–123.

Evans, D. J., Hoffman, R. G., Kalkhoff, R. K., & Kissebah, A. H. (1984). Relationship of body fat topography to insulin sensitivity and metabolic profiles in premenopausal women. *Metabolism, 33*, 68–75.

Feldman, R., Sender, A. J., & Siegelaub, A. B. (1969). Difference in diabetic and nondiabetic fat distribution patterns by skinfold measurements. *Diabetes, 18*, 478–486.

Friedman, G. D., Kannel, W. B., & Dawber, T. R. (1966). The epidemiology of gall-bladder disease: Observations in the Framingham study. *Journal of Chronic Disease, 19*, 273–292.

Frohlich, E. D., Messerli, F. H., Reisen, E., & Dunn, F. G. (1983). The problems of obesity and hypertension. *Hypertension, 5* (Suppl. III), 71–78.

Garfinkle, L. (1985). Overweight and cancer. *Annals of Internal Medicine, 103*, 1034–1036.

Garn, S. M., Hawthorne, V. M., Pilkington, J. J., & Pesick, S. D. (1983). Fatness and mortality in the west of Scotland. *American Journal of Clinical Nutrition, 38*, 313–319.

Garrison, R. J., & Castelli, W. P. (1985). Weight and 30-year mortality in the Framingham study. *Annals of Internal Medicine, 103*, 1006–1009.

Hartz, A. J., Rupley, D. C., Kalkoff, R. K., & Rimm, A. A. (1983). Relationship of obesity to diabetes: Influence of obesity level and body fat distribution. *Preventive Medicine, 12*, 351–357.

Hartz, A. J., Rupley, D. C., & Rimm, A. A. (1984). The association of growth measurements with disease in 32,856 women. *American Journal of Epidemiology, 119,* 71–80.

The health implications of obesity: NIH consensus development statement. (1985). *Annals of Internal Medicine, 103,* 983–988.

Heyden, S., Bartel, A. G., & Hames, C. G. (1969). Elevated blood pressure in adolescents in Evans County, GA. 7-year follow-up of 30 participants and 30 controls. *Journal of the American Medical Association, 209,* 1083–1089.

Hubert, H. B., Feinleib, M., McNamara, N. M., & Castelli, W. P. (1983). Obesity as an independent risk factor for cardiovascular disease: A 26-year follow-up of participants in the Framingham Heart Study. *Circulation, 67,* 5.

Jarret, R. J., Shipley, M. J., & Rose, G. (1982). Weight and mortality in the Whitehall Study. *British Medical Journal, 285,* 535–537.

Johnson, A. L., Cornoni, J. C., Cassel, J. C., Tyrola, H. A., Heyden, S., & Hames, C. G. (1975). Influence of race, sex and weight on blood pressure behavior in young adults. *American Journal of Cardiology, 35,* 523–530.

Joos, S. K., Mueller, W. H., Hanis, C. L., & Schull, W. J. (1984). Diabetes alert study: Weight history and upper body obesity in diabetic and non-diabetic Mexican American adults. *Annals of Human Biology, 11,* 167–171.

Kannel, W. B. (1983). High density lipoproteins: Epidemiologic profile and risks of coronary artery disease. *American Journal of Cardiology, 52,* 9B–12B.

Kannel, W. B., Brand, N., Skinner, J., Dawber, T. R., & McNamara, P. M. (1967). Relation of adiposity to blood pressure and development of hypertension. The Framingham study. *Annals of Internal Medicine, 67,* 48–59.

Kannel, W. B., & Gordon, T. (1979). Physiological and medical concomitants of obesity: The Framingham study. In A. G. Bray (Ed.), *Obesity in America* (pp. 79–359). Bethesda, MD: National Institutes of Health, NIH Publication No. 4.

Keys, A. (1980). Overweight, obesity, coronary heart disease and mortality. *Nutrition Reviews, 38,* 297–307.

Kissebah, A. H., Vydelingum, N., Murray, R., Evans, D. J., Hartz, A. J., Kalkoff, R. K., & Adams, P. W. (1982). Relationship of body fat distribution to metabolic complications of obesity. *Journal of Clinical Endocrinology Metabolism, 54,* 254–260.

Krotkiewski, M., Bjorntorp, P., Sjostrom, L., & Smith, A. (1983). Impact of obesity on metabolism in men and women. Importance of regional adipose tissue distribution. *Journal of Clinical Investigation, 72,* 1150–1162.

Lapidus, L., Bengtsson, C., Larsson, B., Pennert, K., Rybo, E., & Sjostrom, L. (1984). Distribution of adipose tissue and risk of cardiovascular disease and death: A 12-year followup of participants in the population study of women in Gothenburg, Sweden. *British Medical Journal, 288,* 1257–1261.

Larsson, B., Svardsudd, K., Welin, L., Wilhelmsen, L., Bjorntorp, P., & Tibblin, G. (1984). Abdominal adipose tissue distribution, obesity and risk of cardiovascular disease and death. A 13-year follow-up of participants in the study of men born in 1913. *British Medical Journal, 288,* 1401–1404.

Lew, E. A. (1985). Mortality and weight: Insured lives and the American Cancer Society studies. *Annals of Internal Medicine, 103*:6(2):1024–1029.

Lew, E. A. & Garfinkle, L. (1979). Variations in mortality by weight among 750,000 men and women. *Journal of Chronic Disease, 32,* 363–376.

Mann, G. V. (1974). The influence of obesity on health. *New England Journal of Medicine, 291*(4)(Pt. 1):178–185 and 291(5)(Pt. 2):226–232.

Mueller, W. H., Joos, S. K., Hanis, C. L., Zalaveta, A. N., Eichner, J., & Schull, W. J. (1984). The diabetes alert study: Growth, fatness and fat patterning, adolescence through adulthood in Mexican Americans. *American Journal of Physiological Anthropology, 64,* 389–399.

Nonpharmacologic approaches to the control of high blood pressure. (1986). Final report of the Subcommittee on Nonpharmacological Therapy of the 1984 Joint National Committee on Detection, Evaluation and Treatment of High Blood Pressure. *Hypertension, 8,* 444–467.

Oberman, A., Lane, N. G., Harlan, W. R., Graybiel, A., & Mitchell, R. E. (1975). Trends in systolic blood pressure in the 1,000 aviator cohort over a 24-year period in young adults. *American Journal of Cardiology, 35,* 523–530.

Olefsky, J. M. (1976). The insulin receptor. Its role in insulin resistance of obesity and diabetes. *Diabetes, 25,* 1154–1162.

Paffenbarger, R. S., Jr., Thorne, M. C., & Wing, A. L. (1968). Chronic disease in former college students. VIII: Characteristics in youth predisposing to hypertension in later years. *American Journal of Epidemiology, 88,* 25–32.

Reisen, E., Frohlich, E. D., Messerli, F. A., Dreslinski, G. R., Dunn, F. G., Jones, M. M., Batson, H. M., Jr. (1983). Cardiovascular changes after weight reduction in obesity hypertension. *Annals of Internal Medicine, 98,* 315–319.

Salans, L. B., Knittle, J. L., & Hirsch, J. (1968). The role of adipose cell size and adipose tissue insulin sensitivity in the carbohydrate intolerance of human obesity. *Journal of Clinical Investigation, 47,* 53–165.

Shurtleff, D. (1974). *Some characteristics related to the incidence of cardiovascular disease and death. The Framingham study. 18-year follow-up.* Monograph Section #30 Washington, D.C.: USDHEW Publication No. (DHEW) (NIH) 74-599, February 1974.

Sims, E. A. H. (1979). Definitions, criteria and prevalence of obesity. In G. A. Bray (Ed.), *Obesity in America* Ch. 1, (pp. 20–36). Bethesda, MD: National Institutes of Health, NIH Publication No. 4:79–359. (Also reprinted in 1980 80:359)

Stallones, R. A. (1985). Epidemiologic studies of obesity. *Annals of Internal Medicine, 103,* 1003–1005.

Stamler, R., Stamler, J., Riedlinger, W. F., Algera, G., & Roberts, R. H. (1979). Family (parental) history and prevalence of hypertension. *Journal of the American Medical Association, 241,* 43–46.

Stokes, J., Garrison, R. J., & Kannel, W. B. (1985). The independent contributions of various indices of obesity to the 22-year incidence of coronary heart disease: The Framingham study. In J. Vague, (Ed.), *Metabolic complications of human obesities* (pp. 49–57). In: The Proceedings of the Fifth Int'l Symposium of the Metabolic Complications of Obesities. Amsterdam, The Netherlands: Elsevier.

United States Department of Health, Education, and Welfare. (1985). *Vital and health statistics. Weight by height and age for adults 18–74 years, U.S. 1971–1974.* Washington, D.C.: National Center for Health Statistics.

Vague, J. (1956). The degree of masculine differentiation of obesities: A factor determining predisposition to diabetes, atherosclerosis, gout and uric acid dalculous disease. *American Journal of Clinical Nutrition, 4,* 20–34.

Van Italli, J. B. (1985). Health implications of overweight and obesity in the United States. *Annals of Internal Medicine, 103,* 983–988.

Voors, A. W., Webber, L. S., Frerichs, R. R., & Berenson, G. S. [1977]. Body height and body mass as determinants of basal blood pressure in children: The Bogalmsa Heart Study. *American Journal of Epidemiology, 106,* 101–112.

Wadden, T. A., & Stunkard, A. J. (1985). Social and psychological consequences of obesity. *Annals of Internal Medicine, 103,* 1062–1067.

Ward, W. K., Johnston, C., Beard, J. C., Benedetti, T. J., Hatter, J. B., & Porte, D. (1985). Abnormal fat distribution in subjects predisposed to NIDDM. *Clinical Research, 33,* 67A.

8

SLOW-WAVE SLEEP AS A "PROTECTIVE" FACTOR

David J. Kupfer, M.D.
Charles F. Reynolds, III, M.D.
Department of Psychiatry,
University of Pittsburgh School of Medicine

This manuscript will explore the psychobiological hypothesis that the specific amount and temporal distribution of slow-wave sleep (SWS) indexes a set of protective factors against pathological aging and the onset and development of various psychiatric and medical diseases. This distribution, which may be reflected in amplitude, frequency, incidence, and other measures of SWS appears to represent a set of biological protective factors. Furthermore, SWS as a protective factor appears to be a facilitator and perhaps even a synchronizer of a variety of biological rhythms whose dissociation may be the signature for specific psychiatric and medical diseases. Thus, this manuscript will present a brief overview of the available data base in normals from infancy to later life. Available data on various psychopathological and medical diseases, as well as the relatively minimal data based on provocative testing, can also be examined to assess the "strengths" of SWS parameters as protective factors.

This review will cover the following areas: the organization of SWS throughout the night and in relation to aging; advances in SWS physiology from the application of computer technology; sleep-neuroendocrine interactions; aging as a potential vulnerability factor; SWS and selected neuropsychiatric syndromes (dementia and depression); and sleep deprivation as a probe.

TEMPORAL AND ONTOGENETIC ORGANIZATION OF SWS

The seminal observations on rapid eye movement (REM) sleep first published more than 30 years ago have led to considerable interest, not only in the psychology and physiology of REM sleep, but in various aspects of non-REM (NREM) sleep as well. This division of sleep into REM and NREM, in turn, stimulated the development of generally accepted scoring criteria for specific EEG-derived stages of sleep which have been in use for almost 20 years (Rechtschaffen & Kales, 1968). While these criteria for conventional scoring have been associated with advances in our understanding of sleep patterns, various psychopathological states, and aging, the advent of computers has radically increased the possibilities of using detailed quantitative measures to study these phenomena. For example, parameters that could not be recognized or measured on the basis of traditional scoring techniques (such as marked progressive alterations of NREM sleep delta activity as observed by all-night spectral analysis) have led to renewed interest in various aspects of NREM sleep. That the levels of delta-wave activity and REM activity are frequently more pronounced near the beginning of both REM and NREM periods has long been recognized (Aserinsky, 1971). Indeed, the "exponential" decline of EEG amplitude and the linear decline of slow-wave activity over successive sleep cycles have inspired the formulations of various models of sleep regulation, both for the sleep of normal individuals and the sleep abnormalities found in various pathological conditions such as affective disorders (Borbély, 1982; Borbély & Wirz-Justice, 1982; Feinberg et al., 1978).

By the conceptual age of 32 weeks, both sleep and waking states display predominantly slow (delta) wave activity mixed with periods of inactivity and low-voltage fast activity (5.0-8.0 Hz). The consolidation of SWS activity is apparent by about the 40th week, and the association is typically complete by the 44th week. By one-month post-partum, sleep spindles occur along with slow-wave activity and begin linearly to occupy their place in the NREM sleep period. Recently, we have applied computer-based analytical techniques to examine SWS in EEG sleep recordings of 85 healthy children aged 6 to 16 (Coble, Reynolds, Kupfer, & Houck, 1987). Highly significant age effects were demonstrated for both total and average whole-night delta-wave counts. Among these children, differences in SWS appear to be accounted for primarily by decreases across age groups in delta counts in the 2.0-3.0 Hz frequency band. Such differences may be related to other aspects of maturation and development. Age was significantly and inversely related to average delta counts in all but the first NREM period of the night, and there did not appear to be significant night or gender effects on delta sleep in this sample (Coble et al., 1987).

While earlier descriptions of the relation of SWS to age have consistently noted a marked decline in SWS beginning at about 30 years of age, the availability and use of computer-based measures has yielded data suggesting that this apparent decline may be due largely to our traditional scoring criteria, which include both amplitude and frequency components. While there is a marked decline in the amplitude of SWS with aging, the decline in the presence of SWS, as measured by frequency, is limited (Webb, 1982).

In recent years, considerable advances in computer technology have allowed a more sophisticated approach to the study of sleep physiology, particularly the investigation of NREM sleep. This work on SWS, especially delta-wave sleep, has proceeded in two directions. One involves the actual count of the delta-wave frequency by period-amplitude analysis (Ktonas & Gosalia, 1981); the second employs all-night spectral analysis. A review of all-night spectral analysis records has graphically demonstrated that delta sleep, particularly the first two NREM periods, is associated with a rapid delta sleep fall-off (Borbély, Baumann, Brandeis, Strauch, & Lehmann, 1981). We, therefore, were interested in learning whether another technique using period-amplitude analysis of delta-wave activity would demonstrate similar results. As shown graphically in our normative control population, findings similar to those of Koga (1965) and Borbély (1982) emerged (see Figure 8.1). Statistical analyses have demonstrated that the maximum increases in the number of delta waves were significantly less than the maximum decreases, despite the fact that this is not true for REMs. However, these data do not tell us whether REM sleep is directly turning off delta-wave activity or whether the delta-wave generator is being turned off by an independent mechanism, in turn allowing REM sleep to occur. What these findings do suggest, however, is that the rapid fall-off seen at the end of each of the NREM periods may be indicative of an underlying "on-and-off process" that occurs in the transitional period between REM and NREM periods. While these observable alterations between NREM and REM periods are found in normals, it remains to be seen whether the same level of organization is present in the sleep of older individuals or individuals suffering from various psychopathological states.

With respect to the organization of NREM sleep throughout the night, the first

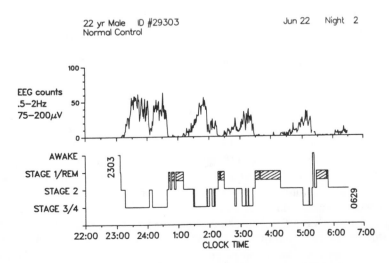

FIGURE 8.1. Automated Delta Wave Sleep in a Normal Control.

two to three sleep cycles that contain SWS (stage 3 and particularly stage 4 sleep) and the associated REM sleep (i.e., about half of total REM sleep) seem to be an essential or obligatory form of sleep (Horne, 1983b). As the night progresses, however, a more "facultative" form of sleep seems to emerge, which is more flexible and can be reduced or extended according to need, energy conservation, circadian factors, and mood changes. Horne has argued that analogues of obligatory-facultative sleep also seem to be present in other mammals. A variety of experimental findings support this obligatory-facultative sleep hypothesis, including the following data: (a) Age-matched natural short and long sleepers have similar absolute amounts of SWS, as so do very short sleepers when their sleep is compared with the first two sleep cycles of age-matched controls. It seems that short sleepers have dispensed with the latter cycles of sleep. (b) Sleep-reduction studies (Horne, 1983b) all show that sleep losses are at the expense of sleep stages other than 3 and 4 for reductions down to about five hours of sleep per night. (c) Only about 30% of the total sleep lost during sleep deprivation appears to be made up on subsequent nights, and calculations (Horne, 1983b) from 2- to 11-day total deprivation studies show that about 80% of the lost stage 4 sleep is reclaimed, compared to less than half of the lost REM sleep and none of the lost stage 2 sleep.

Within normal subjects there is a remarkable lack of correlation between individual levels of SWS and psychometric measures of mental states or personality traits. Further, the relationship between psychometrically measured state variables, such as mood or state anxieties, or experimentally reduced sets of energy expenditure levels have limited relationships to levels of SWS. Only in pathological conditions such as schizophrenia, depression, dementia, and some pharmacologically induced states does the SWS seem to deviate from its time-bound variations.

SLEEP/NEUROENDOCRINE INTERACTIONS

Quabbe's report of a nocturnal elevation in the plasma concentrations of human growth hormone (hGH) (Quabbe, Schilling, & Helge, 1966) and Sassin's polygraphic confirmation of a sleep-linked peak for GH (Sassin et al., 1969) marked the beginning of endocrinological sleep research and opened a field of insights into the neurochemistry of sleep (Parker et al., 1980). Growth hormone, prolactin, luteinizing hormone, testosterone, thyrotropin, and cortisol all show a rhythmicity that is synchronized across time and between subjects. Sleep, itself being part of a circadian rhythm, may be masking the overt rhythm of these hormones. In fact, the intensity of this masking effect, that is, the resistance of hormonal rhythms to the influence of sleep, is revealing. For example, the influence of sleep is maximal on hGH but minimal on the adrenocorticotropic hormone (ACTH)/cortisol rhythms; the masking effect of sleep is stimulatory for hGH, prolactin, and testosterone, but inhibitory for ACTH/cortisol and thyrotropin.

GH release, which is temporally associated with SWS under basal conditions, produces a peak under free-running conditions which coincides both with the fall of cortisol and with SWS (Weitzman, Czeisler, Zimmerman, & Moore-Ede, 1981). Finally, the hormones that are stimulated by sleep have anabolic effects, whereas those that are inhibited have catabolic properties.

GH secretion has frequently been associated with the first NREM period of sleep, although there is a growing body of evidence in controls to suggest that this occurrence may be fortuitous. We and others (Jarrett, Coble, Kupfer, & Greenhouse, 1985) have shown that even though nocturnal GH secretion can occur before sleep onset, the serum concentration at sleep onset is often significantly greater than the value 40 minutes previously.

In a recent examination of the sleep of 23 normals whose sleep was relatively unperturbed by intravenous cannulation (Jarrett et al., 1984), we re-examined 0.5-2.0 Hz delta waves and their relationship to plasma GH concentration. As in previous studies, we compared the average delta count to cortisol and GH on the basis of 20-minute sampling epochs throughout the night. We also conducted a precise examination of individual subject correlations throughout the night. Indeed, the female group ($N=15$) failed to demonstrate any consistent relationship between GH and delta activity. While delta activity was similar for both men and women, GH secretion was less in women than in men. This set of findings stands in contrast to the males studied in this group ($N=8$), in whom the first 160 minutes provided a significant correlation between GH and either average delta count or total delta count. These sets of correlations are consistent with the apparently positive relationship between the peaking of GH and of delta-wave density in the first part of the night. Such findings would suggest that increased attention to sex differences, as well as to the age of the groups, is essential in future studies.

Second, it is apparent that GH is secreted at a time when secretory activity in the hypothalamic-pituitary-adrenal (HPA) axis is relatively quiescent. Indeed, there is frequently a specific inverse relationship between the serum concentrations of GH and cortisol in both depressed patients and healthy control subjects. Using 20-minute sampling epochs, we examined the relationship between serum cortisol and GH concentration. Individual subject correlations throughout the night were used to provide an average correlation. Using the test of homogeneity, it became apparent that this inverse relationship was most significant during the first NREM period ($r= -0.59$, $p < 0.01$).

Recent investigations on both healthy controls and depressed patients have drawn our attention to several major tentative conclusions: (a) The complexity of the interaction between GH and SWS is considerably greater than previously thought. (b) The 24 hour distribution of GH in the preliminary Belgian studies suggests a further need for studies on GH release (Mendlewicz et al., 1985). (c) hGH peaking and SWS can be dissociated under clinical and pharmacological conditions in humans, as well as under normal conditions in the rat, cat, and dog. The functional significance of sleep-linked pituitary activity is, therefore, only poorly understood unless its anabolic potency is seen in the context of the body restitutional concept of Adam and Oswald (1983), which has been challenged by Horne (1983a). There is no evidence that hGH or any other pituitary hormone enhances SWS after systematic application in normals.

In summary, since the original observation of Takahashi and colleagues (Takahashi, Kipnis, & Daughaday, 1968), the nocturnal secretion of GH has been associated with the first NREM period of sleep and, in particular, the first burst of SWS. However, using automated delta-wave analysis and acknowledging individual variability, we have been unable to establish any similar linear statistical relationship between delta-wave activity and GH secretion, even in the first 100 minutes of sleep when these two events appear to be temporally related, suggesting more complex mediating factors. This lack of simple combination has led to the hypothesis that sleep onset is permissive to both processes, and the relationship of delta-wave activity to GH secretion may be mediated by neuroendocrine pathways involving growth-hormone-releasing factor (GRF) and somatostatin (SRIF).

AGING AS A POTENTIAL VULNERABILITY FACTOR

In a recently completed EEG sleep study of 40 healthy seniors (19 men and 21 women) aged 58-82 years, men could not maintain sleep as well as women and experienced less stage 3 sleep (Reynolds, Kupfer, Taska, Hoch, Sewitch, & Spiker, 1985). The increased wakefulness after sleep onset among the men was particularly marked during the last two hours of recording. In both men and women, regardless of age, the temporal distribution of REM sleep and REM density during the night was flat. Finally, only a mild degree of sleep-disordered breathing was noted, with positive age effects on the apnea/hypopnea index and maximal duration of apnea. The current data confirm the earlier findings of Williams and colleagues (Williams, Karacan, & Hursch, 1974) that there are important sex effects on the sleep continuity and architecture of healthy aged subjects. The proportion of aged men with scorable stage 3 sleep is lower than among women, a condition that is also reflected in the diminished stage 3 percentage among men. The current data also confirm a virtual absence of stage 4 sleep in both elderly men and women, noted in most previous reports.

SWS AND SELECTED NEUROPSYCHIATRIC SYNDROMES

Dementia

The nocturnal sleep of elderly depressed and Alzheimer's dementia patients can be distinguished by differences in REM sleep and sleep-maintenance indices

(Reynolds, Kupfer, Taska, Hoch, Spiker et al., 1985; Reynolds, Spiker, Hanin, & Kupfer, 1983). Other studies have also reported decreased SWS time and decreased percentage of time spent asleep in Alzheimer's patients (particularly the more severely demented), as compared with controls (Feinberg, Koresko, & Heller, 1967; Prinz et al., 1982), as well as decreased numbers of sleep spindles and K-complexes correlating with severity of dementia (Feinberg et al., 1967; Prinz et al., 1982; Reynolds, Kupfer, Taska, Hoch, Spiker et al., 1985; Smirne, Comi, Franceschi, Mariani, & Rodocanachi, 1977). In general, however, the manually scored standard all-night summary measures of SWS (minutes, percentage of time asleep) are limited in their ability to demonstrate group differences among healthy elderly controls, patients with probable Alzheimer's dementia, and elderly depressive patients. This may reflect the "masking" influence of the age-dependent decrease in SWS (Roffwarg, Muzio, & Dement, 1966; Smith, Karacan, & Yang, 1977; Williams et al., 1974) Moreover, all-night summary indices convey no information about differences in the intranight temporal distribution, or incidence, of slow-wave activity in the sleep EEG, or differences in the frequency composition of SWS (Feinberg et al., 1967). The use of computer-assisted techniques sharpens the precision by which such comparisons can be made. Our data on 0.5-3.0 Hz (75-200 μV) activity suggest that all-night SWS measures can be enhanced by using a baseline crossing technique with an amplitude criterion among elderly normal and neuropsychiatrically impaired individuals (Reynolds, Kupfer, Taska, Hoch, Sewitch, & Grochocinski, 1985). Using such techniques, significant differences in average delta activity [counts per minute (cpm)] and in the temporal distribution of delta activity were noted among groups of geriatric normal, demented, and depressed patients (Reynolds, Kupfer, Taska, Hoch, Sewitch, & Grochocinski, 1985).

Depression

While SWS decreases have been discussed for many years in relationship to depressive syndromes, it is only with the advent of computerized measures that the issues of specificity with respect to delta-wave decreases can truly be addressed. For example, it has now become clear that there is a significant decrease in delta sleep in the first NREM period, which is more profound in delusional and nondelusional depression than in either patients with schizophrenia or normal controls (Ganguli, Reynolds, & Kupfer, 1987). However, as a greater number of studies are performed with respect to SWS specificity, the issue of aging and SWS changes will need to be examined in greater detail.

Most recently, an examination of relationships between first-NREM-period delta-wave counts and first-REM-period measures showed few significant findings in both the younger and middle-aged depressed patients (Kupfer, Reynolds, Ulrich, & Grochocinski, 1986). As expected, significant differences in sleep continuity between younger and middle-aged depressives were present. Aside from stage 1 sleep, however, this does not seem to be the case with respect to sleep architecture. The increased amount of stage 1 in middle-aged depressives can also be interpreted as a measure of arousal and greater sleep discontinuity in this group of depressed paiients as compared to younger depressed patients.

The average delta counts throughout the night are approximately doubled in the younger depressives, as compared to the middle-aged depressives. The NREM distribution appears to be relatively "flat" between the first and second NREM periods in the younger depressives, but an inverse relationship is present in the middle-aged depressives, with the first NREM period having a lower average delta count than the second. When the average period lengths were examined in the younger and middle-aged depressives, as expected, there appeared to be a shorter first NREM period in the older depressives, with the REM periods themselves being approximately the same length in both groups throughout the night. REM latency/average delta-count correlations for the first NREM period yielded the expected relationships between total delta counts and REM latency and a higher relationship in average delta counts with REM latency in the younger depressives.

These data, taken from different points in the life cycle, suggest the presence of important interactions between age and disease in determining the EEG sleep characteristics of depression. These interactions need to be examined in continuous age groups in order to understand, for example, where major shifts in slow-wave activity may occur and how increasing sleep-maintenance difficulty with advancing age affects the amount and temporal distribution of SWS.

Based on the considerable amount of data available on sleep and other biological rhythms after sleep onset, it would appear that the first 100 minutes of sleep represent an important "window" into central nervous system functioning. As more age-related changes occur in REM and NREM sleep in the first 100 minutes after sleep onset, which is a period of time associated with the usual sleep abnormalities found in depressed patients, we would hypothesize that the similarity of the two "processes" (aging and depression) can be tested in a large sample over an extended age range and that the results would help to clarify a number of issues. Specifically, at what age (if ever) in the life cycle of a normal individual does the sleep pattern of a depressed individual look similar (i.e., is there a 20- or a 30-year "lag" between the sleep patterns of normals and depressives)? Second, are there periods in the life cycle in which the major differences in sleep patterns between patients and normals are less pronounced (e.g., sleep-continuity differences in young depressives versus normal controls)? Third, do the differences between normals and depressives at each decade demonstrate similar rates of aging (e.g., decrease in average delta count as a function of age)? Fourth, within the depressed or normal cohorts, are there gender differences at any decade using automated as well as non-automated sleep-analytic techniques?

SLEEP DEPRIVATION (EXAMPLE OF A PROBE)

Although healthy elderly adults, like young adults (Johnson & MacLeod, 1973; Kollar et al., 1969) and middle-aged adults (Brezinova, Hort, & Vojtechovsky, 1969; Froberg, Karlsson, Levi, & Lidberg, 1972; Webb, 1981), show increased sleep continuity and more SWS on the first recovery night following 36-hour sleep deprivation, our recent studies suggest that healthy elderly women show a more robust increase in sleep continuity and SWS (particularly stage 4) than do elderly men (Reynolds et al., 1986). Among women, the increase in time spent asleep persists to the second recovery night, but not among men. Only 3 of 20 subjects (2 men and 1 woman) failed to show the expected increase in either sleep continuity or SWS. REM latency decreased in response to sleep deprivation despite the increase SWS, with REM-latency reduction in women being delayed to the second recovery night. Indeed, 5 of the 20 subjects (20%) had a total of 7 sleep-onset-REM periods (SOREMPs) on one or both recovery nights, and SOREMP-positive subjects were distinguished by having had higher stage 3 percentages at baseline and higher REM time during the first recovery night. Sleep apnea and nocturnal mycolonus indices were not significantly affected by 36-hour sleep deprivation, except for a modest increase in duration of apnea episodes among elderly men.

These data confirm earlier reports of an increase of SWS and improved sleep continuity in healthy elderly people following either 38 hours (Carskadon & Dement, 1985) or 60 hours (Bonnet & Rosa, 1985) of sleep deprivation. Similarly, we replicated Carskadon's observation of a prolongation of apnea duration (Carskadon & Dement, 1985), albeit only in men, not in women. Like Bonnet and Rosa (1985), but unlike Carskadon and Dement (1985), we observed a decrease in REM latency after sleep deprivation, with 20% of our subjects having a SOREMP on 7 of 40 (17.5%) recovery nights. SOREMPs are distinctly unusual during the baseline or unchallenged sleep of healthy elderly persons but are very common among elderly depressives (Reynolds, Kupfer, Taska, Hoch, Spiker et al., 1985). Our observation of differentially greater stage 4 sleep in women, both at baseline and during recovery sleep, is consistent with the combined observations of Bonnet and Carskadon and underscores the importance of gender in determining late-life sleep structure.

Previous studies in younger adults (Brezinova et al., 1969; Froberg et al., 1972; Johnson & MacLeod, 1973; Kollar et al., 1969; Webb, 1981) have suggested that the first recovery night is characterized specifically by a decrease in sleep-onset time and by an increase in SWS, while later recovery nights show an increase in REM sleep beyond baseline levels. REM sleep changes in the elderly appear to be different (or at least more complex) than those seen in younger subjects who undergo sleep deprivation. Vogel has previously hypothesized that increasing age mediates increasing REM-sleep disinhibition (Vogel, Vogel,

McAbee, & Thurmond, 1980), a suggestion supported by the observations of Hayashi and Endo (1982) and of Reynolds and colleagues (Reynolds, Kupfer, Taska, Hoch, Sewitch, & Spiker, 1985) of a shift of REM sleep to earlier times of the night in the healthy elderly. The current data would appear to support the concept of an age-mediated increase in REM disinhibition following the stress of sleep deprivation, as evidenced specifically by the decrease in REM latency, the occurrence of SOREMPs, and the increase in REM time on the first recovery night. That support must be qualified, however, by the decrease in early REM time and whole-night eye-movement density of the first recovery night. Perhaps, as suggested by Borbély (1982), the first recovery night increase in SWS inhibits the robustness of early REM and diminishes phasic REM activity for the night as a whole.

The functional significance of response to sleep deprivation in the elderly is not well understood. For example, do elderly men and women show differential performance decrements in response to sleep deprivation? Is the apparent increased mood disturbance in elderly women following sleep deprivation related to the observation of greater vulnerability to depression among women generally, or to the higher incidence of sleep complaints in elderly women? Such questions merit further investigation by sleep and aging researchers.

A clue to some of these questions may be provided by a recent study of sleep-deprivation effects in older endogenous depressives (Reynolds et al., 1987). In a drug-free group of 15 depressed inpatients, all-night sleep deprivation (SD) was associated with a significant decrease in Hamilton depression ratings. SD Hamilton depression ratings (at 9:00 a.m. following all-night SD) were inversely correlated with an increase in SWS minutes ($r = -0.60, p < .02$) and percentages ($r = -0.59, p < .02$), from baseline to first recording night. Patients whose SD Hamilton ratings improved 30% or more over pre-SD ratings showed larger increases ($p < .01$) in SWS (54 minutes) than did patients with less clinical response to SD (7 minutes). These data support the concept of an interaction between the process of sleep regulation and the symptoms of depression. More specifically, however, they confirm a prediction from the two-process model of sleep regulation that an increased level of process S (indexed by an increased level of SWS), attained by sleep deprivation, should correlate with clinical improvement.

CONCLUSION

We have reviewed a number of intersecting areas that are relevant to an understanding of SWS. The organization of SWS, its potential for representing an obligatory form of sleep, its relationship to sleep neuroendocrine parameters, its relationship to various psychopathological entities, the effect of such naturalistic probes as sleep deprivation, and the dependence of the overall organization of

SWS on aging all contribute in some detail to various proposed models for sleep regulation. More recently, Borbély and Wirz-Justice (1982) have proposed a two-process model of sleep regulation in depression. This model was first put forth as a model for sleep regulation in normals and has received some empirical support in sleep-deprivation experiments in humans and in animals. The Borbély model, in attempting to provide a framework by which sleep abnormalities in depression can be understood, has emphasized SWS rather than REM sleep. Even more recently, Ehlers and Kupfer (1987) have proposed a refinement of the two-process model of sleep to include the neuropeptide and neuroendocrine pathways that may be involved in affective disorders (Table 8.1).

This model is based on the following empirical findings. A considerable body of data on the first part of the night suggests that both SWS (delta-wave density) and growth hormone are decreased in depressed patients, that the nadir of nocturnal cortisol levels is blunted, and that REM sleep and REM activity distribution are shifted to the earlier hours of sleep. Probes are now needed to assess how these variables can be altered independently in both normals and depressed patients. Any probe that specifically affects any one of these four sets of variables merits consideration. For example, Ehlers and colleagues (Ehlers, Reed, & Hendriksen, 1986) have demonstrated EEG effects following intracerebroventricular GRF administration to animals, suggesting that SWS changes may be stimulated by the GRF-GH axis. It is on the basis of this current data that further investigative activity of possible alterations in GH secretion would be valuable, especially since the mechanisms for nocturnal release of GH are probably different from GH release during the day in response to a variety of metabolic probes. Thus, strategies are predicated on the assumption that GRF may alter sleep EEG patterns and nocturnal GH secretory activity.

Table 8.1
CRF/GRF and the Two-Process Model of Sleep in Depression

	PROCESS S	PROCESS C
Definition	A sleep-dependent process that builds up during the day and is released at night	A sleep-independent circadian process
Sleep Stage Relationship	Slow-wave sleep related	REM sleep related
Neuroendocrine Relationship	GRF and/or GRF/CRF Ratio	CRF-HPA axis
Alteration in Depression	Deficient	Increased
Physiological Consequences in Depression	GH hyposecretion after sleep onset, decreased delta density, delayed sleep onset, lighter overall sleep pattern	Cortisol hypersecretion over 24-hour period, increased REM activity and density

It remains important to conceptualize further how SWS can act as a protective factor in understanding normal aging and various psychopathological states that may be exacerbated by the aging process. In this paper, we have reviewed several lines of evidence supporting the concept that SWS provides a sensitive index of factors which protect against pathological aging and the development of neuropsychiatric disorders: a) the obligatory and preferential nature of SWS rebound following sleep deprivation; b) the association between SWS and anabolic steriod secretion; c) the diminished capacity for SWS rebound in affective-disorder patients, compared to healthy aging persons; and d) the correlation between SWS rebound and improvement in mood following sleep deprivation in endogenous depressives. Further refinements of current models, as well as the introduction of new models, will be required to elucidate these issues in a more comprehensive manner. Furthermore, such models will need to provide suggestions for the empirical testing of their proposed hypotheses.

While this paper has focused heavily on the "protective" role of SWS, it is very likely that elucidating the role of SWS will depend on further understanding of the obligatory interactions between SWS and REM sleep. This point is best illustrated by the ongoing investigations of Rechtschaffen and colleagues (Rechtschaffen, Gilliland, Bergmann, & Winter, 1983) into the effects of prolonged sleep deprivation on rats. These investigators have shown that rats chronically deprived almost totally of sleep show increased energy expenditure and die after 11 to 32 days of deprivation (Everson et al., 1986). What it is that drives this hypermetabolic state resulting from sleep deprivation remains as mysterious as the fundamental "purpose" of sleep. However, the constellation of physiological and biochemical effects that comprise this hypermetabolic state preceding death seem to be related more to paradoxical (REM) sleep deprivation than to SWS loss (Kushida et al., 1986). It may be, therefore, that prolonged REM sleep deprivation "unleashes" or "disinhibits" catabolic processes (an extreme form of the activation seen in the antidepressant effects of REM sleep deprivation), which eventually overwhelm the presumed "restorative" or anabolic functions of SWS.

ACKNOWLEDGMENTS

This work was supported in part by National Institute of Mental Health Grants MH-24652, MH-30915, MH-37869, MH-00295, as well as a grant from the John D. and Catherine T. MacArthur Research Network on the Psychobiology of Depression.

REFERENCES

Adam, K., & Oswald, I. (1983). Protein synthesis, bodily renewal and the sleep-wake cycle. *Clinical Science, 65,* 561–567.

Aserinsky, E. (1971). Rapid eye movement density and pattern in the sleep of normal young adults. *Psychophysiology, 8,* 361–375.

Bonnet, M. H., & Rosa, R. R. (1985). Sleep and performance in young adults and older normals and insomniacs during acute sleep loss and recovery. *Sleep Research, 14,* 69.

Borbély, A. A. (1982). A two process model of sleep regulation. *Human Neurobiology, 1,* 195–204.

Borbély, A. A., Baumann, F., Brandeis, D., Strauch, I., & Lehmann, D. (1981). Sleep deprivation; effect on sleep stages and EEG power density in man. *Electroencephalography and Clinical Neurophysiology, 51,* 483–493.

Borbély, A. A., Wirz-Justice, A. (1982). Sleep, sleep deprivation, and depression. *Human Neurobiology, 1,* 205–210.

Brezinova, V., Hort, V., & Vojtechovsky, M. (1969). Sleep deprivation with respect to age: An EEG study. *Activitas Neurosa Superior, 11,* 182–187.

Carskadon, M. A., & Dement, W. C. (1985). Sleep loss in elderly volunteers. *Sleep, 8,* 207–221.

Coble, P. A., Reynolds, C. F., Kupfer, D. J., & Houck, P. (1987). Electroencephalographic sleep of healthy children. Part II: Findings using automated delta and REM sleep measurement methods. *Sleep, 10,* 551–562.

Ehlers, C. L., & Kupfer, D. J. (1987). Hypothalamic peptide modulation of EEG sleep in depression: A further application of the S-process hypothesis. *Biological Psychiatry, 22,* 513–517.

Ehlers, C. L., Reed, T. K., & Hendriksen, S. J. (1986). Effects of corticotropin-releasing factor and growth hormone releasing factor on sleep activity in rats. *Neuroendocrinology, 42,* 467–474.

Everson, C., Bergmann, B., Fang, V. S., Leitch, C. A., Obermeyer, W., Refetoff, S., Schoeller, D. A., & Rechtschaffen, A. (1986). Physiological and biochemical effects of total sleep deprivation in the rat. *Sleep Research, 15,* 216.

Feinberg, I., Koresko, R. L., & Heller, N. (1967). EEG sleep patterns as a function of normal and pathological aging in man. *Journal of Psychiatric Research, 5,* 107–144.

Feinberg, I., March, J. D., Fein, G., Floyd, T. C., Walker, J. M., & Price, L. (1978). Period and amplitude analysis of 0.5-3 c/sec activity in NREM sleep of young adults. *Electroencephalography and Clinical Neurophysiology, 44,* 202–213.

Froberg, J., Karlsson, C. G., Levi, L., & Lidberg, L. (1972). Circadian variations in performance, psychological ratings, catecholamine excretion, and urine flow during prolonged sleep deprivation. In W. P. Colquhon (Ed.), *Aspects of human efficiency* (pp. 247–260). London: English Universities Press.

Ganguli, R., Reynolds, C. F., & Kupfer, D. J. (1987). Electroencephalographic sleep in young, never-medicated, schizophrenics: A comparison with delusional and nondelusional depressives and with healthy controls. *Archives of General Psychiatry, 44,* 36–44.

Hayashi, Y., & Endo, S. (1982). All night sleep polygraphic recording of healthy aged persons: REM and slow-wave sleep. *Sleep, 5,* 277–283.

Horne, J. A. (1983a). Human sleep and tissue restitution: Some qualifications and doubts. *Clinical Science, 65,* 569–577.

Horne, J. A. (1983b). Mammalian sleep function with particular reference to man. In A. Mayes (Ed.), *Sleep mechanisms and functions in humans and animals: An evolutionary perspective* (pp. 262–312). London: Van Nostrand Reinhold.

Jarrett, D. B., Coble, P. A., Kupfer, D. J., & Greenhouse, J. B. (1985). Sleep-related hormone secretion in depressed patients. *Acta Psychiatrica Belgica, 85,* 603–614.

Jarrett, D. B., Greenhouse, J., Thompson, S. T., McEachran, A. B., Coble, P. A., & Kupfer, D. J. (1984). Effect of nocturnal intravenous cannulation upon sleep-EEG measures. *Biological Psychiatry, 19,* 1537–1550.

Johnson, L. C., & MacLeod, W. L. (1973). Sleep and awake behavior during gradual sleep reduction. *Perceptual and Motor Skills, 36,* 87–97.

Koga, E. (1965). A new method of EEG analysis and its application to the study of sleep. *Folia Psychiatrica Neurologica Japanica, 19,* 269–278.

Kollar, C. J., Pasnau, R. O., Rubin, R. T., Naitoh, P., Slater, G. G., & Kales, A. (1969). Psychological, psychophysiological and biochemical correlates of prolonged sleep deprivation. *American Journal of Psychiatry, 126,* 488–497.

Ktonas, P. Y., & Gosalia, A. P. (1981). Spectral analysis vs. period-amplitude analysis of narrowband EEG activity: A comparison based on the sleep delta-frequency bank. *Sleep, 4,* 193–206.

Kupfer, D. J., Reynolds, C. F., Ulrich, R. F., & Grochocinski, V. J. (1986). Comparison of automated REM and slow wave sleep analysis in young and middle-aged depressed subjects. *Biological Psychiatry, 21,* 189–200.

Kushida, C., Bergmann, B., Fang, V. S., Leitch, C. A., Obermeyer, W., Refetoff, S., Schoeller, D. A., & Rechtschaffen, A. (1986). Physiological and biochemical effects of paradoxical sleep deprivation in the rat. *Sleep Research, 15,* 219.

Mendlewicz, J., Linkowski, P., Kerkhofs, M., Desmedt, D., Golstein, J., Copinschi, G., & Cauter, E. (1985). Diurnal hypersecretion of growth hormone in depression. *Journal of Clinical Endocrinology and Metabolism, 60,* 505–512.

Parker, D. C., Rossman, L. G., Kripke, D. F., Hershman, J. M., Gibson, W., Davis, C., Wilson, K., & Pekary, E. (1980). Endocrine rhythms across sleep-wake cycles in normal young men under basal state conditions. In J. Orem & C. D. Barnes (Eds.), *Physiology in sleep* (pp. 145–179). New York: Academic Press.

Prinz, P. N., Peskind, E. R., Vitaliano, P. P., Raskind, M. A., Eisdorfer, C., Zemcuznikov, N., & Gerber, C. J. (1982). Changes in the sleep and waking EEGs of nondemented and demented elderly subjects. *Journal of the American Geriatrics Society, 30,* 86–93.

Quabbe, H. J., Schilling, E., & Helge, H. (1966). Pattern of growth hormone secretion during a 24-hour fast in normal adults. *Journal of Clinical Endocrinology and Metabolism, 26,* 1173–1177.

Rechtschaffen, A., Gilliland, M. A., Bergmann, B. M., & Winter, J. B. (1983). Physiological correlates of prolonged sleep deprivation in rats. *Science, 221,* 182–184.

Rechtschaffen, A., & Kales, A. (Eds.). (1968). *A manual of standardized terminology, techniques, and scoring system for sleep stages of human subjects.* Bethesda, MD: U.S. Department of Health, Education and Welfare, Public Health Service.

Reynolds, C. F., Kupfer, D. J., Hoch, C. C., Stack, J. A., Houck, P. R., & Berman, S. R. (1987). Sleep deprivation effects in older endogenous depressed patients. *Psychiatry Research, 21,* 95–109.

Reynolds, C. F., Kupfer, D. J., Hoch, C. C., Stack, J. A., Houck, P. R., & Berman, S. R. (1986). Sleep deprivation in healthy elderly men and women: Effects on mood and on sleep during recovery. *Sleep, 9,* 492–501.

Reynolds, C. F., Kupfer, D. J., Taska, L. S., Hoch, C. C., Sewitch, D. E., & Grochocinski, V. J. (1985). Slow wave sleep in elderly depressed, demented, and healthy subjects. *Sleep, 8,* 155–159.

Reynolds, C. F., Kupfer, D. J., Taska, L. S., Hoch, C. C., Sewitch, D. E., & Spiker, D. G. (1985). Sleep of healthy seniors: A revisit. *Sleep, 8,* 20–29.

Reynolds, C. F., Kupfer, D. J., Taska, L. S., Hoch, C. C., Spiker, D. G., Sewitch, D. E., Zimmer, B., Marin, R. S., Nelson, J. P., Martin, D., & Morycz, R. (1985). EEG sleep in elderly depressed, demented, and healthy subjects. *Biological Psychiatry, 20,* 431–442.

Reynolds, C. F., Spiker, D. G., Hanin, I., & Kupfer, D. J. (1983). EEG sleep, aging, and psychopathology: New data and state of the art. *Biological Psychiatry, 18,* 139–155.

Roffwarg, H., Muzio, J. N., & Dement, W. C. (1966). Ontogenetic development of the human sleep-dream cycle. *Science, 152,* 604–619.

Sassin, J. F., Parker, D. C., Mace, J. W., Gotlin, R. W., Johnson, L. C., & Rossmann, L. G. (1969). Human growth hormone release: Relation to slow-wave sleep and sleep-walking cycles. *Science, 165,* 513–515.

Smirne, S., Comi, G., Franceschi, M., Mariani, E., & Rodocanachi, M. (1977). Sleep in presenile dementia. *Electroencephalography and Clinical Neurophysiology, 43,* 521–522.

Smith, J. R., Karacan, I., & Yang, M. (1977). Ontogeny of delta activity during human sleep. *Electroencephalography and Clinical Neurophysiology, 43*, 229–237.

Takahashi, Y., Kipnis, D. M., & Daughaday, W. H. (1968). Growth hormone secretion during sleep. *Journal of Clinical Investigation, 48*, 2079–2090.

Vogel, G. W., Vogel, F., McAbee, R. S., & Thurmond, A. J. (1980). Improvement of depression by REM sleep deprivation. *Archives of General Psychiatry, 37*, 247–253.

Webb, W. B. (1981). Sleep stage responses of older and younger subjects to sleep deprivation. *Electroencephalography and Clinical Neurophysiology, 52*, 368–371.

Webb, W. B. (1982). The sleep of older subjects fifteen years later. *Psychological Reports, 50*, 11–14.

Weitzman, E. D., Czeisler, C. A., Zimmerman, J. C., & Moore-Ede, M. C. (1981). Biological rhythms in man: Relationship of sleep-wake, cortisol, growth hormone, and temperature during temporal isolation. In J. B. Martin & S. B. Reichlin (Eds.), *Neurosecretion and brain peptides* (pp. 475–499). New York: Raven Press.

Williams, R. L., Karacan, I., & Hursch, C. J. (Eds.). (1974). *Electroencephalography (EEG) of human sleep: Clinical applications.* New York: John Wiley and Sons.

9

THE NATURE OF SLEEPINESS: CAUSES, CONTEXTS, AND CONSEQUENCES

David F. Dinges, Ph.D.
The Institute of Pennsylvania Hospital
and
Department of Psychiatry,
University of Pennsylvania School of Medicine

Although the function of sleep remains obscure (Rechtschaffen, 1979; Webb, 1979), the need for sleep requires no scientific demonstration. With rare exception, when sleep is lost or disrupted, by whatever means, the inevitable consequence is sleepiness during the wake period. If sleepiness becomes excessive, the person ceases to function effectively because ultimately the brain imposes sleep, typically in the form of overwhelming drowsiness or microsleeps, despite the individual's best efforts to stay awake.

Because the brain will "slip into" light sleep after varying degrees of sleep loss, no one has yet proven that human sleep can be completely denied for more than a day or two. Although dozens of human sleep-deprivation studies have prevented all but this light sleep for durations ranging from 26 to 260 hours, no pathological consequences of human sleepiness have yet been demonstrated (Horne, 1985); healthy human beings do not become ill or die from sleep loss, at least under the conditions in which it has thus far been studied. Rats, apparently, are not so fortunate; Rechtschaffen and colleagues (Rechtschaffen, Gilliland, Bergmann, & Winter, 1983) have recently demonstrated that rats die from both total and partial sleep loss. Whether the rodents become sleepy before death depends on how one operationalizes sleepiness.

Despite the lack of demonstrated pathophysiology associated with human sleepiness, operationalizing sleepiness has become an increasingly important issue in the fields of sleep and human chronobiology. The neuroscience and biochemical approaches to questions concerning how sleep intrudes into wakefulness (or, stated more generally, how sleep alternates with wakefulness) continue to require a much better understanding of sleepiness (and alertness) to elucidate the function of sleep. Beyond this basic issue, however, a renewed impetus for assessing sleepiness has come from the application of the newly coalesced and expanding specialty of sleep disorders medicine (Carskadon, 1982).

The identification of serious and even life-threatening sleep disorders, such as obstructive sleep apnea syndrome and narcolepsy, has led to the discovery of daytime hypersomnolence or excessive daytime sleepiness (EDS) as part of their symptomatology. By recording nocturnal sleep and measuring daytime sleepiness and sleep tendency, practitioners of sleep disorders medicine have been able to develop a nosology of sleep disorders that has, as two of its broad diagnostic categories, disorders of excessive somnolence (DOES) and disorders of initiating and maintaining sleep [DIMS; Association of Sleep Disorders Centers (ASDC), 1979]. An essential characteristic in this distinction is the extent of the daytime sleepiness. DOES have in common behaviors indicative of daytime sleepiness (e.g., excessive tendency to fall sleep, sleep "attacks," unavoidable napping, decreased performance), while DIMS, which include the insomnias, do not present with daytime hypersomnolence behaviors as a symptom, although the person may subjectively report "sleepiness" (p. 58). It should be obvious that a key issue in sleep disorders medicine is, therefore, the operationalization and assessment of sleepiness; in particular, those aspects of sleepiness that have been conceptualized variously as "objective sleepiness," "physiological sleepiness," "excessive daytime sleepiness," and "pathological sleepiness" (Dement & Carskadon, 1982; Carskadon & Dement, 1982a, 1982b).

A second impetus for the study of sleepiness derives from a growing concern for the occupational health consequences of sleep loss and disturbed sleep-wake cycles brought about by shift work, sustained military operations, and transmeridian flight. As post-World War II industrialized societies increase, through technological and economic pressure, the need for around-the-clock operations, sleep loss and disturbed sleep-wake cycles affect the functioning of a growing proportion of the population (Folkard & Monk, 1985). Aside from the direct medical consequences of this activity (Moore-Ede & Richardson, 1985), there is a need to assess the functional incapacity brought about through sleepiness resulting from these work schedules. This is particularly true in automated, around-the-clock industries that rely on humans to vigilantly monitor operations and where human error can have consequences for the health and safety of many persons, such as in the operation of nuclear power plants, the transportation of hazardous waste, and airline flights. The need for early identification of on-the-job sleepiness and its operational consequences is especially acute in these areas.

Assessing the nature of sleepiness is, therefore, not only essential to our understanding of the function of sleep, but it is also a central issue within the practice of sleep disorders medicine and the application of sleep hygiene to issues of occupational health and safety. The need to assess sleepiness in these areas has led to significant questions: Are there different kinds of sleepiness? What is "pathological sleepiness" and at what point does sleepiness reflect central nervous system (CNS) impairment? What are the most sensitive measures of sleepiness? What are the direct and indirect effects of sleepiness on behavioral functioning? What are the endogenous and exogenous factors that determine the level of sleepiness? Is there a common dimension that underlies all sensitive sleepiness measures?

Such questions transcend subspecialities within sleep research and cannot be adequately addressed by reviewing the literature on sleepiness from any one subfield; others have already provided thorough reviews of the effects of human sleep deprivation (Horne, 1978; Johnson & Naitoh, 1974; Naitoh, 1976; Wilkinson, 1965, 1968), of chronobiological influences on sleep and alertness (Colquhoun, 1971a; Moore-Ede, Sulzman, & Fuller, 1982; Webb, 1982; Winfree, 1982), of factors affecting vigilance and alertness in the work place (Folkard & Monk, 1985; Johnson, Tepas, Colquhoun, & Colligan, 1981), and of the standardization of sleepiness measures in clinical sleep disorders medicine (Carskadon, 1982; Carskadon et al., in press). This paper seeks to address the issue of human sleepiness by reviewing the major ways in which it has been conceptualized and measured throughout sleep research, in an effort to focus on common behavioral themes that underlie these somewhat diverse traditions.

SOURCES OF SLEEPINESS

Sleep Loss and Circadian Phase

Despite a still-popular misconception, sleepiness is not simply a linear function of either sleep loss or prior wakefulness. A ubiquitous finding that is taken for granted in the sleep literature but overlooked by many persons outside the sleep field is that measures of sleepiness that change in response to prior wakefulness also vary in a circadian manner as a function of an endogenous biological clock (Aschoff, 1965; Takahashi & Zatz, 1982); this includes most performance and physiological measures. Even among the multitude of subjective self-report measures, it appears as though those that are responsive to sleep loss also vary in a circadian pattern (Gillberg & Akerstedt, 1981).

These two sources of sleepiness covary in studies of experimental sleep deprivation to produce functions that typically cycle every 24 hours but that change in mean 24-hour level over days (see Figure 9.1). The effects appear to be additive; for example, the sleep-deprived person is sleepiest within each 24-hour period at the circadian trough in the body-temperature cycle and most alert within each 24-hour period near the circadian peak (Froberg, Karlsson, Levi, & Lidberg, 1975; Kleitman, 1963). It is because of this additive effect that virtually any measure thought to index sleepiness should have changed from baseline, at the very latest, by the first 8 hours of the third day (i.e., 0000-0800 hours)—after approximately 40 hours of wakefulness and while in the circadian nadir. By this point in time,

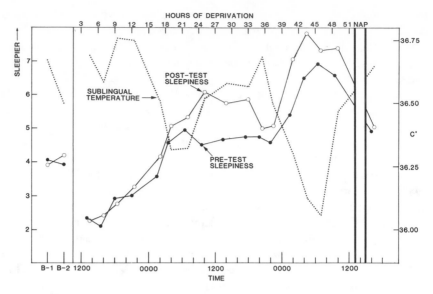

FIGURE 9.1. Mean sublingual temperature recordings and subjective sleepiness
ratings on a 10-point analogue rating scale from 12 healthy young adults undergoing 52 hours of sustained wakefulness in an environment devoid of time cues.
Recordings were made at the beginning and end of 45-minute performance test
bouts, which were carried out every 2 to 3 hours throughout the sleep-loss period.
Plotted separately are the sublingual temperature readings taken at the end of
performance bouts, subjective sleepiness ratings made at the beginning of performance bouts (pre-test sleepiness), and sleepiness ratings made at the end of performance bouts (post-test sleepiness). Pre-test and post-test sleepiness ratings were
compared within subjects at each performance bout; shaded areas indicate statistically significant differences between ratings at those performance times. Subjects
were not permitted to see their previous responses—they did not know when a test
bout would occur or how long it would last. Between test bouts, they interacted
socially with staff. Ratings made pre-test and post-test on two separate baseline
days (B-1, B-2) showed no differences. A 2-hour nap ended the sleep-loss
protocol.

measures of sleepiness have generally shown a greater change than is likely to
occur from this time onward, even if deprivation continues for 2 to 9 days more!
Assuming that no stimulants are taken, subjects cannot maintain continuous
alertness during and after the circadian nadir of the second full day without sleep.

Although prior wakefulness and circadian phase are covariates, they also
appear to be independent sources of sleepiness and sleep regulation (Borbély,
1982). Controversy continues, however, over the extent to which sleep regulation is controlled by either one or both processes (Daan, Beersma, & Borbély,
1984; Moore-Ede & Czeisler, 1984; Strogatz, Kronauer, & Czeisler, 1986;
Winfree, 1982). Each was recognized as an important predictor of sleepiness in

the earliest experiments on the topic (Michelson, 1897; Patrick & Gilbert, 1896), but nature's unkind temporal confounding of the two has made it difficult to separate the contributions of each to sleepiness. In studies of sustained wakefulness, a linear relationship between sleep loss and sleepiness measures can be observed only if procedures are used to average out the contribution of circadian variation (e.g., Lubin, Hord, Tracy, & Johnson, 1976). Conversely, circadian changes in sleepiness measures are evident even when normal amounts of sleep are being obtained, although it requires a special time-free environment to demonstrate them clearly (e.g., Czeisler, Weitzman, Moore-Ede, Zimmerman, & Knauer, 1980).

In everyday life, it is often impossible to fully separate the differential contributions of sleep loss and circadian factors to sleepiness. Aside from a direct effect on sleepiness, circadian factors can contribute to increased sleepiness indirectly through effects on sleep itself. For example, the increase in on-the-job sleepiness experienced by many night-shift workers can be the result of both circadian decreases in alertness at night and partial sleep loss due to circadian truncation of daytime sleep. They are not only working at a time when they are less alert, but they are less alert because they did not sleep as long or as well as they desired to during the day.

Similarly, sleep loss can consist of any number of sleep alterations, including total sleep loss, cumulative partial sleep loss resulting from repeated truncation of sleep length, or sleep fragmentation associated with repeated disruptions of sleep-stage continuity. While we have known for some time that the first two classes of sleep loss are associated with intense sleepiness, recent work suggests that sleep fragmentation or discontinuity is also associated with severe daytime sleepiness (Bonnet, 1985, 1986; Stepanski, Lamphere, Badia, Zorick, & Roth, 1984). It is fragmentation of nocturnal sleep continuity that occurs in certain serious sleep disorders. For example, in obstructive sleep apnea syndrome resulting in EDS, air flow during sleep is restricted, often leading to repeated transient microarousals during sleep; over time, a severe sleep debt is thought to accumulate and result in intense daytime sleepiness.

Sleep

Ironically, another source of sleepiness is sleep itself. Rather than the sleepiness associated with microsleeps intruding into wakefulness due to sleep loss or circadian variation, this is the sleepiness associated with terminating sleep or beginning the awakening process. It is a paradox of sleep that we generally function less effectively and feel sleepier upon awakening from sleep than we do immediately before going to sleep (Kleitman, 1963)! Even awakening from a one-hour midafternoon nap, near the circadian peak in arousal and on a day after a full night's sleep, will result in intense sleepiness and an inability to function effectively for a few minutes (Dinges, Orne, Evans, & Orne, 1981). While this "sleep inertia" (Lubin et al., 1976) or "postdormital disorientation" (ASDC, 1979) is often more intense than the sleepiness due to circadian variation and even to extreme sleep deprivation, it is typically very transient, lasting only from 5 to 30 minutes. The intensity and duration of the sleepiness will depend on the depth of sleep, which in turn is affected by the amount of prior wakefulness, sleep length, the sleep stage at awakening, the amount of time spent in specific sleep stages, and the phase of the circadian cycle in which the sleep occurs. In general, the deeper the sleep, particularly the more the slow wave sleep (SWS) or the more intense the SWS (in terms of lengthy prior wakefulness), the more severe the sleepiness on awakening; although the subject may not subjectively report sleepiness at awakening, performance measures and other behavioral signs indicate profound drowsiness.

This form of sleepiness can be especially severe in a person abruptly awakened from only a few hours of sleep after 24 or more hours without sleep (Dinges, Orne, & Orne, 1985). The intense disorientation and sleepiness seen upon abrupt awakening from very deep sleep in experimental paradigms with healthy sleepers is quite similar to that seen in disorders of arousal (Broughton, 1968), also called "parasomnias" (ASDC, 1979), which involve inappropriate arousal from sleep, such as that found in sleep walking, sleep talking, sleep-related enuresis, and pavor nocturnus. In such clinical cases, some undesirable physical activity intrudes into sleep and produces only a partial arousal. Why this should be especially true for very deep sleep remains unknown.

The other way in which sleep can contribute to feelings of sleepiness is through oversleeping; that is, sleeping for periods of 10 hours or more when not making up a sleep deficit (Globus, 1969, 1970; Taub, Globus, Phoebus, & Drury, 1969). Although Broughton (1982) has argued that the nature of the sleepiness resulting from sleep extension is qualitatively different from that found for sleep deprivation, it remains unclear to what extent the dysphoric effects of oversleeping are reflecting sleepiness per se and to what extent circadian effects and sleep inertia contribute to this primarily subjective phenomenon (e.g., Carskadon, Mancuso, Keenan, Littell, & Dement, 1986).

Age, Health, and Drugs

At any given time, sleepiness is the composite result of different temporal patterns for the effects of prior wakefulness, sleep disturbance, the preceding state (sleep or wakefulness), and the circadian phase. While this presents a complex picture, it is far from complete for most of us. Variations within and between persons in sleepiness are also associated with age (maturational level; Carskadon et al., 1980; Richardson, Carskadon, Orav, & Dement, 1982); infants, young children, and the elderly appear to have increased daytime sleepiness relative to adolescents and adults (who are not otherwise sleep-deprived).

Physical health also plays a role in sleepiness aside from nocturnal sleep disruption per se. Various pathophysiological states can produce sleepiness through somewhat different processes (Broughton, 1982). For example, some disorders of excessive somnolence, such as narcolepsy, may also produce severe daytime sleepiness directly by impairing the ability of the CNS to maintain wakefulness. Many medical and psychiatric conditions will affect nocturnal sleep and increase daytime sleepiness and sleep behaviors. Moreover, virtually all drugs that act as CNS depressants (e.g., hypnotics, alcohol, antianxiety and antipsychotic agents) will also increase sleepiness and sleep tendency.

Environment and Context

Although it is relatively easy to show that sleep loss, illness, and certain psychoactive agents will increase daytime sleepiness, it is more problematic to hypothesize that certain conditions and contexts, such as a heavy meal, warm room, boring lecture, or long automobile drive, might also be soporific. Yet these are precisely the kinds of situations to which most of us are quick to attribute our daytime sleepiness, although we are rarely fully aware that such attributions require some special relationship between sleepiness and conditions of boredom, heat, low stimulation, and satiety.

There are data to suggest that high-carbohydrate, low-protein meals increase sleepiness and lethargy (Fernstrom & Wurtman, 1971), ostensibly through the uptake of amino acids that are brain neurotransmitter precursors, such as tryptophan, a serotonin precursor known to affect sleepiness (Hartmann, 1982/1983; Lieberman, Corkin, Spring, Growdon, & Wurtman, 1982/1983). It is not clear, however, whether every experience of a meal inducing sleepiness is necessarily due solely to the relationship between dietary amino acids and CNS sensitivity to them. Moreover, other explanations for postprandial sleepiness, such as those based on digestive effort, have not been adequately formulated or tested. While specific foods or digestive processes may ultimately be shown to account for all of the sleepiness experienced after eating, parsimony requires that we ask whether satiety has anything in common with the other conditions that are often associated with increased sleepiness.

Boredom, heat, a large meal, and an uninteresting task are the most common contexts in which attributions of sleepiness are made (usually without reference to sleep need or nocturnal sleep disturbance), but they do not always result in sleepiness. Accounting for why they are sometimes associated with feelings of intense sleepiness and daytime sleep behaviors (e.g., napping) is essential for a coherent theory of sleepiness. The key theoretical question that needs to be addressed is: Do these behaviors or contexts actually *cause* sleepiness (in a manner similar to the way sustained prior wakefulness or chronic sleep disruption produce sleepiness), or do they serve to *expose* sleepiness (due to overall sleep need and/or circadian phase) that is not obvious in other contexts?

Carskadon and Dement (1982a) have offered a conceptual framework for answering this question. They have distinguished between *physiological* sleepiness, which is thought of as the underlying tendency for sleep to occur, and *manifest* sleepiness, which is the subjective or behavioral expression of sleepiness within a given context and as a function of a host of factors.

These factors may include such diverse stimuli as light, noise, room temperature, activity level, motivation, recumbency, anxiety, bladder fullness, hunger, thirst, excitement, attention, and many others. When a person is asked, "How sleepy are you?" or when observational assessment is made, all of these factors will influence the response. Thus, even a sleepy person will not feel or appear sleepy when he is on a tennis court or at Disneyland. Yet, the same sleepy person driving a car through Kansas on a warm summer's afternoon would exhibit greatly augmented subjective and behavioral sleep tendencies.

We do not feel that this type of environment augmentation actually causes sleepiness to appear. Rather, the reduction of impinging stimuli serve to *unmask* [italics added] the physiological sleep tendency. Thus, we believe that *a truly alert individual does not feel or appear to be sleepy when placed in a low stimulus environment.* [italics added (Carskadon & Dement, 1982a, p. S69)]

When viewed in this way, the environment becomes a critical moderating variable in the overt expression of basal or physiological sleepiness associated with sleep need. Because behavioral and subjective expressions of sleepiness are manifest expressions, they depend on the context in which they are taken. They will only reflect physiological sleep tendency when alerting factors in the environment are removed.

While this conceptualization of sleepiness by Carskadon and Dement (1982a) was developed from the perspective of explaining what the Multiple Sleep Latency Test (MSLT) measures, it was also intended to account for differences among various measures of sleepiness. Other attempts to understand the diverse effects of sleep deprivation on a variety of subjective, behavioral, performance, and physiological measures have also concluded that situational factors and the interaction of the sleepy person with the environment determine the nature of sleepiness expression (Bohlin & Kjellberg, 1973; Kjellberg, 1977a; Murray, 1965). More broadly, theories of arousal and activation have generally posited two basic determinants of arousal level—endogenous conditions (e.g., sleep need) and exogenous stimulation and demands on the person (Malmo, 1959; Malmo & Belanger, 1967; Schachter & Singer, 1962).

The role of the environment in determining the expression of sleepiness has become a central issue in the measurement of sleepiness. Despite years of attempts to measure pure sleep loss or chronobiological effects on mood, behavior, or physiology in humans, sleepiness measures always and necessarily involve a measurement context, demand characteristics (Orne, 1962), and interpersonal motivational factors that influence the expression of sleepiness; this is likely to remain true even if we ultimately find discrete biochemical measures of sleepiness.

Many investigators have bemoaned the fact that these environmental and psychosocial factors influence assessment. What has not been undertaken, however, but is clearly needed, is a discussion of the various measures of sleepiness with reference to this issue. For example, rather than dismissing boredom (i.e., an uninteresting environment that requires attention) as a confounding variable in measuring sleep loss effects on performance, we might ask how boredom potentiates the expression of sleepiness in performance, what this suggests about the nature of sleepiness, and what similarity this has to an objective sleep tendency measure that relies on the subject to do nothing other than go to sleep. The following analysis of measures of sleepiness will be developed from this perspective.

MEASURES OF SLEEPINESS

The basic observation of increased sleepiness following sleep loss, sleep disruption, or circadian variation has been solidly established through a variety of subjective self-report, behavioral, performance, and physiological measures. The issues of greatest interest currently center on how one best measures sleepiness in a given context and what the measurement conveys about the nature of sleepiness in the population under study.

Early reviews of drowsiness have noted how different conceptualizations of it result in different measurement methods and problems (e.g., Kamiya, 1961; Morris & Singer, 1966). Sleepiness can be measured in numerous ways, not all of which always yield the same result. There are at least two theoretical explanations for the discrepancy among hypothesized measures of drowsiness or sleepiness. The first assumes that sleepiness is a basic physiological process, but that not all measures of sleepiness are equally sensitive to variations in it. The second view is predicated on the assumption that there are different kinds of sleepiness and that this multidimensionality is reflected in the different measures (e.g., the ability to go to sleep versus the ability to resist a sleep attack, or the ability to perform versus the subjective experience of sleepiness).

It is not yet possible to empirically distinguish between these two views; the resolution rests with the as yet unknown neurophysiology and biochemistry of the sleepy brain. Rather than reviewing correlational data among diverse measures in an unsatisfactory effort to find support for one or the other hypothesis, it is more informative to consider the various attempts and traditions of measuring sleepiness and noting, where possible, the similarities among them, particularly with regard to contextual variables.

Subjective Self-Report

In the vernacular, words like "sleepiness," "tiredness," "fatigue," and "drowsiness" are often used synonymously, while "alertness" and "attentiveness'' are used as their antonyms. There are long traditions of trying to operationally distinguish among these terms. Ultimately, such distinctions rest on the dependent variables used in experiments that ask subjects to rate themselves on these dimensions. When sleep is deprived and a subject reports intense fatigue or tiredness, it is reasonable to assume that the descriptor is being applied to feelings of sleepiness, whereas reports of increased fatigue after a treatment condition involving heavy exercise would not permit such a leap of faith. When the session involves sleep loss *and* strenuous mental or physical work, the meaning of fatigue ratings, and even sleepiness ratings, blur further.

The heterogeneity of sensory/perceptual criteria underlying the descriptors people give to their experiential states is perhaps the greatest single difficulty plaguing self-report scales. Nevertheless, subjective impressions often serve as powerful determinants of behavior and of these, feelings of sleepiness result in what is perhaps the most pervasive behavioral control on the planet—sleep itself.

There is no reason to attempt to distinguish in this discussion between self-reports of sleepiness, drowsiness, fatigue, and lowered alertness. There is, however, a need to discuss other dimensions of mood reports and the manner in which the context of asking for these reports influences the meaning of sleepiness. What kinds of self-reported phenomenal experiences are engendered by sleep need?

MOOD DESCRIPTORS AND DIMENSIONS.   The earliest and most consistent finding of sleep-deprivation studies was the effect of sleep loss on self-reported measures of sleepiness, alertness, drowsiness, vigor, tiredness, fatigue, lethargy, activation, and energy—subjective descriptors that are often intercorrelated. Other subjective ratings on dimensions such as irritability, tension, anxiety, aggression, and unhappiness have not consistently been shown to change with sleep loss, but when this has been observed, it appeared to depend on factors other than sleep loss per se, such as whether subjects were deceived, the difficulty of the performance demands, or the availability of adequate food (Murray, 1965). Thus, while we may be convinced from personal experience that sleep loss results in increased irritability, this is apparently a secondary consequence of certain sleep-loss scenarios. One of these might include a situation where sleep is chronically disrupted or lost, but for whatever reason, the individual is not aware that this is the case; perhaps because the chronic nature of the loss has caused a phenomenal redefinition of alertness on the part of the person. The sleepiness and effort to maintain alertness, which the person does not recognize but may report as a difficulty in concentration, is such that it acts as a stressor and results in expressions of irritability. The latter situation may characterize certain patients with hypersomnolence who report, among other things, feelings of irritability and lassitude, without necessarily a phenomenal awareness of sleepiness.

The problem with this explanation is that it also accounts for the data when used the other way around. One can argue, for example, that irritability is a result of sleep loss, but that it is not generally manifested in modern sleep deprivation experiments, where subjects are extremely motivated and cooperative and are treated with great care and respect, which in turn may attenuate the dysphoric and anger-inducing aspects of sleep loss or provide salient demand characteristics that inhibit subjects from reporting such feelings. Whether or not this explanation is correct, at least one mood scale has been developed that is known to reflect sleep-loss effects through an increase in negative mood states and a decrease in positive mood state (NPRU; Johnson & Naitoh, 1974).

SLEEPINESS REPORTS IN DIFFERENT ENVIRONMENTS.   The second way in which contextual variables influence mood reports associated with sleep need concerns the changes in sleepiness ratings as a function of the context in which they are obtained. Unfortunately, as with all subjective self-report measures, sleepiness ratings can vary greatly between subjects, no matter how psychometrically valid the measuring instrument; there is no way of knowing whether someone is twice as sleepy as another person just because the rating is twice as high. But as long as one is comparing sleepiness ratings within subjects rather than between them, subjective ratings of sleepiness can be a useful and sensitive index of sleep loss.

The Stanford Sleepiness Scale (SSS; Hoddes, Zarcone, Smythe, Phillips, & Dement, 1973) represented a major effort to develop and standardize a psychometrically valid measure of self-reported sleepiness. Despite its "better" psychometric construction, it generally yielded data that were similar to those obtained using other self-report measures of sleepiness/fatigue/alertness/activation. It appears that regardless of the type of scale a subject is asked to use, sleepiness ratings generally increase over three days without sleep, provided the subject perceives the situation as one in which it is permissible to express such feelings; the data look similar for analog scales with anchored ends, for adjective checklists, for equal-interval scales, for ratio-estimation scales, and for Likert-type scales (e.g., Angus & Heslegrave, 1985; Dinges, Orne, & Orne, 1984; Froberg et al., 1975; Gillberg & Akerstedt, 1981; Kollar et al., 1969; Murray, Williams, & Lubin, 1958; Richardson et al., 1982). This suggests that there is some experiential dimension that all people invoke when they rate sleepiness, and it probably matters less how you ask them to do it than what the context is in which you ask them to do it.

Although it has been reported that sleepiness ratings are often higher in the middle or at the end of a performance bout during sleep deprivation than prior to it (Carskadon, Harvey, & Dement, 1981; Glenville & Broughton, 1979; Herscovitch & Broughton, 1981), this observation has only recently been studied systematically (Angus & Heslegrave, 1985; Dinges et al., 1984). As is evident in Figure 8.1, the shape of the subjective sleepiness function during sleep deprivation differs when based only on those ratings made during or at the end of performance test bouts versus sleepiness reports taken at the beginning of a performance bout. Interestingly, the functions are not distinct from each other until a full night of sleep loss has taken place. Throughout the second day, until roughly 8:00 p.m., when the circadian peak in the oral temperature cycle occurs, the two functions are significantly different. After the temperature peak, they separate again. Other sleepiness/fatigue/activation scales, including the SSS, show this same pattern (Dinges et al., 1984). However, with the exception of ratings on the confusion-bewilderment subscale of the Profile of Mood States (POMS; McNair, Lorr, & Druppleman, 1971), many other subjective dimensions, such as tension, anger, and depression do not show the pattern. The covariation of the confusion subscale with sleepiness was often supplemented by subjects' spontaneous comments that they did not understand why they felt ''fine'' before coming into the performance room, and now (at the end of the performance bout) they felt so sleepy. Some went so far as to misattribute the increased sleepiness to lower illumination levels in the room and to the air being different in the room (in neither case was it so).

What these and other data seem to suggest is that as sleep need increases, subjective estimates of sleepiness become dependent on the amount of interesting environmental and contextual information afforded us. When the environment is stripped of its interesting qualities (*social* stimulation is the most salient of these) and the sleepy brain is left to remain alert in the face of repetitive performance testing or otherwise boring activity, our phenomenal sense of sleepiness is markedly increased. If we are sleep-deprived, but in the presence of social stimulation, we do not appear to be aware of our diminished capacity to sustain alert functioning. When we are suddenly confronted with the task of remaining alert in the absence of a stimulating environment, we adjust our sleepiness estimates upward, but we also tend to misattribute the reason for the sleepiness because it is not clear why we feel so sleepy when 30 minutes earlier we felt more alert. Has the pressure for sleep changed, or merely our awareness of it?

Behavior

Although subtective self-reports, performance tests, and even most physiological measures of sleepiness involve behaviors or behavioral requirements, this section addresses the extent to which subjects' behavioral acts, choices, and complaints reflect sleepiness. The emphasis is on observed changes in human behavior as sleep need and sleepiness increase.

Studies of human sleep deprivation have noted some characteristic changes in subjects' behaviors over time. Perhaps the most dramatic of the effects attributed to sleep loss were psychotic-like behaviors that were observed in a few subjects with psychiatric histories. Controlled studies soon revealed, however, that neither total sleep loss nor specific sleep stage loss (e.g., REM sleep deprivation) necessarily precipitate psychotic episodes in otherwise normal persons (e.g., Dement, Greenberg, & Klein, 1966; Gulevich, Dement, & Johnson, 1966; Kollar et al., 1969; Murray, 1965), although they do appear to *potentiate* psychotic symptoms in schizophrenic patients (Koranyi & Lehmann, 1960) but *ameliorate* depressive symptoms in many endogenously depressed patients (Vogel, 1975).

Intense sleepiness may not lead to psychosis, but it does produce transient perceptual distortions that are rarely severe enough to be called hallucinations (Murray, 1965). These misperceptions involve visual experiences of diplopia, transient illusions (e.g., flashes of light or airborne particles), and experiences of dreaming while awake (Kleitman, 1963). They are typically reported only by very sleepy individuals. Fantasy intrusion while the person is thinking and less frequently, while the person is speaking (a particularly dramatic behavior to observe), also occurs with intense sleepiness; it is seen in both sleep-deprived persons and following abrupt awakening from deep sleep.

The visual misperceptions, fantasy intrusions, and wake dreams appear to coincide with and result from involuntary slips or lapses into stage 1 microsleeps during the course of prolonged wakefulness. Stage 1 sleep onset is characterized by slow rolling eye movements and hypnogogic reverie. Unfortunately, studies of sleep-deprived subjects have not reported *when* these visual misperceptions and wake dreams are most likely to occur, but our own experience indicates that they are most common during performance test bouts and when the environment is least stimulating. For example, fantasy intrusion while a subject is speaking occurred far more frequently during performance tasks that required oral output than during social conversation outside the performance room. That they are associated with other measures of sleepiness is suggested by the observation that they are more frequent at those times when other measures indicate maximum sleepiness, such as during the circadian nadir.

Other behavioral effects of sleep loss are not particularly dramatic, but even without subjects reporting visual illusions and intruding fantasy into speech, many people feel that they can readily recognize a sleepy person. At least one early study demonstrated that observers rated sleep-deprived subjects as being sleepier than the subjects rated themselves (Murray et al., 1958). Some behaviors indicative of sleepiness are obvious, such as an increase in yawning (a contagious behavior that is not well understood), ptosis, reduced activity, and diminished social interaction. Other behavioral changes observed in sleepy persons are not, however, as conspicuous; these include a cessation of reading, occasional forgetfulness, and an increase in nocturnal eating (sleep is, after all, a period of forced fasting).

In general, when attempting to maintain wakefulness, sleep-deprived subjects will prefer to engage in game playing, (Dinges, 1983) and performance of this kind of activity shows few decrements with prolonged sleep loss (Wilkinson, 1964). Games, of course, typically involve intense social interaction and competitiveness and at least a moderate amount of motor activity without overexpenditure of energy, and performance on them involves little or no extrinsic costs. In performing other activities, such as reading or vigilance tasks, there may be high interest on the part of the sleepy person, but there is little or no social interaction, minimal motor activity, and errors can be costly (e.g., rereading material). The preference among sleepy persons for games involving social interaction suggests that the effort required to sustain wakefulness (which is one way to operationalize sleepiness) in the face of intense sleep need is lessened when the environment and context provide enjoyable social stimulation.

VOLUNTARY SLEEP ONSETS.   If it is reasonable to assume that people elect to go to sleep when they feel sleepy, then voluntary selection of sleep times is another potentially useful way of assessing sleepiness. The selection of a long sleep period every 24 hours, located in the nocturnal phase of the diurnal cycle, is a function of endogenous circadian rhythms that also reflect changes in alertness and sleep tendency. Daytime sleep, however, particularly daytime *napping,* has not been as easily accounted for by chronobiological models of sleepiness and sleep tendency (e.g., Gander, Kronauer, & Graeber, 1985; Zulley & Campbell, 1985). Daytime napping typically occurs when the circadian clock is on the rising phase of the cycle (e.g., rise in body temperature) and after the person has been awake for about eight hours (Dinges, Orne, Orne, & Evans, 1980). Thus, it is not obvious that either circadian or prior wakefulness factors contribute to the napping tendency, which is probably why it has often been attributed to postprandial sleepiness. What is the basis for the daytime sleepiness that results in napping—if that is what napping truly reflects?

Napping has largely been ignored by sleep researchers, being viewed either as an activity of the very young and the very old, or as an anomaly of the variable lifestyles of college students, a population that naps a great deal (Evans & Orne, 1975). More recently, many practitioners of sleep disorders medicine have tended to view it as a sign of EDS, since patients with DOES often nap frequently during the daytime, and have warned against its practice in patients with DIMS because it was thought to contribute to disruption of subsequent nocturnal sleep.

Napping is, however, quite common in healthy adults who have variable or irregular work/rest schedules, such as shiftworkers (Akerstedt, Torsvall, & Gillberg, 1982), short-haul flight crews (Graeber, in press), long-haul transmeridian flight crews (Nicholson, Pascoe, Spencer, Stone, & Green, 1986; Wegmann et al., 1986), and long-haul truck drivers (Mackie & Miller, 1978; R. R. Mackie, personal communication, September 26, 1985). In such groups, as well as in college students, it is not indicative of a sleep disorder (Dinges, Orne, & Orne, 1982), but it is often associated with either a prior night of slightly reduced sleep (due to the subject's work schedule; Dinges et al., 1980, 1981a) or an upcoming lengthy work period (Nicholson et al., 1986). Thus, most napping appears to be voluntary and either a compensatory response to shortened sleep or an anticipatory activity to maintain future alertness.

While compensatory napping is more common in college students (Evans,

Cook, Cohen, Orne, & Orne, 1977) and likely reflects daytime sleepiness, "prophylactic napping" (Orne's concept of napping in anticipation of sleep loss) also appears to affect subsequent alertness by preventing the increase in sleepiness resulting from prolonged periods of wakefulness (Dinges, Orne, Orne, & Whitehouse, 1986). Since the bulk of napping in college students, at least, appears to result from a chronic reduction in nocturnal sleep, it is reasonable to assume that their napping behavior is largely a reflection of increased daytime sleepiness produced by this sleep loss.

There also appear to be chronobiologically based changes in sleepiness that contribute to the tendency to nap during the day. Regardless of the reasons for napping, naps among healthy adults tend to occur at a specific phase of the circadian cycle (circa 1400-1600 hours) approximately 12 hours (i.e., 180°) from the circadian nadir in alertness (Dinges et al., 1980). While performance measures, oral temperature, and subjective sleepiness ratings have occasionally been reported to show a midday "dip" at the time naps are taken, this is not a consistent finding for these measures. Other measures of sleepiness, however, show a midday dip at the time of naps; these include the time of day young adults (nappers and non-nappers) report that they are most alert (Dinges, Orne, Orne, & Evans, 1981) and the time it takes healthy persons to fall asleep on the MSLT (e.g., Richardson et al., 1982). The amount of stage 2 sleep during 5-minute sleep episodes, taken every 20 minutes throughout the day, peaks at this nap time (Lavie & Scherson, 1981), and SWS during 15-hour sleep episodes reappears in this zone (Gagnon, De Koninck, & Broughton, 1985). Studies have also shown that this midday nap zone is a time when sleep onsets are common in healthy young adult subjects confined to bed for more than 24 hours (Campbell, 1984), even if they are instructed to "stay awake" (Nakagawa, 1980; Zomer & Lavie, 1983). Finally, naps occur during the time of day when subjective estimates of sleepiness are significantly increased in sleep-deprived subjects relative to estimates obtained after social interaction (see Figure 9.1).

Although often attributed to a heavy noon meal, the midday sleepiness and nap tendency clearly occurs independent of postprandial effects (Carskadon & Dement, 1985; Colquhoun, 1971b). It has been suggested that it is the second phase of a circasemidian, or about 12-hour rhythm in human sleep tendency (Broughton, 1975, 1985), and that it underlies the siesta pattern of equatorial countries (Dinges, Orne, & Orne, 1983). However, since daytime napping is nowhere near as prevalent as nocturnal sleep onset, this may indicate that the endogenous sleepiness tendency underlying the former is somewhat weaker than that of the latter, although the MSLT data suggests that they are equally intense. Alternatively, since the bulk of human social activity occupies our daytime hours, perhaps the level of environmental stimulation is sufficient to attenuate the sleepiness tendency, thereby obviating the desire or the opportunity to nap for many individuals.

INVOLUNTARY SLEEP ONSETS. The occurrence of voluntary sleep onsets and increased sleep tendency in the middle of the night and the middle of the day should, if they are indicative of increased daytime sleepiness, be accompanied by involuntary sleep onsets at these same times. This is an exceedingly important hypothesis because it suggests that sleepiness and sleep tendency have overt functional consequences for humans working on schedules that increase sleepiness—something that most sleep researchers firmly believe. Sleepiness should not only affect voluntary selection of sleep, but when this selection is interfered with or when there is a pathology of hypersomnolence, there should be behavioral consequences.

The psychosocial and operational consequences of EDS in patients with DOES, particularly narcoleptic patients, is clearly evident (e.g., Broughton & Ghanem, 1976; Broughton, Nevsimalova, & Roth, 1978; Dement, 1983). But the relationship between sleepiness and behavioral functioning in healthy persons is more controversial.

To the extent that we can predict precisely when and under what conditions on-the-job sleepiness should lead to accidents and errors resulting from involuntary sleep onsets and lapses in attention, we have provided support for the hypothesis. Based on everything discussed thus far, accidents and errors should be more prevalent a few hours before and after the circadian nadir at night (i.e., circa 1:00 a.m. to 7:00 a.m.) and to a lesser extent during the midafternoon (circa 1:00 p.m. to 5:00 p.m.). Moreover, they should be most easily demonstrated in human activities that involve relatively low or monotonous environmental stimulation; that is, in contexts that afford little of interest to sustain alertness or hold attention.

There is a surprising amount of data that are consistent with these predictions. The classic data are from a retrospective study of the time of day that errors occurred for 62,000 meter readings in a Swedish gas works (Bjerner, Holm, & Swensson, 1955). Two peaks in errors were found, a large one around 3:00 a.m. and a smaller one around 3:00 p.m., coincident with the voluntary sleep onset data. Studies of the speed with which telephone operators responded to call lights (Browne, 1949) and the speed with which industrial workers joined threads (Wojtczak-Jaroszowa & Pawlowska-Skyba, 1967) also showed slowing around 4:00 a.m., with small secondary peaks around noon. Even data on accidents in hospitals over a five-year period (Folkard, Monk, & Lobban, 1978) and the time of day that 432,000 deaths occurred (Smolensky, Halberg, & Sargent, 1972) reveal a major peak between midnight and 5:00 a.m., and a smaller secondary peak between 3:00 and 4:00 p.m.

Driving, no matter what the vehicle, seems especially prone to drowsiness, errors, missed signals, and accidents at the predicted times. A study of 2,238 failures to respond to warning switches (which then induced automatic brakings) by 15,000 German train drivers revealed a temporal function with two peaks,

3:00 a.m. and 2:00 p.m. (Hildebrandt, Rohmert, & Rutenfranz, 1974). The time of day that 569 Polish automobile drivers reported dozing off at the wheel displayed a peak at 4:00 a.m. and a secondary peak at 1:00 p.m. (Prokop & Prokop, 1955). When 390 "sleep-related" vehicular accidents were separated from all traffic accidents occurring in Israel from 1978 to 1985, two peaks were seen in the frequency histogram, a prominent one at 4:00 a.m. and a lesser one at 4:00 p.m. (Lavie, Wollman, & Pollack, 1986).

Not all data reveal the midafternoon peak in accidents. An analysis of 493 accidents by "dozing" American truck drivers showed a large peak at night (circa 5:00 a.m.), but no midday peak (Mackie & Miller, 1978). Similarly, air-transport accidents that involve fatigue are more frequent between midnight and 6:00 a.m. (Graeber, Foushee, Gander, & Noga, 1985). Finally, some of the more serious nuclear industry accidents in recent times have occurred during this time: The Chernobyl meltdown is officially reported to have involved human error at 1:23 a.m.; the Three Mile Island near-meltdown of Reactor Unit 2 began at 4:00 a.m. and involved eight human errors; the Davis-Beese nuclear reactor reportedly went into automatic shutdown after a control-room operator pushed the wrong two buttons (closing two valves in the backup coolant system) at 1:35 a.m.; and operators were slow to reverse an automatic cooldown after a loss of electrical power to the control room at 4:30 a.m. at the Rancho Seco nuclear reactor.

Clearly it appears as though accidents and errors are far more frequent at the predicted times of increased sleepiness or lowered alertness, especially at night and in occupations that involve minimal environmental stimulation or boring vigilance. Although these data are unquestionably valid because they are actual real-world performance assessments, they also suffer from that very fact. Simply put, we cannot prove that the accidents and errors occurred as a result of height-ened sleepiness or lowered alertness. A skeptic might argue that the nocturnal peak, particularly in transportation functions, could be attributed to darkness and other environmental changes that accompany it, or to alcohol consumption in the evening, while the midafternoon peak could be attributed to a daytime peak in the number of people, vehicles, activities, and processes occurring at this time. Other explanations are also possible; for example, the large midday meal of Swedish workers was suggested as the basis for the midafternoon peak in errors.

The crucial issue is not whether most accidents and errors are primarily caused by lowered alertness, as opposed to other mechanical, behavioral, physi-ological, and psychosocial factors, but, instead, whether alertness can play a key role in accounting for some accidents and errors (or the human response to those problems), particularly when sleepiness has likely been increased for any reason. Once sleepiness is recognized as an important operational variable, counter-measures can be considered to minimize its impact.

Performance

While real-world or field data have superb face validity, the assessment of functional incapacity due to sleepiness ultimately also requires an extensive laboratory performance approach to the problem. Some performance does deteriorate with increased sleep loss, and laboratory-based performance assessments of sleepiness have yielded important insights into the functional nature of sleepiness.

An astounding number of performance tests have been studied in sleep deprivation, and, with the possible exception of memory results (Williams, Gieseking, & Lubin, 1966), many of the effects observed appear to result from a single basic process. As the pressure for sleep increases with time and circadian phase, *lapses* in responding begin to appear (Bjerner, 1949; Williams, Lubin, & Goodnow, 1959). Electroencephalographic recordings during performance bouts indicate that the lapses result from *microsleeps,* which are transient (1-10 seconds) fluctuations by the brain into stage 1 sleep (e.g., Williams, Granda, Jones, Lubin, & Armington, 1962). The effect of lapses on performance varies with the nature of the task, however, such that subject-paced tasks show response slowing when lapses occur, while experimenter-paced tasks show increased errors when lapses occur (Broadbent, 1953). More problematical, however, is the fact that not all tasks are equally sensitive to sleep loss. Subjects appear to be able to motivate themselves to perform near peak levels on many tasks despite overwhelming sleepiness. For this reason, the generalizability of laboratory performance tasks to sleep disorders medicine and real-life occupational contexts has been limited.

The most sensitive laboratory tasks are considered to be those that are long and monotonous, but not too complex, that require continuous attention, that provide little feedback of results, and that offer minimal incentive (Johnson & Naitoh, 1974; Wilkinson, 1968; Woodward, 1974); in keeping with these criteria, a one-hour auditory vigilance task has become the standard behavioral measure of laboratory-induced sleepiness. By implication, short-duration, interesting tasks that provide knowledge of results should not reflect sleepiness. If the performance context is uninteresting, behavioral deficits in performance are evident.

There is, however, increasing evidence that the "lapse hypothesis" does not account for all of the effects of sleep loss on performance (e.g., Kjellberg, 1977a, 1977b, 1977c; Valley & Broughton, 1983), and more importantly, that a diminution in the capacity to perform after increased sleep need can be measured on some simple, short-duration (e.g., 10-minute) tasks, such as reaction time (e.g., Dinges et al., 1986; Glenville, Broughton, Wing, & Wilkinson, 1978; Herscovitch & Broughton, 1981; Lisper & Kjellberg, 1972). Lapses into stage 1 sleep appear to represent the more extreme forms of drowsiness. Lesser degrees of "fragmented wakefulness" also result in performance decrements (Valley &

Broughton, 1983), which are not necessarily confined to lapses in responding (i.e., the longest responses) but also appear in other responses and as a function of time on task (Dinges et al., 1986; Lisper & Kjellberg, 1972).

What this suggests is that the lapse hypothesis and our conceptualization of the most useful performance measure of alertness need to be revised. A sleepy brain appears to fluctuate in level of self-sustained attentiveness before overt behavioral lapses of a few seconds' duration are observed and their operational effects are felt. These fluctuations may occur on the order of milliseconds, and as long as the task has a relatively high and unrelenting signal load, the brain can be "caught" going to sleep. To be sure, long, boring tasks are still among the best behavioral measures, and if the work load is extended to the limit (i.e., continuous performance demands for two or three days without sleep), the effects are profound and evident early on (e.g., Mullaney, Kripke, Fleck, & Johnson, 1983).

Although motivation to perform at one's best for a brief period of time may make it difficult to demonstrate a vulnerability of some types of performance due to sleepiness, performance measures will reflect increased sleepiness if the appropriate ones are used and analyzed correctly. Moreover, these performance deficits tend be maximal at the same times that other sleepiness indicants are increased; for example, the reaction time on a 10-minute task increases significantly with time on the task during the zone when subjective sleepiness ratings change as a function of pre-rating activity (see Figure 9.1; Dinges et al., 1984). Incentive may prop up performance on some cognitive tasks (e.g., Haslam, 1983), but this lasts for only a short period of time (e.g., Horne & Pettitt, 1985).

Because of the effects of motivation and incentives, the traditional "ideal" performance tasks have been long and tedious, and they have been rejected for clinical and field applications. But this situation has partly resulted from a lack of effort in the past 15 years to develop alternative performance measures that are of short duration, highly sensitive, prone to minimal practice effects, and reliable. Albeit quite simple, reaction time appears to have potential as a practical field measure of alertness—it is not unreasonable to suggest that if one cannot do a simple 10-minute reaction-time task without showing significant decrement, then perhaps other more complex tasks might also be at risk when the environment or context ceases to exogenously maintain the alertness level. As long as the goal is to assess the capacity to function or the functional consequences of sleepiness, there is a need for rededicated efforts at documenting sleepiness expressions in behavioral measures that can readily be used in the field.

Psychophysiology

The final class of sleepiness measures to be considered includes all those that rely on a human subject to behave a certain way while a physiological measure is obtained. These psychophysiological or biobehavioral measures have had considerable intuitive appeal as the most "valid" measures of sleepiness, in part because they are thought to be free of the intrapsychic and social-psychological factors that plague behavioral, self-report, and performance measures (e.g., experiential differences, motivational changes, demand characteristics). Unfortunately, this is seldom the case, which is why the more sensitive of these measures (vis-à-vis sleepiness) must be obtained in a highly structured context, where explicit instructions for cooperation are given to subjects. Nevertheless, the idea that the subject is less consciously aware of physiological measures or less able to consciously modify them relative to self-report and behavioral measures has resulted in this class of measures being considered more "objective."

Whether they are measures of objective or physiological sleepiness, however, depends on the extent to which they directly or indirectly measure the increasing tendency of the brain to impose sleep either as a function of experimental manipulations designed to induce varying amounts of sleepiness or as a result of disorders of sleep that are characterized by hypersomnolence. As with other measures of sleepiness considered thus far, the context in which even these ostensibly objective measures are taken appears to affect the sensitivity of the measures. To consider this issue, psychophysiological measures will be arbitrarily divided into those recorded in a wake context, those obtained while the subject is sleeping, and those measures of sleep latency that fall in between these extremes.

WAKE.   Perhaps the most useful measure of sleepiness that could be developed would be one that involves a physiological diagnostic criterion that is easily, perhaps unobtrusively, obtained from an awake human subject, much the way a laboratory test might permit diagnosis of strep throat or pneumonia, or an analysis of breath or blood might indicate alcohol intoxication. At some point the test could indicate "pathological" sleepiness, suggesting that unless corrective action is taken to prop up waking alertness (directly or through improved sleep), potentially catastrophic behavioral consequences will ensue.

This ambitious but laudable goal has long been sought in one form or another. Studies of CNS and autonomic nervous system (ANS) psychophysiology (including everything from electrophysiology of muscles to biochemistry of cerebral spinal fluid) during sustained wakefulness in humans have been numerous. Wake peripheral or ANS electrophysiology has received a good deal of attention in this regard.

Among the peripheral physiological measures of arousal or sleepiness are heart rate (perhaps the most often studied), blood pressure, electrodermal activity, electromyography, and pupillometry. When these measures show changes with increased sleep pressure, the effect is one typically characterized by hypoarousal; the changes are often subtle and inconsistent both within and between subjects until the point at which severe sleepiness is clearly manifested in overt behavioral functioning and mood.

Increased sleepiness has been more reliably indexed by measures that directly assess CNS functions. The use of electroencephalography permitted the discovery of microsleeps (Williams et al., 1962) occuring during lapses in sleep-deprived subjects who were trying to stay awake and function. This was a major step toward understanding that true physiological sleepiness involves the unwanted imposition of light sleep into wakefulness. More recent advances in ambulatory EEG analysis that reflect frequency changes prior to actual stage 1 sleep onsets (e.g., Valley & Broughton, 1983) hold further promise in this area. Of course, such CNS measures are only informative to the extent that the subject is actively attempting to remain awake and alert. In such a context, they reflect the inability of the person to sustain wakefulness.

Evoked potentials (EPs), including auditory and visual EPs, as well as many other EPs ranging from contingent negative variation to electroretinograms have also been used to evaluate the status of the sleepy brain (e.g., Broughton, 1982; Pressman, Spielman, Pollak, & Weitzman, 1982; Williams, Tepas, & Morlock, 1962; Zarcone, Hock, & Barnes, 1982). In general, these measures reveal changes in the amplitude or latency of certain waveform components (depending on the measure) whenever drowsiness is present. Other CNS measures, such as analysis of cerebrospinal fluid, have also been found to reflect hypersomnolence (e.g., Guilleminault & Faull, 1982), but as with EPs, their practical value as assays of sleepiness appears to be limited. Then, too, it is unclear what effect extensive or intrusive measurement procedures themselves have on the response obtained. In the case of EPs, for example, sustained attention to repetitive stimulation may result in accelerated habituation (cf., Kjellberg, 1977a), which, in turn, could accentuate the sleepiness indicator. In this way, EP procedures might function much as a monotonous reaction-time task.

SLEEP.   Although sleep latency tests were reputed to be among the first sleep-based measures of sleepiness, various other measures of sleep have served as indices of the pressure to sleep or need for sleep since the earliest sleep-deprivation studies. Most notably, these measures consist of total sleep time and the amount of specific sleep stages, especially slow wave sleep; others include the depth of sleep as assessed by auditory awakening threshold and the amount of body movement during sleep. These are all legitimate sleep-based measures of sleep tendency. Unfortunately, they are effective measures only when based on the kind of prolonged deep sleep that characterizes recovery from a period of sleep deprivation. This rules out most patients with hypersomnolence because they cannot engage in such undisturbed recovery sleep. In many cases, the EDS they experience is at least partly associated with disturbed sleep; no amount of sleep deprivation, which is what many of them are suffering from, "improves" the sleep as it might for an insomniac (e.g., Spielman, Saskin, & Thorpy, 1983) or an otherwise healthy volunteer undergoing experimentally induced sleepiness. This brings us to the final and perhaps the most exciting development in the measurement of sleepiness since the seminal work by the Walter Reed scientists in the late 1950s and early 1960s.

LATENCY FROM WAKE TO SLEEP.   The time from wakefulness to sleep onset, also known as sleep latency, has been shown to be exquisitely sensitive to increased sleepiness or sleep tendency, particularly the hypersomnolence and EDS that results from serious sleep pathologies (see Carskadon, 1982). Indeed, sleep-latency tests are fast becoming the most widely used clinical tool for assessing EDS in sleep disorders medicine. Foremost among these measures is the MSLT, which consists of repeated naps (e.g., one taken every two hours) during which the latency to stage 1 sleep is measured (Carskadon et al., in press). The naps are limited to only a few minutes of sleep and in the case of the MSLT, they are done on a bed in a dark, quiet room; the subject or patient is asked to "try to go to sleep," and the latency is measured from the time that this instruction is given until stage 1 sleep is present.

The MSLT reflects the increase in sleepiness early on in sleep deprivation (Carskadon & Dement, 1977, 1979) and the sleepiness resulting from varying amounts of truncated nocturnal sleep (e.g., Carskadon & Dement, 1982b). For example, after a night without sleep, healthy college students who normally have sleep latencies that average between 5 and 10 minutes will have latencies that plunge to an average of 1 minute by 7:00 a.m.; if the sleep loss continues for days thereafter, the MSLT remains virtually at zero latency! In addition, the measure has been shown to reflect developmental changes in daytime sleepiness (e.g., Carskadon et al., 1980), and the daytime carryover effects of hypnotic medications on sleepiness (e.g., Dement, Seidel, & Carskadon, 1982). As mentioned earlier, it also shows a 12-hour pattern with shorter latencies occurring around midnocturnal sleep and midafternoon nap time (e.g., Richardson et al., 1982).

The value of the MSLT as an "objective" sleepiness measure has been considerable in sleep disorders medicine. In patients suspected of having EDS as part of narcolepsy, sleep apnea syndrome, CNS hypersomnolence, or other medical disorders, daytime MSLT naps will often reliably yield sleep latencies from 0 to 5 minutes, which is the zone of "pathological" sleepiness (e.g., Dement, Carskadon, & Richardson, 1978; van den Hoed et al., 1981; Zorick et al., 1983). Moreover, the MSLT appears to be sensitive to differential treatment effects in DOES patients (e.g., Zorick et al., 1983). While the increase in sleepiness measured by the MSLT also tends to be correlated with changes in other self-report and behavioral sleepiness indicators in healthy persons undergoing experimentally altered sleep, the MSLT is at times the only measure of sleepiness in patients with EDS that clearly demonstrates the heightened daytime sleep tendency associated with their pathology.

The MSLT is thought to reflect basal or physiological sleepiness that is present in the brain and manifest in low-stimulus situations (Carskadon & Dement, 1982a). As such, it is considered by Carskadon to be an index of vulnerability to falling asleep. It is difficult to argue with this concept when the sleep latency is from 0 to 5 minutes, as it is in many seriously ill patients. But the MSLT does involve a motivated attempt on the part of the subject or patient to try to go to sleep; that is, not to resist sleep in an environment that is deliberately structured to induce sleep. Remarkably, in such a context, most adults, including those who are not sleep deprived, can go to sleep within 20 minutes; many adults, especially college students, can go to sleep during the daytime within 5 to 10 minutes, which approaches the zone of pathological sleepiness. There are even reports of sleep latencies at 11:00 p.m. of less than 5 minutes in 40% of 85 ostensibly healthy adults between the ages of 16 and 59 (Agnew & Webb, 1971).

Short and clinically significant sleep latencies in otherwise healthy populations who are not reporting daytime sleepiness raise an important question: Do these people have especially good control over their sleep onset or are they sleepier than they think? The fact that many college students also engage in a regular midafternoon nap and average nocturnal sleep lengths of under 7 hours suggests that the sleep-latency data may indeed reflect sleepiness in these individuals, albeit only at a specific circadian phase (the nap zone). Alternatively, following a night of sleep deprivation, volunteers will continue to change through the second and third day in their subjective, behavioral, and performance expressions of sleepiness according to a circadian pattern that is accentuated every 24 hours by the additional sustained wakefulness, but they will have long since (i.e., after the first 24 hours) ceased to show any change in the MSLT—it has "bottomed out." Are these continued fluctuations in other sleepiness indices no longer reflecting physiological changes in alertness level? It is doubtful.

The problem, in such cases, is that the MSLT measures the person's "vulnerability to falling asleep" upon request in a sleep-conducive environment, but not necessarily the ability to *resist* falling sleep in this or any other environment. This is a subtle but important qualification concerning what the MSLT measures; without it one has the impression that the MSLT also includes an index of the ability to resist falling asleep and the vulnerability to falling asleep in *any* context. It does neither of these, but in many clinical cases this may not matter, for these reasons.

The data suggest that being vulnerable to falling asleep when encouraged to do so occurs before one loses the ability to resist falling asleep altogether. For example, sleep latency tests that instruct subjects to "try to stay awake" in otherwise sleep-conducive or comfortable environments often show sleep latencies that are much longer than those of the MSLT (e.g., Hartse, Roth, & Zorick, 1982; Mitler, Gujavarty, & Browman, 1982; Mitler, Gujavarty, Sampson, & Browman, 1982). To be sure, even with such instructions, sleep-deprived subjects and patients with DOES fall asleep—it just takes longer. They also are not particularly good at predicting that they will be able to stay awake.

It appears, therefore, that once sleepiness is present, the vulnerability to falling asleep rapidly on request (as measured by the MSLT) reveals this fact clearly—the person goes into stage 1 sleep much sooner than a non-sleepy individual is capable of doing. But the ability to resist sleep may remain relatively intact for some time longer, depending on endogenous (e.g., circadian oscillations in CNS physiology) and exogenous factors (e.g., a stimulating environment or psychologically important interaction); these modulate the latter after the former measure has shown its maximum change. This accounts for why college students may be sleepy, but they can resist it sufficiently to avoid napping everyday and avoid falling asleep in all but the most boring lectures.

In many patients with EDS, measures of vulnerability to falling asleep rapidly on request and ability to resist sleep attacks appear to be highly correlated. Virtually every difference between DOES patients and healthy control subjects that is found with the "stay-awake" instruction is also found with the usual MSLT instruction, but no additional differentiation is obtained; in fact, information needed to further clarify the diagnosis may be more readily available in the MSLT (e.g., REM sleep onsets in narcoleptic naps). For these reasons, the sleep latency tests that involve instructional variants designed to assess the ability to resist sleep do not offer any greater clinical utility than the MSLT.

But assessing the operational consequences of sleep schedules and hygiene in healthy persons may require measurement beyond the MSLT. While the vulnerability to falling asleep on request and the ability to resist falling asleep may also be correlated in nonclinical populations (e.g., in sleep-deprived persons during the circadian nadir of the second night without sleep), this will likely occur only in very extreme circumstances, and the correlation itself may depend on the contexts in which the measures are taken. The ability to resist sleep is much more akin to questions of functional incapacity and optimum performance capability that underlie concerns about sleepiness in the work place. Much more information is needed on the relationship between sleep latency tests and the functional incapacity associated with sleepiness before these tests should be used in the assessment of occupational health to the exclusion of other measures.

CONCLUSIONS

The study of sleepiness is fundamental to understanding the function of sleep itself. Efforts to elucidate the nature of sleepiness, its causes, and its consequences have been prodigious in the past 30 years. Although it can be caused or at least influenced by a host of factors, it can also be operationalized and measured in a variety of ways, some more practical and/or sensitive than others, but most of which provide another dimension vital to understanding it. The history of sleep research has, to some extent, been one of selective emphasis on these different measures of sleepiness.

Within some of these traditions of measurement, most notably the areas of performance (Kjellberg, 1977a) and sleep latency (Carskadon & Dement, 1982a), there has been explicit recognition of the role of the environment and situation in the expression of sleepiness, but the importance of this interactive process in understanding sleepiness in all its manifestations has not generally been recognized. Yet many of the differences among dependent variables designed to index sleepiness are reduced when this contextual factor is taken into account. By "context," I mean variations in amount and type of stimulation and interest afforded by the environment (e.g., low or monotonous stimulation maximizes the expression of the basal sleepiness level), and the meaning of the environment to the subject (e.g., anticipating meeting a loved one near the end of a long, boring ride through Kansas generates an excitement that can attentuate expressions of sleepiness by virtue of what the environment signifies to the person).

This way of conceptualizing the *expression* of sleepiness, as a *contextually-dependent phenomenon,* is not synonomous with an explanation for the cause of sleepiness. There is no evidence to dispute the hypothesis of Carskadon and Dement (1982a) that "a truly alert individual does not feel or appear to be sleepy when placed in a low stimulus environment" (p. S69). On the other hand, the expression of sleepiness in a sleepy person will depend on the context, but there is no way to empirically distinguish between the hypothesis that the uninteresting environment merely unmasks the inherent sleepiness (Carskadon & Dement, 1982a) versus the hypothesis that, for sleep-deprived subjects at least, such an environment actually causes the sleepiness through processes such as habituation (Kjellberg, 1977a, 1977b).

Whatever its physiological substrate in the brain, the overt expression of sleepiness at any given time in voluntary and involuntary behavior, in self-reported sleepiness and mood, in performance, in sleep latency, and in other biobehavioral measures depends on the interaction of the person with the environment. *It appears as though, within limits, the greater the physiological sleepiness, the more dependent we become on the environment to maintain our wakefulness.* Motivation and incentive can contribute to, or override, this environmental effect, but only for a limited period of time. Ultimately, it is the physical and psychological stimulation afforded by the environment that determines whether sleepiness will manifest itself in overt behavioral functioning. Only in very extreme cases, such as prolonged sleep deprivation or pathological daytime sleepiness associated with conditions of CNS hypersomnolence, does the interaction between subject and environment seem to play a less crucial role in the expression of sleepiness. For most of us, however, when sleepiness is heightened for whatever reason, the level of interaction with the environment may ultimately determine whether the sleepiness will be functionally incapacitating (e.g., inability to remain awake while driving for sustained periods).

The contextual dependence of sleepiness expression has implications for the way in which we define alertness or the ability to function vigilantly. If the intrusion of sleepiness into wake functioning is contextually dependent, then alertness does not simply refer to being wide awake and attentive. Rather, *alertness refers to the ability of the brain to sustain attentive wakefulness with little or no interesting stimulation.* This definition is consistent with the seemingly contradictory results of sleep-loss experiments, where performance in a *Monopoly* game can be maintained after 52 hours without sleep, while performance on a simple reaction-time task deteriorates after 24 hours of wakefulness. Moreover, it accounts for the relatively high proportions of accidents and errors occurring at predicted times of sleepiness in occupations that require vigilance in monotonous environments, such as transportation. It also explains how our subjective impression of alertness or sleepiness level changes rapidly as a function of the context we are in when we are sleepy, making it more difficult for us to predict the extent of our ability to remain awake and to know what our alertness level is likely to be in the future.

In terms of understanding the relationship between sleepiness and the capacity to function, the most effective measures of sleepiness for experimental, clinical, and occupational health applications will continue to be those that tap the inherent alertness level of the person through this veil of contextual variability. The best behavioral and physiological tests have this feature in common; as Roth, Roehrs, and Zorick (1982) have noted, "the MSLT is like a performance test constructed with the aim of optimizing performance decrements" (p. S133). The same could be said of the 1-hour Wilkinson Vigilance Test. While long, boring vigilance tasks and sleep latency tests provide much information, the development of brief, yet highly sensitive behavioral measures of alertness continues to require attention if we are to assess crucial questions of functional vulnerability to sleepiness. Such questions take on ever-increasing importance at a time when many industrial and governmental policies concerning health and safety are formulated without regard to the basic biological processes that cause sleepiness or those that permit its unwanted expression into on-the-job wakefulness.

REFERENCES

Agnew, Jr., H. W., & Webb, W. B. (1971). Sleep latencies in human subjects: Age, prior wakefulness, and reliability. *Psychonomic Science, 24,* 253–254.

Akerstedt, T., Torsvall, L., & Gillberg, M. (1982). Sleepiness and shift work: Field studies. *Sleep, 5*(Supplement 2), S95–S106.

Angus, R. G., & Heslegrave, R. J. (1985). Effects of sleep loss on sustained cognitive performance during a command and control simulation. *Behavior Research Methods, Instruments, & Computers, 17*(1), 55–67.

Aschoff, J. (1965). Circadian rhythms in man. *Science, 148,* 1427–1432.

Association of Sleep Disorders Centers (1979). Diagnostic classification of sleep and arousal disorders (1st ed. prepared by the Sleep Disorders Classification Committee, H. P. Roffwarg, Chair.). *Sleep, 2,* 1–137.

Bjerner, B. (1949). Alpha depression and lowered pulse rate during delayed actions in a serial reaction test. *Acta Physiologica Scandinavica, 19,* Supplement 65, p. 93.

Bjerner, B., Holm, A., & Swensson, A. (1955). Diurnal variation in mental performance: A study of three-shift workers. *British Journal of Industrial Medicine, 12,* 103–110.

Bohlin, G., & Kjellberg, A. (1973). Self-reported arousal during sleep deprivation and its relation to performance and physiological variables. *Scandanavian Journal of Psychology, 14,* 78–86.

Bonnet, M. H. (1985). Effect of sleep disruption on sleep, performance, and mood. *Sleep, 8,* 11–19.

Bonnet, M. H. (1986). Performance and sleepiness as a function of frequency and placement of sleep disruption. *Psychophysiology, 23,* 263–271.

Borbély, A. A. (1982). Sleep regulation: Circadian rhythm and homeostasis. In D. Ganten & D. Pfaff (Eds.), *Current topics in neuroendocrinology, Volume 1. Sleep: Clinical and experimental aspects* (pp. 83–103). New York: Springer-Verlag.

Broadbent, D. E. (1953). Neglect of the surroundings in relation to fatigue decrements in output. In W. F. Floyd & A. T. Welford (Eds.), *Fatigue* (pp. 173–178). London: Lewis.

Broughton, R. J. (1968). Sleep disorders: Disorders of arousal? *Science, 159,* 1070–1078.

Broughton, R. J. (1975). Biorhythmic fluctuations in consciousness and psychological functions. *Canadian Psychological Review, 16,* 217–239.

Broughton, R. (1982). Performance and evoked potential measures of various states of daytime sleepiness. *Sleep, 5*(Supplement 2), S135–S146.

Broughton, R. J. (1985). Three central issues concerning ultradian rhythms. In H. Schulz & P. Lavie (Eds.), *Experimental brain research supplementum 12: Ultradian rhythms in physiology and behavior* (pp. 217–233). New York: Springer-Verlag.

Broughton, R., & Ghanem, Q. (1976). The impact of compound narcolepsy on the life of the patient. In C. Guilleminault, W. Dement, & P. Passouant (Eds.), *Narcolepsy* (pp. 201–220). New York: Spectrum.

Broughton, R., Nevsimalova, S., & Roth, B. (1978). The socioeconomic effects (including work, education, recreation and accidents) of idiopathic hypersomnia. In M. H. Chase, M. M. Mitler, & P. L. Walter (Eds.), *Sleep research: Volume 7* (p. 217). Los Angeles: University of California.

Browne, R. C. (1949). The day and night performance of teleprinter switchboard operators. *Occupational Psychology, 23,* 121–126.

Campbell, S. S. (1984). Duration and placement of sleep in a "disentrained" environment. *Psychophysiology, 21,* 106–113.

Carskadon, M. A. (Ed.). (1982). Current perspectives on daytime sleepiness. *Sleep, 5*(Supplement 2), S55–S202.

Carskadon, M. A., & Dement, W. C. (1977). Sleep tendency: An objective measure of sleep loss. In M. H. Chase, M. M. Mitler, & P. L. Walter (Eds.), *Sleep research: Volume 6* (p. 200). Los Angeles: University of California.

Carskadon, M. A., & Dement, W. C. (1979). Effects of total sleep loss on sleep tendency. *Perceptual and Motor Skills, 48,* 495–506.

Carskadon, M. A., & Dement, W. C. (1982a). The multiple sleep latency test: What does it measure? *Sleep, 5*(Supplement 2), S67–S72.

Carskadon, M. A., & Dement, W. C. (1982b). Nocturnal determinants of daytime sleepiness. *Sleep, 5*(supplement 2), S73–S81.

Carskadon, M. A., & Dement, W. C. (1985). Midafternoon decline in MSLT scores on a constant routine. In M. H. Chase, D. J. McGinty, & R. Wilder-Jones (Eds.), *Sleep research: Volume 14* (p. 292). Los Angeles: University of California.

Carskadon, M. A., Dement, W. C., Mitler, M. M., Roth, T., Westbrook, P., & Keenan, S. (in press). Guidlines for the multiple sleep latency test (MSLT): A standard measure of sleepiness. *Sleep.*

Carskadon, M. A., Harvey, K., & Dement, W. C. (1981). Sleep loss in young adolescents. *Sleep, 4,* 299–312.

Carskadon, M. A., Harvey, K., Duke, P., Anders, T. F., Litt, I. F., & Dement, W. C. (1980). Pubertal changes in daytime sleepiness. *Sleep, 2,* 453–460.

Carskadon, M. A., Mancuso, J., Keenan, S., Littell, W., Dement, W. C. (1986). Sleepiness following oversleeping. In M. H. Chase, D. J. McGinty, & G. Crane (Eds.), *Sleep research: Volume 15* (p. 70). Los Angeles: University of California.

Colquhoun, W. P. (Ed). (1971a). *Biological rhythms and human performance.* New York: Academic Press.

Colquhoun, W. P. (1971b). Circadian variations in mental efficiency. In W. P. Colquhoun (Ed.), *Biological rhythms and human performance* (pp. 39–107). New York: Academic Press.

Czeisler, C. A., Weitzman, E. D., Moore-Ede, M. C., Zimmerman, J. C., & Knauer, R. S. (1980). Human sleep: Its duration and organization depend on its circadian phase. *Science, 210,* 1264–1267.

Daan, S., Beersma, D. G. M., & Borbély, A. A. (1984). Timing of human sleep: Recovery process gated by a circadian pacemaker. *American Journal of Physiology, 246,* R161–R178.

Dement, W. C. (1983). Signs and symptoms of sleep disorders. In J. K. Walsh, A. D. Bertelson, & P. K. Schweitzer (Eds.), *Clinical aspects of sleep disorders: Proceedings of a symposium* (pp. 13–32). St. Louis: Deaconess Hospital.

Dement, W. C., & Carskadon, M. A. (1982). Current perspectives on daytime sleepiness: The issues. *Sleep, 5*(Supplement 2), S56–S66.

Dement, W. C., Carskadon, M. A., & Richardson, G. S. (1978). Excessive daytime sleepiness in the sleep apnea syndrome. In C. Guilleminault & W. C. Dement (Eds.), *Sleep apnea syndromes* (pp. 23–46). New York: Alan R. Liss.

Dement, W. C., Greenberg, S., & Klein, R. (1966). The effect of partial REM sleep deprivation and delayed recovery. *Journal of Psychiatric Research, 4,* 141–152.

Dement, W. C., Seidel, W., & Carskadon, M. A. (1982). Daytime alertness, insomnia, and benzodiazepines. *Sleep, 5,* S28–S45.

Dinges, D. F. (1983). *Prophylactic napping to sustain performance and alertness in continuous operations* (Contract No. N00014-80-C-0380, Progress Report 0001AN). Arlington, VA: Office of Naval Research.

Dinges, D. F., Orne, E. C., Evans, F. J., & Orne, M. T. (1981a). Performance after naps in sleep-conducive and alerting environments. In L. C. Johnson, W. P. Colquhoun, D. I. Tepas, & M. J. Colligan (Eds.), *Advances in sleep research: Volume 7. Biological rhythms, sleep and shift work* (pp. 539–552). New York: SP Medical & Scientific Books.

Dinges, D. F., Orne, E. C., & Orne, M. T. (1982). Napping: Symptom or adaptation. In M. H. Chase, W. B. Webb, & R. Wilder-Jones (Eds.), *Sleep research: Volume 11* (p. 100). Los Angeles: University of California.

Dinges, D. F., Orne, E. C., & Orne, M. T. (1983). Napping in North America: A siesta rhythm? In M. H. Chase, W. B. Webb, & R. Wilder-Jones (Eds.), *Sleep research: Volume 12* (p. 29). Los Angeles: University of California.

Dinges, D. F., Orne, M. T., & Orne, E. C. (1984). Sleepiness during sleep deprivation: The effects of performance demands and circadian phase. In M. H. Chase, W. B. Webb, & R. Wilder-Jones (Eds.), *Sleep research: Volume 13* (p. 189). Los Angeles: University of California.

Dinges, D. F., Orne, M. T., & Orne, E. C. (1985). Sleep depth and other factors associated with performance upon abrupt awakening. In M. H. Chase, D. J. McGinty, & R. Wilder-Jones (Eds.), *Sleep research: Volume 14* (p. 92). Los Angeles: University of California.

Dinges, D. F., Orne, M. T., Orne, E. C., & Evans, F. J. (1980). *Voluntary self-control of sleep to facilitate quasi-continuous performance.* (U.S. Army Medical Research and Development Command Report No. 80). Fort Detrick, Frederick, MD: U. S. Army Medical Research and Development Command (NTIS No. AD-A102264).

Dinges, D. F., Orne, M. T., Orne, E. C., & Evans, F. J. (1981b). Behavioral patterns in habitual nappers. In M. H. Chase, D. F. Kripke, & P. L. Walter (Eds.), *Sleep research: Volume 10* (p. 136). Los Angeles: University of California.

Dinges, D. F., Orne, M. T., Orne, E. C., & Whitehouse, W. G. (1986). Napping to sustain performance and mood: Effects of circadian phase and sleep loss. In M. Haider, M. Koller, & R.

Cervinka (Eds.), *Studies in industrial and organizational psychology: Volume 3. Night and shiftwork: Longterm effects and their prevention: Proceedings of the VII International Symposium on Night- and Shiftwork, Igls, Austria, 1985* (pp. 23–30). New York: Verlag Peter Lang.

Evans, F. J., Cook, M. R., Cohen, H. D., Orne, E. C., & Orne, M. T. (1977). Appetitive and replacement naps: EEG and behavior. *Science, 197,* 687–689.

Evans, F. J., & Orne, M. T. (1975). *Recovery from fatigue.* (U.S. Army Medical Research and Development Command Report No. 60). Washington, D.C.: U. S. Army Medical Research and Development Command (DTIC No. A100347).

Fernstrom, J. D., & Wurtman, R. J. (1971). Brain serotonin content: Increase following ingestion of carbohydrate diet. *Science, 174,* 1023–1025.

Folkard, S., & Monk, T. H. (Eds.). (1985). *Psychology and productivity at work series. Hours of work: Temporal factors in work-scheduling.* New York: John Wiley & Sons.

Folkard, S., Monk, T. H., & Lobban, M. C. (1978). Short- and long-term adjustment of circadian rhythms in "permanent" night nurses. *Ergonomics, 21,* 785–799.

Froberg, J. E., Karlsson, C-G., Levi, L., & Lidberg, L. (1975). Circadian rhythms of catecholamine excretion, shooting range performance and self-ratings of fatigue during sleep deprivation. *Biological Psychology, 2,* 175–188.

Gagnon, P., De Koninck, J., & Broughton, R. (1985). Reappearance of electroencephalogram slow waves in extended sleep with delayed bedtime. *Sleep, 8,* 118–128.

Gander, P. H., Kronauer, R. E., & Graeber, R. C. (1985), Phase shifting two coupled circadian pacemakers: Implications for jet lag. *American Journal of Physiology (Regulatory Integrative Comparative Physiology), 18,* R704–R719.

Gillberg, M., & Akerstedt, T. (1981). Possible measures of "sleepiness" for the evaluation of disturbed and displaced sleep. In A. Reinberg, N. Vieux, & P. Andlauer (Eds.), *Advances in the biosciences: Volume 30. Night and shift work: Biological and social aspects* (pp. 155–160). Oxford: Pergamon.

Glenville, M., & Broughton, R. J. (1979). Reliability of the Stanford Sleepiness Scale compared to short duration performance tests and the Wilkinson auditory vigilance task. In P. Passouant & I. Oswald (Eds.), *Pharmacology of the states of alertness* (pp. 235–244). Oxford: Pergamon.

Glenville, M., Broughton, R. J., Wing, A. M., & Wilkinson, R. T. (1978). Effects of sleep deprivation on short-duration performance measures compared to the Wilkinson auditory vigilance task. *Sleep, 1,* 169–176.

Globus, G. G. (1969). A syndrome associated with sleeping late. *Psychosomatic Medicine, 31,* 528–535.

Globus, G. G. (1970). Sleep duration and feeling state. *Int. Psychiatry Clinics, 7,* 78–84.

Graeber, R. C. (in press). Sleep and fatigue in short-haul flight operations: A field study. *Proceedings of the Flight Safety Foundation, Inc., 38th International Air Safety Seminar.*

Graeber, R. C., Foushee, H. C., Gander, P. H., & Noga, G. W. (1985). Circadian rhythmicity and fatigue in flight operations. *Journal of UOEH, 7*(Supplement), 122–129.

Guilleminault, C., & Faull, K. F. (1982). Sleepiness in non-narcoleptic, non-sleep apneic EDS patients: The idiopathic CNS hypersomnolence. *Sleep, 5*(Supplement 2), S175–S181.

Gulevich, G., Dement, W. C., & Johnson, L. (1966). Psychiatric and EEG observations on a case of prolonged (264 hours) wakefulness. *Archives of General Psychiatry, 15,* 29–35.

Hartmann, E. (1982/1983). Effects of L-tryptophan on sleepiness and on sleep. *Journal of Psychiatric Research, 17,* 107–113.

Hartse, K. M., Roth, T., & Zorick, F. J. (1982). Daytime sleepiness and daytime wakefulness: The effect of instruction. *Sleep, 5*(Supplement 2), S107–S118.

Haslam, D. R. (1983). The incentive effect and sleep deprivation. *Sleep, 6,* 362–368.

Herscovitch, J., & Broughton, R. (1981). Performance deficits following short-term partial sleep deprivation and subsequent recovery oversleeping. *Canadian Journal of Psychology, 35,* 309–322.

Hildebrandt, G., Rohmert, W., & Rutenfranz, J. (1974). Twelve- and 24-hour rhythms in error frequency of locomotive drivers and the influence of tiredness. *International Journal of Chronobiology, 2,* 175–180.

Hoddes, E., Zarcone, V., Smythe, H., Phillips, R., & Dement, W. C. (1973). Quantification of sleepiness: A new approach. *Psychophysiology, 10,* 431–436.

Horne, J. A. (1978). A review of the biological effects of total sleep deprivation in man. *Biological Psychology, 7,* 55–102.

Horne, J. A. (1985). Sleep function, with particular reference to sleep deprivation. *Annals of Clinical Research, 17,* 199–208.

Horne, J. A., & Pettitt, A. N. (1985). High incentive effects on vigilance performance during 72 hours of total sleep deprivation. *Acta Psychologica, 58,* 123–139.

Johnson, L. C., & Naitoh, P. (1974). *The operational consequences of sleep deprivation and sleep deficit* (NATO/AGARDograph No. 193). London: Technical Editing and Reproduction.

Johnson, L. C., Tepas, D. I., Colquhoun, W. P., & Colligan, M. J. (1981). *Advances in sleep research: Volume 7. Biological rhythms, sleep and shift work.* New York: Spectrum Publications.

Kamiya, J. (1961). Behavioral, subjective, and physiological aspects of drowsiness and sleep. In D. W. Fiske & S. R. Maddi (Eds.), *Functions of varied experience* (pp. 145–174). Homewood, IL: Dorsey.

Kjellberg, A. (1977a). Sleep deprivation and some aspects of performance: I. Problems of arousal changes. *Sleeping and Waking, 1,* 139–143.

Kjellberg, A. (1977b). Sleep deprivation and some aspects of performance: II. Lapses and other attentional effects. *Sleeping and Waking, 1,* 145–148.

Kjellberg, A. (1977c). Sleep deprivation and some aspects of performance: III. Motivation, comment and conclusions. *Sleeping and Waking, 1,* 149–153.

Kleitman, N. (1963). *Sleep and wakefulness* (rev. ed.). Chicago: The University of Chicago Press.

Kollar, E. J., Pasnau, R. O., Rubin, R. T., Naitoh, P., Slater, G. G., & Kales, A. (1969). Psychological, psychophysiological, and biochemical correlates of prolonged sleep deprivation. *American Journal of Psychiatry, 126,* 488–497.

Koranyi, E. K., & Lehmann, H. E. (1960). Experimental sleep deprivation in schizophrenic patients. *Archives of General Psychiatry, 2,* 534–544.

Lavie, P., & Scherson, A. (1981). Ultrashort sleep-waking schedule. I. Evidence of ultradian rhythmicity in "sleepability." *Electroencephalography and Clinical Neurophysiology, 52,* 163–174.

Lavie, P., Wollman, M., & Pollack, I. (1986). Frequency of sleep related traffic accidents and hour of the day. In M. H. Chase, D. J. McGinty, & G. Crame (Eds.), *Sleep research: Volume 15* (p. 275). Los Angeles: University of California.

Lieberman, H. R., Corkin, S., Spring, B. J., Growdon, J. H., & Wurtman, R. J. (1982/1983). Mood, performance, and pain sensitivity: Changes induced by food constituents. *Journal of Psychiatric Research, 17,* 135–145.

Lisper, H.-0., & Kjellberg, A. (1972). Effects of 24-hour sleep deprivation on rate of decrement in a 10-minute auditory reaction time task. *Journal of Experimental Psychology, 96,* 287–290.

Lubin, A., Hord, D., Tracy, M. L., & Johnson, L. C. (1976). Effects of exercise, bed rest and napping on performance decrement during 40 hours. *Psychophysiology, 13,* 334–339.

Mackie, R. R., & Miller, J. C. (1978). *Effects of hours of service, regularity of schedules, and cargo loading on truck and bus driver fatigue* (Human Factors Research, Inc., Technical Report No. 1765-F). Washington, D.C.: Department of Transportation, Bureau of Motor Carrier Safety, FHWA, and National Highway Traffic Safety Administration.

Malmo, R. B. (1959). Activation: A neurophysiological dimension. *Psychology Review, 66,* 367–386.

Malmo, R. B., & Belanger, D. (1967). Related physiological and behavioral changes: What are their determinants? *Proceedings of the Association for Research in Nervous and Mental Disorders, 45,* 288–318.

McNair, D. M., Lorr, M., & Druppleman, L. F. (1971). *EITS manual for the profile of mood states*. San Diego: Educational and Industrial Test Services.

Michelson, E. (1897). Untersuchungen ueber die tiefe des schlafes [Investigation into the depth of sleep]. *Psychologische Arbeiten, 2,* 84–117.

Mitler, M. M., Gujavarty, K. S., & Browman, C. P. (1982). Clinical note: Maintenance of wakefulness test: A polysomnographic technique for evaluating treatment efficacy in patients with excessive somnolence. *Electroencephalography and Clinical Neurophysiology, 53,* 658–661.

Mitler, M. M., Gujavarty, K. S., Sampson, M. G., & Browman, C. P. (1982). Multiple daytime nap approaches to evaluating the sleepy patient. *Sleep, 5*(Supplement 2), S119–S127.

Moore-Ede, M. C., & Czeisler, C. A. (Eds.). (1984). *Mathematical models of the circadian sleep-wake cycle*. New York: Raven Press.

Moore-Ede, M. C., & Richardson, G. S. (1985). Medical implications of shift-work. *Annual Review of Medicine, 36,* 607–617.

Moore-Ede, M. C., Sulzman, F. M., & Fuller, C. A. (1982). *The clocks that time us*. Cambridge, MA: Harvard University Press.

Morris, G. O., & Singer, M. T. (1966). Sleep deprivation: The context of consciousness. *Journal of Nervous and Mental Disease, 143,* 291–304.

Mullaney, D. J., Kripke, D. F., Fleck, P. A., & Johnson, L. C. (1983). Sleep loss and nap effects on sustained continuous performance. *Psychophysiology, 20,* 643–651.

Murray, E. J. (1965). *Sleep, dreams, and arousal*. New York: Meredith Publishing.

Murray, E. J., Williams, H. L., & Lubin, A. (1958). Body temperature and psychological ratings during sleep deprivation. *Journal of Experimental Psychology, 56,* 271–273.

Naitoh, P. (1976). Sleep deprivation in human subjects: A reappraisal. *Waking and Sleeping, 1,* 53–60.

Nakagawa, Y. (1980). Continuous observation of EEG patterns at night and in daytime of normal subjects under restrained conditions. I. Quiescent state when lying down. *Electroencephalography and Clinical Neurophysiology, 49,* 524–537.

Nicholson, A. N., Pascoe, P. A., Spencer, M. B., Stone, B. M., & Green, R. L. (1986). Nocturnal sleep and daytime alertness of air crew after transmeridian flights. In R. C. Graeber (Ed.), *Crew factors in flight operations: IV. Sleep and wakefulness in international aircrews* (NASA Technical Memorandum 88231, pp. 69–84). Ames Research Center, Moffett Field, CA: National Aeronautics and Space Administration.

Orne, M. T. (1962). On the social psychology of the psychological experiment: With particular reference to demand characteristics and their implications. *American Psychologist, 17,* 776–783.

Patrick, G. T. W., & Gilbert, J. A. (1896). On the effects of loss of sleep. *Psychology Review, 3,* 469–483.

Pressman, M. R., Spielman, A. J., Pollak, C. P., & Weitzman, E. D. (1982). Long-latency auditory evoked responses during sleep deprivation and in narcolepsy. *Sleep, 5*(Supplement 2), S147–S156.

Prokop, O., & Prokop, L. (1955). Ermudung und einschlafen am steuer [Fatigue and falling asleep while driving]. *Deutsche Zeitschrift fur gerichtliche Medizin, 44,* 343–355.

Rechtschaffen, A. (1979). The function of sleep: Methodological issues. In R. Drucker-Colin, M. Shkurovich, & M. B. Sterman (Eds.), *The functions of sleep* (pp. 1–17). New York: Academic.

Rechtschaffen, A., Gilliland, M. A., Bergmann, B. M., & Winter, J. B. (1983). Physiological correlates of prolonged sleep deprivation in rats. *Science, 221,* 182–184.

Richardson, G. S., Carskadon, M. A., Orav, E. J., & Dement, W. C. (1982). Circadian variation of sleep tendency in elderly and young adult subjects. *Sleep, 5*(Supplement 2), S82–S94.

Roth, T., Roehrs, T., & Zorick, F. (1982). Sleepiness: Its measurement and determinants. *Sleep, 5*(Supplement 2), S128–S134.

Schachter, S., & Singer, J. E. (1962). Cognitive, social, and physiological determinants of emotional state. *Psychology Review, 69,* 379–399.

Smolensky, M., Halberg, F., & Sargent, F. (1972). Chronobiology of the life sequence. In S. Ito, K. Ogata, & H. Yoshimura (Eds.), *Advances in climatic physiology* (pp. 515–516). Tokyo: Igaku Shoin.

Spielman, A. J., Saskin, P., & Thorpy, M. J. (1983). Sleep restriction treatment of insomnia. In M. H. Chase, W. B. Webb, & R. Wilder-Jones (Eds.), *Sleep research: Volume 12* (p. 286). Los Angeles: University of California.

Stepanski, E., Lamphere, J., Badia, P., Zorick, F., & Roth, T. (1984). Sleep fragmentation and daytime sleepiness. *Sleep, 7,* 18–26.

Strogatz, S. H., Kronauer, R. E., & Czeisler, C. A. (1986). Circadian regulation dominates homeostatic control of sleep length and prior wake length in humans. *Sleep, 9,* 353–364.

Takahashi, J. S., & Zatz, M. (1982). Regulation of circadian rhythmicity. *Science, 217,* 1104–1111.

Taub, J., Globus, G., Phoebus, E., & Drury, R. (1969). Extended sleep and performance. *Nature, 233,* 142–143.

Valley, V., & Broughton, R. (1983). The physiological (EEG) nature of drowsiness and its relation to performance deficits in narcoleptics. *Electroencephalography and Clinical Neurophysiology, 55,* 243–251.

van den Hoed, J., Kraemer, H., Guilleminault, C., Zarcone, V. P., Jr., Miles, L. E., Dement, W. C., & Mitler, M. M. (1981). Disorders of excessive daytime somnolence: Polygraphic and clinical data for 100 patients. *Sleep, 4,* 23–37.

Vogel, G. W. (1975). A review of REM sleep deprivation. *Archives of General Psychiatry, 32,* 749–761.

Webb, W. B. (1979). Theories of sleep functions and some clinical implications. In R. Drucker-Colin, M. Shkurovich, & M. B. Sterman (Eds.), *The functions of sleep* (pp. 19–35). New York: Academic.

Webb, W. B. (Ed.). (1982). *Wiley series on studies in human performance: Biological rhythms, sleep, and performance.* New York: John Wiley & Sons.

Wegmann, H. M., Gundel, A., Naumann, M., Samel, A., Schwartz, E., & Vejvoda, M. (1986). Sleep, sleepiness, and circadian rhythmicity in air crews operating on transatlantic routes. In R. C. Graeber (Ed.), *Crew factors in flight operations: IV. Sleep and wakefulness in international aircrews* (NASA Technical Memorandum 88231, pp. 85–104). Ames Research Center, Moffett Field, CA: National Aeronautics and Space Administration.

Wilkinson, R. T. (1964). Effects of up to 60 hours' sleep deprivation on different types of work. *Ergonomics, 7,* 175–186.

Wilkinson, R. T. (1965). Sleep deprivation. In O. G. Edholm & A. L. Bacharach (Eds.), *The physiology of human survival* (pp. 399–430). New York: Academic.

Wilkinson, R. T. (1968). Sleep deprivation: Performance tests for partial and selective sleep deprivation. In L. E. Abt & B. F. Riess (Eds.), *Progress in clinical psychology: Volume 8. Dreams and dreaming* (pp. 28–43). New York: Grune & Stratton.

Williams, H. L., Gieseking, C. F., & Lubin, A. (1966). Some effects of sleep loss on memory. *Perceptual and Motor Skills, 23,* 1287.

Williams, H. L., Granda, A. M., Jones, P. C., Lubin, A., & Armington, J. C. (1962). EEG frequency and finger pulse volume as predictors of reaction time during sleep loss. *Electroencephalography and Clinical Neurophysiology, 14,* 64–70.

Williams, H. L., Lubin, A., & Goodnow, J. J. (1959). Impaired performance with acute sleep loss. *Psychological Monographs: General and Applied, 73*(44), 1–26.

Williams, H. L., Tepas, P. I., & Morlock, H. C. (1962). Evoked responses to clicks and electroencephalographic stages of sleep. *Science, 138,* 685–686.

Winfree, A. T. (1982). Circadian timing of sleepiness in man and woman. *American Journal of Physiology, 243,* R193–R204.

Wojtczak-Jaroszowa, J., & Pawlowska-Skyba, K. (1967). Praca nocna i zmianowa: I. Dobowe wahania sprawnosci a wydajnosc pracy [Work at night and shiftwork: I. Day and night oscillations of working capacity and the work efficiency]. *Medycyna Pracy, 18* (1), 1–10.

Woodward, D. P. (1974). *A user-oriented review of the literature on the effects of sleep loss, work-rest schedules, and recovery on performance* (Office of Naval Research, Technical Report No. ACR-206).

Zarcone, V. P., Jr., Hock, P. A., & Barnes, D. L. B. (1982). The effect of partial sleep deprivation on the electroretinogram. In M. H. Chase, W. B. Webb, & R. Wilder-Jones (Eds.), *Sleep research: Volume 11* (p. 197). Los Angeles: University of California.

Zomer, J., & Lavie, P. (1983). The effect of sleep deprivation the temporal structure of sleepability and wakeability. In M. H. Chase, W. B. Webb, & R. Wilder-Jones (Eds.), *Sleep research: Volume 12* (p. 338). Los Angeles: University of California.

Zorick, F., Roehrs, T., Conway, W., Fujita, S., Wittig, R., & Roth, T. (1983). Effects of UPPP on the daytime sleepiness associated with sleep apnea syndrome. *Bulletin of European Physiopathology and Respiration, 19,* 600–603.

Zulley, J., & Campbell, S. S. (1985). Napping behavior during "spontaneous internal desynchronization": Sleep remains in synchrony with body temperature. *Human Neurobiology, 4,* 123–126.

AUTHOR NOTES

The review and substantive evaluation on which this article is based was supported in part by Office of Naval Research Contract N00014-80-C-0380, in part by National Institute of Mental Health Grant MH-19156, and in part by a grant from the Institute for Experimental Psychiatry Research Foundation to David F. Dinges.

I am grateful to Wayne G. Whitehouse, Michael Bonnet, Martin T. Orne, and Emily Carota Orne, for their helpful comments and suggestions, and to Stephen R. Fairbrother for his expertise and assistance in finalizing the manuscript.

10
THE COGNITIVE-BEHAVIORAL TREATMENT OF INSOMNIA

Peter Hauri, Ph.D.
Mayo Medical School

Chronic and serious insomnia is a widespread problem. The incidence rate of patients complaining seriously about insomnia has been consistently placed at about 15 percent of the general U.S. population. About six percent of the population complain to their physicians about insomnia, and about three percent receive prescription hypnotics (Institute of Medicine, 1979).

Although there are some insomniacs whose problem lies beyond the scope of behavioral intervention, the majority of chronic insomnias are related to stress, anxiety, mild depression, maladaptive conditioning, and poor sleep hygiene. These are factors that are obviously treatable with behavioral techniques. Despite this, however, there are few behavioral insomnia clinics in this country in the same sense as there are behavioral pain or headache clinics. Rather, if chronic insomnia is treated at all, it is most often treated with hypnotics. This is unfortunate, because treatment with hypnotics is effective only in the short and intermediate range—days, weeks, months (Kales, Bixler, Tan, Scharf, & Kales, 1974)—while chronic insomnias typically last years or decades.

This paper will focus on some of the problems and issues in the behavioral treatment of insomnia. The goal is to explore some of the reasons why we do not yet have thriving behavioral insomnia clinics. After a short review of the behavioral treatments and concepts about insomnia that are currently available, some basic neurological mechanisms of sleep induction will be discussed. This is done because it appears that behavioral therapists are not currently using up-to-date knowledge on insomnia. Finally, the paper calls attention to a very individualized cognitive treatment of insomnia. It appears that such a treatment can be quite effective if it is well focused on the individual insomniac's specific problem.

CURRENTLY AVAILABLE BEHAVIORAL TECHNIQUES

Most behaviorists use one or a combination of the following four techniques when treating insomnia:

1. *Relaxation therapy* attempts to establish a hypometabolic, deeply relaxed state. This can be done with any of the recognized relaxation techniques such as biofeedback, progressive muscle relaxation, meditation, self-hypnosis, or autogenic training. It is assumed that patients will fall asleep naturally once they have learned how to relax, and there are many studies to verify this assumption (e.g., Borkovec, Grayson, O'Brien, & Weerts, 1979; Borkovec & Weerts, 1976; Coursey, Frankel, Gaardner, & Mott, 1980; Freedman & Papsdorf, 1976).

2. *Stimulus-control therapy* explains to patients that lying in bed frustrated and awake does harm because it strengthens a learned association between the stimuli in the bedroom and arousal (Bootzin, 1972). Therefore, patients are asked to go to bed only when expecting to fall asleep easily and to get up as soon as they realize that they are not falling asleep with ease. They are then asked to remain outside the bedroom until they feel that they might fall asleep easily. This process is repeated all night, if necessary. Patients may initially have to get up 5 to 15 times during a treatment night, but many learn quickly to reassociate the bedroom with relaxation and sleep. There are three additional restrictions: First, get up in the morning at the usual time, even if most of the nighttime hours were spent awake, away from the bedroom. Second, take no naps. Third, engage in no other activities in the bedroom except sleeping (and sex). Stimulus-control is a very thoroughly investigated treatment modality with numerous reports showing its superiority over placebo (Haynes, Price, & Simons, 1975; Lacks, Bertelson, Sugerman & Kunkel, 1983; Turner & Ascher, 1979; Zwart & Lisman, 1979).

3. *Sleep restriction* involves first an assessment (by sleep log) of how long the patients themselves feel that they are sleeping. They are then restricted to staying in bed only for about that amount of time, and this is continued until they report at least a 90% "sleep efficiency" (i.e., 90% of the time in bed is actually spent sleeping). Bedtime is then gradually lengthened by 15-minute intervals until the patients sleep normal amounts again. This is a method that initially causes severe sleep deprivation, but it is quite effective in many serious insomniacs (Spielman, Saskin, & Thorpy, 1984, 1985).

4. *Sleep hygiene* involves a set of rules that patients have to follow, such as regular bed and arousal times, slight sleep restriction, increased exercise, decreased coffee intake after lunchtime, etc. (Hauri, 1982). It seems surprising how often patients who complain bitterly about poor sleep violate the most elementary of sleep-hygiene rules.

Although the above four behavioral approaches have all been shown to be effective in the treatment of insomnia, there are some problems. For example, relaxation therapy seems to work whether or not the patient is actually relaxing (e.g., Hauri, 1981). Stimulus-control therapy and sleep-restriction therapy are often rejected by the patients because they involve severe sleep deprivation for at least a few weeks. Therefore, the dropout rate is high. Sleep-hygiene rules seem to be quite useful in treating milder forms of insomnia, but they are often less effective in serious patients who have been sleeping very poorly for months and years.

OBSTACLES AND CONFUSIONS

Reviewing the behavioral treatment of insomnia, there seem to be two main areas of confusion that need to be addressed:

Definition of Insomnia

Many studies, especially those in the psychological and behavioral area, lump together most kinds of insomnia. This means that these studies include almost anyone who complains about a serious inability to sleep. For example, Monroe (1967) and Kales, Caldwell, Soldatos, Bixler, and Kales (1983), among others, report that insomniacs generally have elevated MMPI scores, particularly concerning the neurotic triad. Similarly, Coursey, Buchsbaum, and Frankel (1975) report that insomniacs typically are anxious, obsessive worriers; and there are dozens of other studies where most insomniacs are lumped together.

The lack of differentiation in many psychological and behavioral studies of insomnia stands in marked contrast to the opinions of most sleep-disorder clinicians, who think that the majority of insomniacs are not alike. According to their view, insomnia may be the final common pathway of very different underlying problems. For example, the Association of Sleep Disorders Centers (ASDC) in 1979 published a sleep nosology which distinguishes nine different major categories of insomnia and 19 subcategories. Similarly, in the psychiatric literature, one frequently finds insomnia subdivided into three groups (e.g., Klerman, 1978): difficulties falling asleep, midcycle awakenings, and early-morning awakenings. In another attempt to ''slice the pie,'' *DSM-III-R* also subdivides insomnia into three categories, but they are not early, middle, and late wakefulness, but rather those insomnias related to another mental disorder, those related to a physical condition, and primary insomnia (i.e., those insomnias secondary to neither a psychiatric nor a physical problem). No matter how one subdivides the group, if there are truly different kinds of insomnia, this would probably imply that behavioral treatment may be more effective in some cases and less effective in others.

Attempting to clarify the issue of insomnia ''in general'' versus ''subtypes of insomnia,'' it appears that the symptom of insomnia may well be akin to the symptom of fever. There are some overall statements that one can make about most fevers and about their treatments (e.g., hypothalamic dysregulation, treatment with aspirin), just as there are some overall, general statements that pertain to all insomnias and their treatments. However, knowing the etiology of a fever can make its treatment much more effective and focused. Similarly, assessing the specific subtypes and the many different etiologies of any given insomnia can focus its treatment. To date, behaviorists have only rarely contributed to this goal of subcategorizing insomnia, and they have only halfheartedly attempted the empirical task of delineating the subtypes of insomnia in which their treatment may work best.

Theories of Insomnia

Because of their unique views about the roots of psychophysiological "disease," behaviorists have a major contribution to make in our thinking about insomnia. Some have done this (e.g., Bootzin, 1972; Borkovec, 1982), but more typically behaviorists have simply taken one of the prevailing theories or common-sense assumptions about insomnia and devised a treatment for it. There are four main theories of interest here:

INSOMNIACS ARE MUSCULARLY TOO TENSE. Certainly, if good sleepers occasionally have a sleepless night, they feel muscularly tense. However, there is good evidence that elevated muscle tension may not be the culprit in chronic insomnia. Frontalis EMG does not seem to be elevated in insomniacs as compared with normals (Good, 1975; recently replicated in our own lab). Further, we have found that frontalis EMG tension at the time of "lights out" is not predictive of sleep latency. Also, different individuals can fall asleep with very different levels of muscle tension. Nevertheless, if one trains insomniacs to lower their frontalis EMG, many start sleeping better (Borkovec, Kaloupek, & Slama, 1975; Freedman & Papsdorf, 1976; Hauri, 1981). Paradoxically, as indicated earlier, whether or not these patients actually learn how to relax their frontalis EMG does not correlate with the amount of sleep improvement, suggesting that muscle tension, in itself, is unlikely to be the crucial variable (Hauri, 1981).

INSOMNIACS ARE PHYSIOLOGICALLY HYPERAROUSED. While many studies do show elevated physiological arousal in poor sleepers (e.g., Coursey et al., 1975; Haynes, Follingstad, & McGowan, 1974; Monroe, 1967), others have not replicated this finding. Johns, Gay, Marston, and Bruce (1971) failed to replicate Monroe's rectal-temperature differences, and Frankel, Buchbinder, Coursey, and Snyder (1973) detected no difference in 17-hydroxycorticosteroids between insomniacs and controls.

In addition, although Freedman and Sattler (1982) did find a group of sleep-onset insomniacs who were physiologically hyperaroused when going to bed, these differences "washed out" quickly, before sleep started. Even more damaging to the idea that physiological hyperarousal causes insomnia is Hauri's

(1969) work: When physiological arousal was artificially induced by intensive presleep exercise, it did not affect sleep. People fell asleep as easily after exercise as after relaxation, even though their heartbeat was, on the average, 10 beats higher; their breathing 1 breath faster; and their core temperature .3 degrees warmer after exercise. Although there seems to be little question that some insomniacs show higher physiological arousal, how this relates to the process of falling asleep is unclear.

INSOMNIACS ARE COGNITIVELY HYPERAROUSED. A "racing mind," general worries and concerns about sleep, and other negative, worrisome thoughts have been documented in many studies (Borkovec et al., 1979; Geer & Katkin, 1966; Kales, Caldwell, Preston, Healey, & Kales, 1976; Roth, Kramer & Lutz, 1976). In addition, Freedman (1986) described more beta EEG activity and less alpha activity in insomniacs both during wakefulness and during stage 1 (the transition between waking and sleeping). This would suggest that insomniacs continue to think actively, even into the transition stage between waking and sleeping, while good sleepers do not. However, Haynes, Adams, and Franzen (1981) shortened, rather than lengthened, sleep latency in insomniacs when they introduced a short presleep stressor (mental arithmetic), possibly because this "stressor" drew the insomniacs' attention away from their own cognitions which might have been more threatening.

Neither Freedman and Sattler (1982) nor Kuisk, Bertelson, and Walsh (1986) could document differences in presleep cognitive activity between insomniacs and normals, and Beutler, Thornby, and Karacan (1978) found that MMPI anxiety and depression were not associated with disturbed sleep. Further, Coursey, Buchsbaum, and Frankel (1975) found that insomniacs showed dampened cortical reactivity to auditory stimuli. In a slight tour-de-force, they speculated that insomniacs may be sensory reducers because they may be inherently hyperreactive and then try to compensate for it. If so, the amount of cognitive stimulation that insomniacs receive may be normal, but it may cause more arousal in them than it does in normals.

Although a racing mind is a common clinical phenomenon in insomnia, it is difficult to know whether it is cause or effect (Freedman & Sattler, 1982). Do racing thoughts occur because we cannot sleep, or do these thoughts keep us from sleeping? Also, if cognitive hyperarousal is indeed the culprit in insomnia, why do behaviorists work with relaxation training and stimulus-control treatment rather than use cognitive strategies which most of them know well?

INSOMNIACS HAVE BAD SLEEP-HYGIENE HABITS. According to Bootzin (1972), many insomniacs show a conditioned arousal to their own bedroom, that is, they become tense and aroused when lying in bed in their own room, but they can sleep well elsewhere. Spielman et al., (1985) see a major sleep-hygiene problem in the insomniacs' lying in their beds too long. Hauri (1982) speculates that a major problem lies in the insomniacs' trying too hard to sleep—the harder they try, the more aroused they get. The specific treatments based on each of these points of view have all been effective, even though the recommendations flowing from them are often diametrically opposed to each other. For example, Hauri (1982) encourages insomniacs to read in bed or watch television, while Bootzin (1972) forbids it. Similary, most behavior therapists using sleep hygiene discourage daytime naps for their insomniacs, while others encourage it on the theory that patients will fall asleep more easily at night if they do not seek sleep so desperately.

Obviously, even if a treatment based on a certain theory is effective for many insomniacs, this does not mean that the underlying theory is necessarily correct. One might speculate that the divergent, often-opposed advice given to insomniacs (exercise versus relax your muscles, read versus don't read, nap versus avoid naps, etc.) all touches tangentially on some core issue, which could be addressed more directly. Might it be that these treatments are all just distractors or that they all give the patients more self-confidence, and that it is this similarity which helps the patients to sleep better?

The following is an attempt to develop a more focused theory of behavior therapy for insomniacs. To do this, a detour through some neurological issues seems necessary.

BASIC NEUROLOGICAL MECHANISMS IN THE
SWITCHING PROCESS FROM WAKEFULNESS TO SLEEP

Although many psychological and behavioral factors affect them, sleeping and waking are basically neurological states, manifested by different brain waves on the EEG. To understand these neurological states, it may be well to first understand how the switching from waking to sleep occurs.

There seem to be two wide-ranging circuits whose interplay determines sleeping and waking: the ascending reticular activating system (ARAS) associated with wakefulness (Moruzzi & Magoun, 1949; Siegel, 1979), and the hypnagogic circuits involved in sleep (Dinner, 1982; Hess, 1943). Both of these opposing systems seem to be continuously active (Morgane & Stern, 1974; Satoh & Kanamori, 1975). Whether one is sleeping or waking depends on which of the two systems is dominant at any given time (Bremer, 1975). This also means that a deeply relaxed, hypometabolic state, in itself, is not equivalent to sleep. On the EEG, such a state seems to be indexed only by stage 1, the transition stage between waking and sleeping. Although most of us fall asleep (make sleep spindles) shortly after we have entered this transition state, experienced meditators can stay in this deeply relaxed, marginally awake state for much longer times (Elson, Hauri, & Cunis, 1977).

Hypnagogic circuits are found on various interacting levels in the brain stem and the hypothalamus. Important foci are the region of the solitary-tract muclei, the raphe nuclei in the pons, and the basal forebrain circuits in the preoptic region. Unfortunately, the state of the hypnagogic system is difficult to assess and in influence. Some have suggested that the power of 12-16 cycles per second (cps) activity (sleep-spindle frequency) in the central EEG may be related to it (Sterman & Macdonald, 1978). Although these spindle frequencies seem to be based more on "idling" in certain thalamocortical circuits, they may possibly reflect the influence of more basic, sleep-related structures (Shouse & Sterman, 1979; Sterman, 1977).

The hypnagogic system seems to be strengthened by sleep deprivation, which may well be an essential part of both stimulus-control therapy and sleep-restriction therapy mentioned above. This system also seems to be affected by hypnotics, most of which increase 12-16 cps EEG activity, both during wakefulness and sleep. Behaviorally, however, it seems to be very difficult to affect this system directly. The only time this was even tried was with sensory motor rhythm (SMR) biofeedback, a technique directed at increasing power in the 12-16 cps EEG band recorded over the sensory-motor strip while awake. Although the technology to do so is complex, this technique was effective with certain insomniacs, namely those who could not sleep even though they were physiologically and psychologically quite relaxed (Hauri, 1981; Hauri, Percy, Hellekson, Hartmann, & Russ, 1982).

Behaviorally, it seems to be much easier to affect the ARAS rather than the hypnagogic circuits. Activity levels in the ARAS depend on environmental stimulation (sound, touch, comfort level), on physical activity (movement), but most of all on psychological factors (anxiety, stress, thought content, etc.) This clearly is the area where behaviorists can make a difference.

To deal effectively with the ARAS, one has to remember its time constants. This system has a very fast rise time (in the order of seconds), but a slow decay time (in the order of minutes). For example, if a gun suddenly went off next to you, you would be maximally aroused within seconds. If you then found that someone had played a prank and only fired a blank, your arousal level would not decrease as fast as it had increased. For at least a few minutes, if not longer, you would still show increased physiological and cognitive activity, even though you could now understand the noise as essentially harmless.

For the treatment of insomnia, we need to remember that it first takes some time to relax deeply enough to enter stage 1. It then takes another few minutes of stage 1 before true sleep (stage 2) can develop. Thus, to fall asleep, we need about 5 to 15 minutes without any transient arousals in the ARAS, otherwise, the whole process has to be restarted. In this context, the general (tonic) arousal level of the ARAS seems to be much less important than the occasional (phasic) arousal-producing thoughts that might intrude. Thus, instead of working behaviorally with the general level of tonic muscle tension or with the average physiological arousal, it appears to be much more important to work with those occasionally intruding thoughts that phasically override the basal level. In other words, the goal of behavior therapy should not be to teach a patient generalized relaxation techniques, but to provide the patient with about 15 minutes at bedtime that are totally anxiety free.

DIAGNOSTIC INTAKE PROCEDURES TAILORED TO A COGNITIVE-BEHAVIORAL MODEL

Faced with an insomniac patient, it would seem to be important to first carry out a careful diagnostic interview. Over half of all insomnias are apparently associated with serious psychiatric disorders (Tan, Kales, Kales, Soldatos, & Bixler, 1984). For these, it would seem to be better, initially, to deal with the psychiatric issues directly during wakefulness, rather than focusing on the associated insomnia.

During the diagnostic interview, the behaviorist also needs to be aware that there are some physical conditions that may cause insomnia, such as sleep apnea or myoclonus. Such conditions may not be apparent during wakefulness, but only manifest themselves during sleep. Occasionally, a bed partner might shed light on such a condition (e.g., talk about the nocturnal twitching of the legs in sleep-related myoclonus or about the breathing pauses in the various forms of sleep apnea). Certainly, if the psychiatric and behavioral treatments of a seriously disturbed insomniac do not lead to improvement over a number of weeks or months, these physical conditions (associated with about 20% of all insomnias) need to be investigated, most likely in a sleep-disorder center.

Following the initial diagnostic interview, the behaviorist should then focus in exquisite detail on the events that occur when the patient cannot sleep. The clue to effective treatment most often lies in the feeling tones and the content of individual thoughts and small actions, not in some global "tension state." However, these events are often unavailable to the patient if one asks what happens "in general." Therefore, the best strategy, apparently, is to ask in minute detail, What happened "last night?" Each thought that the patient remembers having had the previous night should be examined for its arousal-producing affective and cognitive components. "Random" thoughts, when analyzed, are often much less random than they appear. Similarly, each behavior that occurred needs to be understood. For example, it is not only important to know when the patient went to bed the previous night, but also how he decided that it was time (e.g., Was it because the clock said it was time or because the patient felt sleepy?), and, once the decision was made, what happened emotionally? Did it trigger tension, apprehension, or a desire to procrastinate? Similarly, if a patient reports that he awakened at exactly 2:00 a.m. last night, one investigates how he knew that it was exactly 2:00 a.m. and what thoughts went through his mind when he realized that, once again, it was exactly 2:00 a.m. Would the patient be less aroused if the clock had shown 12:30 a.m. or 4:00 a.m.? It then seems to be important to understand exactly what happened in the insomniac's mind in the next 10-15 minutes and also what finally led to the insomniac's falling asleep again. Or did he/she get up a few minutes later in anger and disgust? If so, what led to it? In my experience, in this minute, thought-by-thought analysis of one single night of sleep often lies all of the information one needs to carry out a very specific, highly tailored cognitive treatment program.

COMPONENTS OF THE COGNITIVE-BEHAVIORAL TREATMENT OF INSOMNIA

Overall, the cognitive-behavioral treatment of insomnia focuses on five areas:

REDEFINITION OF THE PROBLEM.   Most insomniacs think of themselves as having a disease. They feel that it is the therapist's job to cure them and that it is the patient's task to muster enough patience to wait until the therapist has figured out the cure. This is *not* so in the behavioral therapy of insomnia! Redefining the problem as a "condition of living" or a handicap that needs to be overcome is often a good first step. One might even agree with the patients that their neurological sleep/wake systems are not ideal, but one can also point to the fact that on some nights they typically sleep much better than on others, even with the same neurological system. The joint job of patient and therapist is to find out what makes some nights better and what aggravates others. To this end, one not only has the patient keep daily sleep logs, but also logs of any daytime or evening events that might possibly be related to either better or worse sleep. Cognitive therapists are at their therapeutic best when, after some weeks of charting and puzzling, the patients themselves start seeing possible relationships of daytime events to sleep without the therapist having seen the relationships first.

It often helps to use analogies in this area of redefining the problem. Being born with a possibly substandard sleep system is less like a disease and more like being born into a poor family. It does not help to rail against the injustice of being born poor. Rather, it is necessary to muster all one's intelligence and "savvy" to overcome the financial limitations. It is difficult, but many have risen above the poverty into which they were born. Similarly, the patient who is born with a relatively poor sleep system needs to be much wiser, more diligent, and more cunning about learning what affects his/her sleep system. After finding what affects the system, the patient then has to systematically go about the task of changing that situation until an acceptable level of sleep is achieved.

SLEEP HYGIENE.   Many insomniacs make obvious sleep-hygiene "mistakes," such as drinking coffee or alcohol close to bedtime, sleeping too late, staying in bed excessively long, etc. Others are unclear about circadian phenomena or about the natural changes in sleep that occur with age. Such individual errors and misunderstandings need to be discussed. However, there are also numerous idiosyncrasies that need to be considered. For example, some sleep best in total darkness, others with an open window and light. Some sleep better with, others without having obtained a daytime nap, with or without the television on, in a warm or a cold room, with or without exercise. Because of the highly idiosyncratic events that help sleep, one cannot simply hand the individual a sheet of sleep-hygiene rules; instead, one has to explore these rules carefully in light of the insomniac's own lifetime experiences. Just as it would be useless to hand the neurotic a sheet with 10 rules for better emotional health, so it is useless to hand the insomniac a sheet of 10 sleep-hygiene rules.

SPECIFIC RECOMMENDATIONS.   As discussed above, most recommendations one gives initially flow directly from the minute-by-minute analysis of the events that occur during a given sleepless night. For example, if the patient attempts to lie very quietly when awake so as not to arouse the bed partner, and this results in increased fidgetiness and arousal, twin beds or even a separate bedroom might be explored. If the patient tries too hard to fall asleep and thereby becomes frustrated and aroused, one might recommend distractions such as reading in bed (Ascher & Efan, 1978). If the patient keeps busy throughout the day in an attempt to suppress worrisome thoughts and these thoughts then occur to him after "lights out," one might schedule a half-hour "worry time" shortly after supper to deal with them. If being unable to sleep, once again, demonstrates to the patient how inferior or neurotic he/she is, that cognitive "error" needs to be addressed directly. The possibilities are endless. The main point in enumerating some ideas here is to emphasize that one tailors these recommendations directly to the patient's experiences. As discussed above, the goal is to provide a 15-20 minute interval at bedtime where the ARAS is not aroused by occasionally occurring worrisome thoughts or behaviors.

CHANGE OF RECOMMENDATIONS DURING SUBSEQUENT VISITS.   Typically, one warns insomniacs that the above-discussed recommendations do not work during the first few nights that they are tried. A patient initially is so curious to find out whether a recommendation will work that he/she becomes highly alert. Sleep may get worse because of that. Each recommendation should, therefore, be tried for at least a week.

To follow up, one then schedules visits about twice per month. During these visits, the therapist explores the effects of the previous recommendations and adjusts them according to the patient's report. Occasionally, one might even recommend the direct opposite of the previous recommendation if the patient reports a deterioration of sleep while he/she tried it. During these meetings, it is important that the patient be re-enlisted as a "co-scientist" trying to puzzle out the scientific problem of poor sleep. The temptation is to become a passive patient again, waiting to be treated by the therapist.

Obviously, there are some patients who are so excessively tense that their general level of arousal needs to be decreased with relaxation training. Others may truly be so conditioned against sleeping in their own bedroom that stimulus-control techniques are to be applied, or they are staying in bed so long that sleep-restriction techniques are necessary. The main point of this paper, however, is to emphasize that extremely careful, individualized attention to the cognitive processes at sleep onset will probably yield faster therapeutic benefits in more insomniacs than the wholesale application of any one of the behavioral techniques that were mentioned at the beginning of this paper. In the past, these behavioral techniques often seem to have worked not because they had intrinsic merit, but because they changed the cognitive climate at bedtime. This, it appears, can now be done much more directly.

MEDICATIONS.   Although the chronic, daily use of medications is not recommended in insomnia because these medications often lose efficacy when used for long time periods (Kales et al., 1974) most insomniacs need occasional hypnotics to break the vicious conditioning cycle of a few poor nights following each other. Thus, in my experience, most insomniacs should have a few prescription hypnotics to be used no more than once or twice per week. (An exception to this rule is the insomniac with high addiction proneness.) Simply knowing that some hypnotics are available in case of an emergency often lessens the fear and panic of chronic insomnia.

OUTLOOK FOR THE FUTURE

Research on this cognitive-behavioral model of insomnia therapy is just beginning. To date, only clinical, anecdotal data exist. Nevertheless, of 12 chronic, serious insomniacs that were treated over a year ago in this mode (each for no more than 6 cognitive sessions), 6 claimed that their problem had entirely disappeared, 4 said that they still had an occasional sleepless night but were much less concerned about it now, while 2 had not benefited and were then referred to our sleep-disorder center for an evaluation (as it happened, both turned out to have sleep-related myoclonus). Considering the chronicity of the patients treated (each had over 2 years of serious insomnia) and the shortness of treatment (6 sessions or less), the future of cognitive insomnia treatment looks very bright. Our task is to get hold of the patient's state of mind at the time of sleep onset and provide a climate where 10-20 tensionless minutes can occur.

REFERENCES

Ascher, L. M., & Efran, J. S. (1978). Use of paradoxical intention in a behavioral program for sleep onset insomnia. *Journal of Consulting and Clinical Psychology, 3,* 547–550.

Association of Sleep Disorders Centers. (1979). *Diagnostic classification of sleep and arousal disorders* (1st ed.). *Sleep, 2,* 1–137.

Beutler, L. E., Thornby, J. I., & Karacan, I. (1978). Psychological variables in the diagnosis of insomnia. In R. L. Williams, & I. Karacan (Eds.), *Sleep disorders: Diagnosis and treatment.* (pp. 61–100). New York: John Wiley & Sons.

Bootzin, R. (1972). A stimulus control treatment for insomnia. *Proceedings of the American Psychological Association, 1,* 395–396.

Borkovec, T. D. (1982). Insomnia. *Journal of Consulting and Clinical Psychology, 50,* 880–895.

Borkovec, T. D., Grayson, J. B., O'Brien, G. T., & Weerts, T. C. (1979). Relaxation treatment of pseudoinsomnia and idiopathic insomnia: An electroencephalographic evaluation. *Journal of Applied Behavior Analysis, 12,* 37–54.

Borkovec, T. D., Kaloupek, D. G., & Slama, K. M. (1975). The faciliative effect of muscle tension-release in the relaxation treatment of sleep disturbance. *Behavior Therapy, 6,* 301–309.

Borkovec, T. D., & Weerts, T. C. (1976). Effects of progressive relaxation on sleep disturbance: An electroencephalographic evaluation. *Psychosomatic Medicine, 38,* 173–180.

Bremer, F. (1975). A further study of the inhibitory processes induced by the activation of the preoptic hypnogenic structure. *Archives Italiennes de Biologie, 113,* 79–88.

Coursey, R. D., Buchsbaum, M., & Frankel, B. L. (1975). Personality measures and evoked responses in chronic insomniacs. *Journal of Abnormal Psychology, 84,* 239–249.

Coursey, R. D., Frankel, B. L., Gaardner, K. R., & Mott, D. E. (1980). A comparison of relaxation techniques with electrosleep therapy for chronic, sleep-onset insomnia. A sleep-EEG study. *Biofeedback and Self-Regulation, 5,* 57–73.

Dinner, D. S. (1982). Physiology of sleep. *American Journal of EEG Technologists, 22,* 85–98.

Elson, B. D., Hauri, P., & Cunis, D. (1977). Physiological changes in yoga meditation. *Psychophysiology, 14,* 52–57.

Frankel, B. L., Buchbinder, R., Coursey, R., & Snyder, F. (1975). Sleep patterns and psychological test characteristics of chronic primary insomniacs. In M. H. Chase, W. C. Stern, & P. L. Walter (Eds.), *Sleep research* (Vol. 2, p. 149). Los Angeles: Brain Information Service/Brain Research Institute.

Freedman, R. R. (1986). EEG power spectra in sleep-onset insomnia. *Electroencephalography and Clinical Neurophysiology, 63,* 408–413.

Freedman, R. R., & Papsdorf, J. D. (1976). Biofeedback and progressive relaxation treatment of sleep-onset insomnia: A controlled, all-night investigation. *Biofeedback and Self-Regulation, 1,* 253–271.

Freedman, R. R., & Sattler, H. L. (1982). Physiological and psychological factors in sleep-onset insomnia. *Journal of Abnormal Psychology, 91,* 380–389.

Geer, J. H., & Katkin, E. S. (1966). Treatment of insomnia using a variant of systematic desensitization: A case report. *Journal of Abnormal Psychology, 71,* 161–164.

Good, R. (1975). Frontalis muscle tension and sleep latency. *Psychophysiology, 12,* 465–467.

Hauri, P. (1969). The influence of evening activity on the onset of sleep. *Psychophysiology, 5,* 426–430.

Hauri, P. (1981). Treating psychophysiologic insomnia with biofeedback. *Archives of General Psychiatry, 38,* 752–758.

Hauri, P. (1982). *The sleep disorders.* Kalamazoo, MI: The Upjohn Company.

Hauri, P., Percy, L., Hellekson, C., Hartmann, E., & Russ, D. (1982). The treatment of psychophysiologic insomnia with biofeedback: A replication study. *Biofeedback and Self-Regulation, 7,* 223–235.

Haynes, S. N., Adams, A., & Franzen, M. (1981). The effects of presleep stress on sleep-onset insomnia. *Journal of Abnormal Psychology, 90,* 601–606.

Haynes, S. N., Follingstad, D. R., & McGowan, W. T. (1974). Insomnia: Sleep patterns and anxiety level. *Journal of Psychosomatic Research, 18,* 69–74.

Haynes, S. N., Price, M. G., & Simons, J. B. (1975). Stimulus control treatment of insomnia. *Journal of Behavior Therapy and Experimental Psychiatry, 6,* 279–282.

Hess, W. R. (1943). Symptomatik des durch elektrischen Reiz ausgelösten Schlafes und die Topographie des Schlafzentrums. *Helvetische Physiologische und Pharmacologische Akten, 1,* C61.

Institute of Medicine. (1979). *Report of a study: Sleeping pills, insomnia, and medical practice.* Washington: National Academy of Sciences.

Johns, M. W., Gay, T. J. A., Marston, P., & Bruce, D. W. (1971). Relationship between sleep habits, adrenocortical activity and personality. *Psychosomatic Medicine, 33,* 499–508.

Kales, A., Bixler, E. O., Tan, T. L., Scharf, M. B., & Kales, J. D. (1974). Chronic hypnotic-drug use: Ineffectiveness, drug-withdrawal insomnia, and dependence. *Journal of the American Medical Association, 227,* 513–517.

Kales, A., Caldwell, A. B., Preston, T. A., Healey, S., & Kales, J. D. (1976). Personality patterns in insomnia: Theoretical implications. *Archives of General Psychiatry, 33,* 1128–1134.

Kales, A., Caldwell, A. B., Soldatos, C. R., Bixler, E. O., & Kales, J. D. (1983). Biopsychobehavioral correlates of insomnia. II: Pattern specificity and consistency with the Minnesota Multiphasic Personality Inventory. *Psychosomatic Medicine, 45,* 341–356.

Klerman, G. L. (1978). Affective disorders. In A. M. Nicholi (Ed.), *The Harvard guide to modern psychiatry.* (pp. 115–281). Cambridge, MA: The Belknap Press of Harvard University Press.

Kuisk, L. A., Bertelson, A. D., & Walsh, J. K. (1986). Presleep cognitive activity in objective and subjective disorders of initiating and maintaining sleep (DIMS). In M. H. Chase, D. J. McGinty, & G. Crane (Eds.), *Sleep research* (Vol. 15, p. 140). Los Angeles: Brain Information Service/Brain Research Institute.

Lacks, P., Bertelson, A. D., Sugerman, J., & Kunkel, J. (1983). The treatment of sleep-maintenance insomnia with stimulus-control techniques. *Behavior Research and Therapy, 21,* 291–295.

Monroe, L. J. (1967). Psychological and physiological differences between good and poor sleepers. *Journal of Abnormal Psychology, 72,* 255–264.

Morgane, P. J., & Stern, W. C. (1974). Chemical anatomy of brain circuits in relation to sleep and wakefulness. In E. Weitzman (Ed.), *Advances in sleep research* (Vol. 1, pp. 1–131). New York: Spectrum Publications, Inc.

Moruzzi, G., & Magoun, H. W. (1949). Brain stem reticular formation and activation of EEG. *Electroencephalography and Clinical Neurophysiology, 1,* 455–473.

Roth, T., Kramer, M., & Lutz, T. (1976). The nature of insomnia: A descriptive summary of a sleep clinic population. *Comprehensive Psychiatry, 17,* 217–220.

Satoh, T., & Kanamori, N. (1975). Reticulo-reticular relationship during sleep and waking. *Physiology and Behavior, 15,* 333–337.

Shouse, M. N., & Sterman, M. B. (1979). Changes in seizure susceptibility, sleep time and sleep spindles following thalamic and cerebellar lesions. *Electroencephalography and Clinical Neurophysiology, 46,* 1–12.

Siegel, J. M. (1979). Behavioral functions of the reticular formation. *Brain Research Reviews, 1,* 69–105.

Spielman, A. J., Saskin, P., & Thorpy, M. J. (1984). Sleep restriction therapy for chronic insomnia: Outcome as a function of pretreatment total sleep time. In M. H. Chase, W. B. Webb, & R. Wilder-Jones (Eds.), *Sleep research* (Vol. 13, p. 167). Los Angeles: Brain Information Service/Brain Research Institute.

Spielman, A. J., Saskin, P., & Thorpy, M. J. (1985). The disruptive effects of increased time in bed in chronic insomnia. In M. H. Chase, D. J. McGinty, & R. Wilder-Jones (Eds.), *Sleep research* (Vol. 14, p. 218). Los Angeles: Brain Information Service/Brain Research Institute.

Sterman, M. B. (1977). Clinical implications of EEG biofeedback training: A critical appraisal. In G. E. Schwartz & J. Beatty (Eds.), *Biofeedback: Theory and research.* (pp. 389–411). New York: Academic Press.

Sterman, M. B., & Macdonald, L. R. (1978). Effects of central cortical EEG feedback training on incidence of poorly controlled seizures. *Epilepsia, 19,* 207–222.

Tan, T. -L., Kales, J. D., Kales, A., Soldatos, C. R., & Bixler, E. O. (1984). Biopsychobehavioral correlates of insomnia. IV: Diagnosis based on DSM-III. *American Journal of Psychiatry, 141,* 357–362.

Turner, R. M., & Ascher, L. M. (1979). A within-subject analysis of stimulus control therapy with severe sleep-onset insomnia. *Behavior Research and Therapy, 17,* 107–112.

Zwart, C. A., & Lisman, S. A. (1979). Analysis of stimulus control treatment of sleep-onset insomnia. *Journal of Consulting and Clinical Psychology, 47,* 113–118.

11

LOW SEXUAL DESIRE: BIOLOGICAL IMPLICATIONS

Patricia Schreiner-Engel, Ph.D.
Department of Psychiatry,
Mount Sinai School of Medicine

Loss of sexual desire is one of the most prevalent sexual dysfunctions; yet, it is extremely resistant to therapeutic intervention and carries the poorest prognosis. One reason may be that no systematic information has been gathered on the determinants of this disorder, which has been labeled "Hypoactive Sexual Desire Disorder (HSD)" by DSM III-R (American Psychiatric Association, 1987). It is likely that both biological and psychological factors interact in a complex way to reduce sexual desire. For example, clinicians frequently observe that illnesses, interpersonal problems, sexual trauma, and depression can each severely reduce interest in sexual activity (LoPiccolo, 1980). However, when these causes are not present in an individual, disordered central nervous system (CNS) processes become suspect.

Unfortunately, little is known about the role of neuroendocrine and psychophysiological processes in the regulation of normal sexual desire in nondysfunctional persons. There is, though, abundant evidence that biological factors participate in the motivational aspects of sexual behavior in animals (Davidson, Gray, & Smith, 1979). In a related development, there is increasing evidence that central monoaminergic mechanisms in humans are involved in psychopathological conditions, such as affective disorders, which are frequently associated with decreased sexual desire.

There has been speculation that diminished brain dopaminergic activity may be associated with lowered sex drive, but direct evidence that these CNS processes are involved in patients with disorders of sexual desire does not exist at this time (Everett, 1975; Gessa & Tagliomonte, 1974). One might, however, examine the prevalence of affective disorders in the life histories of individuals not recently or currently depressed, who have little or no desire for any sexual activity. If histories of affective diagnoses were found to occur significantly more frequently in persons with HSD than in those with normal desire, the notion of a biological contribution to the etiology of HSD would be supported.

HSD is generally defined by DSM III-R as "persistently or recurrently deficient or absent sexual fantasies and desire for sexual activity" . . . which does not occur "exclusively during the course of another Axis I disorder" (American Psychiatric Association, 1987, p. 293). Complaints of HSD, however, have different clinical manifestations. A person may situationally no longer desire sexual activity with one's spouse but will experience desire for another individual and will still masturbate regularly; another individual will not desire one type of sexual activity, such as intercourse, but will continue to masturbate. Some will have a secondary loss of sexual desire following the development of another sexual dysfunction, such as impotence or anorgasmia; still others report that they either have never experienced sexual desire for any sexual activity or partner or that they have similarly lost all desire for sex.

If a biological etiology for loss of sexual desire exists, it most likely will be evident in the latter form of HSD disorder—the generalized loss or lack of desire. Thus, a multivariate study was initiated to investigate this and other hypotheses about the determinants of low sexual desire in men and women with generalized HSD.

SUBJECT SELECTION

In order to control for the possible confounding effects of disease, aging, and partner availability, only persons who had been living in a sexual relationship for at least one year and who were free from all illnesses, medication use, drug abuse, and other Axis I psychiatric disorders were selected. All male subjects had to be between the ages of 25 and 55 and all females between the ages of 21 and 45. Lack of desire also had to be a source of distress to one of the partners.

Because normative data on many parameters of sexual desire in healthy persons do not exist, a control group of nondysfunctional couples was also studied. They met the same inclusion criteria of health as HSD subjects and were matched to the HSD samples on the variables of sex, age, and relationship duration and status (i.e., married or living in a stable relationship).

To maximize the possibility of identifying the determinants of low sex drive, HSD subjects had to be quite impaired. The parameters of their desire disorder were operationally defined as follows: (a) their reported frequency of all sexual activity being twice per month or less over at least the previous six months; and (b) a corresponding lack of subjective desire for engaging in any sexual behavior. For control couples, the total frequency of their sexual activities (coitus and masturbation) was required to average at least twice per week if they were between the ages of 25 and 40, and at least once per week if older than 40.

Eighty-two couples participated in the research study. In 46 couples, one of the partners had hypoactive sexual desire; 22 of the HSD partners were male, and

24 were females. These HSD couples were selected from a sex-therapy clinic population and from self- or therapist referrals generated by announcements of the investigation published in journals and lay magazines. Thirty-six control couples were recruited by placing notices in the hospital where the study was conducted and in surrounding community centers.

Over a period of three years, 438 individuals and couples were evaluated in the Mount Sinai Human Sexuality Clinic. Three-hundred-ninety-five patients were diagnosed as having a sexual dysfunction; 88 of them complained of insufficient sexual desire. Of these, 35 men and 23 women were diagnosed as having HSD according to DSM-III-R criteria (14.7% of those with sexual dysfunctions), but 45 of them failed to meet one or more of the study's selection criteria. Of the 13 remaining eligible clinic couples, 5 consented to participate in the investigation.

During the same three-year period, 249 men and women were referred to the study. After a preliminary screening over the phone, 96 HSD couples were seen for a clinical evaluation. Forty-one met our selection criteria and agreed to participate in the investigation.

STUDY DESIGN

The question of whether biological factors participate in the etiology of generalized HSD was investigated by assessing and comparing life histories of psychiatric illness, current psychological profiles, and (for women) premenstrual symptomatology in individuals with well-defined generalized HSD and their matched controls (Schreiner-Engel & Schiavi, 1986). The Schedule for Affective Disorders and Schizophrenia—Lifetime Version (SADS-L) (Endicott & Spitzer, 1978) was used to elicit information about diagnoses of psychiatric illness in the lives of all 46 HSD subjects and in 34 of the 36 controls. The current psychological symptom status was derived for each subject from the SCL-90R (Derogatis, 1977). The occurrence and severity of premenstrual mood disorders in the female sample was rated from data gathered from the clinical assessment and the Personal History Questionnaire-C (Heiman, 1981).

The SADS-L is a structured interview that records data on a subject's current level of psychological functioning and psychopathology, as well as his or her lifetime mental status. Subjects are classified on the research diagnostic criteria, which are a set of operational diagnostic definitions with specific inclusion and exclusion criteria.

The SCL-90R is a self-report inventory composed of 90 items, each evaluated on a 5-point scale of distress from "not at all" to "extremely." It is composed of 9 primary symptom dimensions and a global index of psychological distress called the "Global Severity Index (GSI)."

Premenstrual syndrome (PMS) was operationally defined as short-term periodic mood changes occurring in the premenstruum severe enough to cause impaired functioning. A cluster of items from the Personal History Questionnaire

(PHQ-C) assesses frequency, severity, and PMS symptoms. The PHQ-C has a total of 432 questions which elicit detailed psychosexual information. The PHQ-C and its larger forerunner, the PHQ-A, have been used in several prior investigations of sexual functioning and have proven to be useful in gathering systematic data about past and current sexual behavior.

Each HSD and control subject (with the spouse) was first interviewed to gather information on the subject's medical, psychiatric, and psychosocial histories and the couple's sexual functioning and marital satisfaction. Each subject then received a comprehensive medical examination and was given laboratory tests for the evaluation of endocrine disorders and medical illnesses. At the next interview, the SADS-L was administered by one of the investigators, and, during another visit, a battery of psychological, sexual, and personal-history inventories were completed by each subject.

SAMPLE CHARACTERISTICS

Demographically, the paired samples of HSD and control subjects were well matched on all selection criteria. Clinically, the sex drive of the HSD sample was considerably impaired, in keeping with the operational criteria. The mean frequency with which male and female HSD subjects initiated sexual intercourse was once per month or less for the previous six months. Interestingly, 15% of the HSD men and 40% of the HSD women reported averaging coitus more than twice per month, explaining that they had been responding to partner pressure for intercourse but had had no desire themselves to initiate such activity.

The mean duration of reduced sexual desire reported by the male HSD subjects was 5.1 years, ranging from 1 to 30 years. Ten of the 24 HSD women (42% of this sample) claimed to have had a lifelong lack of sexual desire, which none of the HSD men reported. The duration of decreased sex drive in the remaining 14 women was 3.6 years, with a range of 2-14 years. Forty-five percent of the HSD men and 39% of the HSD women masturbated no more than once per month, while 35% of the men and 52% of the women never masturbated. A few subjects reported masturbating occasionally in the hope that it would elicit or rekindle some desire. The reported occurrence of sexual thoughts or fantasies in the lives of these subjects was rare.

CURRENT PSYCHOLOGICAL PROFILES

Very little symptomatic distress was being experienced in either HSD sample, as compared to their matched controls or to the nonpatient normative population of the SCL-90R (Schreiner-Engel & Schiavi, 1986). The HSD and control subjects had nearly identical symptom profiles on all nine psychological dimensions as well as on the Global Severity Index of the SCL-90R. With one exception, all scores for both HSD groups were within one standard deviation of the normative mean for this inventory.

On the subscale indicating depressed affect, the HSD men had a significantly higher elevation. The HSD men's increased feelings of depression are understandable from a psychosocial point of view. As carriers of the burden of sexual initiation, these men seemed to be much more distressed by their sexual symptom of HSD. For women, lack of interest in initiating sexual activity is socially accepted and sanctioned behavior. Therefore, having the sexual disorder of HSD would not be as demoralizing to their self-esteem as it would be for men. In fact, several spouses expressed surprise during the initial interview when they discovered that their wives felt little or no sexual desire. These men had always initiated all sexual experiences and had no expectation for their wives to be the initiator. These wives, however, were concerned that they were missing out on something pleasurable in their lives, which they had either read about or had experienced in the past.

Finding normal psychological symptom profiles for both male and female HSD groups confirms the clinical impression, but may be contributing to treatment difficulties. These HSD patients usually seem emotionally and physically healthy, but are unhappy about their lack of interest in the quality of their sexual relationship. This may mislead both therapist and patient to conclude that underlying marital issues are causal.

Derogatis, Meyer, and King (1981) reported that patients with other sexual dysfunctions have markedly higher symptomatology and global psychological distress (as measured by the SCL-90R symptom subscales and summary index) than do nondysfunctional individuals. They found that men with erectile and ejaculatory problems, as well as females with anorgasmia, dyspareunia, and vaginismus, had significant elevations on at least four of the nine subscales. (There were no patients with HSD in their study.) Thus, HSD dysfunctional patients appear to be different emotionally and sexually from persons with other sexual dysfunctions. This, too, is consistent with clinical observations. HSD patients, particularly women, frequently report no difficulties with arousal or orgasm or even in the pleasure derived from their sexual responses. However satisfying or successful, they never quite feel like initiating another such experience. This clinical observation was supported in this study by the reported ability of many female and male HSD patients to become fully aroused during coital activity, to have intercourse, and to experience orgasm. It appears that for generalized HSD patients, it is primarily the motivational aspect of the experience which is lacking.

LIFE HISTORY OF PSYCHOPATHOLOGY

The central hypothesis in this study was supported by several of the findings derived from the psychiatric interview with the SADS-L (Schreiner-Engel & Schiavi, 1986). Although there were no significant differences in histories of schizophrenia, anxiety, or personality disorders, a remarkable and highly significant difference in the life histories of affective disorder was found.

Seventy-three percent of the HSD men met the criteria for lifetime diagnoses of various affective disorders, as compared to 32% of the control men. Thirty-two percent of the HSD men had had bipolar or major depressive disorders, 27% had had episodes of intermittent or dysthymic disorder, and 18% had had minor depressive episodes in their lives. These rates were more than double those of the control men. The male control sample itself was found to have rates of depressive disorder considerably higher than comparable normative epidemiological studies (Boyd & Weissman, 1981). Thus, despite higher rates of depression than expected among the control men, it is noteworthy that the increase in the prevalence of depression in the lives of the HSD men was still highly significant.

Affective illness was equally prevalent in the lives of the HSD women and also significantly higher than the prevalence of depressive disorders in the control sample. Seventy-one percent of the HSD women, as compared to only 27% of the control women, had had lifetime diagnoses of affective disorders: 42% of the HSD women had had bipolar or major depressive disorders; 17% had had intermittent depression; and 25% had had episodes of minor depression in the past. In our view, it is probable that many of the HSD subjects who had no diagnosis of psychopathology in their lives, in fact, may have had a history of affective disorder. In six subjects, an adequate psychiatric evaluation could not be made because they were extremely guarded, evasive, or vague (could not remember) in their descriptions of stressful times in their lives. Thus, a diagnosis of psychopathology could not be made or reliably ruled out. Each of these subjects, however, in our judgment, seemed to have had exceptionally traumatic childhoods; for example, a concentration-camp experience, drunken abusive parents, abandonment, and sexual molestation were reported by these HSD individuals. It seems reasonable that as adults they would develop a personality style that today appears to be constricted, rigid, and humorless. These individuals, in fact, reported experiencing no variations in mood, and prided themselves on maintaining good control over their emotional responses.

The positive association between affective disorder and HSD was further documented by a comparison of the age of onset of each disorder. Remarkably, every HSD woman experienced the beginning of her HSD symptoms during or following her first depressive episode. When her depression lifted, though, her HSD disorder continued. The first affective episode in the lives of the 10 HSD women who had never experienced sexual desire occurred during their teenage years.

In nearly all of the HSD men with histories of affective disorder, their loss of desire also occurred during or subsequent to their first depression episode.

Another finding that supported the hypothesis of a biological contribution to the etiology of HSD was the association found in HSD women between frequency of self-initiated sexual behavior (i.e., female-initiated coitus, masturbation, and fantasy) and affective disorder. Those women who had positive histories of depressive illness had the lowest frequencies of these self-initiated sexual behaviors at the time of the study.

The presence of depressed mood changes associated with menses was investigated because PMS sufferers have been found to have significantly more episodes of depression in their lives than nonsufferers (Halbreich & Endicott, 1985). As hypothesized, the HSD women did, indeed, have a significantly higher incidence of severe PMS symptomatology than did their matched controls.

The evidence from this study offers considerable support for the hypothesis that generalized HSD in part, may have a biological etiology. No other study has investigated the relationship between lifetime prevalence rates of affective disorder and lack of sexual desire. Mathew and Weinman (1982) have reported that a disturbance in "libido," defined as the desire to have sex, was the only sexual dysfunction to occur significantly more frequently among depressed patients than among nondepressed controls. Among sex-therapy patients, Lief and Slowinski (1985) reported a high prevalence of depressive symptoms in their sex- and marital-therapy patients. However, they did not report the rate of depression among the HSD group alone. Others (Merikangas, Prusoff, Kupfer, & Frank, 1985; Ruestow, Dunner, Bleeker. & Fieve, 1978; Weissman & Paykel, 1974) have also reported that, among women, depression is the most frequent determinant of marital problems. Similarly, in our initial screening of referrals to the study, we excluded over 24% of individuals presenting with complaints of sexual desire for reason of current depression. Only individuals who were clearly without recent or current depressive illnesses were accepted for this investigation.

Thus, the speculation that CNS mechanisms are involved in the development of hypoactive sexual desire is supported by the findings of this investigation. Individuals not recently or currently depressed but who had little or no desire for any form of sexual activity had significantly higher rates of affective disorder in their lives than persons with normal sexual desire.

This finding must be viewed with caution, however. As with other biological abnormalities, psychosocial, learning, and experiential factors usually play a role in the development of any disordered behavior. In this study, evidence of traumatic early-life experiences and marital pathology was found in a substantial number of the HSD subjects. The significance of these factors for the pathogenesis of generalized HSD is not clear. It is possible that they interact with a biological predisposition in the development of the disorder. However, in some individuals, they may be the sole determinants of HSD as in the situational forms of this sexual dysfunction.

Clinically, this investigation demonstrated that there is a link between generalized HSD and a history of affective psychopathology. The challenge ahead is to explore the nature of the biological processes that underlie both disorders.

REFERENCES

American Psychiatric Association. (1987). *Diagnootic and Statistical Manual of Mental Disorders.* (Third Edition, Revised.) Washington, DC: The American Psychiatric Association.

Boyd, J. H., & Weissman, M. M. (1981). Epidemiology of affective disorders. A reexamination and future directions. *Archives of General Psychiatry, 38,* 1039–1045.

Davidson, J. M., Gray, G. D., & Smith, E. R. (1979). Animal models in the endocrinology of reproductive behavior. In N. Alexander (Ed.), *Animal models for research on contraception and fertility* (pp. 61–81). Hagerstown, MD: Harper & Row.

Derogatis, L. R. (1977). *SCL-90R: Administration, scoring and procedures manual I.* Baltimore: Clinical Psychometrics Research.

Derogatis, L. R., Meyer, J. K., & King K. M. (1981). Psychopathology in individuals with sexual dysfunction. *American Journal of Psychiatry, 138,* 757–763.

Endicott, J., & Spitzer, R. L. (1978). A diagnostic interview: The schedule for affective disorders and schizophrenia. *Archives of General Psychiatry, 35,* 837–844.

Everett, G. M. (1975). Role of biogenic amines in the modulation of aggressive and sexual behavior in animals and man. In M. Sandler & G. L. Gessa (Eds.), *Sexual behavior: Pharmacology and biochemistry* (pp. 81–85). New York: Raven Press.

Gessa, G. L., & Tagliomonte, A. (1974). Possible role of brain serotonin and dopamine in controlling male sexual behavior. In E. Costa, G. L. Gessa, & M. Sandler (Eds.), *Advances in biochemical psychopharmacology* (Vol. 2, pp. 217–228). New York: Raven Press.

Halbreich, U., & Endicott, J. (1985). Relationship of dysphoric premenstrual changes to depressive disorders. *Acta Psychiatrica Scandinavica, 71,* 331–338.

Heiman, J. (1981). *Personal history questionnaire (PHQ-C)* Copyright.

Lief, H. I., & Slowinski, J. (1985, June). *Sexual dysfunction and accompanying depression: Implication for therapy.* Paper presented at 11th Annual Meeting of the Society for Sex Therapy and Research, Minneapolis.

LoPiccolo, L. (1980). Low sexual desire. In S. Lieblum & L. Pervin (Eds.), *Principles and practice of sex therapy* (pp. 29–64). New York: Guilford.

Mathew, R. J., & Weinman, M. L. (1982). Sexual dysfunctions in depression. *Archives of Sexual Behavior, 11,* 323–328.

Merikangas, K. R., Prusoff, B. A., Kupfer, D. J., & Frank, E. (1985). Marital adjustment in major depression. *Journal of Affective Disorders, 9,* 5–11.

Ruestow, P., Dunner, D., Bleeker, B., & Fieve, R. R. (1978). Marital adjustment in primary affective disorders. *Comparative Psychiatry, 19,* 565–571.

Schreiner-Engel, P., & Schiavi, R. C. (1986). Psychopathology and low sexual desire. *Journal of Nervous & Mental Disease, 174,* 646–651.

Weissman, M. M., & Paykel, E. S. (1974). *The depressed woman—a study of social relations.* Chicago: University of Chicago Press.

12
THE ORGANIC TREATMENT OF VIOLENT SEXUAL OFFENDERS

John Bradford
Director, Forensic Service,
Royal Ottawa Hospital

The organic treatment of violent sexual offenders involves three distinct but related treatments:

1. Antiandrogen or hormonal treatment.
2. Surgical castration.
3. Stereotactic neurosurgery.

To understand these organic treatments, a fundamental understanding of the biobehavioral basis of male sexual behavior and, specifically, sexual aggression is required. This includes the neuroendocrinology and neurochemistry of sexual aggression. When considering these aspects, it is important to note that the androgen hormones (primarily testosterone) are the most important correlates to the maintenance and control of male sexual behavior in all mammalian species. Testosterone is regarded as the most important hormone in sexual aggression.

   Animal research has shown that aggressive behavior is accompanied by physiological changes, including changes in blood chemistry due to the secretion of andrenocorticotropic hormones (McKenna, 1983). In addition, the levels of plasma testosterone can significantly affect aggressive behavior. In humans, there is also evidence that other internal biochemical events, such as hypoglycemia, may act significantly to induce aggression. Research into aggressive behavior led to Lorenz's (1966) hypothesis (Lorenz, 1966; McKenna, 1983) that aggression is a basic biological drive separate from other drives such as sex, and its manifestation was inevitable in order to discharge neurohormonal energy. Similarly, Ardrey (1966) examined aggressive instincts and defined them as part of territorial ambitions and sexual competition (Ardrey, 1967; McKenna, 1983). Psychodynamic theorists have also contributed to the understanding of aggression, and their description of an innate aggressive instinct is similar to both Lorenz's and Ardrey's theories.

Social biologists studying aggression claim that it can be affected by heriditary factors and is also a factor in the natural selection of individuals resulting in individual or species reproduction and survival (McKenna, 1983). In sociobiology, aggressive and sexual behavior are regarded as closely related. This theoretical assumption is based on studies of nonhuman primate aggression, particularly studies of aggression in chimpanzees, our closest relatives in the ape species. Other studies of social behavior and infanticides in primates are also quoted. These socioecological studies have significantly advanced our understanding of the biological basis of aggression (McKenna, 1983). They generally agree that androgens, specifically testosterone, are a major factor in the development of aggression in nonhuman primates. In addition to this, stimulation of various brain areas, including the amygdala and the pre-optic region of the hypothalamus, can similarly precipitate aggressive acts in primates (McKenna, 1983).

Studies have shown that testosterone, during the prepubertal period, has an activating role in the development of aggressive behavior. Similarly, "dominance" behavior has been found to correlate with the level of androgens. There are also studies where prenatal exposure to testosterone was found to be essential in establishing sex-orientation differences, as well as a propensity for aggression (Coe & Levine, 1983). This "organizational" effect of testosterone has been demonstrated in primates, as well as rodents. At puberty, when the sex hormones drastically increase, the emergence of adult social and sexual behavior is highly correlated with hormone levels (Coe & Levine, 1983). In addition, males become more aggressive during post-puberty, which directly relates to testosterone levels (McKenna, 1983). Castration leads to a change in the "dominance" behavior of certain primates. Animal research has also shown that sexual aggression is related to the reproductive cycle and can be significantly influenced by the introduction of a suitable mate (a female in estrus), as well as other extraneous factors (Coe & Levine, 1983). Aggressiveness can also independently affect the adrenal and genital systems (Coe & Levine, 1983).

In summary, therefore, the main male sex hormone testosterone has a significant influence in aggressive behavior in animals. This ranges from the organizational effects of testosterone in the prenatal and prepubertal periods to the activating effects in both adult sexual and nonsexual aggression. It is not surprising, therefore, that the effects of testosterone in sexual aggression in man have also been studied. This forms part of the research into the identification of the violent sexual offender.

Despite considerable research, knowledge in both the identification and the treatment of the violent sexual offender is deficient. As with animals, the primary question is whether sexual aggression is caused or precipitated by the

sexual hormones or whether the endocrine system is responsive to the manifestation of sexual aggression (Coe & Levine, 1983). Studies of men involved in
mock combat or competitive sports show testosterone changes very similar to
those observed in primates (Mazur & Lamb, 1980; Rose, 1980). It is possible
that the changes in testosterone levels are a result of the activating effect of
aggression, but also may reinforce certain aspects of the behavior of violent
sexual offenders (Mazur & Lamb, 1980). A considerable amount of work has
been published on the psychoendocrinology of stress, which includes the measures of adrenocortical hormones, growth hormone, prolactin, and also testosterone (Rose, 1980). Testosterone, unlike cortisol, catecholamines, growth hormone, or prolactin, generally decreases in response to exposure to stressful
stimuli. It has also been documented that certain social situations in primates can
be associated with an increase in testosterone. This is seen in victorious primates,
as opposed to submissive males which show a decrease in testosterone levels
(Rose, 1980).

The relationship of testosterone to aggressive behavior in man has been stud-
ied, and the various studies have attempted to correlate plasma-testosterone
levels mostly with self-report questionnaires on aggression. Some studies have
also sought a link between violent sexual offenders and testosterone (Bradford &
McLean, 1984; Brown & Davis, 1975; Ehrenkranz, Bliss, Sheard, 1974; Kreuz
& Rose, 1972; Meyer-Bahlburg. Nat, Boon, Sharma, & Edwards, 1974; Monti,
Brown, & Corriveau, 1977; Olweus, Mattson, Schalling, & Low, 1980; Persky,
Smith, & Basu, 1971; Rada, 1981; Rada, Kellner, & Winslow, 1976a; Rada,
Laws, & Kellner, 1976b; Rada, Laws, Kellner, Stivastava, & Peak, 1983;
Scaramella & Brown, 1978). Studies that have been completed on plasma-
testosterone levels and human aggression have produced somewhat conflicting
results. Persky et al. (1971) looked at the plasma-testosterone level and production rate in 18 healthy young men, 15 healthy older men, and 6 hospitalized
dysphoric male patients, with an average age of 39 years. Aggressive feelings, as
measured by the Buss-Durkee Hostility Inventory, a self-report questionnaire
measure of aggression, were found to correlate highly with the production rate of
testosterone (Persky et al., 1971).

Kreuz and Rose (1972) looked at plasma-testosterone levels, levels of fighting, and verbal aggression, as well as past criminal behavior in 21 young prisoners. The plasma-testosterone level of the individuals was reasonably stable
over a two-week study period, and highly significant differences were observed
between individuals. Plasma-testosterone levels did not, however, differentiate
between fighting and nonfighting subjects. Ten of the subjects with a history of
the most violent crimes in adolescence had a significantly higher level of testosterone compared to the 11 without. They concluded that testosterone levels may
be an important factor in indicating those individuals at risk to commit aggressive
crimes during adolescence (Kreuz & Rose, 1972).

Meyer-Bahlburg et al. (1974) also looked at the production rate of plasma testosterone, as well as the urinary excretion of androgens in two groups of young men. One group had high scores on the Buss-Durkee Hostility Inventory and the other group had low scores. Essentially this was a negative study and failed to show any significant correlations.

Ehrenkranz et al. (1974) estimated the plasma-testosterone levels of 36 male prisoners, one third of whom had chronically aggressive behavior, one third of whom were socially dominant without physical aggression, and 12 who were not physically aggressive or socially dominant. A variety of psychological tests was also used, including the Buss-Durkee Hostility inventory (Buss & Durkee, 1957). There was a significant association between a high level of plasma testosterone in the aggressive group compared to the nonaggressive group or compared to the other two groups combined. The socially dominant group also had a significantly higher level of testosterone than did the nonaggressive group.

Brown and Davis (1975) looked at how aggressive behavior could be related to plasma-testosterone levels in man. Fifteen healthy undergraduate males, with an average age of 18.4 years, volunteered to have their blood sampled and completed a battery of personality inventories, including the Buss-Durkee Hostility Inventory. The irritability scale of the Buss-Durkee was positively correlated with the mean plasma-testosterone level. They concluded that an association between plasma testosterone and angry feelings was valid, but how this would translate into behavioral action was subject to a number of other factors.

Rada et al. (1976b) examined the plasma-testosterone levels of 52 rapists and 12 child molesters who had also completed the Buss-Durkee Hostility Inventory and the Megargee Overcontrolled Hostility Scale, as well as the Michigan Alcoholism Screening Test. In addition, the rapists were classified according to degree of violence used during the commission of the rape. Plasma-testosterone levels for the rapists and child-molester controls were within normal limits. The group of rapists who were the most violent did, however, have significantly higher mean plasma-testosterone levels than did the normals. The mean Buss-Durkee Hostility rating scores for rapists were significantly higher than the mean for normals.

Rada et al. (1983), in a follow-up study, looked at plasma testosterone, dihydrotestosterone, and luteinizing hormone levels in rapists and child molesters to examine the range and means of plasma androgens in rapists and child molesters, and to compare the plasma-androgen levels between those sex offenders who were violent during the offense and those who were not. In addition, other characteristics of rapists and child molesters, such as age, alcohol consumption and length of incarceration, were also studied. They found in 18 rapists, 26 child molesters, and 11 controls that the mean testosterone levels of the rapists were higher than were those of the child molesters or control subjects. Mean testosterone levels of violent and nonviolent rapists were similar, while violent child molesters had the highest mean testosterone levels of any group. No statistically significant differences were noted between dihydrotestosterone and luteinizing hormone levels. Plasma androgens in alcoholic versus nonalcoholic rapists and child molesters showed no significant differences. Plasma-testosterone levels and subscale Factor II (a motor component of hostility) of the Buss-Durkee Hostility Inventory were positively correlated (Rada, 1981, Rada et al., 1976b, 1983).

Monti et al. (1977), in a study of 101 healthy males, found positive correlations with plasma-testosterone levels on the Buss-Durkee suspicion subscale and masturbation frequency, but not hostility or attributed aggression. Olweus et al. (1980) looked at 58 16-year-old boys and found that their plasma-testosterone levels correlated significantly with self-reports of physical and verbal aggression on the Olweus Aggression Inventory. There was also a correlation with a lack of frustration tolerance. There was, however, only weak, nonsignificant correlation between plasma testosterone and self-reports of antisocial behavior.

Scaramella and Brown (1978) studied the relationship between plasma testosterone and the degree of aggressive response to threat in hockey players and found that this correlated significantly with plasma-testosterone levels. Matthews (1979) examined 11 incarcerated offenders with a history of violent crime, compared to a matched sample of controls with no history of violent behavior, and found no significant difference in plasma-testosterone levels.

Mattson, Schalling, Olweus, Low, and Stevenson (1980) compared 40 male delinquent recidivists with a control group on a number of variables, including plasma-testosterone level, aggressive behavior, and personality variables. No significant correlations were found between plasma-testosterone levels and violent behavior.

In a previous study, Bradford and McLean (1984) looked at sexual offenders, violence, and testosterone levels and did not find a statistical correlation between a high-violence group and plasma-testosterone levels, when compared to low-violence and no-violence groups. It was noted, however, that the most violent individuals in the high-violence group had the higher plasma-testosterone levels. Schiavi, Theilgäard, Owen, and White (1984) looked at a double-blind controlled study of men with sex-chromosome abnormalities and found that those with XYY syndrome had higher concentrations of testosterone, LH, and FSH than did matched control groups and that the mean testosterone level in the 15 subjects of the total sample with records of criminal convictions was significantly higher than in those without criminal convictions. Testosterone levels were, however, almost identical for XYYs with and without criminal convictions. No significant relationships were found between plasma testosterone and measures of aggressiveness from the interview and projective tests that were used in the assessment.

As related in detail above, there have been a number of studies looking at plasma-testosterone levels in sexually aggressive men. A recently completed, unpublished study by this author on 150 sexual offenders clearly shows high levels of plasma testosterone associated with a high level of sexual violence. In this study, documented violent behavior and plasma testosterone were highly correlated. This was clearly a biobehavioral correlation. This was planned to avoid an inherent defect in previous studies which attempted to prove a correlation with questionnaires on aggression. It is clear that there is a complex interaction of a number of different factors that results in sexual violence, and some of the other factors are just as important as hormone levels. Specifically, sexual arousal to sadistic and sexually aggressive stimuli directed toward both women and children is also very significant. Alcohol and drug abuse are important components in the sexually aggressive male. To a lesser extent, there has been evidence of an association between organic brain damage and sexual violence.

Prior to considering any of the organic treatment approaches, a full sexual-behavior assessment must be completed. This should include a sex-hormone profile, chromosome studies (if indicated), penile tumescence testing, and the use of self-report questionnaires and investigations for organic brain damage, as indicated. Careful psychiatric evaluation must exclude obvious primary causes of aggression, such as those associated with schizophrenia and organic personality disorder syndrome. The primary condition can be treated with antipsychotic and anticonvulsive agents such as carbamazepine (Tegretol), which can be very effective in preventing subsequent aggressive episodes. The association between sexual aggression and antisocial personality disorder remains controversial, but, generally, the number of sexual crimes committed by this group is small as compared to the paraphiliac sexually aggressive male. It is this individual who must be very carefully evaluated in a sexual behaviors clinic. A detailed description of this type of assessment has been published elsewhere (Abel, Becker, Blanchard, & Djenderedjian, 1978; Abel, Becker, Murphy, & Flanagan, 1981; Abel, Becker, & Skinner, 1980). Penile tumescence is the most reliable and valid measure of sexual arousal and provides the most accurate means of assessing deviant sexual arousal, including arousal to sexual aggression. Theoretically, paraphiliac rapists and violent child molesters are more sexually aroused to acts of rape against adult women and children than are normal males (Abel et al., 1978, 1981; Barlow, 1977).

The single most important factor is in relation to violence, including sexual violence, is alcohol. It is widely accepted that acute alcohol intoxication at the time of the commission of a violent offense and a history of chronic alcoholism are significant factors in relation to rape. Surprisingly, very few studies have looked at the specific effects of alcohol on sexual arousal of the rapist (Barbaree, Marshall, Yates, & Lightfoot, 1983; Borzecki, Bradford, Pawlak, Zohar, & Wormith, 1985; Wormith Bradford, Pawlak, Zohar, & Borzecki, 1988; Bridell & Wilson, 1976; Farkas & Rosen, 1976; Lansky & Wilson, 1981; Wilson & Lawson, 1976). A recently completed study shows that the sexual arousal of rapists to rape was, in fact, increased when compared to nonrapists under the influence of alcohol (Borzecki et al., 1985).

It is also well known that certain specific organic brain syndromes can be associated with both sexually deviant and sexually aggressive behavior. Specifically, temporal-lobe abnormalities have been reported in conjunction with sexual aggression (Blumer, 1970; Epstein, 1961; Hoenig & Kenna, 1979; Taylor, 1969). In addition, from the neurosurgical techniques that have been practiced, operations such as amygdalotomy have had reasonable success and significant effects on sexual aggression (Kelly, 1976). The classic description of medial-hypothalamic lesions and their dramatic tranquilizing effects have also been examined (Bradford & Pawlak, 1987). The experiments of Klüver and Bucy (1939), and the subsequent description of the Klüver-Bucy syndrome, are well known in psychiatry (Bradford & Pawlak, 1987).

ORGANIC TREATMENTS FOR SEXUAL AGGRESSION

Presently, the most significant organic treatment of the violent sexual offender is the use of antiandrogen medication, specifically cyproterone acetate, in addition to the hormonal treatment approach using medroxyprogesterone acetate. The differentiation between hormonal treatment and antiandrogens is based on the fact that cyproterone acetate is a true antiandrogen, blocking the androgen receptors in the body as its mechanism of action, whereas medroxyprogesterone acetate reduces plasma-testosterone levels by other means. Both cyproterone acetate and medroxyprogesterone acetate reduce the plasma testosterone, and both are highly effective in reducing sexual drive and sexual fantasy and have been described as reducing sexual aggression.

Cyproterone Acetate (CPA)

Cyproterone acetate is the first commercially available antiandrogen and has been used for the medical treatment of a number of different conditions, such as prostatic carcinoma, paraphilias, androgenization in women, and, more recently, acne. In children, it has also been used in the treatment of idiopathic precocious puberty (Schering, 1983). First synthesized in 1961 (Laschet, 1973), CPA has antiandrogenic, progestational, and antigonadotropic effects (Liang, Tymoczko, & Chan, 1977).

The mechanism of action of CPA is through competitive inhibition of androgen at the androgen receptors. Receptors exist in the body both for dihydrotestosterone and testosterone, and these receptors have different affinities for the two androgens (Liang et al., 1977). The androgens have a high affinity for the cytoplasmic receptor protein in the androgen-receptor areas of the target organs. As a result, a steroid-receptor complex is formed, which then migrates into the nuclear chromatin, and this remains at specific sites and is responsible for various changes in intracellular metabolism. Almost all of these androgen-receptor responses are disrupted by CPA, particularly in receptors that have a high affinity for dihydrotestosterone. CPA affects the intracellular testosterone uptake, the intracellular metabolism of testosterone, and the high-affinity receptor binding (Mainwaring, 1977).

The negative-feedback system of the hypothalamic-pituitary-gonadal axis is blocked by the antiandrogens. Two pure antiandrogens, cyproterone (i.e., CPA without the acetate radical) and flutamide are available, and there are antigonadotropic and antiandrogenic compounds, specifically CPA and chlormadinone acetate. When cyproterone or flutamide (i.e., the pure antiandrogens) is administered, an androgen deficit is registered in the hypothalamus, and there is an outpouring of LHRH and LH and a subsequent rise in plasma testosterone. It is the acetate radical of the cyproterone acetate that is antigonadotropic and prevents this from happening.

CPA has been used in a number of clinical studies for the treatment of paraphilia, including treatment of violent sexual offenders. Laschet and Laschet (1971) reported on the CPA treatment of 110 male sexual offenders. A wide range of paraphilias was treated, including sexual aggression and sexually motivated homicide. The largest group, however, was exhibitionists. They found that by six weeks, in all patients, plasma-testosterone levels, number of erections, and volume of ejaculate were decreased. Significantly, sexual fantasies either decreased or disappeared, and there was a substantial reduction in sexual drive. In addition, the researchers noted that psychopathology accompanying hypersexuality was also decreased, including restlessness, agitation, and labile affect. They noticed adverse side effects, including a transient depression, some fatigue, and hypersomnia. Also, there was a negative nitrogen balance and weight gain for the first three months. After three months they noted that the nitrogen balance returned to normal, and no disturbances of calcium and phosphate metabolism were documented. In about one fifth of cases there was gynecomastia.

Ott and Hoffet (1968) reported on 26 psychiatric hospital patients, ranging from chronically recidivistic sexual offenders to mentally ill or severely subnormal individuals. Mothes et al reported on a study of 547 men treated with CPA, some of whom were sexually aggressive (Mothes, Lehnert, Samimi, & Ufer, 1971).

Davies (1974) reported on 50 patients treated with CPA over a period of 5 years. The 50 cases included what were described as hypersexual males and were divided into 6 groups:

1. men convicted of a sexual assault or indecent exposure (exhibitionism);
2. men who complained of distressing, vivid sexual fantasies;
3. oligophrenics with disturbed sexual behavior;
4. homosexuals;
5. men with chromosomal abnormalities; and
6. elderly men with sexual behavior problems.

In the first group, they found that no sexual offenses were committed while the patients were receiving the drug, and even when the drug was stopped for periods up to four years, no further offenses occurred. In one case where the individual had been on the drug for a short period of time, there was a reoffense. In the second group, there were four patients with distressing sexual fantasies. One 22-year-old man started to develop violent fantasies toward women, including strangulation. Within three months, all of his thoughts of violence toward women had disappeared. The third group was schizophrenics who persisted with aggressive sexual behavior, including masturbation in public. They showed a remarkable improvement after treatment with CPA. The group classified as homosexuals was a combination of egodystonic homosexuality and homosexual pedophilia, all of whom noticed an improvement on CPA in that their libido was reduced, but the direction of the sexual orientation was unchanged. Four individuals with chromosomal abnormalities composed the fifth group. A seriously sexually aggressive young man with XYY syndrome showed a marked decrease in sexual aggression on treatment with CPA. Another individual, with a chromosome mosaic of XO XYY, XY, with a homosexual pedophilic orientation, was also considerably improved. A young boy of 16 years, with trisomy 21 (Down's syndrome) and a severe cardiac defect to the point that his excessive masturbation endangered his life, reported a marked reduction in his sexual activity and thus less risk from the cardiac lesion. In addition, he had been seriously self-mutilating, trying to bite his own penis and attacking and biting penises of other patients in his immediate environment. There was a marked decrease in all of his activities. The elderly men were mostly pedophiles who were also exhibitionists. In two of the patients who had a long history of sadomasochistic behavior, including reciprocal beating of and by prostitutes, considerable improvement on CPA was noted.

Laschet and Laschet (1975), describe cases with organic brain syndrome (post-traumatic, post-encephalitic, or cerebrosclerotic defects in the region of the hypothalamus and temporal lobes) as unsuitable for treatment with CPA. They describe this behavior as being less androgen dependent (Cooper, 1981). Twenty-five patients who were followed up between one and five years after the cessation of treatment showed no recurrence of sexually deviant behavior. They describe a limitation in the therapeutic spectrum of CPA with regard to aggression. Aggression which is not sexually driven or eroticized is not affected by treatment with CPA.

Cooper (1981), in a placebo-controlled study of CPA, treated nine individuals, mostly hypersexuals with no reported evidence of any sexual aggression. He noted significant reduction in all sexual parameters with CPA, but also reported a tranquilizing action of CPA, with the majority of the patients noticing that they were less irritable and more relaxed. Zbytovsky and Zapletalek (1979) reported on the treatment of 10 male outpatients. Their study included penile tumescence testing, which showed a flattened response. Deviant sexual behavior was decreased in all of the patients. They described a tranquilizing effect of CPA (Zbytovsky & Zapletalek, 1979).

Berner, Brownstone, and Sluga (1983) treated 21 patients who were recidivistic sexual offenders and who were dissatisfied with traditional treatment. The patients were on CPA for one to two years, with the usual daily dose of 100 mg. Follow-up between one and eight years, with an average of 5.28 years, showed a re-arrest rate of 28%. These individuals were all on CPA for a relatively short period of time.

Ortmann carefully evaluated a number of studies reporting on recidivism rates in sexual offenders who have been treated with CPA (Appelt & Floru, 1974; Baron & Unger, 1977; Fähndrich, 1974; Horn, 1972; Jost, 1974; Ortmann, 1980). Lemaire studied the relapse rate of sexual offenders in Denmark and noted that out of 3,185 sexual offenders over a 10-year period, comprising 85% of all of the recorded male sexual offenders during that time, there was a relapse rate of 16.8% (Lemaire, 1956; Ortmann, 1980). The highest rate for the different paraphilias was 2.4% for exhibitionism; 3.7-9.2% for incest; 16.3% for heterosexual pedophila; and 27.9% for homosexual pedophilia. It was also found that individuals committing more than one sexual offense appeared to recidivate more frequently. A follow-up study confirmed this trend (Ortmann, 1980; Ortmann, 1984a; Ortmann, 1984b; Ortmann, 1984c).

Against this background, Ortmann reviewed studies using CPA where recidivism rates post-treatment were reported. He also looked at the results of these studies, correcting for insufficient dosage of CPA. Prior to treatment with CPA the recidivism rate was close to 100%, ranging from 50-100%. When the results were corrected for adequate dosage, all of the studies except one showed a recidivism rate of 0% (Ortmann, 1980, 1984a, 1984b, 1984c). The follow-up period ranged from one to five years. Some of the studies included sexually aggressive offenders.

Bradford et al. (1987) evaluated the effects of CPA on the sexual arousal patterns of a sadistic homosexual pedophile, measured by penile-tumescence testing with standard audiotape narratives. He suffered cerebral damage as a result of a severe antepartum hemorrhage and a severly obstructed delivery. From a young age, he developed abnormal behavior patterns with features of aggressiveness, head banging, and hyperactivity. He developed epilepsy and was mildly mentally retarded. When he was an adolescent, he committed a sadistic, sexually motivated homicide of a young boy. At this time, a pretrial forensic psychiatric evaluation showed left-sided paroxysmal abnormalities in the temporal lobe of the EEG. A CAT scan showed evidence of dilation of the left anteriotemporal horn. He was treated with CPA, and his sexual arousal patterns while under treatment were monitored. Initially there was very strong sexual arousal to nonviolent and violent homosexual, pedophilic stimuli. Under treatment with CPA, a significant positive correlation was found between plasma-testosterone levels and sexual arousal to aggressive pedophilic tendencies (i.e., as the testosterone decreased, so did his deviant sexual arousal to these stimuli). This decrease included sexual arousal to sadism and physical coercion of young boys to engage in sexual activity; in other words, eroticized sexual aggression responded clearly to treatment with CPA. The effect on eroticized nonsexual aggression was more variable (Bradford & Pawlak, 1987). There was a considerable improvement compared to no treatment, and considerable improvement in his behavior overall. Eroticized nonsexual aggression did not correlate to plasma-testosterone levels. In this case, it was also observed that responses to mutually consenting, heterosexual sex (i.e., the desired response) were maintained on treatment with CPA. This, for the first time, demonstrated differential effects of CPA on the sexual arousal patterns in a man suffering from a paraphilia.

In a double-blind, placebo crossover study of CPA in the treatment of sexual deviation, a number of sexually aggressive men (mostly recidivistic sexual offenders) showed significant treatment responses to CPA as compared to the placebo. Significant reductions in plasma-testosterone levels and sexual arousal both to slides and fantasies were documented. A statistically significant reduction in psychopathology, as measured by the Brief Psychiatric Rating Scale total score, was also documented. On the total score of the Buss-Durkee Hostility Inventory, although the active drug reduced the total score, no statistically significant effect was noted. A "sexual calm" or tranquilizing effect was noted, and there was far less irritability and aggressiveness than was seen previously (Bradford J. & PawlakA, 1986). Another significant facet of the single case study was that a severely brain-damaged, sadistic individual clearly responded to treatment with CPA. In previous studies, particularly those by Laschet and Laschet (1971, 1975), it was maintained that CPA was ineffective in individuals with organic brain damage.

Medroxyprogesterone Acetate (MPA)

Medroxyprogesterone acetate has also been used in the treatment of sexual offenders. This was first described in 1958 (Heller, Laidlaw, & Harvey, 1958). In this study, a group of healthy males receiving MPA described a complete loss of sexual drive while receiving a progesterone-derivative female oral contraceptive. The maximum effect occurred three to four weeks from the onset of treatment and was also reversible within two weeks following withdrawal of the medication. Subsequently, a number of studies have documented the use of MPA in the treatment of paraphilias (Berlin & Meinecke, 1981; Blumer & Migeon, 1975; Gagné, 1981; Money, 1970, 1972; Money, Wiedeking, Walker, Migeon, & Borgoakar, 1975; Rivarola, Camacho, & Migeon, 1968; Wiedeking, Money, & Walker, 1979).

Progestational agents such as MPA exert their sex-drive-reducing effect through different mechanisms from CPA (Albin, Vittek, Gordon, Altman, Olivo, & Southren, 1973; Foote, 1944; Gordon Southren, Tochimoto, Olivo,

Altmank, Rand, et al., 1970). There is interference with the production of testosterone from its precursors. MPA causes a significant increase in the metabolic clearance rate of testosterone (Southren, Gordon, Vittek, & Altman, 1977). MPA also affects the binding of testosterone to sex-hormone-binding globulin.

Money (1970) treated eight cases with MPA in dosage levels ranging from 300-400 mg/week. In a three-year period of follow-up, significant reductions in sex drive without any major side effects were noted. Blumer and Migeon (1975), in a study of 22 cases, found that sex drive was reduced and that aggressive behavior in individuals with temporal-lobe epilepsy also improved. Money et al. (1975) treated 13 males with 47 XYY syndrome genotype and 10 males with 46 XY genotype with MPA in combination with psychotherapy. The 46 XY-genotype patients were all sexual offenders, and those with 47 XYY genotype were antisocial offenders, both with and without sexual offenses. The treatment program was successful in treating all of the sexual offenders, and in three of the 46 XY and two of the 47 XYY men there was a complete remission of the paraphiliac symptoms. The effect of treatment on aggressive and destructive antisocial behavior was less obvious, and was probably due to a placebo response. MPA clearly reduced the frequency of erotic sexual fantasies, reduced the frequency of erection and ejaculation, and suppressed paraphilic behavior. In a follow-up study, it was noted that the recidivism rate increased dramatically when patients disocntinued the MPA. Ten out of 11 patients who discontinued MPA against medical advice experienced a relapse.

Berlin and Meinecke (1981) reported on the treatment of 20 chronic paraphiliac men treated with MPA and confirmed that as long as treatment continued, no relapse seemed to occur, whereas individuals who dropped out of treatment appeared to relapse less than one year after the discontinuation of treatment. Most of the patients treated were pedophiles without any clear evidence of sexual aggression.

Gagné (1981) reported on the MPA treatment of 48 male paraphiliac subjects, of which 39 were sexual offenders. Forty of the patients showed a positive response within the first 10 days to three weeks of the onset of treatment. There was a diminution in the frequency of sexual fantasies and increased control over sexual urges. There was a diminution in the frequency and quality of erections and ejaculations. All of the patients reported side effects, with fatigue the most common complaint, present for two to three days after the injection of MPA. Twenty-eight of the patients had a weight gain of up to 9.1 kg; 14 patients complained of hot and cold flushes. None of the 40 improved patients returned to pretreatment levels of sexual behavior when the testosterone levels returned to normal. Gagné also notes that seven patients with an associated diagnosis of antisocial personality disorder failed to show any significant improvement in sexual behavior. On one occasion, a patient's treatment was terminated due to the development of phlebitis. In reviewing the clinical features of these patients, most of them were hypersexual, masturbating more than once a day, actively seeking out sexual partners, and having difficulty controlling sexual urges as well as having a high level of sexual fantasy and erotic dreams. Patients were initially started on 200 mg of MPA intramuscularly two or three times per week for the first two weeks, then reduced to 200 mg once or twice a week for the next four weeks, and then subsequently 100 mg/week for two weeks for the following three months. A maintenance dosage level varied from 100 mg/week to 100 mg/month.

Estrogens have also been used in the past to treat paraphilia (Foote, 1944; Golla & Hodge, 1949; Scott, 1964; Symmers, 1968; Whittaker, 1959). In addition, sex-drive reduction by phenothiazines has also been described and used in the treatment of paraphilias. To certain extent, a reduction of aggression in relation to the paraphilias has also been described (Bancroft, 1977; Bartholomew, 1964, 1968; Beaumont, Corker, Friesen, Kolakowska, Mandelbrote, Marshall et al., 1974; Field, 1973; Litkey & Feniczy, 1967; Sterkmans & Geerts, 1966).

Castration

Castration is the removal of the testes and can be an effective way of reducing recidivism in violent sexual offenders. It is related to the antiandrogen and hormonal treatments in that approximately 95% of tesosterone is produced by the testes. Castration causes a drastic reduction in plasma-testosterone levels. Castration was first used in 1899 in the U.S. to reduce the sex drive of prisoners (Lemaire, 1956). Subsequently, in the late 19th and early 20th centuries, therapeutic castration for the treatment of sexual offenses occurred in Europe, particularly Switzerland, Holland, Germany, and the three Scandinavian countries. Lemaire (1956) studied 139 castrated sexual offenders, of a total of 3,185 sexual offenders in Denmark, over a 10-year period. The recidivism for the sample varied according to the types of paraphiliac behavior.

Various studies of postcastration recidivism have been reported in the literature. The reported recidivism rates vary between 1.3 and 10.8% in the postcastration period. Periods of follow-up of up to 20 years are also documented (Bremer, 1959; Cornu, 1973; Heim & Hursch, 1979; Langelüddeke, 1963; Stürup, 1968).

Langelüddeke reported on 1,036 sexual offenders with a follow-up period of between 6 weeks and 20 years, and an improvement in recidivism ranging from approximately 84% to 2.3% (Heim & Hursch, 1979). Cornu (1973) examined 127 castrated sexual offenders who had been released for five years, as well as a comparison group of individuals who had been evaluated but had refused castration. The castration group recidivism rate was 7.4%, compared to a pretreatment rate of 76.8%. The comparison group had a recidivism rate of 52% in a 10-year follow-up, compared to a recidivism rate prior to recommendation for castration of 66%. It is interesting that the recidivism rate for nonsexual crimes was also significantly reduced in the castrated sample (Heim & Hursch, 1979).

Bremer (1959) studied 216 castrated subjects. A multiplicity of psychiatric diagnostic groupings was seen. The paraphiliac behavior, however, mostly included sexual aggression in the form of rape, as well as hetero- and homosexual pedophilia, and a small group with exhibitionism. One-hundred-and-two of the sexual offenders who were followed up in a postcastration period had a recidivism rate of 2.9%. The follow-up varied between 5 and 10 years. This compared to a pretreatment recidivism rate of more than 50%.

Ortmann (1980, 1984c) reviewed the Danish data on castrated subjects and concluded that castration reduced an expected recidivism rate of 50% to less than 2%. Stürup (1972) reported on a series of very seriously sexually aggressive men (mostly rapists). Fifty percent of the sample group were castrated, and these men did not recidivate. In a follow-up of a group that refused castration, 20 showed a recidivism rate of 10% (Heim & Hursch, 1979; Ortmann, 1980; Stürup, 1968). In addition, Stürup reported on another sample of approximately 900 castrated individuals with a follow-up period of up to 30 years. A recidivism rate of 2.2% was noted.

Ortmann, (1984a, 1984b, 1984c) reviewed all of the studies of sexual recidivism in Denmark. He noted that castration was used most frequently in seriously sexually deviant men. Although these studies do not have control groups and some questions on the calculation of recidivism rates can be raised, the results are nonetheless dramatic. At the present time, surgical castration as an intervention in the treatment of paraphilias is not acceptable, since it is irreversible.

Psychosurgery

Psychosurgery has also been used for the treatment of sexual deviation, using various stereotaxic techniques. A stereotractotomy and limbic leukotomy are the most significant operations (Kelly, 1976). Roeder (1966) has reported on the treatment of pedophilia with a stereotactic lesion in the hypothalamus. At follow-up, no serious side effects were documented, and erotic fantasies were suppressed (Roeder, 1966). Further discussion of psychosurgery is not warranted, as it is unlikely to be considered as a serious treatment in the future since it is irreversible.

In conclusion, CPA and MPA clearly have a role in the treatment of paraphiliac males and specifically the violent sexual offender. Further research in this area, both in the identification of the violent offender and his treatment, is imperative.

FUTURE RESEARCH

Future research in the treatment of sexual offenders is likely to be in neuroendocrinology. The use of luteinizing hormone releasing hormone (LHRH analogue; Tolis, Ackman, Stellos, Mehta, Labrie, Fazekas et al., 1982) is one such approach. Further studies using the nonsteroid true antiandrogen flutamide should also be conducted. In addition, the antiandrogen treatment approach to sexual offenders, specifically violent sexual offenders, should include measurements of the sexual-arousal patterns of these persons. This will help to improve the identification of the violent sexual offender as well as allow for improved treatment planning and monitoring of the treatment's success.

The hypothalamic-pituitary-gonadal axis appears to show some disturbances in violent sexual offenders. Further research using various hormonal challenges to the axis should be conducted (Gaffney & Berlin, 1984; Gladue, Green, & Hellman, 1984). It is quite conceivable that disturbances in the hypothalamic-pituitary-gonadal axis form the etiological basis for violent sexual behavior and disturbances in sex drive. They could also be factors in sexual orientation disturbances and pedophilia.

ACKNOWLEDGMENT

This is published with the knowledge and permission of Wayne Quan, M.D., Managing Editor Psychiatric Journal of the University of Ottawa with specific reference to "Sexually Aggressive Men" Bradford, J. M. W., Bourget, D. Vol. XII, No. 3. September 1987.

REFERENCES

Abel, G. G., Becker, J. V., Blanchard, E. B., & Djenderedjian, A. (1978). Differentiating sexual aggressives with penile measures. *Criminal Justice and Behavior, 5,* 315–333.

Abel, G. G., Becker, J. V., Murphy, W. D., & Flanagan, B. (1981). Identifying dangerous child molesters. In R. Stuart (Ed.), *Violent Behavior* (pp. 116–137). New York: Brunner/Mazel.

Abel, G. G., Becker, J. V., & Skinner, L. J. (1980). Aggressive behavior and sex. *The psychiatric clinics of North America, 3,* 133–151.

Albin, J., Vittek, J., Gordon, G. G., Altman, K., Olivo, J., & Southren, A. L., (1973). On the mechanism of the antiandrogenic effect of medroxyprogesterone acetate. *Endocrinology, 93,* 417–422.

Appelt, M., & Floru, L. (1974). Erfahrungen über die Beeinflussung der Sexualität Durch Cyproteron acetat (Androcur, Schering), *Int. Pharmacopsychiatry, 19,* 61–76, from Ortmann, J. (1985), *How antihormone treatment with cyproterone acetate influences on relapsing into sexual criminality among male sexual offenders.* Unpublished manuscript.

Ardrey, R. (1967). *The territorial imperative.* New York: Atheneum.

Bancroft, J. (1977). Hormones and sexual behavior. *Psychological Medicine, 7,* 553–556.

Barbaree, H. E., Marshall, W. L., Yates, E., & Lightfoot, L. O. (1983). Alcohol intoxication and deviant sexual arousal in male social drinkers. *Behavior Research and Therapy, 21,* 365–373.

Barlow, D. H. (1977). Assessment of sexual behavior. In A. R. Ciminero, K. S. Calbour, & H. E. Adams (Eds.), *Handbook of behavioral assessment (pp. 461–508). New York: Wiley.*

Baron, D. P., & Unger, H. R. (1977). *A clinical trial of cyproterone acetate for sexual deviancy. New Zealand Medical Journal, 85,* 366.

Bartholomew, A. A. (1964). Some side effects of thioridazine. *Medical Journal of Australia, 1,* 57–59.

Bartholomew, A. A. (1968). A long-acting phenothiazine as a possible agent to control deviant sexual behavior. *American Journal of Psychiatry, 124,* 917–923.

Beaumont, P. J. V., Corker, C. S., Frieson, H. G., Kolakowska, B. M., Mandelbrote, B. M., Marshall, J., Murray, M. A. P., Wiles, D. H. (1974). The effects of phenothiazines on endocrine function, I: Patients with inappropriate lactation and amenorrhea; II: Effects in men and post-menopausal women. *British Journal of Psychiatry, 124,* 413–430.

Berlin, F. S., & Meinecke, C. F. (1981). Treatment of sex offenders with antiandrogenic medication: Conceptualization, review of treatment modalities and preliminary findings. *American Journal of Psychiatry, 138,* 601–607.

Berner, W., Brownstone, G.. & Sluga, W. (1983). The cyproteronacetate treatment of sexual offenders. *Neuroscience and Biobehavioral Review, 7,* 441.

Blumer, D. (1970). Changes of sexual behavior related to temporal lobe disorders in man. *Journal of Sex Research, 6,* 173–180.

Blumer, D., & Migeon, C. (1975). Hormone and hormonal agents in the treatment of aggresion. *Journal of Nervous and Mental Disease, 160,* 127–137.

Borzecki, M., Bradford, J., Pawlak, A., Zohar, A., & Wormith, J. S. (1985). Two psychophysiological measures of deviant sexual arousal and their relationship to instruction, intelligence, hormone level and alcohol ingestion. Ottawa: Programs Branch User Report, Ministry of the Solicitor-General of Canada, #1985-39.

Bradford, J. M. W., & McLean, D. (1984). Sexual offenders, violence and testosterone: A clinical study. *Canadian Journal of Psychiatry, 29,* 335–343.

Bradford, J. M. W., & Pawlak, A. (1986). *A double-blind placebo crossover study of cyproterone acetate.* Submitted for publication, Edited Resubmitted 1987.

Bradford, J. M. W., & Pawlak, A. (1987). Sadistic homosexual pedophilia: treatment with cyproterone acetate. A single case study. *Canadian Journal of Psychiatry, 32,* 22–31.

Bremer, J. (1959). *Asexualization: A follow-up study of 244 cases.* New York: MacMillan.

Bridell, P. W., & Wilson, G. T. (1976). Effects of alcohol and expectancy set on male sexual arousal. *Journal of Abnormal Psychology, 85,* 225–234.

Brown, W. A., & Davis, G. H. (1975). Serum testosterone and irritability in man. *Psychosomatic Medicine, 137,* 87.

Buss, A., & Durkee, A., (1957). An inventory for assessing different kinds of hostility. *Journal of Consulting Psychology, 21,* 343–349.

Coe, C. L., & Levine, S. (1983). Biology of aggression. *Bulletin of the American Academy of Psychiatry and the Law, 2,* 131–148.

Cooper, A. J. (1981). A placebo controlled trial of the antiandrogen cyproterone acetate in deviant hypersexuality. *Comprehensive Psychiatry, 22,* 458.

Cornu, T. (1973). *Catamnesic studies on castrated sex delinquents from a forensic psychiatric viewpoint.* Kargel: Basel.

Davies, T. S. (1974). Cyproterone acetate for male hypersexuality. *Journal of International Medical Research, 2,* 159.

Ehrenkranz, J., Bliss, D., & Sheard, M. H. (1974). Plasma testosterone: Correlation with aggressive behavior and social dominance in man. *Psychosomatic Medicine, 36,* 469–475.

Epstein, A. W. (1961). Relationship of fetishism and transvestism to brain and particularly to temporal lobe dysfunction. *Journal of Nervous and Mental Disease, 133,* 247–253.

Fähndrich, E. (1974). Cyproteronacetat in der Behandlung von Sexual Deviationen. *Bei Mannern Deutsch Med Wochr, 99,* 234.

Farkas, G. M., & Rosen, R. C. (1976). Effects of alcohol on elicited male sexual response. *Journal of Studies of Alcohol, 37,* 265–272.

Field, L. H. (1973). Benperidol in the treatment of sexual offenders. *Medicine Science and the Law, 3,* 195.

Foote, R. M. (1944). Diethylstilbestrol in the management of psychopathological states in males. *Journal of Nervous and Mental Disease, 99,* 928–935.

Gaffney, G. R., & Berlin, F. S. (1984). Is there hypothalamic-pituitary-gonadal dysfunction in pedophilia? A pilot study. *British Journal of Psychiatry, 145,* 657–661.

Gagné, P. (1981). Treatment of sex offenders with medroxyprogesterone acetate. *American Journal of Psychiatry, 138,* 644–646.

Gladue, B., Green, R., & Hellman, R. E. (1984). Neuroendocrine response to estrogen and sexual orientation. *Science, 225,* 496–498.

Golla, F. L., & Hodge, S. R. (1949). Hormone treatment of sex offenders. *Lancet,* 1006–1007.

Gordon, G., Southren, A. L., Tochimoto, S., Olivo, J., Altman, K., Rand, J., & Lemberger, L. (1970). Effect of medroxyprogesterone acetate (Provera) on the metabolism and biological activity of testosterone. *Journal of Clinical Endocrinology, 30,* 449–456.

Heim, N., & Hursch, C. J. (1979). Castration for sex offenders: Treatment or punishment? A review and critique of recent European literature. *Archives of Sexual Behavior, 8,* 281–304.

Heller, C. G., Laidlaw, W. M., & Harvey, H. T. (1958). Effects of progestational compounds on the reproductive processes of the human male. *Annals of the New York Academy of Science, 71,* 649–665.

Hoenig, J., & Kenna, J. (1979). EEG abnormalities in transsexualism. *British Journal of Psychiatry, 134,* 293–300.

Horn, J. H. (1972). Die Behandlung von Sexual Deliquenten mit Cyproteronacetat. In G. Rasne (Ed.), *Life Sciences Monograph* (Vol. 2, p. 113). Oxford: Pergamon Press.

Jost, F. (1974). Klinische Beobachtungen und Erfahrungen in der Behandlung Sexueller Deviationen mit dem Antiandrogen Cyproteron-Acetat. *Schweiz Rundschau Med* (Praxis), *63,* 1318.

Jost, F. (1975). Zur Behandlung Abnormen Sexualverhaltens mit dem Antiandrogen Cyproteronacetat. *Der Informierte, ARZT, 3,* 303.

Kelly D. (1976). Neurosurgical treatment of psychiatric disorders. In J. Granville-Grossman (Ed.), *Recent advances in clinical psychiatry* (Vol. II, pp. 227–261). Edinburgh: Churchill Livingstone Longman Group, Ltd.

Kluver, H., & Bucy, P. C. (1939). Preliminary analysis of functions of temporal lobes in monkeys. *Archives of Neurology and Psychiatry, 42,* 979–1000.

Kreuz, L. E., & Rose, R. M. (1972). Assessment of aggressive behavior and plasma testosterone in a young criminal population. *Psychosomatic Medicine, 34,* 321–332.

Langelüddeke, A. (1963). *Castration of sexual criminals.* Berlin: de Gruyjer.

Lansky, B., & Wilson, G. T. (1981). Alcohol expectations and sexual arousal in males: An information processing analysis. *Journal of Abnormal Psychology, 90,* 39–45.

Laschet, U. (1973). Antiandrogen in the treatment of sexual offenders: Mode of action and therapeutic outcome. In J. Zubin, & J. Money (Eds.), *Contemporary sexual behavior: Critical issues in the 1970s* (p. 311). Baltimore: Johns Hopkins University Press.

Laschet, U., & Laschet, L. (1971). Psychopharmacotherapy of sex offenders with cyproterone acetate. *Pharmakopsychiatrie Neuro-Psychopharmakologie: Advances in Clinical Research, 4,* 99.

Laschet, U., & Laschet, L. (1975). Antiandrogens in the treatment of sexual deviations of men. *Journal of Steroid Biochemistry, 6,* 821.

Lemaire, L. (1956). Danish experiences regarding the castration of sexual offenders. *Journal of Criminal Law: Criminology and Police Science, 47,* 294–310.

Mainwaring, W. I. P. (1977). Modes of action of antiandrogens: A survey. In L. Martini, & M. Motta (Eds.), *Androgens and antiandrogens* (p. 151). New York: Raven Press.

Liang, T., Tymoczko, J. L., Chan, K. M. B., Hung, S. C., & Liao, S. (1977). Androgen action: Receptors and rapid responses. In L. Martini, & M. Motta (Eds.), *Androgens and antiandrogens* (p. 77). New York: Raven Press.

Litkey, L. J., & Feniczy, P. (1967). An approach to the control of homosexual practices. *International Journal of Neuropsychiatry, 3,* 20–23.

Lorenz, K. (1966). On aggression. London: Methuen.

Matthews, R. (1979). Testosterone levels in aggressive offenders. In M. Sandler (Ed.), *Psychopharmacology of aggression* (pp. 123–131). New York: Raven Press.

Mattson, A., Schalling, D., Olweus, D., Low, H., & Stevenson, J. (1980). Plasma testosterone, aggressive behavior and personality dimensions in young male delinquents. *Journal of American Academy of Child Psychiatry, 19,* 476–490.

Mazur, A., & Lamb, R. A. (1980). Testosterone, status and mood in human males. *Hormones and Behavior, 14,* 236–246.

McKenna, J. J. (1983). Primate aggression and evolution: An overview of sociobiological and anthropological perspectives. *Bulletin of the American Academy of Psychiatry and the Law, 2,* 105–130.

Meyer-Bahlburg, H. F. L., Nat, R., Boon, D. A., Sharma, M., & Edwards, J. A. (1974). Aggressiveness and testosterone measures in man. *Psychosomatic Medicine, 36,* 269–274.

Money, J. (1970). Use of an androgen depleting hormone in the treatment of male sex offenders. *Journal of Sex Research, 6,* 165–172.

Money, J. (1972). The therapeutic use of androgen depleting hormone. *International Psychiatry Clinics, 8,* 165–174.

Money, J., Wiedeking, C., Walker, D., Migeon, C., Meyer, W., & Borgoankar, D. (1975). Forty-seven XYY and 46 XY males with antisocial and/or sex-offending behavior: Antiandrogen therapy plus counseling. *Psychoneuroendocrinology, 1,* 165–178.

Monti, P. M., Brown, W. A., & Corriveau, D. P. (1977). Testosterone and components of aggressive and sexual behavior in man. *American Journal of Psychiatry, 134,* 692–694.

Mothes, C., Lehnert, J., Samimi, F., & Ufer, J. (1971). *Schering Symposium uber Sexual Deviationen und Ihre Medikametöse Behandlung.* Oxford: Pergamon Press, Berlin Braunschweig.

Olweus, D., Mattison, A., Schalling, D., & Low, H. (1980). Testosterone, aggression, physical and personality dimensions in normal adolescent males. *Psychosomatic Medicine, 42,* 253–296.

Ortmann, J. (1980). The treatment of sexual offenders, castration and antihormone therapy. *International Journal of Law and Psychiatry, 3,* 443.

Ortmann, J. (1984a). *A comparison between castration and cyproterone acetate regarding treatment of sexual offenders.* Unpublished manuscript.

Ortmann, J. (1984b). *How antihormone treatment with cyproterone acetate influences on relapsing into sexual criminality among male sexual offenders.* Unpublished manuscript.

Ortmann, J. (1984c). *How castration influences on relapsing into sexual criminality among Danish males.* Unpublished manuscript.

Ott, F., & Hoffet, H. (1968). The influence of antiandrogens on libido, potency and testicular function. *Schweizerische Medizinische Wochenschrift, 98,* 1812.

Persky, H., Smith, K. D. & Basu, G. K. (1971). Relation of psychological measures of aggression and hostility to testosterone production in man. *Psychosomatic Medicine, 33,* 265–277.

Rada, R. T. (1981). Plasma androgens and the sex offender. *Bulletin of the American Academy of Psychiatry and the Law, 8,* 456–464.

Rada, R. T., Kellner, R., & Winslow, W. W. (1976a). Plasma testosterone and aggressive behavior. *Psychosomatics, 17,* 138–142.

Rada, R. T., Laws, D. R., & Kellner, R. (1976b). Plasma testosterone in the rapist. *Psychosomatic Medicine, 38,* 257–268.

Rada, R. T., Laws, D. R., Kellner, R., Stivastava, L., & Peake, G. (1983). Plasma androgens in violent and non-violent sex offenders. *Bulletin of the American Academy of Psychiatry and the Law, 11,* 149–158.

Rivarola, M. A., Camacho, A. M., & Migeon, C. J. (1968). Effect of treatment with medroxyprogesterone acetate. *Journal of Clinical Endocrinology, 29,* 506–513.

Roeder, F. D. (1966). Stereotaxic lesion of the tuber cinereum in sexual deviation. *Confinia Neurologica, 27,* 162–163.

Roeder, F. D., Orthner, H., & Müller, D. (1972). The stereotaxic treatment of paedophilic homosexuality and other sexual deviations. In E. Hitchcock, L. Laitinen, & K. Vaernet (Eds.), *Psychosurgery* (pp. 87–111). Thomas, Springfield, IL.

Rose, R. M. (1980). Endocrine response to stressful psychological events. *The Psychiatric Clinics of North America, 3,* 251–275.

Scaramella, T., & Brown, W. A. (1978). Serum testosterone and aggressiveness in hockey players. *Psychosomatic Medicine, 42,* 253–296.

Schering, A. G. (1983). *Androcur Antiandrogen.* Berlin: Bergkamen.

Schiavi, R. C., Theilgaard, A., Owen, D. R., & White, D. (1984). Sex chromosome anomalies, hormones and aggressivity. *Archives of General Psychiatry, 41,* 93–99.

Scott, P. D. (1964). Definition, classification, prognosis and treatment. In I. Rosen (Ed.), *Pathology and treatment of sexual deviation* (p. 87). London: Oxford University Press.

Southren, A., Gordon, G. G., Vitter, J., & Altman, K. (1977). Effect of progestagens on androgen metabolism. In L. Martini & M. Motta (Eds.), *Androgens and antiandrogens* (pp. 263–279). New York: Raven Press.

Sterkmans, P., & Geerts, F. (1966). Is benperidol (RF 504) the specific drug for the treatment of successive and disinhibited sexual behavior? *Acta Neurologica et Psychiatrica Belgica, 66,* 1030–1040.

Stürup, G. K. (1968). Treatment of sexual offenders in Herstedvester, Denmark: The rapists. *Acta Psychiatrica Scandinavica,* Suppl. 204, 44.

Stürup, G. K. (1972). Castration: The total treatment. In H. L. P. Resnik & M. E. Wolfgang (Eds.), *Sexual behaviors: Social, clinical and legal aspects* (pp. 1361–1382). Boston: Little Brown.

Symmers, W. St. C. (1968). Carcinoma of the breast in trans-sexual individual after surgical and hormonal interference with primary and secondary sex characteristics. *British Medical Journal, 2,* 83–85.

Taylor, D. C. (1969). Sexual behavior and temporal lobe epilepsy. *Archives of Neurology, 21,* 510–516.

Tolis, G., Ackman, D. Stellos, A., Mehta, A., Labrie, F., Fazekas, A. T. A., Comaru-Schally, A. M., & Schally, A. V. (1982) Tumor growth inhibition in patients with prostatic carcinoma treated with luteinizing hormone-releasing hormonic agonists. *Proceedings of the National Academy of Science, 79,* 1658–1662.

Whittaker, L. H. (1959). Oestrogens and psychosexual disorders. *Medical Journal of Australia, 2,* 547–549.

Wiedeking, C., Money, J. & Walker, P. (1979). Follow-up of 11 XYY males with impulsive and/or sex-offending behavior. *Psychological Medicine, 9,* 287–292.

Wilson, G., & Lawson, D. M. (1976). Expectancies, alcohol and sexual arousal in male social drinkers. *Journal of Abnormal Psychology, 85,* 225–234.

Wormith, J. S., Bradford, J. M. W., Pawlak, A., Zohar, A., Borzecki, M. (1988). The assessment of deviant sexual arousal as a function of intelligence, instructions and alcohol ingestion. *Canadian Journal of Psychiatry.*

Zybtovsky, J., & Zapletalek, M. (1979). Cyproteronacetate in the therapy of sexual deviations. *Activitas Nervosa Superior* (Praha), *21,* 162.

13

BEHAVIORAL TREATMENT
OF CHILD MOLESTERS

Gene G. Abel, M.D.
Department of Psychiatry,
Emory University School of Medicine

INTRODUCTION

Violence, particularly sexual violence, is a serious problem in our culture. The increasing incidence of serial, sadistic murders, brutal rape, and more graphic media coverage of child molestation have all contributed to society's increasing concern about sexual violence. Recent victim surveys in the United States and Canada (committee on Sexual Offenses Against Children and Youths, 1984) suggest that approximately 20% of all females and 10% of all males have been or will be sexually assaulted in some way before reaching the age of 21.

With regard to child molestation, recent surveys (Finkelhor, 1984) have raised serious questions concerning the validity of information gathered from victim surveys. Finkelhor observes that the following factors tend to influence the validity of victim self-reports:

1. Sexual assaults are so traumatic for the victim that (s)he attempts to deal with the emotional consequences of the assault by denial and forgetting. Therefore, victim surveys are only as valid as the victim's recall of such events.

2. Brief paper-and-pencil questionnaires administered anonymously in an attempt to gain a representative sample of the population lack the sensitivity and humaneness of a clinical interview, and, as a result, participants are reluctant to write down the details of their sexual assault.

3. Much information from victims is gathered without the strong assurance of confidentiality of the data. Many participants are reluctant to report their

own victimization, fearing that others will become aware of the stigmatizing event.

4. Especially critical in understanding child molestation is the reality that all of the victims are children and, as such, lack the cognitive abilities to appreciate the nature and characteristics of their victimization.

The alternative to gathering sexual-assault information from the victim is gathering it from the perpetrator. The value of this source of information is that the perpetrator himself is most knowledgeable about his intent, and the longevity and frequency of his behavior. A critical aspect of this data collection approach, however, is the need for assured confidentiality (Kaplan, 1985).

The information reported in this chapter is gathered from interviews conducted with 571 outpatient sex offenders whose data were collected under the assurance of a Certificate of Confidentiality from the Department of Health and Human Services of the U.S. Government. The data were collected over an eight-year period at two different sites in the United States (Memphis, TN and New York City). In contrast to many large surveys of child sexual-abuse victims which report less than 500 incidents, this survey reports on over 76,000 child molestations (Abel, Becker, Mittelman, Cunningham-Rathner, Rouleau, & Murphy, 1987).

WHO IS MOLESTED?

All types of child molestations reported by 453 child molesters are presented in Table 13.1 in terms of the total number of victims, total acts committed, and various characteristics of the victims. Victim characteristics included age (under

Table 13.1
All Types of Child Molestation Victims and Acts by Behavior,
Age, Gender, and Relationship

Victim	# of Offenders	Total Victims	% All Victims	Total Acts	% All Acts
All	453	67,112	100.0	106,916	100.0
<14	331	35,901	53.5	50,542	47.3
14–17	191	31,211	46.5	56,374	52.7
Female	308	42,511	63.3	58,218	54.5
Male	167	24,601	36.7	48,698	45.6
Incest	181	392	.6	19,962	18.7
Nonincest	310	66,720	99.4	86,954	81.3
Hands on	371	38,671	57.6	77,919	72.9
Hands off	97	28,441	42.4	28,997	27.1

Table 13.2
Nontouching Child Molestation Victims and Acts by Behavior,
Age, Gender, and Relationship

Victim	# of Offenders	Total Victims	% Total Victims	% All Victims	Total Acts	% Total Acts	% All Acts
All	97	28,441	100.0	42.4	28,997	100.0	27.1
<14	73	17,411	61.3	25.9	13,425	46.3	12.6
14–17	50	11,030	38.8	16.4	15,572	53.7	14.6
Female	86	28,166	99.0	42.0	28,618	98.7	26.8
Male	20	275	1.0	.4	379	1.3	.4
Incest	21	38	.1	.1	4,276	14.8	4.0
Nonincest	90	28,403	99.9	42.3	24,721	85.3	23.1

14 years of age or 14–17 years of age), gender, familial relationship (incest or nonincest), and whether the molestation involved tactile (physical assault) or nontactile behavior (voyeurism or exhibitionism).

Results showed that, in terms of victims, slightly over one half were under 14, 63% were female, and 58% of victimizations involved tactile behavior. The most surprising finding was that, according to offender self-reports, less than 1% of all victims were family members.

Table 13.2 reflects those cases of child molestation that involved nontactile behaviors. A total of 97 offenders reported that 61% of their victims were less than 14 years of age, 99% were female, and virtually all (99.9%) of these acts involved nonincestuous activities against females.

In terms of the total number of nontouching acts committed, 54% were committed against adolescents (14–17 years of age), 99% were targeted toward female victims, and 15% were incestuous acts. As was the case when considering all types of child molestation, the percentage of incestuous victims involved in nontouching child molestations remained small, but due to the highly repetitive nature of the crimes against family members, the percentage of total incestuous acts was somewhat high.

Although nontouching crimes are offensive to the victim, society is most concerned with child molestations that include actual touching, fondling, oral sex, or intercourse. This category of crime is viewed as innately more problematic for the victim, more likely to involve verbal or physical coercion, and more likely to lead to arrest. For these reasons, the final analysis of the data involved only child molestations involving touching of the child (Table 13.3) committed by 371 child molesters.

In terms of the total number of victims, slightly over half of the victims were adolescents and, once again, less than 1% of the victims had been victimized by a family member. The most startling finding was that 63% of all victims were male.

Table 13.3
Touching Child Molestation Victims and Acts by Behavior,
Age, Gender, and Relationship

Victim	# of Offenders	Total Victims	% Total Victims	% All Victims	Total Acts	% Total Acts	% All Acts
All	371	38,671	100.0	57.6	77,919	100.0	72.9
<14	304	18,490	47.8	27.6	37,117	47.6	34.7
14–17	164	20,181	52.2	30.1	40,802	52.4	38.2
Female	277	14,345	37.1	21.4	29,600	38.0	27.7
Male	162	24,326	62.9	36.3	48,319	62.0	45.2
Incest	174	354	.9	.5	15,686	20.1	14.7
Nonincest	275	38,317	99.1	57.1	62,233	79.9	58.2

In terms of the total number of touching acts committed by these paraphiliacs, again slightly over 50% were committed against adolescent victims, but 20% of the total acts were committed against family members. The low percentage of total victims who had been molested by family members (less than 1%) compared with a much higher percentage of total acts involving touching of the family member (20%)—once again, a result of the repetitious nature of incestuous, hands-on touching. Nonetheless, of the total child molestation acts involving touching, 80% were against nonfamily members.

Of the child molestation acts involving touching, 62% of the cases were committed against males, while only 38% were committed against females. These results are especially impressive given the fact that, of the molesters evaluated, only 162 had molested males and 277 had molested females. (Each category contained some individuals who had molested both males and females.)

When the number of victims per offender was examined, paraphiliacs who victimized females had, on the average, 51.8 victims each, while paraphiliacs who victimized male children had 150.2 victims each. Of paraphiliacs who carried out touching acts against females, the average offender had committed 106.9 acts, but of those molesters who carried out touching acts against males, the average paraphiliac had committed 298.3 acts. The ratio of acts against male versus female victims is 2.9 : 1. If offenders are brought to the attention of others because of the number of acts they commit, one would expect that child molestations perpetrated against males would be overrepresented because the number of male victims (or acts) per offender is three times the number of female victims (or acts). Since molesters come to the attention of others in part because of the frequency of their child molestation behavior, it would be expected that the relative frequency of molesters of boys would be overrepresented.

These results present different pictures of a child molester depending on one's definition of "child molestation." If one ignores any discrimination among the types of child molestation and examines all varieties of child molestation, these results are not surprising, since the greatest number of victims are female, usually involving nonassaultive behavior perpetrated against girls outside the home. However, if one is most concerned about assaultive child molestation, child molestation takes on an entirely different appearance. In 62% of cases, acts of assaultive child molestation were perpetrated against males, and, in 80% of cases, the act involved nonincestous activities.

If child molestation is to be effectively prevented, treatment programs must focus more directly on the reported specific deviant activities of molesters; that is, the touching of boys outside the family.

WHEN DO CHILD MOLESTERS BECOME INTERESTED IN CHILD MOLESTATION?

Because the consequences of a chronic condition are usually very difficult to correct, public health providers should treat the patient's illness as early as possible. Therapists should apply this principle of early intervention to the treat-

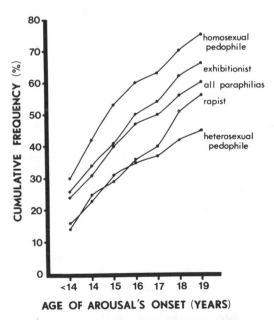

FIGURE 13.1 Onset of paraphiliac arousal. Reprinted with permission from Abel, G. G., Mittelman, M. S., & Becker, J. V. (1985). Sexual offenders: Results of assessment and recommendations for treatment. In M. H. Ben-Aron, S. J. Hucker, & C. D. Webster (Eds.), *Clinical Criminology: The Assessment and Treatment of Criminal Behavior* (pp. 191–205). Toronto: University of Toronto.

ment of child molesters in order to prevent the deterioration that follows repetitive molestation and incarceration.

Child molesters report early onset of paraphilic interests. When each of the 571 outpatients in our study was questioned (Abel, Mittelman, & Becker, 1985), 42% reported deviant sexual arousal by age 15, and 57% by age 19, as shown graphically in Figure 13.1.

Child molesters attracted to boys (homosexual pedophiles) reported the earliest onset of any paraphilic interest, as 53% reported arousal by age 15, and 74% by age 19. In contrast, molesters attracted to girls (heterosexual pedophiles) had a later onset, with 31% reporting attraction to inappropriately young girls by age 15, and 44% by age 19. Applying the principle of early intervention, public health officials could deal with the rising incidence of child molestation by assessing and treating adolescents when they first begin to show paraphilic arousal patterns. Society must confront three realities about child molestation if its increasing frequency is to be halted: (1) sexual behavior begins in adolescence; (2) adolescent sexual exploration is sometimes committed by adolescents who have sexual deviations; and (3) reinforcement follows if deviant behaviors are ignored. Making effective treatment available to the pedophile as early as possible and before deviant patterns become habitual may be the best strategy for containing adult pedophilic behavior.

CHILD MOLESTATION AND OTHER DEVIANT SEXUAL INTERESTS

Psychiatry has traditionally classified paraphiliacs into separate, individualized categories according to one and only one diagnosis, to the exclusion of any other form of deviant sexual behavior. Exhibitionists were considered only to be exhibitionists, for example, while child molesters were thought to be involved only in sexual contact with children. A different picture emerges, however, from the responses given by our 571 subjects regarding their participation in the 21 different categories of paraphilias as listed in Table 13.4. The table indicates the percentage of men in each diagnostic category who reported involvement in only one paraphilia. (Paraphilic categories containing fewer than 12 men were excluded from Table 13.4 because such small numbers are not reliably representative. Pedophilia was further subdivided into four categories because of differences between pedophiles choosing male or female child targets, and between those choosing incestuous or nonincestuous targets). Of those individuals reporting only one paraphilia, the highest percentage (52%) were involved in transsexualism. In each of the other 17 categories of paraphilias, fewer than 30% of the men limited their sexual behavior to only one deviant activity. In 10 categories, fewer than 10% of men reported participating in only one type of paraphilic behavior. Especially striking is the finding that no instance of festishism, bes-

Table 13.4
Percentage of Subjects with Only One Diagnosis and Average Number
of Paraphilias Per Subject

Diagnosis	Number of Subjects*	% with only One Diagnosis	Average # of Paraphilias	Total Paraphilias
Pedophilia (nonincest), female target	224	15	3.6	806
Pedophilia (nonincest), male target	153	19	3.4	520
Pedophilia (incest), female target	159	28	3.1	493
Pedophilia (incest), male target	44	4.5	4.5	198
Rape	126	27	3.3	416
Exhibitionism	142	7	4.2	596
Voyeurism	62	1.5	4.8	298
Frottage	62	21	3.8	236
Transsexualism	29	52	1.7	49
Transvestitism	31	6.5	3.8	118
Fetishism	19	0	4.4	84
Sadism	28	0	4.6	129
Masochism	17	0	4.4	75
Homosexuality	24	25	2.3	55
Obscene phone calling	19	5.5	5.1	97
Public masturbation	17	6	5.1	87
Bestiality	14	0	4.8	67
Total	1,170			4,324

*A subject is included in each diagnostic category in which he reported a completed act of paraphilic behavior. Therefore, overlapping of subjects across categories occurs.

tiality, sadism, or masochism was reported by an individual who had only one paraphilic diagnosis. It is apparent that paraphiliacs with only one paraphilia are rare.

Table 13.4 also presents the average number of different paraphilias reported by the individuals in our study. They reported an average of 3-5 paraphilias per diagnostic category, with the exception of men diagnosed as transsexuals or ego-dystonic homosexuals, who reported fewer paraphilias. Of special concern is the finding that pedophiles traditionally thought to have only one paraphilia (i.e.,

Table 13.5
Percentage of Cross Diagnosis by Paraphilia

		Female nonincest pedophilia	Male nonincest pedophilia	Female incest pedophilia	Male incest pedophilia	Rape	Exhibitionism	Voyeurism	Frottage	Obscene mail	Transsexualism	Transvestism	Fetishism	Sadism	Masochism	Homosexuality	Obscene phone calling	Public masturbation	Bestiality	Urolagnia	Coprophilia	Arousal to Odors
Female nonincest pedophila	n	224	78	78	27	55	65	32	24	1	0	7	10	11	6	1	8	5	10	2	4	0
	%	100	35	35	12	25	29	14	11	1	0	3	5	5	3	1	4	2	5	1	2	0
Male nonincest pedophilia	n	78	153	19	30	17	31	16	12	0	0	4	6	7	6	3	3	2	5	1	2	0
	%	51	100	12	20	11	20	10	8	0	0	3	4	5	4	2	2	1	4	1	1	0
Female incest pedophilia	n	78	19	159	19	30	31	11	10	1	1	7	5	9	5	2	5	4	6	2	3	0
	%	49	12	100	12	19	20	7	6	1	1	4	3	6	3	1	3	3	4	1	2	0
Male incest ped- ophilia	n	27	30	19	44	7	7	6	4	0	0	2	3	1	1	2	0	1	3	2	1	1
	%	61	68	43	100	16	16	14	9	0	0	5	7	2	2	5	0	2	7	5	2	1
Rape	n	55	17	30	7	126	35	23	14	1	0	6	5	13	3	0	7	4	3	0	0	1
	%	44	14	24	6	100	28	18	11	1	0	5	4	10	2	0	6	3	2	0	0	1
Exhibitionism	n	65	31	31	7	35	142	39	23	1	1	11	4	6	6	3	12	12	5	2	3	1
	%	46	22	22	5	25	100	28	16	1	1	8	3	4	4	2	9	9	4	1	2	1
Voyeurism	n	32	16	11	6	23	39	62	14	0	0	3	4	7	1	0	9	5	6	1	2	2
	%	52	26	18	10	37	63	100	23	0	0	5	7	11	2	0	15	8	10	2	3	3
Frottage	n	24	12	10	4	14	23	14	62	0	0	1	3	7	0	0	4	2	1	2	2	1
	%	39	19	16	7	23	37	23	100	0	0	2	5	11	0	0	7	3	2	5	5	2
Obscene mail	n	1	0	1	0	1	1	0	0	3	0	0	0	0	0	1	0	0	0	0	0	0
	%	33	0	33	0	33	33	0	0	100	0	0	0	0	0	33	0	0	0	0	0	0

Diagnosis																													
Transsexualism	n	0	0	0	0	0	0	1	0	0	0	0	0	0	0	0	29	9	0	0	0	7	0	0	0	0	0	0
	%	0	0	0	0	0	0	4	0	0	0	0	0	0	0	0	100	31	0	0	0	24	0	0	0	1	0	0
Transvestitism	n	7	4	2	6	2	3	11	3	1	0	6	4	3	2	4	9	31	2	3	10	6	4	1	4	2	2	1
	%	23	7	7	19	7	10	36	10	3	0	19	13	10	7	13	29	31	7	10	13	19	13	3	7	1	3	1
Fetishism	n	10	5	3	5	4	4	21	5	16	0	2	5	2	3	5	0	2	7	11	5	4	0	0	5	2	5	0
	%	53	26	16	26	21	21	63	12	7	0	11	11	11	2	11	0	11	0	0	5	0	0	0	2	0	5	0
Sadism	n	11	9	1	13	6	6	6	29	7	0	3	28	5	4	18	0	3	0	0	2	14	7	7	2	7	2	0
	%	39	32	4	46	21	21	21	71	25	0	11	100	18	100	17	0	11	2	2	7	0	7	7	2	2	2	0
Masochism	n	6	6	1	3	6	6	6	6	0	0	4	5	2	2	5	0	4	5	0	0	0	0	0	2	12	2	0
	%	35	35	3	18	35	35	35	13	0	1	24	29	8	12	17	7	24	29	8	0	0	0	6	12	12	0	0
Homosexuality	n	1	3	2	0	3	3	3	1	0	4	6	0	0	8	2	29	25	0	0	0	0	0	1	0	0	1	0
	%	4	13	8	7	13	13	13	4	0	0	25	0	0	24	8	29	25	0	0	0	0	0	4	4	4	5	0
Obscene phone calling	n	8	5	0	7	5	5	9	4	4	0	3	4	0	0	0	0	3	21	11	11	19	11	4	2	0	1	0
	%	42	26	0	37	26	26	63	21	21	4	16	21	0	0	0	0	16	100	11	17	100	11	2	0	0	0	0
Public masturbation	n	5	2	1	4	2	2	12	5	2	0	2	2	1	0	0	0	1	2	12	100	2	6	6	1	0	1	0
	%	29	12	6	24	12	12	71	29	12	0	12	12	6	0	0	0	6	12	100	100	14	6	6	1	0	6	0
Bestiality	n	10	6	3	3	6	6	5	6	1	0	4	14	7	1	7	0	4	14	1	1	14	6	1	7	7	1	0
	%	71	43	21	21	43	43	36	43	7	0	29	100	7	7	7	0	29	100	7	7	100	6	1	7	7	7	0
Urolagnia	n	2	2	2	0	2	2	2	1	0	0	2	2	2	1	2	0	2	0	0	0	0	25	1	4	50	2	0
	%	50	50	50	0	50	50	50	25	0	0	50	50	50	25	25	0	50	0	25	25	25	100	2	50	50	0	0
Coprophilia	n	4	3	1	1	3	3	3	2	1	0	1	2	2	0	2	0	1	0	1	1	1	1	25	2	4	50	0
	%	100	75	25	0	75	75	75	25	25	0	25	50	50	0	50	0	25	0	25	25	25	25	100	50	100	0	0
Arousal to Odors	n	0	0	0	1	0	0	1	0	0	0	0	0	0	0	0	0	0	0	0	0	0	0	0	0	0	0	2
	%	0	0	0	50	0	0	50	0	0	0	0	0	0	0	0	0	0	0	0	0	0	0	0	0	0	0	100

*Reprinted with permission from: Abel, G. G., Becker, J. V., Cunningham-Rathner, J., Mittelman, M. S., & Rouleau, J.-L. (in press). Multiple paraphilic diagnoses among sex offenders. *Bulletin of the American Academy of Psychiatry and the Law.*

231

female-targeted incest molesters and male-incest molesters) commonly reported multiple paraphilias (Abel, Becker, Cunningham-Rathner, Mittelman, & Rouleau, in press).

Because paraphiliacs engage in additional types of deviant sexual behavior beyond their primary diagnosis, it is important to determine which paraphilias are likely to occur in combination. Table 13.5 presents a cross-diagnosis table that reports the percentage of men reporting additional paraphilias (reading across Columns 2 through 22) for each category of paraphilia listed (reading down Column 1). By examining Row 1, for example, one sees that for men involved in female nonincestuous pedophilia (Column 1), a total of 224 men (Column 2) engaged in this paraphilia. The number 100 directly below the number 224 represents 100% of the total subsample of men involved with girls outside the home. Continuing across Row 1, one sees in Column 3 that 78 of these men (35%) were also involved with boys outside the home; in Column 4, 78 men (35%) were involved in incest with female children; in Column 5, 27 men (12%) who reported nonincestuous female pedophilia were involved in incest with male children; in Column 6, 55 of these men (25%) were involved in rape; and so forth across Row 1. By examining each row in Table 13.5, each total in Columns 2 through 22 represents the likelihood of additional paraphilic behavior accompanying the paraphilia reported in Column 1. From a clinical standpoint, these data clearly show that paraphiliacs frequently engage in other cross-diagnostic paraphilic behavior. Each diagnostic category contained a high percentage of men who had also engaged in other types of paraphilic behavior at one time or another.

The results reported in Table 13.5 for men involved with child molestation are of special concern. Of the 153 men who molested boys outside the home (reading down Column 1 to Row 2 for the category male nonincest pedophilia), 51% had histories of molesting girls outside the home, 12% molested girls within the home, and 20% molested boys within the home. Of the 159 female-incest pedophiles (Row 3), 49% molested girls outside the home, 12% molested boys outside the home, and 12% molested boys within the home. Of the 44 men who had engaged in male-incest pedophilia (Row 4), 61% had engaged in female-nonincest pedophilia, 68% in male-nonincest pedophilia, and 43% in female-incest pedophilia. These data clearly show that many pedophiles do not differentiate between children targets within or outside the home. Contrary to popular belief, pedophiles who molest their own children will frequently molest children outside the family as well.

Also of importance to our understanding of pedophilia is the finding that rapists also engage in cross-diagnostic paraphilic behaviors. Of the 126 men who reported raping a female adult (Row 5), 44% reported having molested young girls outside the home, 14% molested young boys outside the home, 24% molested girls within the family, 28% reported engaging in exhibitionism, 18% reported voyeurism, and the remainder reported involvement in the other categories of paraphilia, although to a lesser degree.

Exhibitionists also have a negative impact on children, since they also report high frequencies of paraphilic involvement in addition to exhibitionism. Of the 142 exhibitionists in our study (Row 6 in Table 13.5), 46% had engaged in female nonincest pedophilia, 22% in male nonincest pedophilia, 22% in female-incest pedophilia, 25% in rape, 28% in voyeurism, and 16% in frottage. Fewer exhibitionists reported engaging in the other paraphilic diagnostic categories. The finding that exhibitionists were frequently involved in many other types of paraphilic activities, some overtly aggressive, impressively contradicts the popularly held view of exhibitionists as harmless eccentrics. The data must be interpreted cautiously, however, since this finding may be limited to this subsample of paraphiliacs, and since not all exhibitionists in this study also engaged in other paraphilias.

Table 13.5 reveals that men diagnosed in the other categories of paraphilias also reported involvement in additional sexually deviant behaviors. Because so few men in our study reported engaging in infrequently seen paraphilias (e.g., senders of obscene mail, arousal to odors), it is difficult to draw conclusions about their occurrence concomitant with other paraphilias of concern, such as child molestation.

In summary, the findings in Tables 13.4 and 13.5 suggest that health practitioners have been naive in viewing paraphiliacs as engaging in deviant sexual behaviors limited to one diagnostic category. If a specific conflict leads to the development of a specific deviant sexual behavior, one would anticipate that many, if not most, paraphiliacs would be diagnosed in one paraphilic category. These data, however, suggest otherwise, for with the exception of transsexuals, paraphiliacs frequently engage in cross-diagnostic behavior. Paraphiliacs do not appear to have a specific conflict that results in a specific paraphilic arousal pattern, but instead have a general deficit that results in a general lack of control across a wide range of sexually deviant behaviors. This finding is more than theoretically interesting, for it should alert therapists to conduct cross-diagnostic evaluations of their paraphilic patients. The assessment strategy must be capable of identifying the paraphiliac's multiple categories of deviant interest beyond any single paraphilia he may initially report. This is especially important when treating child molesters, for as seen in Table 13.5, pedophiles may have additional child targets, male or female, within or outside the home, than previously thought.

TRAINING CHILD MOLESTERS TO CONTROL THEIR SEXUAL INVOLVMENT WITH CHILDREN

Behavioral treatment of sex offenders during the 1950s and 1960s focused almost exclusively on treatment to eliminate deviant arousal that was presumed antecedent to deviant sexual behavior. Throughout the 1970s and 1980s, additional attention has been directed toward other behavioral abnormalities of paraphiliacs, including: (1) cognitive distortions (attitudes and beliefs) which support and justify deviant sexual behavior; (2) social-skills deficits which inhibit appropriate social interaction with adults; (3) assertive-skills deficits, especially an inability to decline social approaches from children; (4) deficits in sexual arousal toward adult partners; (5) deficits of sexual knowledge; (6) excessive alcohol and drug use leading to deviant sexual behavior; (7) excessive attachment to interests similar to those of children; and (8) sexual dysfunctions which inhibit sexual interaction with adult partners. Although this greater awareness of the various personality components of the pedophile has contributed to a better understanding of him as a person, control of deviant sexual behavior with children continues to be the cornerstone of treatment. Many treatment programs, however, ignore the most critical issue of deviant arousal.

The heterosexual male who is attracted to adult females may see a number of women whom he finds sexually attractive. Establishment of a closer relationship with one or more of them, leading to eventual sexual involvement, involves many preliminary behaviors. Similarly, the child molester may see a number of children whom he finds sexually attractive and may initiate the chain of events that leads to his molestation of one or more of them. The chain of events for a typical child molester may begin with periods of unstructured time. His long-standing interest in children may lead to his participation in activities that involve children, such as Boy Scouts, Big Brothers, summer sports, camping or church-sponsored youth activities. Since approaches to children by strangers are likely to provoke suspicion and caution on the part of the child, his parents, or others, the potential offender spends hours, weeks, or months cultivating familiarity and trust in various children whom he finds attractive, helping them in various ways so that they are less frightened and intimidated by his presence. Next, the typical offender will seek to arrange opportunities to be alone with the child (e.g., babysitting) so as to begin the gradual process of seduction, intimacy, close touching, and eventually fondling or sexual intercourse. With increasing time alone with the child, a more personal seduction begins in which the offender learns the interests, fears, and reinforcers of the child so as to reduce the child's anxiety about being alone with this new adult. It is only after all of the previous steps are accomplished that the typical molester then begins to actually molest the child, initially with fondling and eventually with actual oral, vaginal, or anal intercourse.

Treatment of the offender first involves identification and confrontation of his particular chain of events leading to molestation so that he can recount the sequence and begin to identify the early antecedents of his deviant behavior. Disruption of these events occurs by covert sensitization or ammonia aversion—techniques that the offender can then use to disrupt the sequence of events early in the chain leading toward actual child molestation. The offender is taught how to associate various severely negative social consequences with these early antecedents. Ammonia aversion similarly allows the patient to learn the pairing or association of the early antecedents to child molestation with the chemically offensive odor of ammonia in a manner (similar to covert sensitization) in which the early antecedents are repeatedly paired or associated with the aversive ammonia odor.

Child molesters and other varieties of paraphiliacs are adept at denying or concealing their true arousal in order to avoid treatment by noncompliance. Compliance among child molesters becomes even more critical when one considers that failure to respond to treatment and recidivism means that more children will be victimized. In other words, treatment noncompliance among child molesters is not only harmful to the offender (leading to recidivism and re-arrest), but it is of grave consequence to the child (or children) who will be molested within the course of that recidivism. To ensure that compliance to the treatment regimen has occurred, treatment sessions are initially observed directly by the therapist and subsequently audiotaped by the offender. The tape recorded treatments (involving convert sensitization and ammonia aversion) are brought to the therapist and reviewed to ensure that the treatment has been accomplished correctly. This audiotaped treatment check has the additional advantage of permitting the patient to do his treatment any place, any time, whether or not the therapist is present. Furthermore, playback of the offender's audiotape treatments and feedback regarding this taped treatment destroys the secretive nature of the behavior and attraction to children, thus reducing the titillating, erotic character of the relationship between the offender and the child.

The patient's attraction to children that motivates the early antecedent behaviors can also be directly reduced through ammonia aversion and through masturbatory satiation. The latter technique teaches the patient how to extinguish his arousal to children by having him use his most erotic child-molestation fantasies post-orgasm, when he cannot become sexually aroused by such fantasies. This extinction or satiation technique, like ammonia aversion and covert sensitization, is also tape recorded by the patient within the privacy of his home and reviewed in the treatment setting for feedback and recommendations from the therapist and to ensure compliance.

DECREASING COGNITIVE DISTORTIONS ABOUT CHILD MOLESTATION

During adolescence or early adulthood, most young males become aware of their society's mores and expectations concerning sexual behavior. The young pedophile, however, will begin to rationalize any discrepancy between his sexual attraction to children and social sexual mores by developing a system of very individualized beliefs and cognitions to support his arousal. Cognitions are the statements one makes about the appropriateness of one's behavior (i.e., My sexual contact with children is normal or abnormal). In order to maintain his sexual interest in children, the pedophile must develop cognitions to support his position. A non-paraphilic example of how cognitive distortions develop might be the case of a boy, 10 years of age, who begins to steal. Most parents teach their children not to steal, and that any such behavior is inappropriate. The 10-year-old, however, may observe his friends steal small pocket items from stores. If they are not caught and punished, the boy may conclude that no negative consequences result from such behavior. With his peers (or media criminals) providing models, he begins to steal. Although his initial cognitions, based upon his family's attitudes, were that stealing was inappropriate, he begins to modify his cognitions as he watches his friends steal without negative repercussions. He concludes that stealing is fairly common since his friends do it, and not as dangerous as he was led earlier to believe. If time passes without negative consequences following his thefts, the boy's faulty cognitions will become strengthened by the cumulative rewards he receives from stealing successfully. As he discovers that he can obtain with minimum exertion whatever he wants through stealing, and without any significant negative consequences, he will come to believe that stealing is a legitimate manner to make one's living.

Whether an adolescent or adult, individuals aroused to children can likewise develop a set of cognitive beliefs that support and maintain sexual involvement with children. The following section recounts cognitions often held by child molesters, along with an explanation of why these cognitions are distortions.

EXAMPLE I.   "A child who does not physically resist my sexual advances really wants to have sex with me." This cognition assumes that a child knows how to effectively express and assert himself or herself with an adult about activities (s)he does not want. It also assumes that harm results from molestation only when the adult uses physical force. Research has established that the victim suffers as many symptoms from the offender's use of non-physical coercion as from physical force (Becker, Skinner, & Abel, 1983). Furthermore, a child is not likely to object when an adult attempts a sexual activity (especially if the adult is a family member) because parents and adults teach children to obey an adult's requests. Finally, it is a misconception that any child would physically resist sexual abuse, for resistance is only one way to respond to sexual assault. Some child victims (and adult victims of rape) respond out of fear by compliance or silence, which the offender may erroneously interpret as enjoyment of the sexual behavior.

EXAMPLE II.   "Having sex with a child is a good way for an adult to teach the child about sex." Adults attracted to children sometimes justify their molestation by claiming that it brings positive benefits to the child. Sexual activity with the child is justified as educational and will teach the child to be a better sexual partner when he or she reaches adulthood. The pedophile does not confront the question that, if such sex education is advantageous, why does he not share with other adults this insight of the positive educational value of sex between adults and children? If a child is unable to give informed consent to participate as a willing partner to sexual activities with an adult, what is the child learning during such encounters? Pedophiles are often astounded when they hear what child victims actually feel about having sexual activities with adults. Unfortunately, the adult who molests children usually does not stay to obtain feedback on how the victims were negatively affected by his sexual molestations. Because he lacks such feedback, the adult's misperceptions go uncorrected about his impact on the children.

Many people develop distorted beliefs about a variety of situations in the world, and about what behaviors are appropriate or inappropriate. Because we interact with others, we have the opportunity to discuss our attitudes and beliefs, including our cognitive distortions. In this way, erroneous thinking is pointed out to us by others, and we are able to correct idiosyncratic ideas that might otherwise remain unchallenged. The pedophile's cognitive distortions frequently perplex the therapist who treats the offender shortly after his initial arrest or after his deviant behavior first comes to the attention of others. The therapist may wonder how the child molester could maintain such distorted beliefs.

Child molesters keep secret their sexual behavior and its attendant attitudes and beliefs. Molestation is carried out in private, and offenders threaten or coerce the child to ensure the child's silence. As a consequence of no one knowing of the offender's activities, no one can confront his attitudes and beliefs supporting his deviant behavior. As time passes, his repeated successes at molestation produce an increasingly stronger cognitive armor to support additional molestations of children.

The therapist who confronts the faulty cognitions of pedophiles must educate the offender about children's lack of consent to engage in sexual activities with adults, about the impact of such intrusive sex upon children's later lives, and about society's disapproval of the inappropriateness of adults behaving sexually with children.

THE EFFECTIVENESS OF BEHAVIORAL TREATMENTS FOR CHILD MOLESTATION

To determine the effectiveness of behavioral treatments is usually a straightforward task. If one wished to assess the effectiveness of a weight-loss program, for example, self-reports, paper-and-pencil testing, daily weighing, and caloric intake might all be considered appropriate measures of the patient's progress during treatment. Although the patient might feel decreased self-satisfaction if the treatment were not effective, treatment failure is unlikely to pose imminent danger to the patient or to others.

It is an entirely different matter to evaluate the effectiveness of a behavioral treatment program for pedophiles, because recidivism in this case is synonymous with child molestation being committed. Complicating the prediction of recidivism among pedophiles is their extreme reluctance to divulge whether they commit any acts of child molestation post-treatment. Kaplan has observed that the degree of validity of a pedophile's self-reports is directly proportional to the level of confidentiality guaranteed to his disclosure (Kaplan, 1985). In other words, child molesters conceal and falsify their self-reports whenever confidentiality is minimal or nonexistent. The consequences of disclosing recidivism without confidentiality are high. By reporting any recurrence of child molestation activities during or after treatment, the offender would place himself at risk of re-arrest, reincarceration, or loss of parole. The pedophile who reports any recidivism, therefore, places his freedom in severe jeopardy.

Because reducing the reluctance of child molesters to provide valid self-reports of their recidivism would allow a more valid appraisal of the effectiveness of behavioral treatments for pedophiles, we treated 200 child molesters who voluntarily agreed to be treated in an outpatient setting (Abel, Mittelman, Becker, Rathner, & Rouleau, in press). We used a multiple crossover treatment design in which one third of the pedophiles received specific treatment to decrease sexual attraction to children and to increase sexual attraction to adults; one third received social-skills training or assertive-skills training; and the final third received sex-education/sex-dysfunction training and cognitive therapy to eliminate cognitive distortions. Obviously, ethics prohibited using a no-treatment control group. As each group completed its treatment segment, it continued therapy by entering one of the two other treatment segments, so that by the end of the study, all patients had participated in all three segments. Evaluations were conducted before treatment began, after each of the three segments of treatment, and at 6- and 12-month intervals following completion of the entire treatment package. Only patients who recidivated post-treatment received maintenance therapy during the follow-up phase.

As part of the study's original intent to evaluate treatment effectiveness of the three components, we wanted to compare the validity of reports of recidivism based upon the patient's rearrest records, information received from individuals in his environment, and his self-reports. Results showed that re-arrest records were of no value because recidivism post-treatment never led to arrest, in spite of recurrences of molestation behavior. Individuals in the patient's environment were equally non-productive in providing valid information because such individuals were usually only vaguely familiar with the patient's history of pedophilia. The patient's self-reports were the most helpful measures of recidivism. The extensive contact between an offender and his therapist before and during treatment apparently generated a high level of trust. Whenever patients reported molestation activities post-treatment, increased efforts were made to ensure patients' compliance to therapy and to protect, when possible, any children at risk.

In a few instances, the patient's participation in the experimental treatment protocol was discontinued, and he was treated according to the therapist's best clinical judgment.

Recidivism by pedophiles in our study was of two types: recidivism prior to completing treatment and recidivism after completing treatment. Obviously those pedophiles who withdrew from the study before completing treatment did not fully benefit by learning all of the elements that comprise successful therapy. A patient's withdrawal from treatment, however, could not be interpreted as indicative of recommission of child molestation. Those pedophiles who withdrew from the study included those with antisocial personalities, those who felt considerable coercion from others to participate in this voluntary program, and those with multiple categories of child molestation targets (Abel, Mittelman, Becker, Rathner, & Rouleau, in press).

SELF-REPORT STRATEGIES

We found no significant differences in demographic characteristics between patients who completed treatment and those who withdrew. The number of deviant acts committed prior to treatment, the frequency of deviant behavior, and the amount of self-control over deviant behavior did not predict patient withdrawal from the program.

To predict whether a patient was likely to remain in treatment or withdraw, a discriminant-function analysis was performed using a linear combination of those variables found to significantly discriminate the two groups. The variables that successfully discriminated between the groups and predicted a greater likelihood of withdrawing from treatment were, in order of statistical importance:

1. committing both hand-on and hand-off molestations (a dichotomous variable)
2. committing molestations against male and female, child and adolescent targets (a dichotomous variable)
3. committing molestations against both incest and nonincest victims (a dichotomous variable)
4. being under greater pressure to receive treatment
5. having an antisocial-personality diagnosis (a dichotomous variable)

Of these five variables that predicted withdrawal from treatment, the first three concern the pedophiles' inability to discriminate among selected targets (male and female, incest and nonincest, children and adolescents) and among molestation behaviors (hands-on and hands-off). Apparently, pedophiles having multiple types of targets were more likely to withdraw from treatment pre-

Table 13.6
Differentiating Subjects Completing Treatment
from Those Dropping Out During Treatment

Characteristics Not Significantly Different	Characteristics Significantly Different
Referral source	Amount of pressure to participate
Age	Antisocial-personality diagnosis
Race	Multiple-target types
Hollingshead class	
Education	
Employment status	
Religious preference	
Motivation for seeking treatment	
Treatment goals	
Frequency of deviant behavior per week before treatment	
Control over deviant behavior before treatment	
Lifetime completed acts	
Lifetime victims	

Reprinted with permission from Abel, G. G., Mittelman, M. S., Becker, J. V., Rathner, J., & Rouleau, J.-L. (in press). Predicting child molesters' response to treatment. *Annals of the New York Academy of Sciences.*

maturely. The inability of a pedophile to limit his molestation to a specific target type is, therefore, a useful variable for predicting withdrawal from treatment.

A similar analysis was performed to discriminate those pedophiles who recidivated post-treatment from those who did not commit additional molestations. Results showed that pedophiles with the highest frequency of child molestation prior to treatment, those with a life-long high incidence of molestation, or those with the highest number of victims were *not* necessarily more likely to recidivate post-treatment.

A discriminant-function analysis was performed to determine whether molestation recidivism could be predicted using information from the intake evaluation before patients entered treatment. The variables that successfully discriminated between the groups and predicted a greater likelihood of recidivism post-treatment were, in order of statistical importance:

1. committing molestations against male and female, child and adolescent targets (a dichotomous variable)
2. having the treatment goal of increasing communications skills with adults (probably because paraphiliacs with such skills already relate well to adults)

3. committing both hands-on and hands-off molestation (a dichotomous variable)
4. being divorced (a dichotomous variable)
5. committing molestations against both incest and nonincest targets (a dichotomous variable)

It is noteworthy that the first variable on the above list (having had both male and female, child and adolescent targets) was almost as effective alone in predicting recidivism as were all five variables combined. That one variable successfully identified 9 of the 12 patients who recidivated and 73 of the 86 patients who did not recidivate, correctly classifying 83.7% of the total sample.

A limitation of this analysis in identifying recidivists is that the discrimination among groups was based on pretreatment variables that will not be changed regardless of treatment. For example, the target's age, gender, and familial relationship to the offender cannot be modified as a result of treatment. A more critical analysis would involve pre-/post-treatment variables that may change as a consequence of receiving treatment.

In some respects, treatment was highly successful. Compared to the frequency of deviant acts committed by offenders prior to treatment, one sees a 95%

Table 13.7
Differentiating Between Subjects Recommitting Crimes
and Not Recommitting Crimes

Characteristics Not Significantly Different	Characteristics Significantly Different
Referral source	Multiple-target types
Age	Marital status
Race	Treatment goals
Hollingshead class	
Education	
Employment status	
Religious preference	
Motivation for seeking treatment	
Frequency of deivant behavior per week before treatment	
Control over deviant behavior before treatment	
Lifetime completed acts	
Lifetime victims	

Reprinted with permission from Abel, G. G., Mittelman, M. S., Becker, J. V., Rathner, J., & Rouleau, J.-L. (in press). Predicting child molesters' response to treatment. *Annals of the New York Academy of Sciences.*

reduction in their frequency of child molestations committed post-treatment. Although this reduction in molestations is dramatic, many critics would argue that anything less than the total elimination of all molestation behavior by an offender constitutes treatment failure. Those who advocate incarceration of the child molester stress the reality that during his incarceration, additional molestations would be eliminated, since the offender would be removed from his social milieu and from further opportunities to molest. Advocates of incarceration ignore, however, the costs of incarceration and, more importantly, the cost to society's children upon the eventual release from prison of an essentially untreated offender. In contrast, an offender can complete behavioral treatment as an outpatient for one tenth of the cost of incarceration and, at the same time, benefit from immediate and long-term reduction or cessation of his deviant behavior.

REFERENCES

Abel, G. G., Becker, J. V., Cunningham-Rathner, J., Mittelman, M. S., & Rouleau, J. -L. (in press). Multiple paraphilic diagnoses among sex offenders. *Bulletin of the American Academy of Psychiatry and the Law.*

Abel, G. G., Becker, J. V., Mittelman, M. S., Cunningham-Rathner, J., Rouleau, J. -L., & Murphy, W. D. (1987). Self-reported sex crimes of nonincarcerated paraphiliacs. *Journal of Interpersonal Violence, 2(6),* 3–25.

Abel, G. G., Mittelman, M. S., & Becker, J. V. (1985). Sexual offenders: Results of assessment and recommendations for treatment. In M. H. Ben-Aron, S. J. Hucker, & C. D. Webster (Eds.), *Clinical criminology: The assessment and treatment of criminal behavior* (pp. 191–205). Toronto: University of Toronto.

Abel, G. G., Mittelman, M. S., Becker, J. V., Rathner, J., & Rouleau, J. -L. (in press). Predicting child molesters' response to treatment. *Annals of the New York Academy of Sciences.*

Becker, J. V., Skinner, L. J., & Abel, G. G. (1983). Sequelae of sexual assault: The survivor's perspective. In J. G. Greer & I. R. Stuart (Eds.), *The sexual aggressor: Current perspectives on treatment* (pp. 240–266). New York: Van Nostrand Reinhold.

Committee on Sexual Offences Against Children and Youths. (1984). *Sexual offences against children* (Vol. 1) (Catalogue No. J 2-50/1984E). Ottawa, Canada: Canadian Government Publishing Center.

Finkelhor, D. (1984). *Child sexual abuse.* New York: Free Press.

Kaplan, M. (1985). *The impact of parolee's perception of confidentiality on the reporting of their urges to interact sexually with children.* Ann Arbor, MI: University Microfilm International.

AUTHOR INDEX

Martin, W. R., 58, *69*
Martinez, L. J., Jr., 62, *69*
Mason, E., 20, *29*
Mathew, R. J., 201, *202*
Mathews, A., 82, *95*
Matthews, R., 207, *220*
Mattison, A., 205, 207, *220*
Mattson, A., 207, *220*
Mawson, D., 91, *95*
Mayer, J., 9, *29, 30*
Mazur, A., 205, *220*
McAbee, R. S., 140, *145*
McArdle, W. D., 41, *51*
McCabe, M., 88, *97*
McEachran, A. B., 135, *143*
McGaugh, J. L., 53, *69*
McGowan, W. T., 184, *192*
McHugh, P. R., 17, *29*
Mckenna, J. U., 203, 204, *220*
Mckeon, P. E., 25, *29*
McLaughlin, C. L., 55, 58, *69*
McLean, D., 205, 207, *218*
McNair, D. M., 158, *177*
McNamara, N. M., 116, 122, *128*
Meadors, G. F., 109, 123, *127*
Mehta, A., 216, *221*
Meinecke, C. F., 213, 214, *218*
Meigs, J. W., 118, *127*
Melmed, S., 62, *69*
Mendlewicz, J., 135, *144*
Merkangas, K. R., 201, *202*
Messerli, F. H., 122, *127, 129*
Messick, S., 81, *97*
Messing, R. B., 62, *69*
1983 Metropolitan Height and Weight Tables, 99, *106*
Meyer, J. K., 199, *202*
Meyer, W., 213, *220*
Meyer-Bahlburg, H. F. L., 205, *220*
Mezey, E., 55, *67*
Micelli, D., 57, *68*
Michelson, E., 151, *177*
Michelson, O., 41, *51*
Migeon, C., 213, 214, *218, 220*
Miles, L. E., 168, *178*
Miller, J. C., 160, *176*
Minuchin, S., 75, *95*
Mir, P., 62, *70*
Miselis, R. R., 17, *29*
Mitchell, J. E., 58, 62, *68, 70,* 75, *95*
Mitchell, R. E., 122, *129*

Mitler, M. M., 149, 168, 169, *173, 177, 178*
Mittelman, M. S., 225, 228, 231, 232, 238–241, *242*
Mohai, L., 59, *66*
Money, J., 213, 214, *220*
Monk, T. H., 148, 162, *175*
Monroe, L. J., 182, 184, *193*
Monti, P. M., 205, 207, *220*
Moon, T., 64, *69*
Moore, B. J., 34, *37*
Moore, F. E., 109, *127*
Moore, M. E., 10, 11, *29*
Moore-Ede, M. C., 135, *145,* 148–151, *174, 177*
Moran, T. H., 17, *29*
Moretti, C., 58, *68*
Morgan, S. F., 62, *68*
Morgane, P. J., 186, *193*
Morely, J. E., 53–60, 62, 64, *66–70*
Morlock, H. C., 167, *178*
Morrell, W., 76, *96*
Morris, G. O., 155, *177*
Moruzzi, G., 186, *193*
Morycz, R., 137, 139, *144*
Mothes, C., 210, *220*
Mott, D. E., 182, *192*
Mowrer, O. H., 77, *95*
Mueller, W. H., 118, *128*
Mullaney, D. J., 165, *177*
Müller, D., 105, *106,* 122, *127, 221*
Murphy, D., 62, *67*
Murphy, W. D., 208, *217*
Murray, E. J., 154, 156–160, *177*
Murray, M. A. P., 215, *218*
Murray, R., 119, *128*
Murray, S. S., 57, *69*
Muzio, J. N., 137, *144*

N

Naitoh, P., 139, *143,* 149, 157, 158, *176, 177*
Nakagawa, Y., 161, 164, *177*
Nat, R., 205, *220*
Naumann, M., 160, *178*
Nelson, J. P., 137, 139, *144*
Nemzer, E., *96*
Netto, C., 62, 63, *68*
Nevsimalova, S., 162, *173*
New Weight Standards for Men and Women, 99, *106*

SUBJECT INDEX